The Last Lincoln
Conspirator

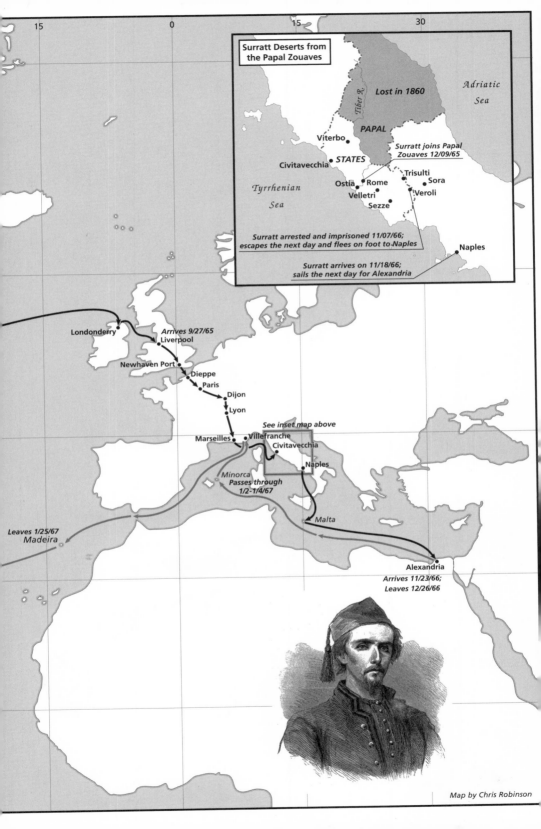

Surratt Deserts from the Papal Zouaves

Lost in 1860

Adriatic Sea

Tiber R.

PAPAL

Viterbo

STATES

Civitavecchia

Tyrrhenian Sea

Ostia • Rome
Velletri
Sezze

Surratt joins Papal Zouaves 12/09/65

Trisulti • Sora
Veroli

Surratt arrested and imprisoned 11/07/66; escapes the next day and flees on foot to Naples

Naples

Surratt arrives on 11/18/66; sails the next day for Alexandria

Londonderry

Arrives 9/27/65 Liverpool

Newhaven Port •
Dieppe
Paris
Dijon
Lyon

See inset map above

Marseilles • Villefranche
Civitavecchia
Naples

Minorca
Passes through 1/2–1/4/67

Malta

Leaves 1/25/67 Madeira

Alexandria

Arrives 11/23/66; Leaves 12/26/66

Map by Chris Robinson

The Last Lincoln
Conspirator

John Surratt's
Flight from the
Gallows

Andrew C. A. Jampoler

NAVAL INSTITUTE PRESS
Annapolis, Maryland

Naval Institute Press
291 Wood Road
Annapolis, MD 21402

Library of Congress Cataloging-in-Publication Data
Jampoler, Andrew C. A., 1942–
  The last Lincoln conspirator : John Surratt's flight from the gallows / Andrew C.A. Jampoler.
    p. cm.
  Includes bibliographical references and index.
  ISBN 978-1-59114-407-6 (alk. paper)
  1. Surratt, John H. (John Harrison), 1844–1916. 2. Lincoln, Abraham, 1809–1865—Assassination.
3. Assassins—United States—Biography. 4. Fugitives from justice—United States—Biography.
5. Conspiracies—United States—History—19th century. 6. Surratt, John H. (John Harrison),
1844–1916—Trials, litigation, etc. 7. Trials (Assassination)—Washington (D.C.) I. Title.
  E457.5.S972J36 2008
  973.7092—dc22
  [B]

                    2008015585

Printed in the United States of America on acid-free paper

14 13 12 11 10 09 08   9 8 7 6 5 4 3 2
First printing

Endsheet: "John Surratt's Flight from Arrest and Return for Trial." The USS *Swatara*'s track from Alexandria to Washington with Surratt on board in irons is from the ship's deck log, held by the Library of Congress. The sketch of Surratt in Zouave uniform is by Andrew McCallum, *Harper's Weekly*, March 9, 1867. (Original map by Christopher Robinson)

Book design: David Alcorn, Alcorn Publication Design

A SHIP HAS COME HOME WITH THIS YOUNG MAN SURRATT. Providence has given him almost two years to illustrate the fugitive and vagabond career of an assassin. He has taken his crime to the oldest parts of the world; put it in contact with the ocean; made partners in it the hereditary enemies of republican freedom; connected it with the strange old cities over our border; striven to forget it in the riot of continental capitals; carried it past the Alps; made the bluest waters of the earth red with it; connected the Sovereignty of the Catholic faith with the murder of the President of Democracy; fled from this discovered secret through the mountain fastness of brigands; uniformed in the livery of the Pope, till the olive and the orange orchards opened upon the Bay of Naples; thence he made this crime a part of the citadel of Malta, associating it with the crusades; bore it to Egypt, within sight of the Pyramids; and had very nearly, like the pursued of the Jews, found a refuge at the grave of Christ.

Here is the most extraordinary theme for an American romance since the days of Cortez. To this romance the flight of Booth was but a highwayman's ride.

"THE STORY OF SURRATT," Chicago Tribune, FEBRUARY 24, 1867

CONTENTS

ILLUSTRATIONS

PREFACE

Lt. William F. Lynch, U.S. Navy, spent the spring and summer of 1848 in command of thirteen young volunteers, teetotalers all, who together made up the first official U.S. expedition to the holy land. This was the only time American sailors under arms and under their own flag were afloat on the ancient waters of the Dead Sea. Remarkably, the expedition into what was then a dusty outpost of the Ottoman Empire achieved its goals—the principal one being to establish precisely the elevation of the Dead Sea—with the loss of only one life. Disease and dangerous Bedouin tribes could have been expected to have levied a much higher toll on the explorers, especially so because 1848 was an epidemic year for cholera, first in South Asia and the Levant and then worldwide, the second great pandemic of this mysterious killer in the nineteenth century.

Lynch succeeded not only thanks to his leadership skills but also because he had the wit to solicit help when he needed it. Once ashore, he recruited a direct descendant of the Prophet Mohammad and an Arab chieftain with his armed and mounted escort to travel with the expedition's supporting land party. Beneath their protective umbrella, Lynch's sailors were able to do their work afloat in small boats on the Jordan River and the Dead Sea largely unmolested. Lynch also hired two expatriate American scholars to perform some of the expedition's scientific specimen collection.

Other help came from U.S. consuls in the major ports of the Mediterranean— some U.S. citizens, some not—who represented the nation's diplomatic and commercial interests in the ports, in foreign capitals, and in the royal and imperial courts bordering that great sea. One such consul was William Winthrop, a Bostonian who served for thirty-five years (essentially his entire adult life; he died there) as the U.S. State Department's representative in Valetta, Malta. At the time, as it would again be one century later, the small island's superb port and chief city was the strategic and geographic center of the British Empire's commanding position in the Mediterranean.

Eastbound from the United States by way of Gibraltar, Lynch rode in the USS *Supply* on the way to the holy land and his historic exploration of the Dead Sea.

He stopped in Malta to pick up a pilot for the tricky passage through the island-studded Aegean Sea. Westbound, Lynch disembarked at Malta from a chartered French barque, *La Perle d'Orient*. He was searching for the *Supply*, months overdue at Beirut, to carry the survivors of his exhausted and diseased expedition back home. Both times he was assisted by Winthrop, who during his years in office would help countless American sailors and landsmen as they went about their business in the central Mediterranean.

Reading about Winthrop's life and career while writing *Sailors in the Holy Land* (Naval Institute Press, 2005), I learned that nearly twenty years after Lynch and the consul parted (in fact, the year after Lynch's death) the doughty Winthrop had a speaking role in another little-known adventure. In late 1866 Winthrop attempted unsuccessfully to arrest a U.S. citizen and passenger aboard a transiting vessel, the Royal Mail Ship (RMS) *Tripoli*, steaming between Naples and Alexandria, Egypt. The man, an escaped deserter from the Pontifical Zouaves, was believed to have participated in the plot to assassinate President Lincoln the year before.

This book about John Harrison Surratt Jr., the fleeing conspirator and deserter, came from the accidental discovery that at least once something on the Maltese waterfront had gotten past Consul Winthrop.

ACKNOWLEDGMENTS

I'M GRATEFUL FOR THE ASSISTANCE OF THE FOLLOWING, who generously contributed their special knowledge to my research efforts or helped otherwise: John Andrew, M.D. (Leesburg, Virginia), Prof. Lewis Becker (Villanova University School of Law, Villanova, Pennsylvania), Jim Burk (Oak Hill, Virginia), Eugene Canfield (Jamestown, New York), Sr. Catherine Clarke (the Vatican Library, Vatican City), André Debois, O.M.I. (Archives Deschâtelets, Ottawa, Canada), John Duerkop (Kingston, Ontario), Robert Ellis, Mark Mollan, and Richard Peuser (National Archives and Records Administration, College Park, Maryland), Mary Fishback (Thomas Balch Library, Leesburg, Virginia), Joseph Geraci (National Postal Museum, Smithsonian Institution), Rev. Dr. J. A. Harding (Clifton Diocese Archives, Bath, England), Valerie Hart (Guildhall Library, London, England), Bart Houlahan (Devon, Pennsylvania), Roger Hull (researcher, Liverpool Record Office), Marilyn Ibach and Virginia Wood (Library of Congress, Washington, D.C.), August Imholtz (Beltsville, Maryland), Sr. Mary Joseph McManamon, O.S.B. (librarian, the Venerable English College, Rome), Dr. Lorenzo Innocenti (Perugia, Italy), Janna Israel (MIT, Cambridge, Massachusetts), Betsy Knight (Houston, Texas), Msgr. Maciej Michalsky, O.M.I. (Archivist General, Oblates of Mary Immaculate, Rome), Mike Musick (Harpers Ferry, West Virginia), Heidi Myers (Navy Department Library, Washington, D.C.), Judge Phil Nichols (Upper Marlboro, Maryland), Michael Pestorius (Austin, Texas), Msgr. Thomas Petrillo (Papal Nunciature, Washington, D.C.), Pat Purcell (National Railway Historical Society, Philadelphia, Pennsylvania), Kimberly Richards (archivist, Booth Library, Elmira, New York), Pier Luigi Rossi (Lucca, Italy), Billy Strasser (park ranger, Dry Tortugas National Park, Florida), John Stevenson (Trinity Research Services, Edinburgh, Scotland), Judge Nicholas Stroumtsos (New Brunswick, New Jersey), Dr. Meg Whittle (diocesan archivist, Liverpool, England), John Winrow (assistant curator, Liverpool Maritime Museum, England), and Marijke Zonneveld-Kouters (Nederlands Zouavenmuseum te Oudenbosch, Holland).

Anyone researching or writing about John Harrison Surratt Jr. owes a great debt to Father Alfred Isaccson of Middletown, New York, who began his own research on Surratt for a master's essay in 1956 and has continued to plumb Surratt's life and times. I also drew extensively on Michael Kauffman's definitive biography of John Wilkes Booth, *American Brutus*, to set the scene for John Surratt's flight from pursuit. I am happy to acknowledge my obligation to both authors' meticulous scholarship.

The staff of the Surratt House Museum of Clinton, Maryland (formerly Surrattsville), including Laurie Verge, Joan Chaconas, and Sandra Walia, are the custodians of the Surratt flame and the prime movers behind the historical society that carries the family name forward. Laurie and Joan are distinguished scholars of the assassination in their own rights, and the research they support and the publications that flow from it, especially the "Surratt Courier," have been another important resource for me, for which I am grateful. Sandra, archivist of the museum's James O. Hall Research Center, has been unfailingly cooperative.

The research librarians at the Rust Library, Leesburg, Virginia (including Karim Khan, Holly Peterson, Marcie Pierson, Oona Pilot, and Betsy Quin), have again been patient and helpful throughout. They, and Bob Boley of the Loudoun County, Virginia, public library interlibrary loan service, made it possible for much research to be done in comfort.

Bob Jones, from neighboring Seaforth, helpfully hosted my research visit to Liverpool, England, and generously shared with me his own knowledge of Liverpool and the Civil War.

Laurie Verge and Joan Chaconas (the Surratt House Museum's director and the museum's resident history specialist, respectively), Prof. Patrick Hayes (St. Johns University, Staten Island, New York), Margaret Wagner (Library of Congress, Publishing Office), and Chief Justice Frank J. Williams (Lincoln Forum) read this book in manuscript and offered candid and useful comments and corrections. This book is much better for each of them having read it. Karin Kaufman ably copyedited the manuscript, the third time she has performed this service for me.

All these people improved this book during two years of research and writing. It remains for me to thank Suzy, my wife, who has immeasurably improved my life for forty-three years. She also assembled the illustrations.

The Last Lincoln
Conspirator

I

"ON THE HONOR OF A LADY"

Washington has been a failure," Anthony Trollope pronounced magisterially in *North America*, his two-volume travelogue published in 1862 following a nine-month tour around the United States. He found the city "but a ragged, unfinished collection of unbuilt broad streets, as to the completion of which there can now, I imagine, be but little hope. Of all the places that I know it is the most ungainly and the most unsatisfactory;—I fear I must also say the most presumptuous in its pretensions."

"Of all the places I know" was an especially cruel phrase. By the early 1860s Trollope was an immensely popular novelist in Great Britain, but his day job was as a senior postal inspector and in this capacity he had recently finished an extended trip to the West Indies and the Spanish Main (the coast of the Caribbean and part of the Gulf of Mexico) for the Royal Mail. Apparently even the town of Charlotte Amalie on St. Thomas in the Caribbean, awash in the pollution of its harbor and famous as a "Dutch oven" for incubating yellow fever, ranked higher in his estimation than the American capital.

Warming up to his critique, Trollope conceded that each of the six principal public buildings in Washington City ("the Capitol, the Post-office, the Patent-office, the Treasury, the President's House, and the Smithsonian Institute") had some small merit, albeit all were "marred by an independent deviation from recognized rules of architectural taste." But the six, together with the incomplete Washington Monument—never to be finished, he predicted myopically—stood apart on unfinished streets in an unpeopled town surrounded by an uncultivated, undrained wilderness. At the end of Massachusetts Avenue, he wrote, "tucking your trousers up to your knees, you will wade through the bogs, you will lose yourself among rude hillocks, you will be out of the reach of humanity. The

3

"A Balloon View of Washington, D.C." Describing a perspective looking toward downtown from Washington City's western limits, Anthony Trollope wrote, "The unfinished dome of the Capitol will loom before you in the distance, and you will think that you approach the ruins of some western Palmyra." This is that unfinished dome in July 1861 in an imagined overhead view looking southwest. (*Harper's Weekly*, July 27, 1861)

unfinished dome of the Capitol will loom before you in the distance, and you will think that you approach the ruins of some western Palmyra." In 1862 it was all hopeless—and hopelessly dirty besides.

Still, it required a moment of amnesia for Trollope to speak about Washington's ruins forthrightly. After all, it had been his countrymen who had burned the capital in late August 1814 during the last war. Fifty years later the city still had not fully recovered from that long-ago abuse. One of the objects of his criticism, the new Treasury Building next to the White House, would not be finished until 1869. Fire, from arson or otherwise, was an enduring problem in the city. Another of the targets of Trollope's architectural criticism, the Smithsonian Institution, suffered a major blaze in January 1865 that resulted in the destruction of its archive and some of its collections.

Trollope's review wasn't original. His mother, Frances, had written an even crankier appraisal following her troubled, four-year-long family encampment in Cincinnati thirty years earlier, a book that her son later described as "a somewhat unjust appraisal of our cousins over the water."[1]

By 1860 a host of other British literary lights—Charles Dickens among them, twice—had also visited the United States, or soon would. Some were drawn to the country by curiosity, the search for new material, or a chance to tour and make money speaking to the rubes. Others came to fight off copyright poachers. Trollope visited the United States again, in late spring and early summer 1868, one year after his retirement from the Royal Mail. When he fell asleep in the Senate gallery during President Johnson's impeachment trial that year, the press, groping for something new to say, had a field day at his expense. *

Even dividing by two to account for a certain smugness about the strange life-styles of foreign provincials that traveling Victorians carried in their hand baggage, however, Trollope wasn't too far off the mark. Washington as the 1860s began was a small, undistinguished southern town that occasionally stirred but then quietly dozed through the many months of the year Congress was not in session. Still much more of a hope than a promise.

Americans thought so, too. A scant decade earlier, the young Henry Adams had stepped from his aunt's house on F Street onto a dirt road, "with wheel-tracks meandering from the colonnade of the Treasury hard by, to the white marble columns and fronts of the Post Office and Patent Office which faced each other in the distance like white Greek temples in the abandoned gravel-pits of a deserted Syrian city. Here and there low wooden houses were scattered among the streets, as in other Southern villages."

---

* Anthony Trollope (1815–1883) was a keen observer of the American scene. He visited the country five times between 1859 and 1875. Beginning in February 1865 and running through July 1868, Trollope's editor published a series of his letters anonymously in the *Pall Mall Gazette*, a new London evening newspaper, in which Trollope revealed himself to be a thoughtful political analyst, firmly on the side of the Union in the Civil War and a foe of slavery. He predicted the victory of the North, based, he later said, "on the merits of the Northern cause, on the superior strength of the Northern party, and on a conviction that England would never recognise the South, and that France would be guided in her policy by England."

In part because of Trollope's admiration for Lincoln (saying in a piece published soon after the assassination that Lincoln was "pre-eminently gifted" with "courage, constancy, patience, moderation, and mercy"), but for other reasons as well, Trollope doubted that the United States would go to war in Canada after the end of its civil war. His was not blanket appreciation, however. Trollope thought that the reconstruction plans of the Radical Republicans were hypocritical, a scheme to use the votes of former slaves in the South as a way to achieve permanent Republican control of Congress by the North. A clear voice against slavery, Trollope nevertheless believed that "a negro is not fitted by his gifts and nature to exercise political power amidst a community of white men."

Like his mother and a brother, he was an enormously fecund writer, thanks to a very workmanlike and unromantic approach to the business of putting words down on paper. Trollope wrote nearly fifty novels focused on the life of the Victorian middle class and published travel books, a substantial number of short stories, and essays. Trollope's *Autobiography* was published posthumously in 1883. In it he had the candor to describe his *North America* as "not well done . . . tedious and confused, and will hardly, I think, be of future value to those who wish to make themselves acquainted with the United States."

The Civil War changed everything. The 1860s saw the population of Washington City grow by nearly 80 percent, from 61,000 to 109,000 in 1870, promoting it to twelfth in size in the nation, between Buffalo, New York, and Newark, New Jersey. "Low wooden houses," yes, but also hotels, boarding-houses, taverns, and "disreputable resorts" everywhere (nearly eighty-five houses of prostitution according to the inventory of the provost marshal, not even one-fifth of the true number), all enjoying full occupancy and handsome revenues even when Congress was not in session.[2]

The war dramatically expanded the federal government's role and hugely enlarged its resources. Between 1861 and 1865 its budget ballooned by over 1,500 percent, and thousands of civilians joined the federal bureaucracy. By midway through the 1860s Washington had been a fortified capital, an armed camp, a cornucopia for government contracts, a hospital center, and a Confederate strategic objective for four years. Powered by population growth and by wartime spending, business of all kinds was good. The annual issue of *Boyd's Washington and Georgetown Directory,* a sort of early combination Yellow Pages and White Pages without phone numbers, now ran to more than four hundred pages each year. Hinting at the future, among Boyd's listings were the names of more than 150 lawyers, most with offices clustered around Judiciary Square in the Fourth Ward.

By spring 1865 citizens and visitors with more elevated tastes than could be satisfied by reference to the provost marshal's roster of sporting places could find their entertainment at Ford's New Theatre—the old one having burned down several years before—on Tenth near F Street or, in the same district along Pennsylvania Avenue, at Grover's Theater, in the Oxford Hall of Music and Pinacotheca (self-described as the "fountainhead of talent"), or at the Odd Fellows' Hall on Seventh Street between D and E Streets. In the same season couples with children could repair to the Stone and Rosston Circus Combination, offering, on "a scale of Unprecedented Magnificence," superb entertainment under the big top at New York Avenue and Sixth Street twice every day at 2 and 7 PM: "Equestrians, Gymnasts, Acrobats, Pancratists, Posturers, Equilabrists, Pantomimists, Humourists, and Danseuses! A profusion of attractions . . . presented with all the fascinating adjuncts essential to render them inimitable in superiority and marvelous in splendor."

Business done or entertainment over, travel out of town could be by horse or carriage on bad roads or afloat on fast steamboats from the docks at the foot of Sixth and Seventh Streets and from the ports of Alexandria and Georgetown.

Trains from Washington connected three times a day with the express trains of the Great Pennsylvania Route, providing daily service north as far as Niagara Falls and west all the way to St. Louis. From its depot on Capitol Hill, at New Jersey Avenue and C Street, the Baltimore and Ohio Railroad ran nine trains a day between just after 6 AM to 7:30 PM, direct or with connections to the major cities north and west.

If out-of-town mail service was too slow, there was always—since 1844, anyway—the telegraph. The first telegraph line in the country was strung between Washington and Baltimore in May that year. (The wires carried bad news as fast as they did good, and some blamed the national recession of 1857 on the swift spread of economic panic by Morse code.) In the early 1860s commercial service was supplemented by the U.S. Military Telegraph, an army system that had its chief node in the telegraph room of the War Department and carried plain and encrypted messages to armies in the field. By the end of the Civil War, Washington was connected to the rest of the country by thousands of miles of wire. Western Union alone had nine telegraph offices in the city, some in hotels; its two small competitors operated four more.

Nine newspapers published daily or Sunday, morning and afternoon in Washington, and twenty out-of-town papers had local offices in the city, providing their readers as far away as Boston, St. Louis, and Detroit with regular information on events in the national capital.

Beneath all the new cosmopolitan glitz, however, still beat the heart of a country town. Washington's population might have put it one up on Newark, but the city wasn't much compared to European capitals. Trollope's London, the metropolis of England and of an empire that spanned the globe, boasted a population of more than three million, making it by far the most populous city in the Western world and some thirty times larger than the U.S. capital on the Potomac. On any given day the *Washington Evening Star*'s lost-and-found column might report that an entire barnyard was adrift on its city's streets: A brown and white spotted cow ("no horns, long tail"), two red calves, a small, black buffalo cow, and a sow with seven spotted piglets were a fraction of a few days' meandering menagerie. The city's feed lots, during the war full of cattle on the way to slaughter, filled the air with the restless lowing and pungent smell of confined beef on the hoof.

And it was a barnyard underfoot. In the rain, wagon wheels churned Pennsylvania Avenue into an adhesive paste that could suck your shoes and socks off in midstride and required improvised bridging to cross. "Hundreds of colored men carried boards around on their shoulders, and, for a consideration, assisted pedestrians to cross the 'thoroughfares,' and aided persons in carriages to reach the sidewalks when their vehicles mired down," former Nevada Senator William Steward wrote in 1908, recalling his war years in the capital. "A trip from the Capitol to the White House frequently occupied an hour, and sometimes two hours, and one's hack would very often be stalled hub deep in the mud . . . and one would have to climb out and wade ashore."

It was a country town and a military garrison, too; by the end of the Civil War nearly thirty thousand armed men—infantry, cavalry, and artillery—were stationed in and around the city. The clatter of everything they did was the soundtrack to life in the capital.

In the nineteenth century, midyear in the swampy capital was notorious for its heat and humidity.[3] Beginning in June and extending well into September, the city was generally thought to be uninhabitable by the better class of people (defined as those with the means to go elsewhere), as demonstrated by the suicide of the French ambassador, Lucien Prevost-Paradol, who shot himself soon after he took up his new assignment in 1870. He was commonly believed to have done it to escape the insufferable heat. If so, his stratagem worked, but other ambassadors found equally effective albeit temporary solutions. Before air conditioning, embassies often relocated their diplomatic staffs to New England over the midyear months, a seasonal migration that continued well into the next century. Newport, Rhode Island, was a favorite refuge.

Ninety-degree temperatures with humidity to match are possible in Washington as early as May, though uncommon. June, however, can see five to seven days of such weather, and July often as many as two weeks. Washington was just such a furnace in the late spring and summer of 1865. On Greenleaf Point—the city's southernmost ground, a low-lying triangle of land that jutted out to separate the Potomac River's main stem from its eastern branch—conditions were particularly enervating. There, at the U.S. Arsenal, today Fort Leslie J. McNair, hot, humid air hung day after day above the surface of the brackish river and its adjacent shore like an enveloping, suffocating vapor.

The heat outside coupled to the congestion of bodies inside must have turned the impromptu courtroom on the third floor of the old penitentiary building on the Arsenal's grounds into a brick oven during late afternoons, despite the room's eleven foot high ceiling and its large volume, making it an airless place that passing early summer thunderstorms could not have freed from the yeasty aroma of unclean clothes on unwashed bodies thickening the air.

While spring gave way to summer, inmates who were jailed on the top floor of the same building stewed in the cauldrons of their tiny cells in what had been the central, women's wing of the old prison block. The penitentiary that held them had been closed in 1862 (forcing the relocation of its complement of more than three hundred prisoners to Albany) and converted to storage, but it was reopened for this special purpose. Inside, until June 11, all but one of the male special prisoners were hooded in confinement in solitary cells, closets really, each several feet wide and not even seven feet long. Less than half the size of solitary confinement cells in federal "supermax" prisons today. The enveloping, padded cloth sacks over their heads were ventilated only at the nose and mouth and tied snugly in the back, the knots far out of reach of manacled hands. No openings for eyes and ears. A regime that would be defined as torture today.

The government went to some expense to prepare the courtroom (formerly the prison hospital) for the trial of the eight Lincoln assassination conspirators it held in custody, fitting the room out appropriately for the historic trial but also taking obvious care to ensure a suitably spare and somber setting.[4]

The entire room (perhaps 1,400 feet square, about the size of half a junior high school basketball court) was freshly painted and whitewashed. New, brown fiber carpeting covered its floor. New or nearly new furniture filled the space, the principal pieces of which, two long tables on either side of the room, were draped in the green felt cloth that even then traditionally decorated court-martial furnishings. Moreover, a new corridor and stairway had been built to provide public access to the court without requiring passage through the prison wing of the building. Behind the prisoners' dock at the west end of the room, a massive, reinforced door of "dungeon-like appearance" led directly to the cells. All four of the courtroom's windows were heavily barred.

Security about the Arsenal and at the trial was seemingly very tight. The approaches to the penitentiary for half a mile around and the building's corridors, stairways, and landings were thick with light blue–coated, armed guards.[5] These were men of the Veterans Reserve Corps, soldiers no longer fit for combat in the field but still capable of garrison duty, all armed and serious. The name of everyone issued a pass to enter the prison was recorded, and a roster was kept of all persons who called on a prisoner when court was not in session.

It's not clear what potential threat to the proceedings was being deflected by these precautions. By the first day of the trial, May 9, all Confederate forces in the military departments east of the Mississippi River had given up the fight, beginning with one-legged Lt. Gen. Richard Ewell's surrender of the Second

Army Corps, Stonewall Jackson's former command, on April 6. Three days later what remained of Gen. Robert E. Lee's Army of Northern Virginia put down its arms at Appomattox Court House.

The end of the Civil War came piecemeal, in a flurry of separate documents signed by generals; each one acknowledged defeat and the onset of peace in some specific place. The evaporation of President Jefferson Davis's government after its displacement from Richmond and flight from Danville in April meant that there could be no single Confederate surrender on the political level. One would not have been accepted in any case: In Union eyes a formal Davis surrender on behalf of the Confederacy would have given inappropriate status to the defeated rebellion.[6] Instead, Lee's decisive act triggered a cascade of other surrenders spread over the next few months as the Confederacy's remaining senior commanders realistically appraised their situations and yielded one at a time to force majeure.

On April 26 Gen. Joseph Johnston surrendered the skeleton of the Army of Tennessee to Maj. Gen. William T. Sherman, who had infamously emptied and razed Atlanta during the previous summer and then in January 1865 loosed three blue-coated columns through Savannah against coastal Georgia and the Carolinas, where they had gnawed their way north across the terrain like a plague of locusts.

Eight days later at Citronelle, Alabama, Lt. Gen. Richard Taylor, the son of former president Zachary Taylor and Jefferson Davis's brother-in-law, surrendered the remnants of his army to Maj. Gen. Edward Canby, a Union officer of no particular military merit. The disarming of Taylor's twelve thousand men on May 4 by Canby marked the end of Confederate resistance in the East.[7]

After Richmond fell and Lee surrendered, Secretary of War Edwin Stanton and Lt. Gen. Ulysses S. Grant moved quickly to start standing down the enormous, and enormously expensive, Union army. Between spring 1865 and autumn 1867 a million and a quarter officers and men were released and sent home, a process slowed only by Washington's anxieties about what mischief the French were doing in Mexico in defiance of the Monroe Doctrine. When demobilization was complete, all that remained of the Union's two thousand–plus regiments of infantry, cavalry, and artillery was a regular army barely twenty-six thousand men strong. One million volunteers, tens of thousands of draftees, and thousands of hired draft substitutes were all gone, and with them the brigades, divisions, corps, and armies that had fought with such horrible determination for so long. (Thirty years later, when a war with Spain loomed, the U.S. Army was scattered in battalion, company, and detachment strength throughout

Indian Territory. The regular army could field no unit larger than a regiment, and no officer under his mid-fifties had experience commanding any formation as large as one thousand men. Volunteers, 216,000 of them eventually, would once again flesh out the ranks.)

In 1865 during that first postwar spring season, however, troops were still everywhere in Washington City, the most heavily defended capital in the world. The city lay behind twenty miles of infantry trenches in a loose ring that was punctuated by sixty-eight forts and ninety-three artillery batteries and connected by thirty miles of military roads and skeins of telegraph lines. All but one of the positions, Fort Washington (erected in 1809 to defend the Potomac River approach to Washington and reconstructed in 1824), were new, built by the Army Corps of Engineers beginning in 1861.[8]

A successful strike across the Potomac River into neighboring Virginia during late May 1861 carved Union footholds from enemy territory immediately south of the city, including the Lee family estate. (Arlington National Cemetery occupies the property today. In 1882 the Lee family accepted $150,000 for the estate from the federal government, after the Supreme Court ruled that its confiscation in 1861 had been illegal.) Hard points stretching across Washington's southwestern approaches, from Battery Rodgers below Alexandria to Fort Marcy near the Chain Bridge, completed the defensive ring and gave the Union effective control of what are today Alexandria, Crystal City, Arlington, and Rosslyn, nearly to the Fairfax County line. This same piece of northern Virginia had been a part of the capital's original one-hundred-square-mile federal district until 1846, when it was returned to the state.

Washington's powerful defenses were never truly challenged during the war. The Confederacy missed what was probably its best opportunity to move against the city in July 1861, right after the First Battle of Bull Run. After that, the closest the capital city came to being threatened was three years later, in July 1864, when Lt. Gen. Jubal Early approached within a dozen miles of downtown with eight thousand infantry, veterans of a battle several days earlier on the banks of Maryland's Monocacy River. Quick Union reinforcements snatched away Early's opportunity to change the course of the war. (The small car ferry thirty-six miles northwest of Georgetown that takes commuters across the Potomac River today on State Route 109 is named after him. A mobile and rusty monument to an exciting moment in Early's career.)

In the midst of the turmoil that marked the end of the fighting and the sudden death of the president, at the edge of a city still bristling like a porcupine with war surplus defensive works, the trial of Lincoln's assassins began.

Thirty or more, perhaps as many as fifty, found places in the courtroom at any one time, one-third or so in Union army uniforms spangling the otherwise drab room with blue and gold.[9] Eight defendants and their individual guards. Corporals from the ubiquitous Veterans Reserve Corps. Counsel for both sides. Nine senior army officers—as stern, bearded, and judgmental as Old Testament prophets—who formed the military commission that served as both judge and jury. Witnesses, several every day shuttling in and out to testify (after the usual morning review of the previous day's proceedings). Court recorders, styled "phonographs" because they wrote a verbatim shorthand record of what they heard. Newspaper correspondents, miscellaneous observers, and other hangers-on who had somehow managed to get a pass and so gain access to the most sensational event of the age.

After Secretary of War Stanton reluctantly agreed to admit spectators, entry was by daily pass signed by Bvt. Maj. Gen. John Hartranft, appointed by President Johnson's executive order on May 1 to be special provost marshal general (the chief policeman and head bailiff) during the trial. His station when court was in session was at a small table near the room's public entrance.*

Gruesomely, John Wilkes Booth, Lincoln's assassin and the mastermind of the attacks on Good Friday, was there too . . . after a fashion.

Booth had fled the city immediately after shooting the president, riding alone into Maryland across the Navy Yard Bridge, which spanned the Potomac's eastern branch (the Anacostia River today), and passing easily by the Union sentries at the river crossing, despite their orders to let no one leave the city after 9 PM.[10] He finally was captured at "Locust Hill," Richard Garrett's farm north of Bowling Green, Virginia, on April 26, after dodging the Union manhunt for twelve days.

---

* Hartranft's Civil War service began with the war's first major fight, when the soldiers of the regiment he raised, the 4th Pennsylvania Volunteer Infantry, walked off the field in Manassas, Virginia, as the guns began to fire because their ninety-day enlistments had just expired. Hartranft (1830–1889) bounced back from that humiliation at the Battle of Bull Run to serve ably through the rest of the war. Hartranft later became active in Republican politics in his home state and was elected and then reelected governor of Pennsylvania. He served from 1872 to 1879.

Between May 1 and July 19, 1865, during the conspirators' trial, Hartranft wrote a daily report to his superior officer, Gen. Winfield Scott Hancock. These reports, an important eyewitness account of the trial and related events, compiled in "letterbooks" were for a time shelved at Gettysburg Lutheran College.

Like everything else to come in this story—John Surratt's fate, Henri Beaumont de Sainte Marie's reward, Andrew Johnson's presidency, and several colorful love affairs involving bit players—the ownership of General Hartranft's letterbooks became the subject of a lawsuit, in this case a three-way dispute in 1995 between his descendants (the Shireman family of Oxford, Pennsylvania), Gettysburg College, and the National Archives. Inevitably, in view of its staying power fueled by public funds, the Archives won. (As this was being written, Hartranft's letterbooks were scheduled to be published in autumn 2008.)

Trapped in Garrett's locked barn after two nights at the farm, Booth was entirely spent and suicidal, so perhaps his death at Garrett's place was inevitable. After a few hours of fruitless palaver through the walls of the barn, Booth was shot mortally between its slats by Sgt. Thomas "Boston" Corbett of the 16th New York Cavalry. The shooting should never have happened; Booth ought to have been captured, disarmed, and brought to trial. The mounted troopers who stumbled on the assassin and his accomplice, however, were poorly led. Corbett, in particular and despite the praise of his commander, was rash.[11] (Odd, too. He is also remembered in history as one of the few men who castrated himself. He shares that special distinction with Dr. William Minor, the demented former Civil War army surgeon made famous by Simon Winchester's book *The Professor and the Madman*.)

Young David Herold, one of the conspirators and the only one to join Booth during his flight through Maryland, was taken prisoner at the same time. The two, dead high priest and living acolyte, were quickly shipped up the Potomac to the Washington Navy Yard in a steamer, the *John S. Ide*. Both were then taken aboard a Union monitor in port, the USS *Montauk*, where Herold was confined temporarily.

The damp, dark interior compartments of the USS *Montauk* and its classmates were the nearest things to a medieval dungeon that could be found in Washington. When it was new the *Montauk*—like its class namesake a doubled-ended, iron-clad hull with very little freeboard, topped with a gun turret amidships that resembled nothing so much as an armored corncrib—had fought off-shore Georgia and the Carolinas.[12] In 1863 it had bravely bombarded Forts McAllister and Sumter and sunk the blockade runner CSS *Rattlesnake*. But in 1865 and not yet three years old then, the *Montauk* was already war surplus. At the end of the year it would be laid up permanently in Philadelphia and finally scrapped in 1904.

Before then the *Montauk* served first as the morgue for Booth's autopsy and later as the escape- and rescue-proof prison afloat in which several male conspiracy suspects were held temporarily awaiting trial. There had been some urgency to get the forensic medical procedure done as quickly as possible. At midmorning on April 27 Commo. J. B. Montgomery, commandant of the navy yard, delicately warned Secretary of the Navy Gideon Welles that Wilkes's remains were "changing rapidly," decaying in the heat of spring, and he asked, "What disposition shall be made of the body?" The scene in the illustrated magazines of the day, the dead Booth lying supine beneath a canvas fly on the *Montauk*'s weather deck surrounded by a covey of somber, bearded men in coats and neck ties, could have been a studio publicity still for a 1930s horror film.

Early that same afternoon, some twelve hours after it had arrived on board, Booth's body was examined by a pair of army surgeons under the supervision of Dr. Joseph Barnes, the surgeon general. Barnes sent Stanton his brief autopsy report late the same day. Booth was killed, Barnes said, sounding like a clinician, by "a gun-shot wound in the neck—the ball entering just behind the sterno-cleido muscle—2½ inches above the clavicle—passing through the bony bridge of fourth and fifth cervical vertebrae—severing the spinal cord and passing out through the body." He then went on more colorfully, and with what sounds almost like satisfaction, to explain to a layman what this single shot had done to its target. "Paralysis of the entire body was immediate, and all the horrors of consciousness of suffering and death must have been present to the assassin during the two hours that he lingered." Debate continues whether the paralyzed and fatally injured Booth could have really uttered his quoted last words, "Useless, useless."

Later, under orders from Secretary Stanton, Col. Lafayette Baker of the National Detective Police faked Booth's burial at sea in an attempt to stymie sympathizers who might make a martyr of the man. At the Arsenal still later, Maj. Edward Stebbins, a storekeeper, and two noncommissioned officers wedged Booth's body into an empty musket shipping crate and covertly buried it under the floor of a locked room in the penitentiary building. The Gothic scene, a secret burial by lamp light inside a vacant room (once the prison dining room), lacked only Bela Lugosi or Boris Karloff to complete it.

Then, as now, it was difficult keeping a secret in Washington, and Booth's grave wasn't a secret for long. On May 10, not two weeks after the interment, the *Washington Evening Star* added this tidbit to its room-by-room description of the Arsenal's prison building: "A morbid interest attaches to this gloomy, sparsely lighted, iron-warded storeroom from the fact that popular report places under the brick flooring of its southern half all that remains mortal of the assassin Booth." The revelation made no difference; Booth was denied martyrdom. Robert E. Lee, the living general, rather than John Wilkes Booth, the dead actor, became the icon of the Lost Cause, the Southern myth that quickly arose to explain the region's defeat and to preserve its pride.

When Richard Montgomery, the first of 366 trial witnesses, took the stand on May 12 to give testimony "relating to the general conspiracy" that allegedly ended in the president's assassination, Booth had been in his grave two stories beneath Montgomery's feet for two weeks. That grave would eventually prove to be temporary, but Booth lay there throughout the trial, a silent presence unknown to many moving about on the floors above. He remained buried on the Arsenal's grounds until exhumed for a second time on February 15, 1869, for reburial in Baltimore's Greenmount Cemetery, where he lies today not far from an obelisk identifying the Booth family plot.

Only one woman sat through the entire proceeding, Mary Surratt, age forty-two, one of the eight accused. Pale, a little stocky, with a plain, guileless face framed by dark hair parted in the middle and pulled back into a prim bun, Mary watched it all quietly and attentively from behind a decorous black veil that entirely covered her head and face. In the private space behind her veil Mary must have suffered from terrible anxiety. Soon after her arrest she refused to eat, and according to Hartranft's notes she ate nothing at all during her first five days locked in her cell. Later she subsisted largely on tea and toast. Later still, and not surprisingly, she fell ill, so seriously that on June 20 she was removed from the courtroom. Her fragility was aggravated, said historian Margaret Leech in 1941, by "disorders incident to the menopause."[13] (Elizabeth Trindal, her first biographer, took this much further in 1996, sympathetically describing the imprisoned Mary Surratt as suffering "agony in her . . . churning uterus.") Mary's dress was black, too, falling to the floor. Unlike those of the other prisoners, her legs were not confined in irons and her hands were not cuffed.

It is not clear how much detail Mary saw of the proceedings that played out around her on this congested stage. During the trial her daughter and others would testify about Mary's weak vision, allegedly so bad that she was unable to thread a needle or read by gaslight. Near-sightedness and a consequent inability to recognize people passing close by were a part of her defense, however, so the testimony might have been exaggerated or even outright invention.

When the trial began on May 9 Mary had already been in prison nearly four weeks. The dragnet that had swept up her and the others into prison, and dozens more besides, had been cast by Secretary of War Stanton with astonishing speed and little discrimination. Stanton (whom Secretary of the Navy Welles, who disliked him, described as "mercurial—arbitrary and apprehensive, violent and fearful, rough and impulsive—yet possessed of ability and energy") ran that search with frenzied effort and determination.

Even before Lincoln died, early morning the day after he had been shot without ever regaining consciousness, his distraught Cabinet led by the secretary of wavr moved swiftly to capture the conspirators in what was obviously, even in the dark of the first night, a plot involving many people to decapitate the Union. The belief in the streets of Washington and soon throughout the shaken nation was that Jefferson Davis lay behind the attacks, that the president of the Confederacy personally and his government collectively had conceived of and ordered the deed, obediently executed by criminals from their safe haven in neutral Canada.

In the early morning of April 15, as part of his immediate response to the crisis and among a stream of telegrams transmitted from his headquarters on the corner of Seventeenth Street and Pennsylvania Avenue launching the search for the perpetrators, Stanton also ordered the arrest of Confederate agents known to be in Quebec, from where the South had mounted covert operations against the North. It would soon become apparent that Union officers of the law had no way to implement that order.

About one o'clock in the morning on April 15, just hours after John Wilkes Booth shot Lincoln and even before the president was dead, four detectives were on the way to the Surratt boardinghouse at 541 H Street, just off Sixth Street.[14] They were led there by a tip from a source lost to history. The four were seeking Mary's youngest son, John Harrison Surratt Jr., rightly suspected to be a Booth confidant but wrongly believed to have savagely assaulted Secretary of State William Seward in the latter's home on Lafayette Park as part of Booth's plot.

Two days later, near midnight on April 17, with several of the assassination conspirators already in custody but Booth and others, whoever they were, still free despite the frantic search underway, police attention turned to the mother. That night Mary, her daughter, tenants, and servants were arrested and jailed.

With them was one Lewis Powell, a large and powerfully built young man who had unaccountably materialized at her front door while the house was being raided by police, and then told an incredible story about his reason for being there. He was promptly hauled away with the others and soon was the solitary occupant of cell number 195 in the prison on Greenleaf Point. Later Powell would be described in the press as the mystery man among the plotters; there was even some question about his real last name. The trial record calls him "Payne," an alias.

Stoic, taciturn almost to the point of silence, and with a face that was remarkably handsome given that he had been kicked in the jaw by a mule as a twelve year old, his head topped by a thick shock of dark hair that fell naturally into a part, Powell in a sleeveless shirt, as a common contemporary photo showed him, could be confused for an athletic young collegian today.[15] In fact, he was a veteran of the 2nd Florida Infantry Regiment (in which he fought at Gettysburg and other places) and had served for a year with the 43rd Battalion,

Virginia Cavalry, Col. John Mosby's raiders. Powell's connection to Booth came through an introduction by Mary's youngest son.

On the night of April 14 Powell had obediently attacked the secretary of state as assigned by Booth, terrorizing the Seward household's several occupants, assembled there tending the bedridden secretary, who had been seriously injured in a runaway carriage accident nine days before. Powell viciously pistol-whipped Secretary Seward's son Frederick into unconsciousness, knifed an orderly on duty in Seward's second floor sickroom, stabbed Seward in the face, nearly killing him, and then, running down the stairs toward the door, slashed a fleeing State Department messenger in passing. Once on the street Powell discovered that David Herold, his assigned guide out of the city, had run away from the sounds of mayhem erupting from the big brick mansion. After hiding out for three days in the unfamiliar city alone, and minus his weapons, horse, hat, and coat, Payne had knocked at 541 H Street.

All inside were taken first for questioning to the District commandant's headquarters and then to the Carroll Branch annex of the Old Capitol Prison at Maryland Avenue and East First Street, in the city's northeast quadrant. Powell was then confined temporarily in the USS *Saugus*, another one of the several homely ironclad monitors in port at the navy yard that week.

The long war's all-consuming appetite had forced many shortages on both sides of the lines. One of these was a dearth of cell space, of secure confinement for the many prisoners of war, deserters, spies and enemy sympathizers, cheating contractors and profiteers, common criminals, drifters and miscellaneous misfits, and innocents caught off base that lent their texture to the population of both sides once fighting started.

The solution was hasty improvisation. In Richmond, the Libby Brothers' ship chandlery and grocery, three four-story brick buildings cut into the hillside across from the James River on the corner of Nineteenth and Cary Streets, was quickly adapted into a downtown prison for Union soldiers. Additional Union prisoners were held in the Confederate capital at approximately twenty-five other lock-ups, almost all of them superfluous tobacco factories or warehouses. In Washington, the Old Capitol and Carroll Row buildings, standing vacant and side by side one block apart on First Street facing the Capitol across East Capitol Park, were converted to the same purpose. All the transformation required was slats of wood on their ground floor windows, hasps and locks on the interior doors, and for each place a guard detachment of an officer and some sixty men on temporary detail from a handy infantry regiment.

Both buildings had seen better days, the Old Capitol Building especially. For four years after the War of 1812, until the original Capitol was rebuilt following the British arson, it had served as the temporary home of both houses of Congress. In July 1861 the dilapidated building, for a time a school and then a boardinghouse, became a four-story jail when the war's first Confederate prisoners, from the Union defeat at Manassas, were confined there. (In time both prison buildings were razed. In 1932 the grand Romanesque temple that is the Supreme Court began to rise in place of the former prison, and the Library of Congress took the place of Carroll Row.)

Locked in the prison annex next door, in one of the rooms of what had once been the elegant downtown property of Maryland's Carroll dynasty, until she was transferred to cell 157 in the Arsenal's penitentiary on May 1, Mary Surratt was for these few weeks more fortunate than the seven others who were to be tried with her. (Cell 157 was tiny, not even twenty square feet of floor space. Secretary Stanton soon directed that she be moved to less grim confinement, and Hartranft put her in a slightly larger cell, number 200, also on the third floor and furnished it with some tokens from H Street.)

Five other alleged conspirators were swiftly swept up in addition to Mary Surratt and Lewis Powell: Edman Spangler, Samuel Arnold, Michael O'Laughlen, Samuel Mudd, and George Atzerodt. David Herold, fleeing with Booth after he had abandoned Powell at LaFayette Park, was the last of the eight to be caught.

Edman Spangler was a former carpenter turned stagehand at Ford's Theatre, where he had worked part and full time for five or six years before the festive evening of April 14, when President Lincoln and his party came to see the last performance of *My American Cousin*. Ned Spangler had known Booth for a long time. Earlier he had agreed to tend a skittish mare that the actor kept in a rented stall in a stable at the end of the alley behind the theater. That evening Booth asked Spangler to hold his horse at the theater's back door. Spangler, unaware of what was to come, arranged instead for Joseph Burroughs ("Peanut John," who sold goobers at the box office) to hold the horse that Booth would ride in his flight from Washington.

Spangler was arrested on April 17 and jailed, first in the Old Capitol Prison, then aboard the USS *Montauk* in the stream off the Washington Navy Yard, and finally in the Arsenal penitentiary, in cell 209.

Samuel Arnold was a Georgetown native, the second son of a prosperous baker, and a classmate of John Wilkes Booth at St. Timothy's Hall, a boarding secondary school on the road west out of Baltimore toward Frederick, Maryland.

By 1864 Arnold had already been invalided out of the 1st Maryland Infantry Regiment in Richmond (one of the few formations that carried the state's name in the Confederate States Army), been in and out of a civilian job in Augusta, Georgia, and gone back to Maryland when he received news of his mother's serious illness. Booth reconnected with Arnold that August after a twelve-year hiatus. Arnold, bored and out of work, immediately joined the plot to kidnap Lincoln. After the group's failure to abduct Lincoln on March 15, Arnold apparently got cold feet. But it was too late. His ties to Booth were indelible.

Arnold was arrested on April 17 in Tidewater Virginia, shipped to Baltimore in irons, jailed briefly at Fort McHenry (in "a dungeon beneath the earthworks of the fort"), and then removed to the Washington Navy Yard, where he joined the USS *Montauk*'s chain gang. He ended up in the Arsenal's cell 184.

Monday, April 17, was a big day. That's when Michael O'Laughlen, another alumnus of the 1st Maryland Infantry and the third conspirator to be taken in custody, nervously turned himself in to police. O'Laughlen was a childhood friend of Booth, dating back to when the two were near-neighbors in Baltimore.

Booth brought O'Laughlen into the plot when its purpose was to kidnap Lincoln as the president rode alone through northwestern Washington and to use him as a bargaining chip to force the resumption of prisoner of war exchanges. As Booth's scheme morphed into something very different, O'Laughlen recoiled, but Booth had cunningly scattered evidence about that made exposure or successful withdrawal impossible. Like Arnold, O'Laughlen was stuck to the tar baby. He went into cell 181.

George Atzerodt was the only foreign-born plotter. He had come to the United States from Prussia in 1844 as a child. After the beginning of the Civil War Atzerodt was living in Port Tobacco, Maryland, no longer painting carriages with his brother as he had done briefly but drinking too much and ferrying border crossers over the Potomac along the "secret lines" that ran from King George County and Westmoreland County in Confederate Virginia across Maryland and into Washington. In January 1865 John Surratt introduced Atzerodt to Booth.

That April, with the kidnapping plot suddenly put aside, Booth assigned Atzerodt to kill Vice President Andrew Johnson in his first-floor suite at the Kirkwood Hotel. On the night of April 14 Johnson went to bed early and was unaware of the mayhem boiling in Washington until an acquaintance, one Leonard Farwell, rushed to his hotel and breathlessly told him about the horror that had just visited Ford's Theatre. At the time Johnson had no idea that he had survived the terrible night intact because George Atzerodt had lost his nerve (or suffered an uncharacteristic flash of good sense) in the Kirkwood's bar a short while earlier.

Atzerodt then stumbled around Washington, Georgetown, and Rockville, Maryland, during the Easter weekend, leaving an unambiguous trail from the Kirkwood Hotel to a relative's farm in Maryland's Montgomery County. He was arrested there by troopers of the 1st Delaware Cavalry in the early morning of April 20. Atzerodt was soon in chains in the windlass room aboard the USS *Saugus*. Presumably, only six days into the manhunt, all the available accommodations in the USS *Montauk* were already full. On May 1 he was locked into cell 151.

The next conspirator to be arrested was Dr. Samuel Mudd, a physician and tobacco farmer in Charles County, Maryland, who, like most of his neighbors, was a Confederate sympathizer. Just after four o'clock in the morning on Saturday, April 15, Mudd had set and splinted Booth's broken left leg. The two, Booth and Herold, then spent the rest of the day resting at Mudd's comfortable home near Beantown (a museum today) before continuing their run to the border around supper time.

Mudd later claimed repeatedly and ingeniously that the invalid who appeared at his door in darkness was unknown to him. Had that been it, innocent acts of care of and hospitality to an injured wayfarer by a good Samaritan, Mudd might have escaped trial, conviction, and confinement altogether. Several others with much less pure motives who assisted Booth and Herold on their way south did. Mudd, however, had recognized Booth that night. In fact, he knew his nocturnal caller well. The two first met in November, and they had met twice since. It was Mudd who had introduced Surratt to Booth in December 1864.

On April 24, after having been questioned four times during the preceding week by increasingly skeptical interrogators, Mudd was arrested and taken to the Carroll Annex from where he would soon be moved to cell number 176 in the Arsenal penitentiary. His status as an educated member of southern Maryland's professional class afforded him one benefit: Unlike the other men, he was not forced to wear a hood over his head.

David Herold was a part-time pharmacy clerk in Washington and enthusiastic Maryland partridge hunter. He led Lewis Powell, Seward's would-be assassin, to his victim's house, deserted him there, and later accompanied Booth during the actor's halting escape attempt through southern Maryland and into Virginia. Herold brought little more to the plot than loyalty to Booth and a lack of imagination, but like Surratt and Atzerodt he knew his way around the open country of southern Maryland. Thursday night, April 20, midway through their escape, Booth and Herold got lost rowing across the Potomac in the dark (Booth on the compass, Herold working the oars), going west upriver instead of south across it. The error cost them two days. Not until Saturday night did they try again. Five days later he was caught at Garrett's farm and became the lone occupant of cell 170.

At forty-two Mary Surratt was the oldest defendant by three years. Spangler, next oldest, was thirty-nine. Arnold, Atzerodt, and Mudd were in their thirties, and the other three were in their twenties. John Wilkes Booth himself was just two weeks short of his twenty-seventh birthday when he was shot to death at Garrett's tobacco farm. (Astonishingly, twenty-six makes Booth only the second youngest in the field of presidential assassins. The distinction of being the junior man on this roster falls to Lee Harvey Oswald, twenty-four when he shot John F. Kennedy in November 1963.)

Two years after this trial was over, when John Surratt sat in the dock alone on June 10, 1867, the correspondent for the New York Times dismissed the eight in a single, offhand sentence: "Those who remembered Wilkes Booth and looked upon [John] Surratt today, at once recalled the fact that of all the conspirators these two only possessed any brains, and that of the two, Surratt's was the best balanced mind."

Like her freedom from the claustrophobic cloth hood the male prisoners were forced to wear over their heads in their cells, the absence of manacles and leg irons in the Arsenal's courtroom was a concession to Mary's sex. So, too, was the fact that she sat apart from her codefendants and wasn't bracketed by an armed guard to either side. The other seven defendants, on a bench behind a railing along the western wall of the room, enjoyed no such delicate treatment. The seven—in their order on the bench, David Herold, Lewis Powell, George Atzerodt, Michael O'Laughlen, Edman Spangler, Doctor Samuel Mudd, and Sam Arnold—wore weighted leg irons and manacles. A corporal of the Veterans Reserve Corps sat at each end of the line of male prisoners and another guard sat between every pair of them, ensuring they didn't speak to one another; when required, guards also carried the cannon ball weights of their shackles to permit the prisoners to shuffle awkwardly into and from the room. (The shackles made bathing difficult, and Powell's leg irons, of a different design than the others, had to be modified on June 1 to permit him changes of underwear.)

Of the group, Mary aside, only Powell commanded spectators' special attention. A contemporary journalist described him as being young, "of splendid muscular development, a massive neck . . . and a most noteworthy face," and as "an extraordinary ruffian" with the physiognomy of an assassin. The others appeared somehow inadequate to have participated in the great crime.

Occasionally a female witness—Mary's adult daughter, Anna, was one, and there were others, both black and white—joined Mary in the chamber, but otherwise the trial of those charged as conspirators in the murder of the president was a distinctly male proceeding.

Maryland was a border state in 1861, one of four in the Union that permitted slavery. As war loomed the state exhibited the same schizophrenia that divided some families, with part loyal to one side of the conflict and part to the other. Southern sympathies were especially virulent around Baltimore and to the city's south, in the tobacco-growing farm country that spread like great, fat fingers between the lower Potomac River and the upper reaches of the Chesapeake Bay. These five counties—Anne Arundel, Prince George's, Calvert, Charles, and St. Mary's—had much more in common with Virginia across the river than they did with the mountainous western panhandle of their own state. In 1860 the five, together with Baltimore City and Baltimore County, were home to more than forty-six thousand slaves, 53 percent of the total in Maryland. The state's other fifteen counties accounted for the remaining 47 percent.[16]

Baltimore would eventually move toward redemption. During Lincoln's progress by rail through the city on his way to inauguration, there were fears for his safety, and in April 1861 street toughs fought a bloody brawl, the "Battle of Baltimore," with the transiting 6th Massachusetts Infantry Regiment on the way to reinforce Washington that cost thirteen lives. (In May 1898 the same regiment passed through Baltimore again, on the way to another war, and was met with wild, patriotic cheering.) Four years later the Republican Party convention that selected Lincoln to run a second time was held in the same city, now presumably safe for the Great Emancipator. Even so, Southern sympathies ran deep in the port at the head of Chesapeake Bay: More than fourteen thousand Baltimoreans petitioned Andrew Johnson in 1866 to release Jefferson Davis from prison; no petition from any city in Dixie had as many names.

Like many of their neighbors, the Surratts of Prince George's County were Southerners in everything but place of abode. In Surrattsville (the hamlet was little more than their farm and boardinghouse with its tavern and post office; today it is Clinton, Maryland) they lived almost exactly midway between Washington and the Potomac border between North and South. Citizens of Maryland, they and many of their relatives and neighbors had the sentiments of plantation Virginians.

The Surratts and southern Maryland's other citizens lived in what amounted to an occupied country. Maryland surrounded the Union capital on three sides (Virginia closed off the fourth), and so Washington was indefensible if the state was neutral or in unfriendly hands. During a turbulent spring and summer Lincoln moved to ensure the security of the capital. The decisive moment came on August 7, 1861, when delegates to the state's general assembly sympathetic to the South were arrested in Frederick, where the assembly was meeting in special session. (They joined a mixed bag of lesser government officials, journalists, and other private citizens already being held on suspicion of their loyalty.) An election in November, marked by a heavy federal thumb on the scales, put a loyal majority into the state legislature and completed the lockdown of the state.

Elizabeth Susanna Surratt, "Anna," twenty-two in 1865, was the middle one of Mary Surratt's children and the only one of the three who appeared at her mother's trial. Hartranft's mercy went further than the simple gentlemanly courtesies he had shown the imprisoned widow. During part of the trial Anna was permitted to sleep near her mother, after Mary's health forced a move from cell 200 into a larger "side room."

Anna's older brother, Isaac Douglas, had left home heading southwest in March 1861. His last glimpse of his mother must have been then, when he was twenty. Reportedly Isaac left Maryland on Inauguration Day in March 1861, and if so the leave taking deliberately underscored his politics. In May 1862 in San Antonio, Texas, Isaac joined a unit that was eventually absorbed into the 33rd Regiment, Texas Cavalry (Duff's Partisan Rangers). He served with his regiment through the war, likely taking part in its several dusty rumbles during the last two years of the war. Apparently his service was creditable. By the time the Confederacy's Trans-Mississippi Department surrendered its forces to the Union in late May 1865, Isaac had risen in the ranks to sergeant and was serving as a unit quartermaster.

Not much is known about the 33rd Regiment, which spent the war in the department's Rio Grande Military District along the lower Rio Grande, under the command of Col. James Duff. Perhaps the best known today of the regiment's officers is Maj. (later Col.) Santos Benavides, the South's senior Mexican officer. It is Benavides and his Hispanic roots rather than his regiment that have received historians' attention recently. According to them, in March 1864 Benavides, then at the head of the forty or so troopers of the regiment, defended his hometown, Laredo, against a Union cavalry formation said to have been some five times larger. Improbably, the Confederates won, leaving the small battle near the Rio Grande to ornament the colonel's reputation.

Not much is known about Isaac Surratt either—one of forty-seven Surratts who appear on the Confederate army's muster rolls. (There were seven other men with the same last name fighting on the side of the Union.) On September 18, 1865, he was paroled in San Antonio, Texas, with the other survivors of his defeated regiment. He arrived back in Maryland that same autumn, some months after his mother's execution. On the first day of his younger brother's trial in June 1867 Isaac came into the courtroom with the accused and sat by his side. The *New York Times* described the pair this way, casually slipping in an ethnic slur: "Surratt was brought into the court . . . appearing rather careworn and despondent. . . . His brother, Isaac Surratt, sat near him, presenting quite a contrast, John being a quiet, refined, student-looking young man while Isaac is much stouter, far less intelligent in countenance, with a bold b'hoyish expression, and far more likely to be picked out as the perpetrator of a desperate deed, although evidently endowed with far less brains."[17]

The Library of Congress holds a single photograph identified as a likeness of Isaac Surratt. A young, clean shaven man dressed in coat and cravat in the style of the time, he looks urban, if not exactly urbane, professional, like a junior clerk or storekeeper, and nothing like the dullard edging toward brutishness described by the *Times*. Perhaps it is not his portrait at all (its provenance isn't certain, and for a time library records identified it as a photo of John Surratt), but possibly it is and the *Times* was being unfair. Isaac was often there, next to his brother in the courtroom, as the summer progressed, perhaps making up in this way for his absence at his mother's trial.

The fact that Mary's first son had fought for the Confederacy would have poisoned opinion against her even before the trial began. But her other connections were more damning still.

Anna's youngest brother, John Harrison Jr., a former seminary student and very briefly a clerk at a package delivery service in Washington, had been a Confederate courier since leaving St. Charles' College in Ellicott City, Maryland, in the summer of 1862. Monthly, or more often, he carried mail and messages and escorted agents across the border up and down the 120-mile-long "secret line" between Richmond and Washington that threaded through his mother's tavern in southern Maryland, the line's last stop before the capital.

Alone among the conspirators John Surratt was unaccounted for at the trial in the Arsenal. A quick pass through Montreal in April to find young Surratt had failed, and there was no immediate follow-up. Still, it's clear that the prosecution regarded Mary's youngest son as unfinished government business. At the arraignment of the accused the absent Surratt's name appeared twice in the charge, both times immediately next to Booth's and four more times in the specification. Even more damning than her son's ties to the actor, however, was Mary's own close connection to John Wilkes Booth.

Mary Elizabeth Surratt (sometimes "Mary Eugenia," using her confirmation name) made three big decisions during her truncated life. Two of them went very badly for her, the last one most especially so.

Her first decision, made as a schoolgirl, was to become a Roman Catholic. In later life the faith gave her great comfort and she served it until death with passion and the fervent piety that often marks converts. Mary raised her children in the religion and persuaded some of her kinsmen and kinswomen to convert. Roman Catholicism was suspect in Protestant America in the mid-nineteenth century, where it was viewed by many as just short of idolatry and unaccountably foreign and antirepublican, subversive. Under these circumstances her decision to leave the much more mainstream Anglican Church was a bold one, even in Maryland, which had its roots in the English Roman Catholic peerage. Her adopted church would return the favor. In May 1865 during her trial, five priests would be character witnesses for the defense, all agreeing that she was a "proper Christian matron" and "a Christian lady in every sense of the word."

To have won his wife John Harrison Surratt should have professed the faith at least outwardly when the two were married in 1840, he at twenty-seven, she only seventeen, but possibly he did not. It is not clear that Surratt, raised an Episcopalian like her, and his bride were married in a Catholic church. Whatever he believed, John Sr. was a backslider at best, and after they were wed he had to be hounded into church by his wife. The few times he went to mass were occasions for letters to her friends. During the next decades her second big decision, to marry this man, led to sad consequences. John proved himself repeatedly to be a poor provider but an accomplished alcoholic. The two vices fit neatly together in the tavern–cum–post office the two ran in their family's new home beginning in 1852, after they moved from property he had inherited from his adoptive parents. Well before John died ten years later, Mary was stoically telling her confessors of his daily drunkenness. His death in August 1862 and their debts forced her out of the country house and into Washington, where she would make her living as a single woman.

Mary's third decision was to enter into a complex and eventually fatal entanglement with the mesmerizing young Baltimore actor John Wilkes Booth. Raised among white supremacists at the very margin of the slave-owning South and an owner of slaves herself (until their ownership became illegal in Maryland at the end of 1864 under the new state constitution), Mary must have found Booth's political views congenial, adapting hers to his as Booth's became progressively more extreme. She would have found his increasingly frequent presence at her house in Washington gratifying, too. Perhaps even exhilarating.

John Ford, the theater proprietor, presumably would have been immune to Booth's manly charms, but he was not unaware of them. Booth, he described in capsule form, "was above ordinary height, very graceful and good looking . . . one of the best gymnasts in the country . . . remarkably handsome . . . an extremely fascinating man in his manner." Years later, when Mary's son was on trial for his life, defense counsel limned Booth as a nearly irresistible figure in the Surratt circle, "of polished exterior and pleasing address, highly prepossessing in appearance and manners, received into the most accomplished circles of society; his company sought after; in conversation he was exceedingly agreeable; his disposition was bold, courteous, considerate, and generous to a fault; and a warm and liberal-hearted friend."

Suave, elegant John Wilkes Booth was Mary Surratt's connection to things more glamorous and thrilling than eking out a living as a widowed landlady in middle age with no prospects for anything better. His proximity must have been intoxicating.[18] Satan could not have been more alluring.

Unlike his jailed accomplices, who soon would face capital charges filed by a government that needed revenge the way its home city needed food and water, Booth had a plan for escape after the act. Once out of Washington, through southern Maryland, and across the Potomac River, Booth intended to make for Richmond and then by train and on horseback to ride twenty-five hundred miles from Richmond to Mexico City, where he expected to find sanctuary from Union pursuit.

The Mexico of Emperor Maximilian, the naïve unemployed Hapsburg archduke who had arrived at Veracruz in April 1864 to discover with surprise that his empire-to-be was in violent revolution, was viewed by some planters as a refuge should they be driven from the United States. Maximilian encouraged these fantasies, responding favorably to initiatives, such as those by Lt. Matthew Fontaine Maury, USN, to stimulate immigration by southern planters and to establish enclaves in Mexico for Confederate expatriates where the past could live on.* He

---

* Lieutenant Maury (1807–1873) is credited by many as the first oceanographer and recognized for his pioneering scientific research and many publications while long-term head of the U.S. Navy's Depot of

and Empress Carlota fancifully hoped that this new blood would dilute the old and usher in an era of progress and prosperity.

That perception, and the expectation that beyond the Rio Grande he would also be out of the reach of American law, must have been the lures that attracted Booth there. Maximilian barely outlived the Confederacy (he bravely went before a Republican firing squad in June 1867) but during his brief reign Mexico appeared as a potential haven to beleaguered southerners.

Thinking in early April about the long trip through nearly the full length of the Confederacy to this foreign bolt hole, Booth must have hoped and imagined that his would be less an escape than a procession through admiring and adoring fans in his adopted nation—people who saw his murder of Lincoln the way he did, thought it brave, and believed him to be a hero.[19] That was not to be: Booth's broken leg, his lack of planning in detail, his delay in crossing the Potomac into Virginia, and the reluctance of some to harbor him allowed Stanton's furious pursuit to catch up. In any case Booth's few days alive in Virginia made reality clear.

Charts and Instruments and first superintendent of the Naval Observatory. It was his genius to observe that the great collection of ships' logs held in the U.S. Naval Observatory was a database that could be mined for valuable information on the seas.

Maury's insight produced an enormously important result: detailed charts that permitted the ocean commerce of the mid-nineteenth century, still largely moving by sail, to benefit reliably from seasonal winds and ocean currents, roughly halving the time at sea between New York and Rio de Janeiro, for example. More generally, Maury's pioneering work made the planet's vast oceans seem knowable for the first time. Before Maury sailing instructions were largely based on local lore and personal experience; after him they were based on global science and public information.

In 1861 Maury (a native Virginian raised in Tennessee) and nearly three hundred other U.S. Navy officers resigned their commissions and later joined the Confederate States Navy. He spent the war years working on torpedoes and as a purchasing agent for the CSN in Europe. Before and during the war Maury studied the possibility that Brazil or Mexico could become a bolt hole where plantation agriculture and slavery could be preserved if or when expelled from the United States. (Earlier, in 1851, he had launched a brother-in-law, Lt. William Herndon, to explore the basin of the Amazon River for this purpose.) Maury went so far in this project as to become Emperor Maximilian's immigration commissioner immediately after the war. Their relationship dated back to the days when the archduke was chief of the Imperial Austrian Navy.

Maury attempted to interest Gen. Robert E. Lee in his and the emperor's resettlement scheme, but Lee (who knew Mexico from his service there during the Mexican-American War) gently turned him down. "The thought of abandoning the country and all that must be lost in it is abhorrent to my feelings," Lee wrote to Maury on September 8, 1865, "and I prefer to struggle for its restoration and share its fate, rather than give up all as lost. I have a great admiration for Mexico; the salubrity of its climate, the fertility of its soil, and the magnificence of its scenery, possess for me great charm; but . . . [Virginia] has need for all her sons and can ill afford to spare you."

After returning from England in 1868, where he went after Maximilian's execution, Maury spent the last five years of his life teaching at the Virginia Military Institute, in Lexington, Virginia. Richmond's Museum of the Confederacy was founded by his niece, Isabel Maury.

For more on "the Southern dream of tropical empire," see Robert Kagan, *Dangerous Nation* (New York: Knopf, 2006), chap. 8.

The Virginians he met there then regarded his deed with horror or consternation. Either way, they feared Yankee retribution if they were caught providing Booth with hospitality, and they begrudged what very little they gave him.[20]

The legal process that followed the capture of the eight proceeded with what would be seen today as astonishing, almost inherently extralegal haste, "a rush to judgment" that on its face threatened the defendants' rights. After three days of legal preliminaries, the taking of trial testimony began May 12. By early July it was all over: The condemned had been executed, the others were on the way to prison.

Compared to the trial of the abolitionist John Brown in 1859, the next most sensational trial of the age, the one on the Arsenal's grounds atop Greenleaf Point moved, however, at an almost stately pace. Brown's raid on Harpers Ferry, Virginia, began on October 16. Two days later, the survivors of his "Provisional Army of the North" were easily winkled out of the building he had seized by Bvt. Lt. Col. Robert E. Lee's troops. Brown's trial on three capital charges (treason, murder, and insurrection) began on October 25 and lasted only six days. On December 2, 1859, Brown was hanged, achieving the martyrdom he had so avidly anticipated. Six weeks, crime to punishment.

In fact, as a pair of proceedings during the next thirty-five years showed, the pace of events in the Arsenal was about average. The trials and executions of America's next two presidential assassins went about as swiftly from crime to punishment as did this one. The second was slower, but the third much faster.

The trial of Charles Guiteau—he was the "deranged and depraved" killer of President James Garfield in July 1881—started in mid-November, and he was not hanged until June the following year. Twenty years later President William McKinley's killer, the self-proclaimed anarchist Leon Czolgosz, was the object of swifter, perhaps even breathlessly quick, disposal. McKinley was shot on September 6, 1901. Czolgosz's one-day trial took place later that month. He was electrocuted on October 29, only forty-five days after he twice fired at and hit the president.

President Andrew Johnson's executive order establishing the military commission that tried the case was signed on May 1. The defendants were then arraigned, defense counsel was selected, and on May 12—less than one month after Booth fired his derringer, plunging a lead ball nearly the size of the tip of your finger "against and upon the left and posterior side of the head of said Abraham Lincoln"—the tribunal of nine officers began hearing testimony, beginning with that of Richard Montgomery. During the next seven weeks, 366 witnesses were heard. The last witness left the stand on June 29.[21]

At first the commission intended to operate in closed session with access barred to the press, but protest soon wrested the proceedings open. In 1865 everything that was reliably known about Booth's plotting and the assassination itself, and more besides, was written into the daily verbatim record of trial as recorded in shorthand by the "phonographs." Immediately after being transcribed, these records were provided to government counsel and to the press. Newspapers in Washington and Philadelphia promptly printed complete accounts. Bound copies of the full text appeared as soon as July 10, not even two weeks after the trial ended. In 1865 only in Maine were defendants permitted to testify at their trials—an injunction elsewhere designed to bar self-incrimination—and the military tribunal adopted this general restriction in its own proceedings. Thus the published trial record encompasses the testimony and examination of witnesses and statements of counsel and the commissioners only. It runs something over four hundred two-column book pages.

On May 10 the defendants were collectively charged by the War Department's judge advocate general, Joseph Holt—a committed abolitionist from Kentucky, he managed the government's case—with "maliciously, unlawfully, and traitorously, and in aid of the existing armed rebellion against the United States of America . . . combining, confederating, and conspiring together with [here the list included not only John Wilkes Booth, John Surratt, and Jefferson Davis but also seven others named and "others unknown"] to kill and murder" Abraham Lincoln, Andrew Johnson, William Seward, and Ulysses Grant. The charge, a single sentence some 325 words and seven semicolons long, went on to accuse the defendants of the murder of President Lincoln, of assault on Secretary Seward, and of lying in wait "to kill and murder" Vice President Johnson and Lieutenant General Grant.*

The amplifying specification mentioned every conspirator by name. "And in further prosecution of said conspiracy," Holt had written,

> Mary E. Surratt did . . . receive, entertain, harbor, and conceal, aid and assist the said John Wilkes Booth, David E. Herold, Lewis Payne

---

* Before September 1862, when he became judge advocate general in Stanton's department, Joseph Holt (1807–1894) had been a lawyer in private practice in Kentucky and Mississippi and under President Buchanan successively the U.S. commissioner of patents, the postmaster general (after 1829 and until 1971 a politically important cabinet position), and the secretary of war.

When Edward Bates, seventy-one, resigned from the office in November 1864, Lincoln offered the attorney generalship to Holt. Holt declined in favor of another Kentuckian, James Speed, who willingly took the post. It was Speed who, retroactively, provided the legal decision that permitted the Arsenal trial to go ahead as a military tribunal rather than in civil court.

[Powell], John H. Surratt, Michael O. Laughlin, George A. Atzerodt, Samuel Arnold and their confederates, with the knowledge of the murderous and traitorous conspiracy aforesaid, and with intent to aid, abet, and assist them in the execution thereof, and in escaping from justice after the murder of the said Abraham Lincoln, as aforesaid.

All eight pleaded "not guilty" to the charge and specification.

The commission began to hear testimony in the case against Mary Surratt on May 13, but that was not the first time that she had been the focus of the proceedings. Mary was defended by the largest and what superficially appeared to be the best legal team any of the eight managed to recruit. Hers included Frederick Aiken and John Clampitt, partners who were soon joined by a third lawyer, Senator Reverdy Johnson of Maryland.

According to Edward Steers, Aiken and Clampitt were both on their first important case as lawyers.[22] Of the three, Johnson, sixty-nine, was the acknowledged star. Eight years earlier he had argued the case of *Dred Scott v. Sanford* before the Supreme Court, one of the landmark race relations cases in U.S. history, and his persuasiveness was commonly believed to have influenced Chief Justice Roger Taney (a colleague from Maryland) and his court to rule that blacks were not and could not be citizens and had no right to sue. The decision, which upended the 1820 Missouri Compromise and opened the western territories to slavery, established Johnson's reputation as a preeminent constitutional lawyer and froze race relations in the United States for decades.

Reverdy Johnson had been President Taylor's attorney general for two years and was at the time he joined the Surratt legal defense team midway through what would eventually be ten years as a U.S. senator. Mary Surratt aside, Johnson might have had a second marquee legal client in 1865. He offered to defend Gen. Robert E. Lee in the event the United States decided to prosecute him for treason. Later he counseled Lee on his approach to President Johnson via General Grant for restoration of his citizenship rights. (Those rights were finally restored by President Gerald Ford in August 1975, more than a century after Lee's death, after relevant documents were discovered at the National Archives.)[23]

Had the commissioners known that on April 5, 1861, Frederick Aiken had "after mature deliberation" enthusiastically volunteered in a personal letter to Jefferson Davis to work for the Confederacy, he might have been the target of an objection to his presence as defense counsel. "I desire now to identify myself with the government of the Confederate States," the young lawyer had written

Davis after first describing his service to the Democratic Party during the past election, "and to offer my services in any civil position of usefulness that you may designate. I have not the military knowledge suiting me for the Army, nor the means for the support of myself and wife that would enable me to serve as a private in the ranks. . . . In the event of war coming on I know the influence I could exert upon Northern Democrats would be marked and important." There is no record of Davis's reply, and so Aiken, with his sympathies apparently unknown, took his place on Mary's team unchallenged.

So it happened that Senator Johnson was the only defense counsel nominated to whom a member of the commission objected. The objection to Johnson, made on May 12 on the grounds that he had failed to sign an obligatory loyalty oath to the Union, was subsequently withdrawn, and the senator joined Mary's defense, in which he was an active partner for a special purpose. After participating on May 13 in the examination of just one prosecution witness, he left the rest of Mary's courtroom defense entirely to Aiken and Clampitt for a month.* (In the ensuing weeks the two did her little good, often calling witnesses or following lines of questioning that inadvertently weakened their client's case.) Not until June 16 did Johnson again stand to speak. That's when he delivered a long and eloquent legal argument citing the constitution and English and American authorities and case law denying that the commission had jurisdiction to try the case it was hearing.

He had made the same argument earlier, at the outset of the trial. "Mary E. Surratt," he wrote the tribunal then, speaking for his client,

> says that this court has no jurisdiction in the proceedings against her, because she says she is not, and has not been, in the military services of the United States. And, for further plea, the said Mary E. Surratt says that loyal civil courts, in which all the offenses charged are triable, exist and are in full and free operation in all places where the several offenses charged are alleged to have been committed. And, for further plea, the said Mary E. Surratt says that the court has no jurisdiction in the matter of the alleged conspiracy . . . said alleged conspiracy and all acts said to have been done in the formation and the execution thereof, are, in the

---

* After his last term in the Senate, Reverdy Johnson (1796–1876) became the U.S. ambassador in Great Britain, serving at his post in London while the former first family of the Confederacy, Jefferson and Varina Davis, lived in the city and country and while his immediate predecessor, Charles Francis Adams Sr., was in Geneva negotiating Civil War damage claims against the United Kingdom related to losses inflicted by Confederate commerce raiders built in British shipyards and manned largely by English crews.

charges and specifications, alleged to have been committed in the city of Washington, in which city are loyal civil courts, in full operation, in which said crimes are triable.

Other defense counsels made similar arguments for their clients, also unsuccessfully. (The argument was neither successful nor novel; by 1865 military tribunals had judged and convicted civilians for three years. In one landmark 1862 case more than three hundred Sioux had been tried by such a body.)

Johnson apparently served without fee. The press showed great interest in the fees paid to Aiken and Clampitt, who might together have eventually received one thousand dollars of an expected three thousand to thirty-five hundred dollars. Not enough, in any case, as their firm of Aiken and Clampitt closed its doors the next year, a victim of embezzlement.

Nine witnesses testified against Mary over the course of nine days, two to especially powerful effect. The first was her tenant at the house in Surrattsville, John Lloyd. His testimony seems to have been taken at face value despite the fact that several other witnesses volunteered that he was a hard drinker and often very drunk during the critical days of April, something Lloyd acknowledged without embarrassment. He testified on May 13 and again two days later about John Surratt concealing weapons and ammunition at the house weeks before, and about Mary's anxiety on April 14 to ensure that the stashed "shooting irons" and two bottles of whiskey would be available for collection by mysterious night riders later that evening. Herold, Lloyd said, then rode up in darkness to the tavern in Surrattsville with another man to empty the cache. During Lloyd's first session on the stand, he quoted Herold as volunteering to him, "I am pretty certain that we have assassinated the President and Secretary Seward."

Louis Weichmann, next up after Lloyd, testified three different times and what he said was equally damaging. Weichmann, a self-described "companion of John H. Surratt's for seven years," her tenant and his roommate on H Street, exposed Mary Surratt as the mistress of a Confederate safe house and as an inn keeper for transiting border runners. Weichmann's description of the many visits of the conspirators (less Arnold and O'Laughlen) to her city home and country place and of their mysterious private conversations together put her in the center of Booth's cabal. His testimony also hinted that the band had been involved in a failed kidnapping attempt on the president in mid-March.

The night she was arrested, Mary, hand raised piously in the air, had sworn to God that the laborer unexpectedly standing in front of her with a pickaxe on his shoulder was a stranger. It soon developed that he was Powell, Seward's assailant, that he had been an overnight guest at number 541 twice before, and that Mary had also called on Powell in April at his hotel. Five of the twenty-nine witnesses called to the stand by the defense in May and June testified to Mary's poor eyesight, an attempt to explain away her apparently false statement. "I assure you," Mary had said to Col. Henry Wells during her first interrogation, "on the honor of a lady that I would not tell you an untruth." But seemingly in an effort to save herself she had, and been caught at it.

Isaac and John Surratt's mother, Booth's frequent hostess, Powell's familiar, and the keeper of the assassin's arms and equipment was not going to escape conviction. The testimony of John Lloyd and Louis Weichmann was simply too damning, the lingering presence of Booth in her home too vital, the sense that she was an improper woman and therefore capable of the crime too strong.

On Thursday, June 29, the nine commissioners finally met in closed session to consider what they had heard during the preceding seven weeks of trial from the witnesses and from counsel on both sides, from everyone but the silent accused, and what had been said to them in hundreds of thousands of words of sworn testimony during legal interrogation. The next Wednesday, its deliberations completed, the commission sent its conclusions to President Andrew Johnson for his review and approval.

The government's attempt to ascribe leadership of the plot to Jefferson Davis, his secretary of state, Judah Benjamin, Beverly Tucker, and a gaggle of other Confederate agents in Canada failed, despite the fact that sixty government witnesses were called to prove the case. (Stanton and Holt both fervently believed this, but there was no evidence for it then. What there is now, combed over thoroughly by William Tidwell and his coauthors, most find unpersuasive still.) The case against the defendants present at the Arsenal, however, succeeded. All were found guilty by the commission, but the votes were not unanimous, nor were they required to be. Conviction required only a simple majority: five votes. Six votes or more to convict equated to a death sentence.

On Wednesday, July 5, approaching three months following his inauguration as Lincoln's successor and only one day after he had received the commission's conclusions, Johnson approved its work. Mary was found guilty of the charge, except as it related to Edman Spangler, and guilty of the specification, except as it encompassed Arnold, O'Laughlen, and Spangler.

Lewis Powell, David Herold, George Atzerodt, and Mary Surratt were condemned to death by hanging, "by proper military authority, under the direction of the Secretary of War, on the seventh day of July, 1865, between the hours of ten o'clock a.m. and two o'clock p.m. of that day." Samuel Arnold, Michael O'Laughlen, and Samuel Mudd were sentenced to life in prison. Edman Spangler, who knew nothing about anything, was sentenced to six years at hard labor, a classic victim of being in the wrong place at the wrong time.

These four were to be confined at hard labor in the county penitentiary at Albany, New York. Ten days later this was changed on presidential order to Fort Jefferson on Garden Key off Florida, a place *Scientific American* quoted military men as calling "the safest fort in the world, and the most useless." Since September 1861 the massive, unfinished coastal defense installation had been used as a military prison. The convict population had jumped in February 1864, eighteen months before the four came ashore there, when imprisonment at Fort Jefferson replaced the death penalty for desertion, a substitution that says something about the quality of life in the Dry Tortugas.

On July 25 Mudd and the others joined a few other civilian "prisoners of state" and some four hundred former military offenders already being held in the hellish heat of the Dry Tortugas at Fort Jefferson. The trip south via Fortress Monroe took the new convicts only one week, first in the USS *State of Maine* and then in the USS *Florida*. In September a regiment of U.S. Colored Troops arrived to relieve the New Yorkers who had been guarding the prisoners until then. In Mudd's eyes the arrival of the black troops on Garden Key made his punishment complete. It prompted his unsuccessful escape attempt two weeks later.

Mary was the object of a brief but fervent campaign to have her sentence mitigated to life in prison. During the commission's closed deliberations on Friday, June 30, five of the nine members (including Maj. Gen. David Hunter, its president) signed an appeal for clemency to President Johnson. The impetus behind the appeal for mercy from the five was not any doubt about her guilt, but rather gentlemanly discomfort with the idea of putting a woman to death. There was, however, real doubt about her guilt elsewhere in the courtroom. Benn Pitman, chief of the five phonographs hired to record the proceedings, revealed many years later that he believed she was "entirely innocent." There was doubt in Johnson's Cabinet, too. Longtime treasury secretary Hugh McCullough, who served in the Cabinets of three presidents beginning with Lincoln's, wrote in his memoir years later, "The evidence on which she was convicted would not have convinced an impartial jury. Her complicity in the assassination was not proven."

The commissioners' clemency recommendation was reportedly delivered to the White House with the rest of the trial documents for the president's review the following Wednesday. Although he denied it later, Johnson might have seen the petition of the five that day or the next and ignored it. Several other pleas for mercy were directed at the president, the most fervent by a hysterical Anna Surratt. They also were ignored.

On July 7, with preparations in the capital completed for that afternoon's executions, the *New York Herald* printed a day-old dispatch from an unnamed Washington correspondent. "In the cases of Payne [Powell], Harold, and Atzerott [*sic*] there is great concurrence of opinion, but that of Mrs. Surratt elicits discussion," the reporter wrote.

> We have not converged [conversed?] with a single individual who has not manifested great sympathy for her, and who does not condemn in some terms the determination of the authorities to make her punishment capital. The feeling springs from a universal repugnance to hanging a woman, no matter for what offense. But few deny its justice. None believe her innocent, but all respect her sex. . . .
>
> Since the sentences of the conspirators were made public the friends of those sentenced to death have been unceasing in their efforts to obtain an interview with the President, in order to endeavor to obtain a commutation of their sentences or at least a respite. . . . There is not the slightest hope of either commutation or reprieve, except in the case of Mrs. Surratt. In her case there is some reason to believe that her sentence may be commuted to imprisonment for life, or at least that she may be reprieved, though it is very slight. The others will undoubtedly be executed, as ordered, tomorrow.

Her lawyers also tried. Working furiously, Frederick Aiken prepared a petition for a writ of habeas corpus and delivered it late Thursday night to a pajama-clad Judge Andrew Wylie, a justice of the District of Columbia's Supreme Court. In several brief paragraphs, he made the same arguments about the military commission's lack of jurisdiction that Senator Johnson had raised at length and unsuccessfully weeks earlier. This was the last time during Mary's life that the authority of the military commission and its verdict were challenged on constitutional grounds. Apparently persuaded (or at least willing to consider that the government was holding Mary unlawfully), Judge

Wylie issued the writ, instructing Major General Hancock to deliver Mary to his courtroom at ten o'clock on Friday.

At 11:30 on Friday morning, July 7, ninety minutes late, Attorney General Speed and General Hancock appeared at the court without Mary. Instead, they handed Judge Wylie President Johnson's written response to the court's writ:

> I, Andrew Johnson, President of the United States, do hereby declare that the writ of *habeas corpus* has been heretofore suspended in cases such as this, and direct that you [General Hancock] proceed to execute the order heretofore given upon the judgment of the Military Commission, and you will give this order in return to the writ.

Johnson's secretary of the interior, Orville Browning, happened to be at city hall that morning, and he witnessed the short proceeding in Wylie's courtroom that sealed Mary's fate.* He recorded in his diary:

> Atto Genl Speed & Genl Hancock came in to refuse to make a return to the writ of Habeas Corpus which the Judge had issued this morning. Hancock returned that the President had directed him to pay no atten-

---

* A native Kentuckian, Orville Hickman Browning (1806–1881) began the practice of law in Quincy, Illinois, in 1831 and soon got into local politics. In the late 1830s Browning (the editor of his diaries describes his subject then as a "handsome, steely, suave college man and finished orator") and Lincoln served together in the Illinois legislature. Later, Stephen Douglas defeated Browning in the latter's only run for statewide office. He was appointed by Illinois' governor in July 1861 to fill Senator Douglas's unexpired term after Douglas's death in June. Thereafter, however, the legislature declined to elect Browning to a term in the U.S. Senate of his own.

Browning and Lincoln were often described as close friends in Washington, as were their wives, but his political support of Lincoln seems never to have been more than half-hearted. Browning backed a rival in the 1860 presidential campaign and was cool to Lincoln's reelection run in 1864, which might explain why he never got his hoped-for place in Lincoln's Cabinet.

Instead, he joined Johnson's Cabinet in July 1866 as secretary of the interior, where his work focused on issues related to railroad construction and Indian affairs. Browning's views about Reconstruction closely matched his president's, and that probably accounts for his selection as interim attorney general when the Senate refused to reconfirm Henry Stanbery in the position after Johnson's impeachment trial.

Despite his adherence to Johnson's line, Browning was horrified by the tribunal that tried the eight and the trial's outcome. His diary entry for Thursday, July 6, was short, little more than a scant commentary on the big news of the day: "The findings of the Military Commission were approved today by the President, and Mrs. Surratt, Atzerot, [sic] Herald and Payne [Powell] were directed to be hung tomorrow. The others are to go to the Penitentiary. This commission was without authority, and its proceedings void. The execution of these persons will be murder."

Browning died impoverished in 1881, the victim of railroad investments gone wrong at the very end of his life. The debacle, a scam in which his son-in-law was a player, left Browning's family destitute.

tion to the writ but to proceed and execute the sentence, and therefore he did not produce the body. The Judge said he was powerless and could do nothing further, and let the Genl go. He [Wylie] should have proceeded against him [Hancock] for contempt, and have seen whether the President would have taken him forcibly from the hands of the court.

And so with Browning looking on in distress, the court yielded to Johnson's suspension, and that ended that. (Only for a time. The root issue, the scope of authority of military tribunals, would come up again and again in U.S. history.)

On July 7 cavalry troopers were poised at the White House grounds, posted to rush a pardon hand to hand from President Johnson to General Hartranft at the penitentiary on Greenleaf Point in the event one was issued. The riders were never exercised. As one o'clock approached the two senior officers present, Hancock and Hartranft, morosely accepted that Mary's execution was inevitable and moved to proceed.

Gen. Winfield Scott Hancock, in command of the Middle Military Division, which encompassed Washington, and Hartranft's superior, was "overwhelmed" with applications for passes to witness the hanging.* Only two hundred were to be admitted to the Arsenal's grounds on Friday, July 7, to watch justice done at 1 PM. That's the number of special signed permits that were available to grant passage through a double ring of sentries with fixed bayonets, and beyond them entry into the two-acre, high-walled prison yard where a gallows had been constructed and tested the day before. Many applicants were disappointed, but the general made a special effort to accommodate newspapermen.

Tests of the drops, the two hinged platforms (the entire front half of the scaffold) that were to fall away beneath the feet of the condemned, had gone on for two hours on Thursday under the personal supervision of the executioner, Capt. Christian Rath, once of the 17th Michigan Infantry and now one of the provost marshals working for General Hartranft.

---

* "Hancock the Superb" (1824–1886) was a career army officer who fought in the Mexican-American War, Seminole War, and with distinction for the Union throughout the Civil War, though he never rose above corps command. He led large formations in the field during many of the major campaigns in the East and was wounded at Fredericksburg and Gettysburg.

Once out of uniform, after a tour in command of the Fifth Military Department (Texas and Louisiana) during Reconstruction, Hancock ran for the presidency as the Democratic candidate against James Garfield. He lost the popular vote very narrowly but went down hard in the Electoral College, 214 to 155. In 1880, Hancock's consolation prize was presidency of the National Rifle Association, an outcome that would have gratified the late actor and NRA president Charlton Heston, who believed himself fit for bigger things, too.

The four condemned learned what was to come the same day, when Hartranft stopped in each cell with the terrible news from the White House. The distinctive noises of that day's macabre practice session on the gallows, with 140-pound weights chained to the ropes standing in for the condemned, would have certainly carried across the yard and to the cells in the adjacent building. It's possible that one or another of the prisoners eventually deduced what the recurrent, unfamiliar sounds echoing from outside their cells meant, even before Hartranft's visit.

They spent their last night alive in shock, stunned by the severity of the punishment and by the swiftness of its imposition. Mary spent the night with her daughter; "Davey" Herold with several of his many sisters; Atzerodt with his common-law wife, the mother of his daughter; Powell alone. All were visited by churchmen. Sometime early the next afternoon steeple bells began to toll in the city, marking that "the hour had come when these people were to be hung."[24]

The four were escorted along a direct path from their cells to chairs atop the raised gallows platform, so it is possible that none saw the open graves dug into the ground on the opposite (south) side of the gallows or the four rustic coffins resting nearby. Another nod to English tradition, which prescribed that even after death the condemned were not to leave prison.

Mary was dressed in black, with a black silk bow tied around her neck and held in place with a cheap arrow clasp that Anna had affixed. (That bit of jewelry would be found on her body later, after it was exhumed.)[25] Lieutenant Colonel McCall, Sergeant Kenny, and two priests, Jacob Walter and Bernardine Wiget, her confessors, walked with her. The latter had been a defense witness at the trial. Atzerodt, Powell, and Herold were next up the stairs in turn, all accompanied by an army escort and a single minister.

In a weird act of delicacy, while Mary's bonnet was removed, her arms and legs bound, the noose fitted, and a white hood installed over her head, she was protected from the sun by an umbrella. So were the others. Powell was positioned next to her, with Herold and Atzerodt side by side atop the other drop. All were trussed for hanging in the shade of parasols.

Executioner Rath had been a sheriff in Michigan before the war, and that experience apparently qualified him for this work. The gallows had been built under his orders. He had supervised the functional tests, falsely promising the "prop kickers" a canteen of whisky each for a job well done.[26] He was the one who knotted four lengths of the prescribed Navy three-quarter-inch Boston hemp rope into nooses the night before in his quarters. With everyone in place and after Hartranft read the death warrants aloud, Rath gave the signal, three claps of his hands, and the traps fell on the last clap.* Rath chose to wear a white suit and hat rather than his uniform that afternoon, making him a standout in Alexander Gardner's photographs of the hanging.**

Hanging kills in one of two ways. The first is by slow strangling of a living, sensate person when the drop has been too short, as it would be from the tailgate of a wagon or from horseback. That's the cliché climactic scene in old Hollywood western movies, such as Twentieth Century Fox's bleak *Ox Bow*

---

* Rath's version of the events on Greenleaf Point was published posthumously in 1911 in *McClure's Magazine* under the byline of John A. Gray, who had interviewed him long before for the piece. The account, in which Rath was reported to have said that Surratt was assigned by Booth to kill General Grant, is fanciful and unreliable.

After growing fruit and raising chickens for years on a large farm near Jackson, Michigan, Rath came to a sad end in 1892. A short page-one story in the *Washington Post* that April 8, under a subtitle that read "Captain Christian Rath Suddenly Becomes Insane in Michigan," reported that the conspirators' executioner "was suddenly bereft of reason yesterday on the run to Jackson with the mail train. He has been mail agent for twenty years between [Grand Rapids, Michigan] and Jackson, and made the latter place his headquarters. . . . An investigation found him in the car surrounded by the bags, staring wildly at vacancy."

Mary's execution was the centerpiece of Rath's life. The *Post's* story was titled "He Hanged Mrs. Surratt," and that legend could just as well have served as Rath's epitaph.

** Alexander Gardner (1821–1882) and his assistant, Timothy O'Sullivan, were the official photographers at the execution. Gardner, his wife, mother, and two children immigrated to the United States from Scotland in 1856. Soon thereafter he joined Matthew Brady's photography studio in New York City. Brady was, and is remembered today as, the dean of Civil War photography, but fading vision made him rely increasingly on others, among them this talented Scot. Two years later Gardner was in charge of the Brady gallery in Washington. Once the fighting began Gardner joined Brady's project to make a photographic history of the Civil War, moving his darkroom around the battlefields of the war. He and other photographers capitalized on the fact that by 1860 photographic equipment was durable and portable enough to permit taking to the field, making the Civil War the first conflict to be substantially recorded in still pictures as well as paintings.

"Captain" Gardner (his military rank was an honorific) had taken portraits of the accused men before they were transferred from the Navy monitors to prison. On July 5 he and Sullivan were admitted secretly to the Arsenal grounds to prepare for the picture taking to come. On the seventh they brought two cameras with them, one a stereo camera and the other a conventional single aperture model, and these took the stark pictures that freeze the image of the conspirators' death into recorded history.

Four months later, on November 10, 1865, Gardner photographed the execution of Maj. Henry Wirz, CSA, at the Old Capitol Prison in Washington. A Swiss-born hydropathic doctor, Wirz had been the commandant of Georgia's Andersonville Prison. He was the only other Civil War figure to be tried, condemned, and executed by the Union after the war. In 1908 Wirz's memory was honored, if not rehabilitated, by the erection of a stone monument at Andersonville by the Georgia Division, United Daughters of the Confederacy. The UDC had resolved three years earlier in a national convention to raise the memorial to "show that the Federal Government was solely responsible for the condition of affairs at Andersonville." One side of it reads, "Discharging his duty with such humanity as the harsh circumstances of the times, and the policy of the foe permitted, Captain Wirz became the last victim of a misdirected popular clamor."

The execution of Mary Surratt and her three codefendants. This detail from one of Alexander Gardner's photographs of the execution has lost none of its power to shock after nearly 150 years. (Library of Congress)

Incident. This results in the dreadful, minutes-long twitching dance that amused ghoulish spectators around the gnarled tree in the Ox Bow Valley. The second is by slow asphyxiation of a comatose person who has suffered an instantaneous fracture at the second cervical vertebrae, severing the nerves in the spinal column and presumably putting the "executee" beyond feeling pain during the minutes it will take for the paralyzed diaphragm to cause asphyxiation. One authority says the goal is to inflict 1,260 foot-pounds of shearing force to the neck to ensure a fracture. More force risks a grisly, accidental beheading.

Mary at, say, 140 pounds (the New York Times described her, cruelly, as "fair, fat, and forty," so that sounds about right) would have to fall seven feet for a clean, unconscious kill. Witnesses reported seeing one hand clench reflexively at the bottom of her drop, but nothing else. Powell, the heaviest at perhaps 210 pounds, would have required only a five-foot fall. He didn't move at all at the end of his rope.

An unknown number of observers stood in the near-100-degree heat watching this, clustered in the vacant spaces around the ranks of armed infantry and beneath the stares of more soldiers aligned along the twenty-foot-high brick wall that blocked the view of James Creek and Buzzard's Point. Gardner's photographs suggest that there were fewer than two hundred civilian observers on the grounds, although some might have been obscured by the open umbrellas held up as parasols for protection against the midday sun. (After two cloudy days and some rain on Thursday, Friday the seventh had come up clear, hot, and dry. Morning temperatures were in the 80s and climbing; by early afternoon the temperature in the open was well into the 90s—unremarkable for Washington in early summer but hard on men in ranks, whose only shade came from their uniform caps.) Others stood looking out of the windows of the penitentiary's first and second floors. Out of the reach of Hancock's pass system, boats filled with oglers crowded the Potomac around the point in the afternoon. Still more spectators might have had a view from the upper floors of nearby buildings.

It's possible that the total count, including these more distant voyeurs, might have exceeded several hundred. Although an audience was present, by midcentury judicial hanging in the United States was less the spectator sport that executions had been earlier and that lynchings would remain for some time to come. Ostensibly, the official audience was there, as execution observers are today, to confirm to society that justice had been done and the sentence carried out, but before and after the event at the Arsenal souvenir hunters ghoulishly collected scraps of rope and chips of wood from the gallows to take home.

Mary Surratt's life and fate crossed over from politics to art not too long thereafter. Few legal proceedings become part of popular culture, but everything about Mary Surratt's trial was extraordinary. In 1879 James Webb Rogers, successively a Confederate veteran, Episcopal minister, Catholic journal editor, patent attorney, and playwright, wrote "Madame Surratt, a Drama in Five Acts," an earnest, overheated, and unproduced epic that reads like a bad Shakespeare imitation. A better written (but no more successful) play on the same subject came out in 1947. *The Story of Mary Surratt*, by John Patrick, opened on Broadway on February 8 that year but closed after only nine performances. Former silent film comedienne Dorothy Gish, chased off the screen by talkies, played the doomed Mary.

Patrick's play, wrote the *New York Times*, "proclaims her innocence and protests against the injustice of the military trial that sent her to the gallows." The author (also the play's director) knew enough of the history not to include Mary's wretched husband in his drama and instead invented a boyhood sweetheart who defended her in the trial. The reviewer took it all on board. "As a chapter out of history, Mr. Patrick's play has the merit of shedding light on a generally glossed-over tragedy of another post-war period," he wrote, referring to World War II, faulting the play as a drama because "it is held to earth by the comparatively minor stature of its heroine."

Patrick's script got a second chance during an airing on the Philco Radio Theater sometime later, but after that and an improbable mention in Burns Mantle's *Best Plays of 1946–47*, it disappeared. (The same 1946–47 New York City theater season first saw Maxwell Anderson's *Joan of Lorraine* played on the stage in New York, and some theatergoers might have stretched and found a connection between Joan of Arc, burned at the stake in Rouen in 1431, and Mary Surratt, hanged in Washington 434 years later.)

Mary Surratt was the first woman executed in the United States after trial and conviction in federal court. The definitive source of historic information on executions in the United States is the so-called Espy File, a database covering the period between 1608 and 1991 complied by two Alabama researchers. It's named after M. Watt Espy, one of the principal researchers. His file has become the source document for all manner of social science and legal studies, most supporting the campaign to end the death penalty in the United States. Among the 14,634 executions tabulated, a national average across the centuries of about one every ten days, are those of 356 women. Twenty-six of these, nearly 7 percent, were convicted during the seventeenth century of witchcraft, some during the famous hysteria in Salem, Massachusetts. As one would expect, executions of women convicted of murder are by far the most common category. They constitute more than three-quarters of the total. The statistics put Mary in a special category.

The best known of Mary's successors in such a special status is Ethel Rosenberg,[27] accused in 1950 with her husband, Jules, of spying for the Soviet Union. The two were convicted in April 1951 and finally executed in June 1953. During the twenty-six months she and her husband were on death row in Sing Sing Prison, and right up to the moment of their execution, Ethel (the mother of two young boys) and her husband were the subjects of a determined international campaign to save their lives, orchestrated in large part by Soviet sympathizers. There was no such swelling campaign in the case of Mary Surratt.

Everything moved too fast, with the result that public protests in her case, and they grew to a clamor as time went on, were all posthumous.

John Surratt was not in Washington when his mother, Mary, was hanged on the greenwood gallows hastily erected on the Arsenal grounds. (Fort McNair's tennis courts occupy the same site today.) Had he been present in the U.S. capital anytime after April 14, it would have been as a codefendant in the dock at the conspirators' trial, and young Surratt surely would have been hanged alongside his parent, a fifth in that dreadful line of suspended bodies made famous by Alexander Gardner's photographs. The simultaneous executions of a mother and son would have been an even more macabre milestone than Mary's death alone.

In midsummer 1865, with the four condemned now in their graves and the four others convicted locked in prison, everyone understood that John Surratt was unfinished legal business. His status was nowhere better depicted than on the frontispiece of the trial transcript published in 1865. Nine faces were artfully arranged there around the caption "The Conspirators." For artistic reasons—she was here, as she had been throughout the last months of her life, the only woman in a world of men—Mary Surratt's face was in the center of the oval, with portraits of the other eight arrayed around her. Only her son, John, at bottom right paired with Ned Spangler, was still at large.[28]

"The Conspirators." Dr. Samuel Mudd is unaccountably missing from this gallery of the conspirators, which includes John Surratt. This plate decorated the frontispiece of the published trial record in 1865.

2

"FLIGHT IS THE CRIMINAL'S INARTICULATE CONFESSION"

T wo years after Mary Surratt's execution the fact that mother and son had not been hanged side by side was presented to John Surratt's jury by government lawyers as proof of his cowardice. In escaping this fate Surratt was then and was still, according to the U.S. district attorney for the District of Columbia, "false to the mother who bore him, and whom he deserted in the hour of danger and distress. The gallows upon which she expired should have been his throne. There he might have palliated or irradiated, with some show of gallantry or parental affection, the horrid crime he had committed." Instead of sharing her fate, on the day of her execution Mary's second son was in French Canada, hiding as "Charles Armstrong" in the hamlet of St. Liboire, some forty-five miles east of Montreal, in the rectory of the parish priest, Abbé Charles Boucher.

John Surratt was the only one of Booth's coterie who was not in the capital or in neighboring southern Maryland the night Lincoln was shot, and this absence enormously simplified his escape from hasty pursuit after he heard about the killing. Throughout that critical first weekend Surratt was well beyond the immediate reach of Stanton's posses, and by the time a single, dilatory search for him briefly passed through Canada he was already burrowing underground.

When Mary died Surratt had been lying low—low by his own peculiar standard of stealth—in Canada for ten weeks or so after heading north from Elmira, New York, in a near-panic on Saturday, April 15, the day after his twenty-first birthday. That morning he had accidentally learned from John Cass, a merchant tailor in Elmira, that Lincoln had been killed by Booth.

How Cass might have known that isn't certain. The *Elmira Advertiser*'s lead story on Saturday was about Lincoln's impromptu speech to a crowd on the

White House lawn on Tuesday, April 11. The *Advertiser* didn't print its story on the death of Lincoln and Surratt's suspected role in the attack on Secretary Seward until its Monday issue. By then Lincoln had been dead for two days. "From the evidence obtained," the *Advertiser* wrote on Monday, mentioning Surratt for the first time, "it is rendered highly probable that the man who stabbed Mr. Seward and his sons is John Surratt, of Prince George County, Md. . . . Surratt is a young man with light hair and goatee. His father is said to have been Post Master in Prince George County."

Surratt's first hideout in Canada was in the Montreal home of John Porterfield, a banker from Nashville, Tennessee, who was prominent among Canada's resident Confederate elite. Not just its convenient location, but also the presence of expatriate Confederate officials and of fraternal coreligionists made French Canada the ideal temporary refuge for a young Catholic man with Confederate links escaping from the Union and its law officers.

Although most Canadians, uncompromising abolitionists by and large, at first sided with the North emotionally when they contemplated the possibility of civil war in the United States, soon after the fighting started in earnest, sentiment in Canada was no longer so unequally distributed. By the end of the war citizens in large parts of "Canada," meaning for this purpose the two provinces of British North America then known as "Canada West" and "Canada East," had switched their sympathies from North to South. (Canada West, or Upper Canada, was Ontario; Canada East, or Lower Canada, was Quebec. Not until the British North America Act was passed by Parliament in London in 1867 did Canada begin to assume something like its modern form, although that process wasn't fully complete for another eighty years.)

In his definitive history of Canada and the United States during the Civil War years, Robin Winks identifies the many reasons for this change of heart. The trigger might have been one of the initial paragraphs in President Lincoln's first inaugural address, given on March 4, 1861. "I have no purpose, directly or indirectly," Lincoln said from in front of the Capitol, quoting himself in part, "to interfere with the institution of slavery where it exists. I believe I have no lawful right to do so, and I have no inclination to do so." Reading these unequivocal words, Canadians thought they saw abolition recede as a Union objective, while soon other political and economic goals seemed to rise that didn't resonate in Canada at all.

The open ambitions, moreover, of some Yankee politicians for outright annexation of their northern neighbor were alarming. The idea of annexation wasn't new in the 1860s. Only grotesque U.S. military incompetence had prevented its achievement earlier in the century, the last time Great Britain and the United States fought a war. North of the border, those who knew of the powerful new U.S. secretary of state, William Seward, a longtime New York politician before his elevation to the cabinet, believed him to be both combative and instinctively anti-British, a potentially explosive combination.

In fact, some in Washington planned for an invasion of Canada up until the end of the Civil War.[1] Senator Zach Chandler of Michigan was father to one such plot. His plan was that 200,000 veterans, half from the North and half from the South, would march into Canada. The purpose, as reported by a supportive contemporary, Senator William Stewart of Nevada, was to confiscate British possessions in Canada as compensation for Union shipping losses to British-built Confederate navy commerce raiders. Not coincidentally, going to war together, "to fight against a common hereditary enemy," was expected to help heal the breach between North and South. Stewart claimed thirty senators (of fifty) supported Chandler's idea and that only Lincoln's assassination, "at almost the very instant the scheme was to be sprung upon the country," derailed it.

Some U.S. newspapers, the *New York Herald* in the van, also contributed to Canadian anxiety about American interest in expansion across the forty-ninth parallel. Whether the case for expansion was cast in terms of some sort of symmetrical compensation for the loss of southern territory or more generally as a part of continental ambitions, Americans' lust for Canada was evident in what many said and wrote. The prospect of this appetite coupled to a huge army was unnerving. Fears were not entirely obviated by the unexpected, humiliating Union defeat at Manassas in July 1861, which simultaneously diminished the North and made open support of the South in Canada seem not only reasonable but low risk.

Lincoln's sudden death nearly four years later affected most Canadians powerfully, as evidenced by an outpouring of government, press, and private sympathy (but not from the *Toronto Leader*, still resolutely adhering to its Confederate perspective) that mirrored the grieving going on south of the border. Most Canadians, in common with most Americans, instantly understood that Lincoln's death as much as Lee's surrender marked a great cleft in history: the end of one thing and the beginning of something else. Several days after the assassination, while local citizens and resident Americans from both sides were first beginning to absorb this new reality, and fully two months before the British Empire officially recognized the onset of peace in North America, Surratt reappeared in Canada.

Nearly simultaneously with Surratt's arrival in Montreal, Secretary Stanton published a poster offering a reward of twenty-five thousand dollars for his apprehension and threatened anyone "harboring or secreting" Surratt (and Booth and Herold) with "trial before a military commission and the punishment of DEATH."[2] It was not the wanted poster, however, but the sudden appearance in the city of a team of Union detectives to search for him that flushed Surratt out of Porterfield's house in town all the way to tiny St. Liboire.

Midafternoon on April 17 a small posse of detectives from the Washington Metropolitan Police left Baltimore by train for Montreal and Quebec to apprehend Surratt. Two of Surratt's familiars, Weichmann and John Holohan, another of Mary Surratt's tenants, were with them to help identify the subject. (Both men were called "special officers" in the written Army orders that sent them north, a formulation possibly designed to grant the two a pretense of a semiofficial role once they crossed the border.) The group traveled via New York City and Burlington, Vermont, and arrived in Montreal on the twentieth. How, with no police power north of the border, U.S. lawmen were to make an arrest in Canada wasn't clear then or now. In any event, everyone was back in Washington, empty-handed, on April 29.

Surratt had been holed up at Abbé Charles Boucher's since April 22, and that fact gave Boucher special status. He was the first in a line of Roman Catholic clerics in North America and Europe—they ranged from this rustic parish priest in arboreal eastern Canada to the rector of the Venerable English College in Rome—who would give the fleeing suspect aid and comfort during the next eighteen months. Until the last month of his flight Surratt moved along what almost appears to have been an underground railroad staffed by Roman Catholic divines. John Surratt had a special claim on this assistance; he too was Catholic, and possibly a former aspirant to holy orders to boot.

St. Liboire was then a country parish of some eight or nine hundred souls. Boucher had been parish priest there for a year or so when Joseph du Tilly, a local farmer with unexplained Confederate connections, appeared late on an April evening in company with a young, homeless American, Porterfield's former house guest. He introduced the man to Boucher as someone who had been "compromised in the American war," and Boucher agreeably took the stranger in. Surratt spent weeks there, reportedly often in bed suffering from *fièvres tremblantes*, the ague. Occasionally, when he didn't feel ill, he was out hiking or hunting. Sometime during the second week of his stay in St. Liboire the house guest revealed to his host who he really was. The knowledge didn't faze the priest, who quietly concealed Surratt for another ten weeks, later visited him frequently in Quebec City, and preserved Surratt's secret for months thereafter.

As a British subject at home in Canada and protected by British law, Boucher shielded Surratt from discovery at little real risk to himself, of course, even if his boarder were unmasked. As it turned out, it was at little risk to Surratt, too. In May the U.S. consul in Montreal, John Potter, reported to Washington that Surratt was in St. Liboire—but nothing happened, despite Secretary Seward's request to Attorney General James Speed for an indictment.[3] Later the secretary of war explained lamely that Canada had not been expected to respond favorably to an American extradition request, so one was not made and Surratt had been allowed to slip away unimpeded.

In late July Surratt was moved from St. Liboire to La Prairie, near Montreal, where his new protector was Abbé Pierre-Larcille Lapierre. Lapierre hid Surratt in the home of his father. And there Surratt stayed until the end of summer.

David Reed had appeared twice as a witness in the stand at the conspirators' trial in the Arsenal in 1865, once on May 15 and again on June 3. Both times he swore that he had seen Surratt in Washington City midafternoon the day Lincoln was shot. In May Reed's testimony had been specific. When he saw Surratt, Reed said, he "was dressed in a country-cloth suit of drab [brown], very fine in texture and appearance, and very genteelly got up. . . . He had a little, round-crowned drab hat . . . a pair of new, brass-plated spurs, with very large rowels." Reed provided another precise detail in June, saying that from his vantage point standing on the stoop of Hunt and Godwin's military store he had watched Surratt, apparently booted and spurred and wearing a color-coordinated hat and suit, passing the National Hotel. When Reed testified at Surratt's own trial two years later his memory was even better; the hat had become "not very low-crowned, but wide brimmed" and straw colored.

Eyewitness accounts are notoriously unreliable, but Reed went beyond simple error all the way to fantasy. Reed must have known Surratt on sight as the "genteelly got up" description is just right for the young dandy, but in this case Reed was wrong or lying, which amounts to the same thing.

This phenomenon, people testifying as eye witnesses to things they had not seen, was to be a feature of Surratt's trial in June 1867, too. As we will see, a procession of witnesses during its first few days, once the jury was finally seated, swore that each of them had seen Surratt in Washington City at the time of the assassination. The most telling of the group was Sgt. Joseph Dye, who said he

Surratt wearing his Canada (Garibaldi) jacket. Several shopkeepers in Elmira testified in 1867 that they remembered Surratt wearing this distinctive pleated coat in their town during Easter weekend 1865. In February 1868 Surratt deposited this carte de visite with the Clerk's Office at D.C. Superior Court and secured copyright to the photograph. (Library of Congress, Lot 7964)

saw Booth talking to a pale "well dressed man" immediately outside of Ford's Theatre that night. During the course of the trial "well dressed" became a short-hand description identifying the defendant. Surratt's fashion sense and particular taste in clothes would anchor defense testimony about his presence elsewhere when Lincoln was attacked. Competing haberdashers would swear to his being in their shops, absolutely certain of their identification because of their customer's peculiar "Garibaldi" jacket (which was "a pleated garment with the pleats in the front; also in the back. The wristbands were plain, same as the shirt, with a belt round the body . . . four buttons in front and one on the belt").

"Did you see the man distinctly?" asked Edwards Pierrepont, one of the government's lawyers, of Sergeant Dye.

"Very distinctly," Dye replied.

"And do you see him now?"

"I do, sir." Dye pointed at Surratt. "There he sits. . . . I have not seen him since until lately, and now the man I saw then was John H. Surratt, the prisoner at the bar."

But on April 14 Surratt was not within several hundred miles of Washington's National Hotel or Ford's Theatre. He had not been there since passing through Washington on a courier mission to Gen. Edwin Lee of the Confederate Secret Service Bureau in Canada for Secretary of State Judah Benjamin on April 3, and he would not be in the city again until February 19, 1867.*

Soon after it first opened in early 1864 the Confederate Secret Service Bureau in Canada was staffed by three commissioners. Professor James Holcombe of Virginia arrived in the country first. He was joined a few months later by former Senator Clement Clay of Alabama and Judge Jacob Thompson of Mississippi.

---

* Secretary Judah Benjamin, "seal-sleek, black-eyed, lawyer and epicure," was the cabinet officer responsible for the operation of the Confederacy's military intelligence apparatus. (The flattering description is from Stephen Vincent Benét's book-length poem, *John Brown's Body*.)

Benjamin (1811–1884) was one of the more remarkable men of an age that had many. Born a Jew in St. Croix, he immigrated as a child to the United States, where he married well (although not happily) and became a wealthy lawyer and sugar planter in southern Louisiana. Historian William Davis attributes Benjamin's strained family life (his wife lived in Paris during most of their marriage) to his homosexuality.

Beginning in 1852 he was the state's U.S. senator for two terms. He resigned his seat when Louisiana seceded from the Union and spent the war in Jefferson Davis's cabinet, first as attorney general, then as secretary of war, and finally as secretary of state. Benjamin had sold his plantation, Bellechasse, and slaves in 1850, and a decade later he was Davis's only cabinet secretary who was not a slave owner. He might have been the first senior official to propose enlisting (and freeing) slaves in the Confederate army, an idea later endorsed by Gen. Robert E. Lee.

Almost alone among his contemporaries, Benjamin landed on his feet after the war. He fled to England—a thrilling escape that featured two stops in the Bahamas and one in Havana, a sinking, and a fire at sea—with enough in hand such that during the first postwar summer he was able to lend twelve thousand dollars to the nearly impoverished Jefferson Davises (Joan Cashin, First Lady of the Confederacy, 172). The next year he joined the English bar and became a successful and prosperous barrister in London. Judah Benjamin is known through the public record and his published books on the law—in Louisiana, *A Digest of Reported Decisions of the Supreme Court of the Late Territory of New Orleans, and of the Supreme Court of Louisiana* (1834), and in England, *Treatise on the Law of Sale of Personal Property* (1868)—but because he destroyed his private papers he remains something of an enigmatic figure.

Benjamin is buried in Paris's famous Cimetèrie du Père-Lachaise, the burial ground of a constellation of figures from history. He lies near the tomb of his daughter's in-laws, so there must have been a family reconciliation of sorts.

The three landed in Halifax, Nova Scotia, from Wilmington, North Carolina, via a one-cushion bank shot off Bermuda. Their indirect route reflected the realities of the Union's naval blockade of the Confederacy, an attempt to interdict traffic through key ports along a three-thousand-mile coastline. Although the blockade strangled cotton exports in bulk, people and high-value freight continued to move relatively easily in and out of the Confederacy through its gaps.

Clay set up shop in the village of St. Catharines on Lake Ontario. The others worked out of Toronto and Montreal. The bureau's branch office in Montreal was in the pricey St. Lawrence Hall Hotel on Rue St. Jacques. A regular factory for plots and counterplots.

Initially, Holcombe, a lawyer, was sent to Canada in connection with the *Chesapeake* affair, the legal imbroglio in Canadian prize court surrounding the capture of the U.S. steamer *Chesapeake* by Confederates and its later recapture by the U.S. Navy. His mission was then expanded to manage the transportation home of former prisoners of war who escaped across the international border from Union prisons along the northern frontier.

Although prisoner recovery remained the focus of the bureau throughout the rest of the war, once Holcombe was joined by Clay and Thompson their mission quickly grew. It soon included launching cross-border raids and sabotage to elicit an attack on Canada in reprisal and provoking disunion among Northern antiwar groups (the "Copperheads"), in hopes that Illinois, Indiana, Ohio, and Missouri could be seduced into secession from the Union.

The notion wasn't complete lunacy. No less a figure than Bvt. Lt. Gen. Winfield Scott, in October 1860 the aged commanding general of the sixteen-thousand-strong Army of the United States, had suggested not two but four confederations as a way around the seemingly irreconcilable differences that divided North and South. Then again, by 1860 "Old Fuss and Feathers," seventy-four and a general officer for more than forty years, was well past his prime. Others had posited equally fantastic geographic constructions as solutions to the political problem slavery posed. One such was amicable separation based on a division of the remainder of the continent: the South would secede and take Mexico; the North would accept secession and get Canada. Thus sated, both sides would go their separate ways. The concept was no less eccentric than Scott's, but it had the virtue of requiring fewer moving parts. The likely response of Mexico, France, Canada, and Great Britain to this high-handed divvying up of things they were profoundly invested in appears not to have been seen as a show stopper.

The Confederate commissioners' more lofty purposes were combined with such capers as a failed attempt to capture the USS *Michigan* at Sandusky, Ohio, guarding a nearby prison, and a raid on St. Albans, Vermont, that involved the robbery of three banks, the theft of $200,000, the murder of a citizen, and a failed attempt to burn the town down. The bureau's Quebec office, however, was more than simply a planning cell conjuring up dirty tricks. It also connected the Confederacy's treasury to European banking systems and served as an important communications node between Richmond and the Confederacy's agents and would-be diplomats in Europe.

The presence and purposes of the three commissioners quickly became no secret, and federal counterspies were soon so thick on the ground that the clandestine work being done was compromised to the extent that Secretary Benjamin eventually ordered the original commissioners home, bowing also to British pressure to remove this aggravation. Prying Union detectives were not the only obstruction to success. Grandiose plans, an organization riddled with moles and snitches, and the commissioners' inability to cooperate with one another got in the way of meaningful achievement, too.

Clay left Canada in November 1864, soon after the raid on St. Albans. Thompson was the last to be recalled. On December 3 he wrote a despairing letter to Benjamin from Toronto bemoaning the presence of Union detectives or stool pigeons "on every corner." In his reply a few weeks later Benjamin directed the transfer of Thompson's correspondence, files, and remaining funds to Brig. Gen. Edwin Lee, who had arrived in Canada carrying the recall letter. Thompson finally left Canada in April 1865 for Great Britain. He arrived there thanks only to Lincoln's willingness to instruct others to look away while he passed through Portland, Maine, on the way to Halifax.

This particular General Lee was yet another of the South's seemingly inexhaustible supply of Lees, a second cousin of the revered Robert E.* Declining health after 1862, the symptoms of advancing and eventually fatal tuberculosis, had forced Lee away from service with troops in the field and into a series of odd jobs in and out of uniform ending with more than a year in Canada beginning

---

* Brig. Gen. Edwin Gray Lee's father, Edmund Jennings Lee II, was Robert E. Lee's first cousin. Edwin Lee (1836–1870), from Loudoun County in Virginia, joined the 33rd Virginia Infantry Regiment as a second lieutenant in 1861 and rose swiftly to command as its third colonel at the second battle of Bull Run (August 1862) and at Antietam (September 1862).

Lee's short adult life was shaped almost entirely by tuberculosis. He was diagnosed with the disease in 1860, at age twenty-four. During the next ten years until it killed him, TB often intruded into his life. It forced his resignation from the Confederate army in 1862 and, after his reinstatement, a six-month

in 1865 as a newly installed brigadier general fresh from commanding reserves in the Shenandoah Valley. He was the last Confederate commissioner in Canada.

The Bureau in Montreal never lived up to Richmond's expectations. It probably never could have. More was wanted from its busy swarm of agents and their amateur sympathizers—many trailed more or less openly by a Union detective—than they could have delivered. As it turned out, there proved to be nothing any group of Southerners could do to sap the Union's greater strength on the ground and afloat and to stave off defeat. But well before this truth became clear, the hope was that from this international sanctuary far behind the lines, Confederate agents would be able to strike powerful, unsettling blows at the Union on its isolated, unprotected rear, and failing that, to provoke a war between the United States and Great Britain that would surely result in recognition of the Confederacy. Initially, this activity was understood to be an adjunct to the real fighting going on hundreds of miles away, a painful distraction but nothing more. Eventually, however, after the Army of Northern Virginia had twice invaded the North unsuccessfully, commerce raiding at sea and cross border raids from Canada were all the Confederacy could do to bring the war to the enemy.

According to Louis Weichmann's testimony on May 13 during the trial of the eight, Surratt had arrived home from a mission to Richmond on April 3 but left hastily a few hours later for Montreal, impelled by the stunning and unexpected news that Richmond had fallen to Grant. Unexpected because, Surratt told Weichmann, he had been personally assured by Davis and Benjamin that Richmond would not surrender, but it had—armed resistance dying out like air leaking from a balloon as Lee abandoned defensive lines near Petersburg in the effort to save his army.

---

medical leave of absence the next year. The disease had the same effect on all its victims, reshaping and shortening their lives.

Edwin Lee returned to Virginia in the spring of 1866 from Texas, where he had gone for his health, and testified at Surratt's trial the following year. He died at the spa at Yellow Sulfur Springs, Virginia, at thirty-four. A photocopy of Lee's 1865 diary is in the James O. Hall Archive at the Surratt House Museum in Clinton, Maryland.

In the United States, says social historian Sheila Rothman, "consumption" was responsible for one death in five through the nineteenth and into the twentieth century. Their search for recovery and health sent sufferers to sea and in search of salubrious climates ashore. Tuberculosis invalids seeking healthy places formed an appreciable fraction of the early settlers in the Far West and were responsible for the popularity of New York state's Adirondack Mountains and for the establishment of towns of cure seekers in California, Colorado, and Texas. Not until 1882, with the discovery of the tubercle bacillus, was tuberculosis properly understood to be an infectious disease caused by bacilli, not a hereditary, noncontagious condition that happened to blight particularly susceptible families.

On his trip north Surratt carried dispatches from Jefferson Davis and Judah Benjamin to Southern agents in Canada. Once there, he was soon turned around. In early April 1865 Edwin Lee, in his late twenties as the war rushed to its conclusion, was enough out of touch with what was really happening on the ground in Virginia that even after the fall of Richmond and his kinsman's surrender of the Army of Northern Virginia at Appomattox one week later, Lee directed John Surratt to reconnoiter the large Union prisoner of war camp in Elmira, New York, on his way back home to Maryland. The idea was to explore the possibility of a jailbreak, presumably returning some of the five thousand–plus inmates then held there to the Confederacy's depleted ranks.

"The news of the evacuation of Richmond did not seem to disturb the General much in his plan," Surratt said years later, "as he doubtless thought then that the Confederacy wanted men more than ever, no one dreaming that it was virtually at an end." How the escaped prisoners would make their way four hundred miles south through Pennsylvania and Maryland to friendly territory, conspicuous by their gaunt appearance and all-gray clothing (no other color of outer garment was allowed them), and what the fortunate, exhausted, and unarmed few could do on arrival are mysteries.

The idea of a prison break from Elmira wasn't original with Lee and Surratt. Charles Dunham, a notorious double agent, had also concocted such a scheme.* In Dunham's plan, about one hundred "resolute and reliable men" were to attack the prison during a change of the guard while off duty camp officers were

---

* Among the host of courageous spies, secret agents, and seedy double dealers who peopled the underside of the Civil War, Charles A. Dunham (1832–1900) was the consummate shape shifter. He made a career, many of them, from the fact that proof of identity was difficult to produce in the nineteenth century. That career included fabrications, accusations, plots, counterplots, and crimes and intrigues of bewildering variety and remarkable originality. Reportedly Durham in one persona once offered a cash reward for his own capture and arrest in another. The index to Carmen Cumming's biography of Dunham, *Devil's Game: The Civil War Intrigues of Charles A. Dunham*, lists fourteen certain aliases for Dunham, with six other "possibles."

Peopled by his twenty avatars, Dunham's story is necessarily a difficult one to unravel. He was born the son of a tanner in Croton, New York. At twenty-one he married Ophelia Auser, the daughter of a successful farmer in Westchester, with whom he had eight children. He studied law for a time in New York City, and he died in Rutherford, New Jersey. Almost everything else is uncertain. Cumming calls Dunham "the Chameleon," but the *Washington Morning Chronicle* had the better name. In one of its columns Dunham was styled "the Napoleon of perjurers."

As "Sanford Conover" Dunham testified three times in the Arsenal at the trial of the eight, the first time to connect Davis, his cabinet, and Canadians in Canada directly to the assassination. Everything he said was a lie. The following autumn Dunham was the principal of the notorious "School for Perjurers" that produced a coterie of play-acting witnesses who swore to three complex fictions, all supporting Stanton and Holt's general conspiracy theory.

distracted by a dance at one of the city's hotels. Under his fantastic scenario, in a few hours the freed Confederates would be aboard trains passing through Elmira and on their way to Pennsylvania and Maryland, where together with armed bands of guerrillas already in place, they could threaten Union forces from the rear.

Manpower was yet another of the "sinews of war" that was in permanent short supply in the Confederacy. In the national census of 1860 the eleven states of what would soon become the Confederacy counted only 1.574 million men aged fifteen to fifty, omitting, of course, male slaves from that total. The same count had the North numbering 4.395 million white males, nearly three times as many. New York state alone was home to just under 1 million. Even accepting that slave labor freed many white men to fight for the South who otherwise would have worked in the economy and that slaves labored to construct fortifications and performed other military-related tasks, the imbalance was significant. The South would manage to put fewer than 900,000 men under arms during the war (3 out of every 4 men eligible), the North some 2,100,000. In this, as in all other quantifiable measures of nineteenth-century military power potential, the Confederate States of America entered the war at a fatal disadvantage.

Many important battles of the American Revolution had been fought by as few as several thousand men on a side—there were fewer than four thousand total at Boston's Bunker Hill in 1775, thirty-eight hundred at Trenton, New Jersey, in 1776, and perhaps three thousand at Cowpens in the Carolinas in 1781—sometimes on isolated battlefields as small as a few square miles. Until the Battle of Baltimore and the postwar Battle of New Orleans, the sides facing each other in the campaigns of the War of 1812 were not appreciably larger.

In the Civil War fifty years later, everything was on a scale entirely new to the Americas: the total number of men in uniform, the size of the formations, the massed artillery batteries, everything. One day's fighting at Antietam in September 1862 produced nearly twenty-three thousand casualties. Fifty-one thousand were killed, wounded, or went missing during the three days of battle at Gettysburg in July 1863. Fourteen other battles during the war saw one or both of the sides suffer ten thousand or more casualties in a few days' time. Hundreds were captured in a single engagement; thousands during a single campaign. The slaughter hinted at what the wars of the next century would bring.

But as in other wars before and since, everyone expected a short war (everyone, perhaps, but old General Scott, who realistically forecast a long and bloody conflict). For their part, Southerners counted optimistically on their natural abilities as horsemen and hunters, buttressed by training in the region's nearly one hundred military schools, and on an unquantifiable élan that came from their cavalier, plantation life-style, to defeat the citified, effete North quickly. The outcome of the Union's initial offensive on Southern soil, the first battle of Bull Run, seemed to bear out that conceit, even though this one time the Rebels actually outnumbered the Yankees.

On July 21, 1861, Gen. Irvin McDowell and 28,452 Yankees in the Army of Northeastern Virginia met 21,883 Rebels in Gen. Pierre Beauregard's Army of the Potomac near Manassas, Virginia. (The Union lines would have been thicker still had not some ninety-day volunteer regiments, their enlistments just then expired, walked off the battlefield as the opposing forces got in line.)[4] Other than a few veterans of the Mexican-American War, the officers and their troops facing each other were as green as rye grass, old boys and young men out on a thrilling outdoor adventure as they closed together over the banks of Bull Run creek. Some dressed fit to kill in the flashy uniforms of the Zouaves, complete with colorful fezzes, vests, and bloused pantaloons, looking like warriors from a different hemisphere—or a different planet.

Just before the crisis, Beauregard was joined by Gen. Joseph Johnston and the nearly nine thousand men of Johnston's Army of the Shenandoah.

To the amazement of rapt civilian observers, day trippers from Washington—sightseers and miscellaneous sports—who had ridden out of town to watch the excitement (and would witness a battle in which nine hundred men would die and another twenty-seven hundred would be wounded), the badly led, scantily trained, and now outnumbered Yanks got thrashed and panicked, all the way back to the city. McDowell got blamed for the debacle into which he had been pushed. (Such was his bad luck that McDowell was also present at the *second* battle of Bull Run little more than one year later, and his generalship was again found wanting on this now familiar ground.)

Shaken by the defeat, the North immediately began a more serious mobilization and training effort, and Lincoln started a frustrating search for a general in chief who could lead and win that would not end until he promoted Ulysses Grant to lieutenant general and gave him command of the Union's armies. The next call for Union volunteers, issued on the day of the battle, sought fully half a million men. By the time the war ended, nearly three million men had taken part in the fighting. More than 620,000 of all those under arms were killed outright in combat or died of disease, wounds, or injury during the forty-nine months of the war.

Any war that lasted longer than one campaign season (and any one with weapons as lethal as were used in this one) inevitably made manpower a decisive factor. Despite leadership in the field that often compensated for imbalances in strength, manpower shortages bedeviled the Southern economy and the Confederacy's ability to fight practically from the outset. After the first battle of Bull Run, Southern formations almost always took to the field inferior in strength and were not as well armed or equipped as their foe. As the war went on those imbalances grew more acute.

In fact, pressures on Confederate States Army recruiters became so great that by autumn 1864, after the unsettling idea had been floating around for months, serious consideration was given to arming slaves and putting them into the ranks. Sending slaves to war, or first freeing and then arming them, raised all sorts of questions that led to pungent debates, to fears that nothing less than traditional society was being threatened with upending and that going forward would let the long-suffering "bottom rail" finally get on top.

The desperate initiative ran headlong into the great boogeyman that terrified Southern society, that a fearsome revolt of their slaves would unleash on the South and especially its women bands of furious blacks seeking revenge for a lifetime of abuse. There was some substance to the fear. Spartacus's revolt during the first century B.C. wasn't the only example in history of what happens when control of an entire underclass is lost. A slave rebellion on the French portion of Hispaniola (then called St. Domingue) that began in 1791, watched anxiously from over the horizon by American plantation owners, had by January 1804 succeeded first in battering an opportunistic British invasion force and then in ejecting a large but disease-wracked French army and establishing a republic. A vision of Toussaint Louverture's army of Caribbean canefield slaves swinging farm tools against whites outnumbered dozens to one was the stuff of every Southern planter's perfect nightmare.[5]

Slaves had revolted in the United States, too. For the most part these were small and ineffective uprisings that were quickly and brutally put down. In 1820 Gabriel Prosser's plan to seize Richmond with fellow slaves was betrayed; he, his brothers, and two dozen others were hanged. Two years later, another slave, Denmark Vesey, plotted to overrun Charleston, South Carolina, at the head of an army of as many as eight thousand blacks and then to flee to Haiti. His plot was betrayed too, and its leadership was either hanged or exiled. The best known revolt today, thanks to the late William Styron's Pulitzer Prize–winning (and hugely controversial) 1966 novel about its leader's jailhouse confession to a journalist, is the one in Southampton, Virginia, in 1831 led by Nat Turner. (Turner's timing had to have been deliberate, forty years to the day after the start of Toussaint Louverture's rebellion.) Some sixty whites were murdered by Turner and his men. The subsequent toll on blacks, of course, was much higher. Twenty were promptly tried and executed, twenty-plus more were later executed in Virginia and North Carolina, and one hundred or so were killed still later by vigilante mobs while white hysteria slowly wound down.

There were sufficient such attempts at insurrection during the prior two hundred years that in 1860 Joshua Coffin, a charter member of the American Anti-Slavery Society, was inspired to publish a chronicle of two centuries of slave revolts. Coffin's timing was incendiary. His book, *An Account of Some of the Principal Slave Insurrections,* which appeared just one year after John Brown's failed attempt to seize the huge stock of weapons at the federal arsenal at Harpers Ferry, Virginia, had reanimated Southern fears of insurrection and sharpened the region's loathing of abolitionists.[6] Brown's bungled raid on the town and its arsenal "was the South's worst nightmare and most paranoid fantasy come to life," Debby Applegate wrote in 2006. "Just as Northerners had taken 'Bleeding Kansas' as definitive evidence of the secret treachery of the South, the massacre at Harper's Ferry was regarded [by Southerners] as undeniable proof that abolitionists were plotting a major slave rebellion."[7]

Once captured, John Brown was swiftly tried and hanged soon thereafter. His death put nothing to rest. In the South and against the backdrop of Brown's frightening plan, Coffin's history would have made enduring fears seem terribly real. It took the increasingly desperate situation on the battlefield five years later to force lurid visions of rampaging blacks armed with John Brown's glistening pikes and captured firearms back into the recesses of the Southern psyche.

On January 11, 1865, Gen. Robert E. Lee wrote a thoughtful reply to a letter from Senator Robert Hunter of Virginia. The salutation over, Lee quickly got to the substance. "I would deprecate any sudden disturbance of [the relation of master and slave] unless it be necessary to avert a greater calamity to both," he explained, and then almost audibly drawing breath went on:

> I should therefore prefer to rely upon our white population to preserve
> the ratio between our forces and the enemy, which experience has shown
> to be safe. But in view of the preparations of our enemies, it is our
> duty to provide for a continued war and not for a battle or a campaign,

and I fear that we cannot accomplish this without overtaxing the capacity of our white population.

Should the war continue under the existing circumstance, the enemy may in the course of time penetrate our country and get access to a large part of our negro population. It is his avowed policy to convert the able-bodied men among them into soldiers and to emancipate them all. . . . His progress will thus add to his numbers, and at the same time destroy slavery in a manner most pernicious to the welfare of our people. . . . Whichever may be the effect of our employing negro troops, it cannot be as mischievous as this . . . we must decide whether slavery will be extinguished by our enemies and the slaves be used against us, or use them ourselves at the risk of the effects which may be produced on our social institutions. My own opinion is that we should employ them without delay. I believe that with proper regulations they can be made efficient soldiers.

Mention of the North's "avowed policy," of course, referred to the Emancipation Proclamation. After its publication the North had begun to enlist huge numbers of blacks into the Union army.

Lee dropped his other shoe in his letter's next paragraph:

There have been formidable armies composed of men having no interest in the cause for which they fought beyond their pay or the hope of plunder. But it is certain that the surest foundation upon which the fidelity of an army can rest . . . is the personal interest of the soldier in the issue of the contest. Such an interest we can give our negroes by giving immediate freedom to all who enlist, and freedom at the end of the war to the families of those who discharge their duties faithfully (whether they survive or not), together with the privilege of residing in the South.

The Confederacy's god of war had spoken. Lee clearly meant his letter, with its implication of the possibility of military collapse, to mark the tipping point in a debate that was then already more than a year old. (The idea of arming slaves seems to have been first proposed in December 1863 by Irish-born Maj. Gen. Patrick Cleburne of the Army of Tennessee.) "I can only say in conclusion," Lee wrote Hunter, "that whatever measures are to be adopted should be adopted at once. Every day's delay increases the difficulty. Much time will be required to organize and discipline the men, and action may be deferred until it is too late." Even so, it took until February 18, 1865, before enlisting slaves became policy. That's when the Confederate Congress very reluctantly enacted, after two weeks' secret debate and by only three votes in its House and one in its Senate, the necessary permissive legislation. The initiative was much too late to make any difference.

Blacks were one source of additional manpower for both sides, repatriated prisoners of war were the other. Until the first battle of Bull Run, when General Beauregard captured hundreds of Yankees, no one seems to have given any serious thought to prisoners, even less to the possibility that there might eventually be hundreds of thousands of them. (This lack of preparedness was not unique. Neither army was ready to treat its sick and wounded or to recover, record, and bury the dead.) Unlike the enlistment of former slaves, however, recycling former captives into combat required no agonizing, mind-bending justification in Richmond—just men released from confinement and at least early in the war not subject to "parole," to their sworn oath not to take up arms again until officially exchanged for a man from the other side.[8]

In theory at least, exchanged prisoners represented a pool of trained soldiers that could be quickly rearmed and put on the front lines, as swiftly as their strength and health would permit. Right after Bull Run and during the first months of the war, when neither side had any intent to build a network of prison camps, that's exactly what happened. Quick, informal exchanges on the battlefield under a flag of truce in 1861 became more commonplace the following year.

As soon as men began to be captured in the field the Confederacy understood prisoners to be a potential resource. The manpower-rich Union was under much less pressure to recycle its former prisoners to the front lines. Despite initial opposition in Washington to the idea of exchanging prisoners, however, a procedure to do just that was eventually formalized under the terms of the Dix-Hill cartel of July 1862, negotiated for the Union and Confederacy by Maj. Gen. John Dix and Maj. Gen. Daniel Hill, respectively ("cartel" here meaning "written agreement").

As evidenced by events during the American Revolutionary War, such cartels, another loan from European military tradition, typically had a difficult history and a short, troubled life-span. During that war the Continental Congress effectively made general prisoner exchanges within its reach impossible, to the intense frustration of Gen. George Washington. Delegates wanted to force language into the cartel document reflecting de facto British recognition of American belligerency, something London refused to permit. Congress was rightly fearful, too, that absent any alternative released British soldiers would rejoin their regiments but that American militiamen with expired enlistments would simply go home, further upsetting the balance in the field. Moreover, exchange protocol required the receiving party to pay for the former prisoner's room and board, such as these had been, and the impoverished Americans didn't have the money to get their soldiers out of hock. For all these reasons, while several general exchanges occurred in the South where the writ of Congress ran smaller, in the North none was possible.

A similar combination of hard-nosed political, economic, and military calculations eighty-odd years later doomed the Dix-Hill cartel. Under the 1862 cartel's terms, prisoners were to be exchanged at Vicksburg, Mississippi, and City Point, Virginia, within ten days of capture according to a specific formula that accounted for all captives in terms of private "equivalents," with a private himself, of course, equal to one. Thus one lieutenant equaled four privates, a captain six, a major eight, and so on. Near the top of the scale, one major general could be exchanged for forty privates. (That ratio was a becoming bit of modesty on the part of the cartel's negotiators, in effect reducing the military worth of a corps commander to less than the riflemen of a single infantry company in the field.)

Thousands of prisoners were exchanged later in the summer of 1862 following big, set-piece battles in Kentucky and Virginia. The cartel lasted, however, only until late December, when the exchange of officers was abrogated by the Union following a Confederate decision to turn over black prisoners to the states coupled to a threat to try and execute their white officers. In retrospect, it's surprising that the formal agreement survived so long. All its military advantages accrued to the hard-pressed South and Secretary of War Stanton had been dubious from the outset.

Beginning in January 1863, immediately after the collapse of the agreement, both sides began to collect large numbers of prisoners, which neither side was ready to house, feed, tend, and confine to anything like a humane standard. Semipermanent prisoner of war camps were new to warfare in the Americas.[9] The North begrudged the money necessary to run a camp system on the scale the war required, although it permitted controlled sales of Southern cotton to fund the maintenance of prisoners it held. The South didn't have the money

A partial view of the Union prison camp at Elmira, New York. The Union operated twenty-three large camps, each of which held a population of over one thousand prisoners, and a number of other, smaller camps. Elmira was one of the few largest camps, with a peak population estimated at nearly ninety-five hundred men. Roughly one-quarter of its prisoners died in the camp. (Chemung Valley Historical Museum)

necessary to support the camps it operated, and with its economy confined by the Union blockade it had no way to raise it. By spring 1865, when the war ended, some 690,000 men had been held as prisoners of war by both sides, all held in camps improvised from civil prisons, factory compounds, vacant buildings, and surplus military facilities or built from scratch in open space. Of that number perhaps 57,000 died in captivity, roughly one in twelve.

By 1865 the Union POW camp at Elmira, New York, on thirty-two low-lying acres just west of the city between downtown and the Chemung River, was home to some eight thousand prisoners held in rude, converted barracks and tents surrounded by a wood post stockade. Two gates pierced the wooden wall. To the north the main gate connected the compound to the city at a point along West Water Street. An auxiliary gate at the south wall gave access to the river.

The Elmira prisoner of war camp had been improvised from a surplus recruiting barracks, but there was nothing slapdash about the camp's design or construction. The heart of the camp was fifty-eight prisoners' barracks. A stout perimeter stockade twelve feet high surrounded the grounds. It was punctuated by elevated sentry boxes at fifty-yard intervals, forty such watchtowers connected to one another by an elevated wooden walk. Guards were stationed along the walk and at key points on the ground inside, a total of one hundred at a time, patrolling around the clock. At night, forty-one kerosene lanterns spaced along the inside of the stockade, each backed by an immense tin reflector, illuminated the interior of the camp. Every two hours the detail on duty turned over its responsibilities to a relief force of equal size.

Conditions at the camp, opened in mid-1864, were predictably terrible. Foster's Pond, a long slough lying in a depression between the river and the prisoners' barracks, was very soon little more than an open cesspool, awash with the drained human waste, trash, and kitchen garbage of thousands of men. A Union medical officer described the pond in an inspection report as "a festering mass of corruption, impregnating the entire atmosphere of the camp with its pestilential odors, night and day, green with putrescence, filling the air with its messengers of disease and death."

To the south, on the low ground between Foster's Pond and the Chemung River, stood the camp's hospital and infirmary tents, the smallpox isolation ward, and the busy "dead house," where bodies were prepared for burial. To the north, prisoner barracks were crowded between the pond and the camp's stockade wall running along the city's West Water Street. The site could have possibly held as many as five thousand prisoners under reasonably humane conditions; army headquarters insisted instead on ten thousand, and that crowding guaranteed high mortality. It has since been calculated that roughly one-quarter of the prisoners at Elmira (2,963 of 12,122) died from exposure and disease during their captivity, some falling to an otherwise unidentified medical condition one Union doctor called at the time "crowd poisoning" and others to pneumonia, small pox, and malnutrition. (The death rate elsewhere was even higher and more appalling. At Camp Sumter, site of the Confederacy's notorious Andersonville Prison, nearly one-third, 13,000 of more than 45,000, died during the camp's fourteen months in operation.)

Obedient to Edwin Lee's instructions, Surratt arrived in Elmira on Wednesday, April 12, after six days in French Canada. In December 1870, at a speech in Rockville, Maryland, he described his mission in New York to the audience:

General Lee came to my room [at St. Lawrence Hall] and told me he had a plan on foot to release the Confederate prisoners then in Elmira, New York. He said he had sent many parties there, but they always got frightened, and only half executed their orders. He asked me if I would go there and take a sketch of the prison, find out the number of prisoners, also minor details of the number of soldiers on guard, cannon, small arms, etc. I readily accepted these new labors, owing to the fact that I could not return to Washington for fear of the detectives.

Although Surratt had complained in a letter to his mother from Quebec about the high cost of room and board in Montreal, on arrival in Elmira he promptly checked into the best of the city's sixteen hotels, the handsome Brainard House. His choice was foolhardy. The Brainard was the billet of the prison camp commandant, Maj. Henry Colt, and several other senior camp administrators. The hotel filled a full city block at the corner of Water and Baldwin Streets, not too far from the Union camp. It stood at the southern end of the city's prosperous business district, across from the islands in the Chemung River. Here, as he had in Montreal, Surratt registered as "John Harrison," his usual alias. In due course that particular hotel register, with its proof that Surratt had been in Elmira the day Lincoln was shot, went missing, and its mysterious disappearance would feed all manner of speculation. Surratt thought he knew the motive, if not the answer. "Now the question is," he asked an audience rhetorically years later, "what became of that register? That some of the government emissaries abstracted that register, I firmly believe, or perhaps it is stored away in some of the other government vaults, under charge of some judge high in position, but this is only a surmise of mine. But the circumstance involves a mystery of villainy which the All Seeing God will yet bring to light." In fact, the deity has not done so, and the whereabouts of the Brainard's desk register covering the spring of 1865 remains a mystery.

Elmira today is a demonstration of entropy on an urban scale. The city's population in the 2000 census was roughly the same as it was one century before, thirty-one thousand, but Elmira's vigor and confidence now seem gone, sucked away by other communities in New York state's "Southern Tier" or absorbed by empty sidewalk pavements alongside shuttered shops and barren storefronts. In an eerie echo of its Civil War past, Chemung County is now home to two New York state maximum security prisons, a local growth industry. Boosters bravely tout the city's heritage, which includes serving for decades as the site of Mark Twain's summer home, Quarry Farm (his in-laws, the Langdons, also lived in the city), and a cluster of exceptionally handsome buildings from another time, but few seem to be listening.

In the 1860s and through the end of the nineteenth century, however, Elmira flourished as the Queen City of the Southern Tier. The 1860 census listed roughly eighty-seven hundred residents. In 1865 the total likely approached twice as many, much of the increase reflecting growth related first to the short-lived Army recruiting depot (one of only three in the entire state) and later the great camp along the river. Thanks to the Junction Canal, connecting to the better known Chemung Canal, and to the Erie and Northern Central Railroads running through its center, Elmira was both a regional transportation hub and a commercial center for surrounding farms. Its 1863 business directory proudly listed fifty-nine categories of business, the total buoyed by government purchasing of local goods and services as the war progressed.

The next morning, Thursday, April 13, Surratt headed west down Water Street to the prison's imposing main gate, facing Foster House from across the street. Earlier during the war some enterprising citizen had erected an observation tower on the northwest corner of Hoffman and Water Streets nine blocks from the hotel, from the top of which one had a perfect view over the walls and into the heart of the camp. (Two copy cats, the Mears Brothers, quickly followed and built a second tourist overlook, but theirs was soon torn down.) If the original were still in place, the tower with its comfortable seats and helpful spyglasses—their use included in the fifteen-cent price of admission—would have been a perfect vantage point for Surratt. But an unimaginative army officer had ordered at least one of the towers and the nearby food and drink booths torn down, perhaps both, and so Surratt might have had to improvise at ground level. He said that he did. He claimed to have gained admission into the compound by bribing a watch officer. Inside the compound the view would have been jarring.

Despite the reduced prisoner population, still 20 percent higher than the maximum capacity the first engineering survey had proposed for the camp, and superficial appearances, conditions inside would have been grim: wizened men aimlessly milling about newly landscaped open ground that just four weeks earlier had been the setting of Elmira's great St. Patrick's Day flood—the terrible result of an early warm spell thawing the snow pack in the mountains coupled with unseasonably heavy rains. At the crest, water stood up to two feet deep in the prisoners' barracks and only a single acre of high ground in the prison remained dry. The bill for postflood camp reconstruction was just over seventy-three thousand dollars, as much as several other camps required for a full year of operation and more than a few cost for the entire war. Even in benign weather, Elmira was the Union's most expensive prison camp to operate.

While Surratt was casing the camp in Elmira, celebrations anticipating the end of the war were still underway in Washington: decorous fêtes in the fine homes, hotels, and restaurants of polite society and more informal ones in the capital's hundreds of saloons and houses of prostitution. An "illumination" was planned for that night that would make the weary city's streets sparkle with torchlight processions under the flickering light of lamps, lanterns, and candles.

His mission for Lee in Elmira accomplished, Surratt was idly killing time clothes shopping and waiting for a return train to Montreal at the start of the week when his world was suddenly turned upside down by the news that Lincoln was dead and that he was a wanted man. Canada was a convenient sanctuary for a few weeks or several months. The condemnation and execution of his mother months later, however, made clear that a temporary bolt hole wasn't enough. After the first week of July, Surratt knew he needed someplace more distant to hide out, perhaps for years to come.

Edwin Lee's diary for Saturday, September 16, reads, "Charlie [Surratt] leaves Quebec today." And so he did. About nine o'clock in the morning, soon after breakfast on board the overnight river steamer from Montreal, Surratt and his minders presented themselves at Quebec's Napoleon Wharf, and from there a tender took him and fellow travelers to where the Royal Mail Ship (RMS) *Peruvian* was moored out in the stream. Among the others riding out to the ship was the usual small sprinkling of former Confederates emigrating to England, including this time Brig. Gen. Roswell Ripley, William Cornell Jewett, and Beverley Tucker. Ripley and "Colorado" Jewett were bit players in the war. So, too, was Tucker, but unlike them he had managed to rise to conspicuous and undeserved notoriety.

Beverley Tucker spent the last two years of the war in Canada on a covert trade mission for the Confederacy.* Immediately after Lincoln's assassination Tucker was named in Union wanted posters as one of the chief co-conspirators, lumped together with Clement Clay and Jacob Thompson, whose missions in Canada, unlike his, had been military not economic. The prospect of bounty

---

* In 1857–61 Nathaniel Beverley Tucker was the U.S. consul in Liverpool. Tucker (1820–1890), a third-generation Virginian from a distinguished family with its roots in England by way of Bermuda, began the war as a Confederate procurement agent in England. He served there for two years without any particular success. Tucker then relocated to Quebec in early 1864 to negotiate trades of Southern cotton for Union foodstuffs, a clandestine commerce made possible because of Davis's and Lincoln's tacit encouragement of this intercourse between belligerents. Not much seems to have come from Tucker's efforts as an agent of the Confederate commissary either, marking yet another lackluster phase of his generally unimpressive career. (This Tucker is not the man of the same name who, in 1836, was author of *The Partisan Leader*,

hunters chasing after the twenty-five-thousand-dollar reward for his capture pushed a fearful Tucker into flight from Canada to England—in the *Peruvian*—then to Mexico and, after Emperor Maximilian's execution in July 1867 (while Surratt was on trial), back to Canada. Much later the prosecution at Surratt's trial tried to make something of the coincidence that these three were on board on the same crossing as Surratt, but nothing came of the attempt.

Earlier the RMS *Peruvian* had loaded coal, cargo, and provisions for the voyage alongside a wharf. It then moved to a mooring off shore, prepared to sail just as soon as passengers and mail came aboard. Abbés Boucher and Lapierre, who had traveled to Quebec City from Montreal with Surratt, said farewell to him on the ship's main deck just before it got underway, but first Lapierre handed Surratt off to the ship's surgeon for safekeeping.

Surratt found the ocean crossing from Canada, the second leg in what became during the next fourteen months a flight spanning two continents, relatively easy. He sailed to England during those few years when transatlantic passenger travel switched suddenly and almost completely from wooden sailing vessels to iron-hulled steam ships, although the combination of technologies that made this possible—a rigid metal hull and the compound steam engine turning a screw propeller—had been visible on the horizon for decades.

Just a few years after Surratt's voyage, beginning in 1870 with the novel deck design of the White Star Line's RMS *Oceanic* and accelerating after 1878 with the introduction of electric lights in the Inman Line's speedy RMS *City of Berlin* (sailing between New York and Liverpool), North Atlantic passenger service began a long process of refinement that ended in the mid-twentieth century with vessels

---

a novel that predicted secession and the Civil War. That Tucker [1784–1851], an ardent secessionist, came from the same roots but spent his life as a lawyer and judge first in Missouri and then in Virginia.)

It took the U. S. chief executive two tries to replace Tucker in Liverpool, which city soon became the center of Confederate machinations in Europe. In January 1861 President Buchanan nominated Robert Magraw, of New Jersey, for the important diplomatic post, but the vacancy was finally filled by a Lincoln nominee, Thomas Dudley, of New Jersey. Dudley, about whom more later, was nominated to the Senate for confirmation just before Christmas that year.

General Ripley's chief distinction was that he adopted the Confederacy. Born in Ohio and raised in New York, Ripley had graduated from West Point and fought in the Mexican-American War and Seminole War before resigning his commission and moving to Charleston, South Carolina, his wife's home state. During the Civil War he commanded infantry in combat in South Carolina, Virginia, and Maryland before surrendering with Lee at Appomattox. In September 1865 Ripley was emigrating to Great Britain in the *Peruvian*. He remained there for twenty years before he returned to the United States in the 1880s to die. William Cornell "Colorado" Jewett was an even more minor character during the war, a Peace Democrat who largely on his own initiative pushed for British mediation between the sides. He later promoted a private audience with Leopold I, king of the Belgians (a closet Confederate sympathizer), to no particular effect.

of almost sybaritic luxury racing each other across the ocean during swift five- and six-day crossings.

Surratt's transatlantic carrier, the Montreal Ocean Steamship Company, commonly known as the "Allan Line" after founders Hugh and Andrew Allan, had been operating steamships across the ocean for almost fifteen years, ever since its *Canadian* went to sea in 1854. In 1865 the Allan Line's autumn schedule included four small steamers (fourteen to fifteen hundred tons, all named after saints) plying between Quebec City and Glasgow, Scotland, and seven larger ones (twenty-five to twenty-six hundred tons, including the RMS *Peruvian*) on weekly sailings between Quebec (leaving there Saturdays for Liverpool) and Liverpool, England (leaving there Thursdays to return to Quebec).[10] Steerage passengers could book passage from Quebec to England for only twenty-five dollars. Cabin class passengers paid more than twice as much, sixty-six, seventy, or eighty dollars, depending on accommodation. The line's fares to Scotland topped out at sixty dollars. Even the priciest fare equated to little more than three cents per nautical mile.[11]

3

"SUCH A WRETCH OUGHT NOT TO ESCAPE"

W ell before noon the *Peruvian* headed out of Quebec for Liverpool, England, with her master, William Ballantine, standing alongside the river pilot on the ship's open bridge. Three days of sailing through famously dangerous waters, "notorious for swift and uncertain tides and currents, for treacherous submerged reefs and rocks, and shoals in long stretches of the river," preceded the ocean crossing to come. Few knew the passage and its dangers better than Ballantine. He had been master of the Allan Line steamship *Nova Scotian* on the same transatlantic run before he moved up to take command of the new-construction *Peruvian*. Experience was important. The leg on the St. Lawrence River between Montreal and Quebec was a notoriously tricky bit of seamanship, often humbling old salts and freshwater pilots alike, despite decades of practice.

The first half day's cautious steaming put his ship past a string of islands to port and into the relatively open water of the lower St. Lawrence River, heading for the gulf of the same name. Past Anticosti Island to starboard and once through the Strait of Belle Isle, between Newfoundland and mainland Labrador, the *Peruvian* with Surratt on board was safely well beyond the uncharted and unmarked hazards of the St. Lawrence and finally at sea in the North Atlantic. Seven hundred fifty miles done, some seventeen hundred still to go.[1]

Whoever paid the $2.50 fare for Surratt's voyage down the St. Lawrence River from Montreal the night before probably also paid for his cabin on the next leg of his escape. In 1870 Surratt implied that he paid it himself, out of $200 in gold received from Secretary Benjamin when he left Richmond for the last time in spring, and that's certainly possible. While in Canada Surratt had received money from General Lee, too: on April 19, $140 for his mission to Elmira, another $100 on May 4, and a final $100 on September 5.[2]

Surratt's ocean crossing in the *Peruvian*, his first time at sea, was likely not uncomfortable, despite being in early autumn when heavy weather could be expected on every North Atlantic passage and the unsettling fact that his ship was reputed to roll noticeably even in good weather and to heave about "terribly" in bad. In 1865, nearly thirty years after the start of transatlantic steam ship travel, ocean crossings by packet late in the year had become routine, though hardly trouble free.[3] Steamship losses in ice and to storms, fires, collisions, and groundings were commonplace—and would be well beyond the end of the century.

In fact, the *Peruvian*'s parent company lost eight steamers in the seven years beginning in 1857 in groundings or ice fields, seven of them in Canadian waters. The first was the RMS *Canadian* on the St. Lawrence near Montreal under a river pilot's command eleven days out of Liverpool, followed by the RMS *Indian* (1859), *Hungarian* (1859), a second *Canadian* (1861), *North Briton* (1861), *Anglo-Saxon* (1863), *Norwegian* (1863), and *Bohemian* (1864). Nearly six hundred lives were lost in these accidents. Happily, not all shipwrecks suffered fatalities. The first *Canadian* did not, and in November 1861, when the Allan Line's RMS *North Briton* ran aground on tiny Mingan Island north of Anticosti in the Jacques Cartier Strait, the passengers and crew made it safely ashore, too, to be rescued a week later after what must have been very like a poorly equipped Outward Bound wilderness winter campout.

All the other transatlantic companies had generally similar safety records, a collective performance so intimidating to underwriters that most shipping companies found commercial insurance to be unaffordable and sailed their vessels without it. Self-insurance was a bold but sometimes very expensive risk to run. When, for example, at the end of October 1867 a late-season, category-three hurricane suddenly hit the eastern Caribbean, it sank three ships of the very well managed Royal Mail Steam Packet Company, including its flagship, the pretty and nearly new steamer RMS *Rhone*. Three other company vessels were pushed hard aground, and its facilities ashore battered. None was insured, forcing the company to eat this very considerable expense alone. Almost everything in nearby Charlotte Amalie, the port of St. Thomas in the Danish Virgin Islands and the company's transshipment hub, sank too. The busy harbor limped along for years while obstructing wreckage was cleared by divers.

By the standards of the 1860s, the *Peruvian* was handsome and big: 312 feet long, almost 39 feet abeam, with a volume of just over twenty-five hundred gross tons, three masts, and a single stack. Reasonably comfortable, too, at least for the cabin-class passengers it could carry, who were assigned two to a compartment and served hot meals from a steam table in the Russian fashion then in vogue: in successive courses on individual dishes.

Hot meals presented à la Russe on the grander ships of the period must have surpassed expectations and provoked gout. The Cunard Line's side-wheel steamship, the *Scotia*, offered her three hundred first-class passengers five meals a day "with the strictest punctuality" while crossing the Atlantic between New York and Liverpool under Captain Judkins's command. (He was described in a fawning *Liverpool Mercury* article as "the very *beau ideal* of the English gentleman.") Breakfast items served from her galley included "beef steak, mutton chops, pork chops, veal cutlets, smoked salmon, broiled chicken, ham, eggs, hot rolls, new milk, cream, and a host of things to tempt the palates of the most fastidious or satisfy the cravings of the most ravenous sea appetites." Four additional meals larded through each day spent aboard the *Scotia* offered even more prodigious spreads of edible ballast. The RMS *Scotia* was a famously good feeder, but it was a big eater too. Thanks to the ship's inefficient steam plant and paddle wheels, on eight-day Atlantic crossings it routinely devoured more than thirteen hundred tons of coal. The *Scotia* was, for that reason, Cunard's last paddle steamer.

In the 1860s second-class passengers generally had to provide their own bedding but benefitted from ship-supplied crockery. On the Allan Line's Quebec-Glasgow route, however, a forty-dollar "intermediate" fare, sixteen dollars more than steerage, got one a "bed, bedding, and all other requisites," likely eating utensils, furnished by the company.

The hundreds of steerage-class passengers who usually rode the ship west enjoyed no such coddling. They were berthed in cramped, single-sex dormitories at opposite ends of the ship and could ease their discomfort only slightly by renting bedding and flatware with which to eat from cold cans. The usual industry practice was to require steerage passengers to bring aboard with them bedding and eating utensils as well as a quart cooking pot and a three-gallon water keg. For migrants—and most in steerage were—this spare kit of household goods and the clothes they wore were often everything they had to start life in the new world.

The *Peruvian* carried auxiliary sails on its masts, but these were set only in unusual situations, most commonly in the event of mechanical problems or in the presence of very favorable winds along course. Ordinarily, the ship made its crossings entirely driven by steam from a boiler that swallowed some sixty to seventy tons of coal every day underway. Under full power it could (allegedly) make eleven knots, about 12.5 statute miles per hour. Despite a difficult introduction into service—it stuck on the ways at Robert Steele's Shipyard at launch into the River Clyde and was then gutted by fire while being fitted out—during the *Peruvian*'s first years at sea it was the pride of the Montreal Ocean Steamship Company. That special status didn't last long, only until the early 1870s, when newer and bigger ships joined the line's fleet, but the *Peruvian* stayed afloat and in service past her fortieth anniversary, impressive longevity in that era.

The *Peruvian* was practically new when Surratt came aboard. Its maiden voyage had been in March 1864, twelve and a half days between Liverpool and Portland, Maine (the line's winter western terminal during the many months when the St. Lawrence River was closed to navigation by ice; the land connection for Allan Line passengers between Portland, Maine, and Montreal, Quebec, was three hundred difficult miles in the cars of the St. Lawrence and Atlantic Railway). Since then it had crossed the Atlantic round trip just over once per month. Eleven days on average each way, infrequently as few as eight or nine, occasionally as many as thirteen. From the first it was under the command of Capt. William Ballantine, who apparently had been forgiven by the Allans for being below in his cabin when the river pilot ran his command (and their property), the *Canadian*, hard aground just above Stone Pillar Island in June 1857 and lost the ship. A few years later a passenger described him admiringly as "a kind Christian captain . . . a churchy Presbyterian . . . evidently well read and a thinker."

In 1865 the *Peruvian*'s arrival at the Montreal docks on May 3 marked the spring season's reopening of the port to Atlantic traffic and consequently won for her master that year's "gold-headed cane" trophy, marking the city's unofficial end of winter. When the *Peruvian* put to sea the following September from Quebec, the law of averages had the Allans past due for another catastrophe, but they and Surratt beat the odds. The next time her bridge watch saw land after Belle Isle was on Sunday, September 24, while the ship was approaching northern Ireland.

Like her skipper, the *Peruvian*'s physician on that voyage, Lewis McMillan, apparently was a congenial travel companion. Or so it would appear on the basis of Surratt's decision during the voyage to disclose to the doctor who he really was and why he was at sea.

Surratt had met McMillan on September 15 aboard the steamer *Montreal*, in which both rode down the St. Lawrence River overnight from Montreal to

Quebec and from where the next day they caught their connection for England. The short voyage might have been an awkward one. Surratt was then in the company of the same two priests who had harbored him one after the other through spring and summer. One of them, Abbé Boucher, knew McMillan and loathed him. When both had lived in Shefford, Quebec, Boucher said at Surratt's trial, they had argued about abortion (the man of science and the man of God allegedly taking predictable, opposing positions) and about five dollars that Boucher owed McMillan. The debt spilled into a lawsuit that later was the subject of some barely relevant testimony at the trial, but Boucher's testimony about their abortion debate might have been an invention, an attempt to discredit McMillan before a jury that would have believed doctor-induced abortion to be criminal and sinful. Defense counsel Richard Merrick deliberately raised the incendiary subject again during McMillan's first cross-examination:

> Merrick: "Did you ever offer your services in any of these places [three towns in Canada], in a professional capacity, for the purpose of *foeticide?*"
> McMillan: "I never did. I swear positively that I never did."
> "That was not part of your business?"
> "It was not."

Perhaps because he was aware of the McMillan-Boucher feud, it was Abbé Lapierre who introduced Surratt to McMillan aboard the *Montreal* and Lapierre who arranged that Surratt stayed out of sight in McMillan's cabin until the *Peruvian* got underway.

In the RMS *Peruvian*, as he had in St. Liboire and as he would in the stops to come, Surratt found it impossible to keep his identity secret from travel companions he barely knew. This odd, dangerous failing afflicted most of Booth's recruits, whose dull wits, immaturity, or lack of caution led them to repeated, impromptu confessions of identity to near-strangers. Surratt's crisis, when it eventually came, arose from what two Canadians, Lewis McMillan and Henri Beaumont de Sainte Marie, knew about him or said they knew and who they told what they knew. McMillan claimed to have received his information directly from its subject. He described Surratt as uncontrollably garrulous aboard the *Peruvian*. "I do not remember asking him during the whole passage a half dozen questions; and the reason that I did not question him is, that he seemed to be so

Looking east at the RMS *Peruvian* on the Mersey River, the city of Liverpool in the background. St. Nicholas Church's distinctive pierced lantern tower, built in 1814, rises just forward of the ship's foremast. The rectangular building between that mast and the *Peruvian*'s forward funnel (red with a white band and black top) is the Tower Buildings at 22 Water Street, where U.S. consul Thomas Dudley had his office in the 1860s. The photograph dates from between 1891, when the second funnel was added, and 1905, when the ship was scrapped. (Photograph by Francis Frith, No. 26629, National Museums Liverpool Maritime Library and Archive)

free in expressing everything that he had done, that I thought he would tell me enough without my questioning him," he recalled. "He was quite free; seemed to be overflowing with the subject."

Whether or not McMillan later embroidered his shipboard conversations with Surratt to make for a better story would be up to a jury to decide.

On one of the last days of September 1865 a slender, dark-haired and mustachioed young man wearing eyeglasses resting atop "a very sharp Roman nose," a Mr. John McCarty according to his ship's passenger manifest (elsewhere sometimes "Macarthy"), stepped ashore at a ferry landing in Liverpool, England. Under the dyed hair and the facial makeup tinting his skin, "McCarty" was John Surratt. The invented name was an addition to the several aliases he had used while a courier during the war.

Surratt came to rest in England after a short stopover in Northern Ireland at Moville, the port of Londonderry at the mouth of Loch Foyle. The *Peruvian*'s call at Moville was a routine mail drop on the way to her destination, but Surratt's exit seems to have been a last-minute gambit to shake off a possible intercept when the ship tied up later that night in Liverpool. The *Peruvian* entered Moville just after midnight Monday morning and was safely in Liverpool's Wellington Dock late Monday night or early the next day, on schedule after an uneventful nine-day crossing. It stayed there until October 26, one full month, until some unidentified repairs were completed, before retaking her place in the line's schedule and returning to Quebec.

If we believe the ship's surgeon, who said he saw him off when the gangplank went down at Moville, Surratt was "rather the worse for his drinking" three half-tumblers of straight brandy in the previous twenty minutes—drunk to the point that McMillan feared Surratt might fall overboard while trying to disembark in the early morning dark. "I said to the chief officer at the gangway," McMillan recounted to the jury later, "will you mind to take this officer [*sic*] by the arm and lead him down. . . . He did."

Once ashore, it's not clear how Surratt then crossed the Irish Sea from Moville to Liverpool, but the heavily traveled, short crossing (190 nautical miles direct, less than one day's steaming) would have offered him several options, including frequent ferries from Belfast and Dublin. A U.S. State Department investigator, George Sharpe, later determined that Surratt reached Liverpool on Wednesday, September 27.* If Sharpe were right, Surratt must have stayed ashore in Ireland a day or so before moving on to Liverpool.

He had good reason to expect a warm welcome in the blue-collar city on the Mersey River, England's Baltimore inflated. Liverpool had a vigorous Roman Catholic community and was famous for its Confederate sympathies. Congested, busy, booming Liverpool and its natives, speaking "scouse," Lancashire-accented English, must have been a marvel to the young man from southern Maryland. Nothing in his prior experience, not Richmond, Washington, or Montreal, would have prepared him for Liverpool, already then a metropolis of near half a million stretched along five miles on the east side of the tidal Mersey estuary with crowded wet docks on both sides of the river as far north and south as one could

---

*   Sharpe (1828–1900), a native New Yorker, was the ideal choice for this mission. An honors graduate of Rutgers College in New Jersey and the Yale Law School, he raised a volunteer infantry regiment at the outbreak of the war (the 120th New York) but soon gravitated into military intelligence. Before demobilizing at the end of the war and returning to the practice of law, Sharpe first succeeded Allan Pinkerton as the Army of the Potomac's intelligence officer and then served successively as the chief of the new Bureau of Military Intelligence for General Hooker and General Meade and finally for General Grant at his City Point, Virginia, headquarters. Grant remembered Sharpe well. In 1870, when he was president, Grant appointed him the U.S. marshal for the Southern District of New York.

see and a busy double-track rail line to the interior.[4] (The Manchester Canal connecting that landlocked city with Eastham on the seacoast would come much later, in 1894.)

The British establishment saw Victorian England as a beehive, an orderly, hardworking society in which everyone had a station in life and willingly performed its duties, the entire structure surmounted by a beloved queen (now widowed after the death in 1861 of her consort, Prince Albert) who gave her identity to the whole and her name to the age.

Mid-nineteenth-century Liverpool—already 650 years old then and ranked as England's second city; thanks to its frenetically busy port the city had sometime since supplanted Bristol in that status—could be described by a better metaphor than a rustic skep. Liverpool's iconic structure was (and recently restored, still is) St. George's Hall, the handsome Greco-Roman municipal building that rose practically at city center. Superb St. George's Hall symbolized the city even better than the miles of wet docks lining the River Mersey. Designed by a young local architect, Harvey Elms, St. George's Hall was finally completed by a successor in 1854, seven years after Elms's death in Jamaica from tuberculosis.

The hall's huge and wonderfully decorated assembly room, the observation galleries above it on two sides, and an adjacent, compact twelve-hundred-seat concert hall could represent the prosperous and privileged among the city's many residents. The same hall's civil and criminal courtrooms on the main floor, connected by a spiral staircase to several holding cells in the brick basement below, could stand in for the city's huge population of suffering poor. Those suspected of crime were shuttled between the court and Liverpool's two ghastly prisons by police wagons, whose access to the hall was through a tunnel built at ground level for just this purpose.

The most evocative images available of Liverpool in the late 1850s and early 1860s come from the contemporary watercolors of W. G. Herdman and a son, William, one of the sixteen Herdman children his durable wife, Elizabeth, bore the hard way, *seriatim*, during an impressive total of twelve years spent in pregnancy. William, W. G.'s first son and namesake, painted until his early death in 1878 at forty-nine and left some nine hundred paintings. Many of these and some done by his father in later life show Liverpool's busy streets and lanes in the city's prime, and in full color, dominated by the brick reds of the city's chief building material. (Liverpool photographer Francis Frith's cityscape photos from the same era are, of course, in black and white.) Although W. G. had three other sons who also painted professionally, it is largely through W. G.'s and William's

St. George's Hall, circa 1855. Liverpool's beautiful and impressive municipal assembly hall opened in 1854. The building's central great hall was the site of both a week-long Confederate fund-raising bazaar in October 1864 and of the lord mayor's eulogy for Abraham Lincoln in April 1865. It was full to overflowing for both events. Watercolor by William Herdman. (Liverpool Central Library)

eyes that we can best see Liverpool as Surratt must have seen it in early autumn 1865, while he hiked uphill from Prince's pier-head ferry landing along Chapel and Tythe Barn streets toward his next sanctuary, the Church of the Holy Cross, rising at the intersection of Great Crosshall and Standish.

In the nineteenth century Liverpool was the principal British seaport for emigrants heading to North America. The city's location and well-developed facilities made it a natural collection point, a sump for Great Britain's poor—the starving farmers and suffering factory workers of Ireland and Scotland and of England's industrial heartlands. Scandinavian and Russian emigrants heading for the New World transited through Liverpool, too, after crossing the North Sea to Hull and moving on from Hull to Liverpool by train.

These unfortunates lived in wretched conditions, in tenement "courts" on the dark, labyrinthine streets just inland of Liverpool's docks near the city's north end. Tiny three-story hovels stacked rooms, ten feet by ten feet, atop one another, the rearmost reached through a low tunnel dug out beneath those in front facing the alley. Each such cluster was served by open public toilets on

Liverpool from the Mersey, 1863. The steam-paddle ferryboats just visible at the piers in front of St. Nicholas' lantern tower suggest one way that Surratt might have crossed from Ireland to England. The perspective is nearly the same as in the *Peruvian* photograph by Francis Frith. Watercolor by William Herdman. (Liverpool Central Library)

the street and a single drinking-water tap nearby. Not surprisingly, lethal disease washed through these congested neighborhoods in waves. Surratt arrived in the city just behind an explosion of typhus that had hit the city's three poorest wards—St. Anne's, Exchange, and Great George—especially hard. Even so, death rates from typhus ("starvation fever"), typhoid, diphtheria, cholera, and tuberculosis did little to reduce population densities that peaked at an astonishing tens of thousands per square mile as new refugees came in on the tide to replace the old.

Crime as well as poverty and disease was rife in Liverpool. In 1865 Head Constable J. J. Greig reported to the city council in part that there were 3,380 known "depredators, offenders, and suspected persons at large" in the city and that his police force was carefully watching 1,345 "houses of bad character," places frequented by fences, thieves, and prostitutes: public houses, beer and coffee shops, brothels, and tramps' lodgings. Greig's report did not mention an estimated forty-five thousand feral waifs, "street Arabs" who roamed the city, living as Oliver Twist had in Charles Dickens's gritty, thirty-year-old novel of life in the impoverished precincts of the hive.

For those with the means of escape to the New World, scores of packets (ships on regular schedules; sail first, steam later) lay in the port's docks offering transatlantic passage in steerage for a few pounds per person and competing vigorously for the business.

In 1825 only five thousand emigrants left Great Britain for America, but by midcentury the number departing in a single year approached a quarter million, most during the summer months of the "emigration season," most from Liverpool, and most originally from Ireland. (The great impetus for Irish displacement to Liverpool in midcentury was the Irish potato famine, which peaked in 1847. Most moved on from there to the New World.) The result was that the port city developed a substantial Catholic community on its waterfront, numbering among them people stranded for one reason or another on that side of the Atlantic, and others whose business or calling it was to provide succor to those about to depart, almost all of whom were desperately poor.

To move this human freight several shipping lines centered their transatlantic business on Liverpool, including the Montreal Ocean Steamship Company, which for the past ten years had specialized in the Liverpool-Quebec route. Emigrant packets sailed full, often more than full, westbound, but the revenue traffic was nearly all one way; until the 1880s, when livestock began to fill steerage spaces on the eastbound leg, these ships usually returned to England in ballast.

The year 1865 might have held a few exceptions to this general rule, because after hostilities ended south of the border London concluded that the American military threat to its Canadian provinces (imputed from the tensions that followed the RMS *Trent* affair in November 1861, when Confederate diplomats James Mason and John Slidell were forcibly and illegally removed from a Royal Mail ship on the high seas by the USS *San Jacinto*) had diminished. The nearly 14,500 British regulars that had been sent during the last half of 1861 to reinforce army garrisons in British North America, for a time quintupling the force already present in Canada, were withdrawn in 1865, and they were transported in steerage back home that year. The huge *Great Eastern* and eighteen other chartered transport vessels had carried the regular troops together with arms and munitions for the militia westbound.[5] When it came time to withdraw them four years later, the *Great Eastern* was no longer part of the mix, and an even larger civilian fleet was required to back haul the force home. A one-time good deal for shipping companies.

Thanks to its extensive system of wet docks on the waterfront, the port of Liverpool was second only to London in the usual measures of commercial vitality. These docks, many featuring basins large enough to hold two dozen oceangoing ships nested side by side like littermates, were closed off from the river at high tide by flood gates. The gates trapped water behind them, keeping the ships inside afloat and erect until the next high tide. In this way the city tamed its river's seventeen-foot tidal fall, but at the cost of a huge capital investment in construction at the river's edge.

Passenger traffic aside, business was generally very good, in large part because Liverpool was the nearest seaport serving land-locked Manchester and the other factory towns of Lancashire, the heartland of industrialization in northwestern England—and the world. All the raw materials (bales of cotton principally) and other imports necessary to feed the textile mills of Lancashire, Yorkshire, and the Midlands and a booming local textile machinery industry necessarily passed across the Liverpool docks. Canny Liverpool shippers and middlemen charged all that the traffic could bear, that is, until 1861, when cotton exports from the embattled South began to collapse.

The Confederacy had many friends in the city on the Mersey, a relationship that had its eighteenth-century roots in the Atlantic trade in Virginia tobacco and then in African slaves, increasingly important to the city beginning in the 1740s. After 1807 American cotton took the place of slaves as the principal commodity moving through the port. (The substitution simply replaced shipping slaves with shipping the product of their labor.) By 1860, two-thirds of the world's supply of cotton came from the plantations and small farms of the American South and West. Liverpool was the principal port of entry into the United Kingdom for American short staple, upland cotton, "King Cotton" the raw material upon which confident Southern planters believed the economy of the United Kingdom and the rest of the industrializing world was based. In 1860 nearly half a million tons of U.S. cotton were landed at Liverpool, an annual level of imports that collapsed to fewer than three thousand tons three years later, and would not rise again to the half-million-ton mark for another twenty years.

These historic ties through generations engendered a natural sympathy in Liverpool for the Confederacy. Given this history, it is not remarkable that supporters of the Confederate States of America were thick on the ground in the city. They included not only those who made money directly from the conflict, shipbuilders or dealers in ship's stores and chandlers, but also cotton merchants and mill owners who hoped to profit again when the war was over. (Scotland, too, harbored Confederate sympathizers with economic motives, especially around the Clydeside shipyards near Glasgow where more than forty blockade runners were built and launched during the war.)

Jefferson Davis's government understood the importance of Liverpool to the success of the Confederate war effort and the leverage prominent Liverpudlians could exert on Her Majesty's government in the South's campaign to gain European diplomatic recognition. To the extent that the Confederate States of America had effective representation in the United Kingdom, its "embassy" was not in London but in Liverpool, at the 10 Rumford Place offices of Fraser, Trenholm and Company, a Charleston, South Carolina–based merchant bank deeply involved in arms purchases and blockade running. (The same offices are today being handsomely restored by a local firm of property managers sympathetic to their new headquarters' nineteenth-century history.) Ties between the merchant bank and the Rebel government were very close, evidenced by the fact that in mid-1864 Jefferson Davis appointed George Trenholm, the firm's senior partner in Charleston and the Confederacy's wealthiest man, to be the new secretary of the treasury for the Confederacy.

Davis and his cabinet wisely salted Liverpool with capable men, chief among them James Bulloch, three-year-old Teddy Roosevelt's maternal uncle, who began his service as the senior Confederate contracting officer in the United Kingdom and ended it living in Liverpool and raising his family there after the war. He lies there still, in the Toxteth Park cemetery amid several relatives.

At the outset of the war cotton (and the other staples from the South: tobacco, sugar, and rice) was embargoed because of Richmond's belief that the ensuing "cotton famine" would simultaneously destabilize the Union's economy and force the United Kingdom into diplomatic recognition and military intervention. In this, as in so much else, Richmond was disappointed. The embargo and later blockade coupled to the demands of the war eventually pauperized the Confederacy.

Although blockade runners managed to move a few hundred bales at a time through the blockade, that trickle was nothing like the flow that was required to sustain England's textile industry. Stocks on hand eased the impact of the "cotton famine" during the earliest months of the war, but as those inventories were quickly spun into thread and woven into cloth (and as other sources, including Egypt, India, and Ottoman Turkey, failed to make up the difference) mills began to shut down and both English workers and the national economy began to suffer. At its peak in the winter of 1862, roughly 400,000 spindle operators in Lancashire were affected by the "famine," of whom nearly a quarter million were unemployed and the rest were on short shifts.

A combination of factors kept Great Britain from supporting the Confederacy decisively, despite the costs of the war to its domestic industry and the aristocracy's sympathy for the South and members of its plantation plutocracy, whom it saw as kindred spirits. These ranged from the philosophical and moral (Britain outlawed the trade in slaves in 1807 and slavery itself in the empire after 1833; after that most Britons regarded the institution as indefensible) to the strategic and political (a suspicion that the badly outmatched South couldn't win in the field which became, after 1862 and the bloody battle of Antietam, a conviction that it could not).

Still, if Liverpool and Richmond were not exactly sister cities during the first half of the 1860s, they were close to it, and Liverpool made no secret of its bias. The great central room in St. Georges Hall was the scene in October 1864 of a fund-raising bazaar sponsored by the kingdom's titled elite to support Southern widows and orphans. Among the charity event's twenty-four "lady patronesses" were one princess, three marchionesses, a marquise, three countesses, one vicomtesse, and a baronness; a handful of less august ladies and mistresses rounded out the list of worthy hostesses. Over five days, booth sales—each booth was named to honor one of the Confederate states—managed by this covey of aristocratic ladies raised £22,000 for the South, perhaps $125,000 in Union money.[6]

In early November 1865, six weeks or so after Surratt arrived in the port, the Confederate screw steam cruiser CSS *Shenandoah* sailed through the Irish Sea to Liverpool, dropped anchor, and hauled down her colors. So quietly ended the ship's superb service as one of the Confederacy's most successful commerce raiders, second only to the CSS *Alabama*.[7]

The *Shenandoah*, built originally on the Clyde for the fast tea trade between China and Great Britain as *Sea King* but surreptitiously purchased for the Confederacy by the tireless Bulloch, was perfect for its mission: driving Yankee ocean commerce from the seas. The twelve-hundred-ton ship was the first to feature iron frames and wooden planking, a step partway between familiar wooden ships and the next generation of all-metal ones. Similarly, its suit of twenty-one square sails was supplemented by a coal-fired steam plant driving a single screw, retractable so that it could be housed to reduce drag when it was underway on sail alone. In October 1863 at sea off Madeira, the *Sea King* was outfitted with eight guns, including two 32-pound Whitworth rifles, manned with a new crew, and provisioned, and almost as simply as that the innocent merchant was transformed into the CSS *Shenandoah*. Its captain's commission signed by Jefferson Davis authorized him and his crew "by Force of Arms, to attack subdue, scuttle, and take all ships belonging to the United States of America. . . . And to take by force if necessary any vessel, barge, or floating transporter belonging to said United States or persons loyal to the same, including Tackle, Apparel, Ladings, Cargoes, and Furniture."

The *Shenandoah's* cruise took her around the world under the Confederate ensign, from London in October 1864 to Liverpool the following November. During these months under Lt. James Waddell's command, the *Shenandoah* sank or captured almost forty U.S. ships and singlehandedly nearly shut down the Union's prosperous North Pacific whale fishery. Supposedly not until August 2 did Waddell learn from a passing English bark, the *Barracouta*, that the Civil War had been over for months.[8] Later still he would discover that his ship had fired the last shots of the war, against Union whalers working the rich grounds off the Aleutian Islands.

Waddell's selection of Liverpool as an internment port for his ship could not have been an accident. The *Shenandoah's* sisters, CSS *Alabama* and CSS *Florida* (the third in the Confederate navy's famous triumvirate of raiders; there were nine others less well known), were both built on the Mersey, the *Alabama* by John Laird Sons and Company and the *Florida* by William C. Miller and Sons. For a while in 1863 it looked like Liverpool would add two more combatant ships to the Confederate navy, two powerful, ironclad rams built by Laird and specifically designed to break the North's blockade. The surprise appearance of the CSS *Virginia* (formerly the USS *Merrimack* below the waterline) in Hampton Roads in March 1862 had illustrated what a single ironclad could do to wooden men of war massed in a roadstead, and the vision of a pair of such super weapons loose among the Union fleet was frightening.

The two rams were scheduled to be completed, one in March and the other in May, and the prospect so inflamed Washington that Ambassador Adams in London was instructed to threaten a breach in diplomatic relations tantamount to a declaration of war if the finished ships were delivered to the Confederacy. They were not. After a bogus sale to Egypt fell through, customs officials in Liverpool seized both ships and they soon reappeared in the Royal Navy as the HMS *Scorpion* and HMS *Wyvern*. But it had been a near thing. The Confederacy's secretary of the navy, Stephen Mallory, and others had foreseen (or imagined) a scenario that had the Laird rams breaking the blockade and attacking Union vessels in their home ports, which successes would have prompted Britain to acknowledge the South's independent status.

The close relationship between Liverpool and Richmond was not unknown in Washington. To protect the Union's interests in this important place, in late 1861

Thomas Dudley, Union consul in Liverpool, 1861–72. A fellow American in diplomatic service described the slender, bearded, six-foot-tall Dudley this way: "He is as intelligent as he looks, and talks with great force . . . a strenuous patriot." Although the *Oreto*/CSS *Florida* and *Enrica*/CSS *Alabama* both slipped past him because Her Majesty's government moved too slowly, Dudley's tireless efforts did prevent the two immensely powerful "Laird rams" from joining the Confederate navy. (Augustus C. Rogers, ed., *United States Diplomatic and Consular Service: Our Representatives Abroad* [New York: Atlantic, 1874], 257)

Secretary of State Steward sent Thomas Dudley to be the U.S. consul in the city. Dudley's credentials for such a sensitive post seemed modest enough: He was a New Jersey–born Quaker, a committed abolitionist who had the wit in 1860 to lead his state's Republican Party delegation to support Abraham Lincoln's campaign for the presidential nomination in Chicago.

Credentials aside, Thomas Dudley turned out to be a natural intelligence station chief. Not long after he arrived in Liverpool on November 19—in all, he would serve there for eleven years—Dudley was running a collection operation targeted against the Confederacy throughout the United Kingdom using anonymous hired "detectives" and with the assistance of consuls on the Continent.

One of his important sources was Matthew Maquire, the retired superintendent of Liverpool's police, freelancing as a "private detective and inquiry officer" out of an office at 6 Doran's Lane. Perhaps excluding Maquire, Dudley described his covert agents as in general not "very estimable men." Thanks to Dudley's zeal, Liverpool was the focal point of Union espionage operations in Europe during the war.

McMillan wasted no time in passing on the remarkable information he had received from his young traveling companion. The day after the *Peruvian* docked in Liverpool, on Tuesday, September 26, McMillan hied himself over to the office of the justice of the peace, one George Melly, where he swore out a statement:

> during the voyage, two or three days after we sailed from Quebec, during a conversation said McCarty spoke of his having great difficulty escaping from the United States into Canada, and asked me if I suspected who he was. I told him that connecting what he had been telling me with what had occurred at the time, I supposed that he had been connected with the assassination of President Lincoln. He made no reply but smiled. Subsequently during the voyage he told me that he had been in the Confederate service, engaged in conveying intelligence between Washington and Richmond; that he had been concerned in a plan for carrying off President Lincoln from Washington, which was concocted entirely by John Wilkes Booth and himself; that he came to Canada just before the assassination of Lincoln took place; that while in Canada he received a letter from Booth saying that it had become necessary to change their plans and requested him to come to Washington immediately; that he did start immediately for Washington, but did not say whether he went there, but he said on the way back to Canada the train he was on was delayed at St. Albans, and while sitting at breakfast a gentleman next to him spoke of the report of the assassination, and that he, McCarty or as he then called himself, Harrison, replied that the news was too good to be true; that the gentleman took a newspaper out of his pocket and read the account of the occurrence, and he, McCarty, was surprised to see his name there, and left immediately; that on Sunday evening last [September 24] he had been telling me of an interview . . . at Richmond, and I said to him, you have told me a great deal, what must I call you, what is your real name? And he said, my name is Surratt.

That interesting work done, McMillan delivered his statement to Henry Wilding, the U.S. vice consul in Liverpool, Dudley's assistant, and momentarily left the stage. Wilding was clearly intrigued but not yet fully persuaded by McMillan's story. The next day Wilding sent a copy of McMillan's affidavit to Ambassador Adams in London and dispatched its text to Secretary of State William Seward.[9] Mindful of his host country's legal procedures, Wilding concluded his cable No. 538 to Seward with "Should there be really anything in it, and a warrant be obtained for Surratt's apprehension, we should scarcely get him delivered up without other evidence than we can obtain here, we should have to ask his remand until you can send us the necessary evidence."

McMillan's sensational disclosure about his fellow traveler on the steamer *Peruvian* to Vice Consul Wilding must have immediately triggered a search through the port city for Surratt. It took Wilding no more than a few days to unearth his prey. Surratt's host in Liverpool turned out to be one Father Charles Jolivet of the Oblates of Mary Immaculate. Between 1856 and 1867 Jolivet was superior of Holy Cross Parish in Liverpool's crowded and impoverished St. Anne's ward.* The mission, originally the inspiration of a French bishop in Marseilles who was appalled by the suffering of Irish Catholics at home and in the slums of Liverpool, Cardiff, and Glasgow, was six years old when Jolivet took over, relieving the first superior, Father Noble. The runaway American was not the usual sort to seek comfort in Father Jolivet's hospitality. It's tempting to assume that Surratt made the French connection thanks to a letter of introduction from either Boucher or Lapierre in Quebec, but no such letter has been found.

In 1865 Liverpool's Roman Catholic Parish of the Holy Cross was in vigorous good health. The parish's mother church on Standish Street, replacing an improvised house of worship at the same place on the third floor of a building that had until then been a cowshed and rag and bone store, had been opened only five years earlier. Within, Father Jolivet and his five fellow priests ministered

---

* Charles Constant Jolivet (1826–1903) was born in Pont-l'Abbé, France, on the southern coast of Brittany. Jolivet's years as a young seminarian saw him progress from a weak start to a strong finish; the master of novices first called him "flighty and lazy" but later described him as "very charming and cheerful." He took holy orders in 1846 and joined the Oblates of Mary Immaculate a year later at age twenty-one, becoming the order's 243rd member. Soon after celebrating his first mass as a priest in Nancy, Jolivet left France for England. He never returned to his native country.

In 1874, after twenty years in England that included more than a decade in Liverpool, during which he met and harbored Surratt, Jolivet was sent to South Africa. There he served for the rest of his life as the apostolic vicar, traveling among the order's residences for six months of each year and presiding over the explosive growth of Roman Catholicism in southern Africa "au milieu de Noirs" (among the blacks). Jolivet died in Durban, South Africa.

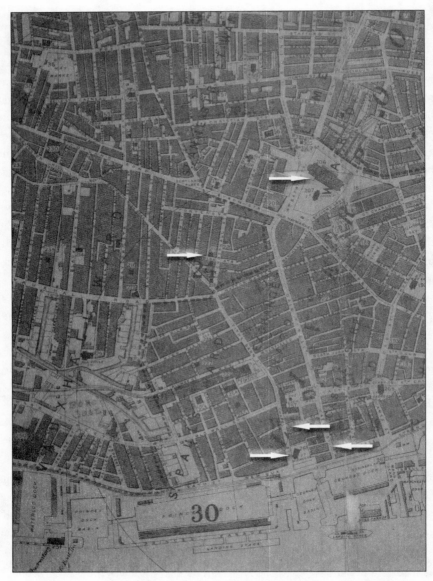

A contemporary street map of several of Liverpool's northern neighborhoods showing the city when Surratt hid with the Oblates of Mary Immaculate. The arrows mark
(*top to bottom*) St. George's Hall, Holy Cross Church (at the intersection of Standish and
Great Crosshall streets), the offices of Fraser, Trenholm and Company on Rumford Place,
Consul Thomas Dudley's office on Water Street, and the Church of Our Lady and St.
Nicholas. (Mawdsley's Map of the Town, Port and Environs of Liverpool, revised and
corrected by T. B. Ryder, 1865. Liverpool Central Library)

to the spiritual needs of thousands in the surrounding Vauxhall Road–St. Anne Street district of the city.

The new church was a handsome one, but when Surratt came upon it, it was not yet complete. Between 1865 and 1882 a new sanctuary and side aisles, a new choir, and a new altar were all inaugurated with proper ceremony. In 1899 Jolivet returned in retirement to his spiritual home to celebrate the installation of 108 electric lights.[10]

By September 30 Wilding had the church's rectory on Great Crosshall Street staked out and Surratt under observation. The existence of the search, so quickly successful, could not have remained secret for long. That the place was being watched wouldn't have escaped the notice of its staff, and plans must have quickly been made to move Surratt away from surveillance and away from Great Britain altogether.

Three days later, Wilding knew more and was more insistent. "The supposed Surratt has now arrived in Liverpool," he wrote to Seward,

> and is now staying at the oratory [sic] of the Roman Catholic Church of the Holy Cross. According to the reports, Mrs. Surratt was a very devout Roman Catholic, and I know that clergymen of that persuasion on their way to and from America have frequently lodged, while at Liverpool, at that same oratory, so that the fact of this young man going there somewhat favors the belief that he is really Surratt. I can, of course, do nothing further in this matter without Mr. Adams' instructions, and a warrant. If it be Surratt, such a wretch ought not to escape.

Clearly, sometime during the end of the week, in between his first cable on Wednesday and his second (No. 359) on Saturday, Wilding had managed to see Surratt, despite a train trip to London Surratt had taken in the meanwhile (where, the *Times* of London later reported without elaboration or identifying a source, "he received from some friend an advance of £70, with a recommendation that he should betake himself to Spain").[11] In his second cable Wilding was able to tell the secretary, "His appearance indicates him to be about twenty-one years of age, rather tall, and tolerably good looking."

Naturally ignorant of what use, or lack of use, had been made of the information he had so breathlessly provided to Vice Consul Wilding, after recrossing the Atlantic McMillan next appeared at the U.S. consulate in Montreal, at John Potter's office, to pass on his exciting intelligence to this man too. On October 25,

John Harrison Surratt Jr. During his flight, Surratt was most often described in prose rather than depicted in photographs. Most of these descriptions revealed as much about their author as their subject. Reporter George Alfred Townsend described Surratt this way: "long, hooked nose, long oblique dark brows, keen blue eyes with eyelids hidden under the brows, outflapping pointer's ears; head, flat on the top, huge and swelling behind the ears, mobile, sensitive, pointed, haughty chin, a type of face expressed in the portraits of the stern and gloomy Stuart Calverts and their pioneers in Catholic Maryland, pear-shaped with cruciform, florid goatee and moustache, the Saxon crossed by the Spaniard." (Library of Congress, LC US262-8583)

the day before McMillan was scheduled to head back to Liverpool as the ship's doctor in *Nova Scotian*, he was in talking to Potter. By then Surratt had already been gone from England for a week. For his part McMillan continued as a company medical officer on the Quebec-Liverpool run, sailing first in the RMS *Belgian* and then in the RMS *Damascus* before leaving the Allan Line.

Surratt's short stay in Liverpool was unusual, but others from America did not fear pursuit as he did. Most Confederates and Confederate sympathizers who came to the city immediately after the war stayed much longer; some made their homes there or jumped from Liverpool to London. The attractions in both places were the English language and the protection of English law. That law protected Surratt, too, but for him the city was a way station, a place where he could make connections and wait for the money he needed to move on.

Surratt's route from England to Italy, his next destination, isn't completely certain. Scheduled service by sea from Liverpool into the Mediterranean was available at least as early as 1853, when steamers of the British and Foreign Steam Navigation Company first sailed between England and Gibraltar, Malta, and other Mediterranean ports. It's possible that Surratt went by ship from one port to the other, and some believe that's what he did. What evidence there is suggests instead that Surratt crossed the English Channel and moved overland to Paris and from there probably to Marseilles on what was swiftly becoming a well-developed French rail system. A short, easy passage by sea from Marseilles to Civitavecchia, the port of Rome on the Tyrrhenian Sea, would have completed the trip.[12]

In the 1860s ships from Liverpool or Southampton (serving London) to the Continent usually arrived at the English Channel port of Calais or Le Havre. From either place, or several other French coastal cities, an international passenger could get to Paris by train and connect there with the rest of the French rail system, a cluster of independent regional operating companies loosely hubbed at the capital. From Paris Surratt could proceed at a swift eighteen miles per hour or so on standard gauge, mainline trackage to any of dozens of domestic destinations, among them the Mediterranean ports of Marseilles, Toulon, and Villefranche sur Mer through Dijon and Lyon. Traveling with a Canadian passport—financed out of the Confederate funds remaining available to Gen. Edwin Lee—and unimpeded by pursuit, Surratt would have had little trouble getting into and out of France.

Marseilles to Civitavecchia was easy too. Although there was no oceangoing papal shipping line, and no Italian shipping lines would have served the two ports in 1865–66, several French ones did. Both Léon Bazin and Gay and Valéry et Fraissenet, headquartered in Marseilles, are known to have offered packet service to Civitavecchia. After May 1865 and through at least October 1866 the French government's state packet boat service connected the two ports on a weekly schedule. A French steamer of the state Ligne d'Italie left Marseille every

Thursday for Messina on the strait between the Italian boot and Sicily with a stop at Civitavecchia southbound on Saturdays.

Henri Beaumont de Sainte Marie, the informer who appears again later in the story, is one source of the information that Surratt passed through Paris en route to Italy. Two defense witness at Surratt's trial in mid-1867, French Canadian lawyers who knew Sainte Marie in Montreal, characterized him as an accomplished (or imaginative) liar, and anything he said is suspect. This, however, sounds credible. The only document that touches on the subject—Surratt's Canadian passport, sent to Washington in 1867 from Rome by George Sharpe but since lost—reportedly confirmed Sainte Marie's report.

In March 1868 an English volunteer, Joseph Powell, went to Rome to join the Zouaves. According to his 1871 published memoir, Powell's route took him from London south to Newhaven Port, then overnight on the Channel steamer to Dieppe, to Paris via Rouen by rail followed by a one-day train ride through Lyon to Marseilles, and nearly two days by steamer to Civitavecchia. Surratt's itinerary in 1865 was likely very similar.

4

"THE ESCAPE OF WATSON SAVORS OF A PRODIGY"

L iving on little and looking for sanctuary, in October 1865 Surratt arrived from Marseilles at Civitavecchia nearly broke. During the last week of the month Washington learned that the papal capital had been Surratt's destination from the outset. "It is Surratt's intention to go to Rome," Consul General Potter wrote the secretary of state from Montreal on October 25, information he almost certainly received from McMillan, who was now back home in Canada between voyages to Liverpool and full of news about his notorious shipmate. On November 13 Secretary of State William Seward, citing Potter's dispatch (No. 237), asked Attorney General James Speed to obtain an indictment against Surratt "as soon as convenient, with the view to demand his surrender," to no apparent effect. The government had failed to snag Surratt in Canada, failed again in England (didn't really even try), and would have failed a third time in Rome, despite this accurate intelligence, were it not for what appeared to be an extraordinary coincidence months later.

Civitavecchia was then, as it is today and has been since imperial times (when it was known as Centum Cellae), the principal port serving the city of Rome, some forty miles away. This status is explained by the fact that inside its protective moles Civitavecchia's harbor was free of the silting that was a chronic problem at its closer-in rival, Ostia, where the Tiber River carried its watershed's sediment into the Tyrrhenian Sea. When Surratt passed through Civitavecchia, its old fortified citadel on the waterfront, Forte Michelangelo, had been recently repaired and the city was defended by a French army contingent stationed there by Napoleon III to preserve the emperor's options and this strategic property for the pope. Local headquarters of the papal army was a quarter mile up a hill from the fort, inside a stout building of vaguely military architecture that could pass today as the lodge of a mystic order. (It is, in fact, the dusty and underfunded Museo Archeologico, housing artifacts of the Etruscan and later Roman civilizations not significant enough to have been skimmed off to the capital's museums.)

Mark Twain found himself in the same port city about eighteen months after Surratt and did not much like what he saw there. "This Civitavecchia is the finest nest of dirt, vermin, and ignorance we have found yet except that African perdition they call Tangier, which is just like it," he recalled in *The Innocents Abroad*. "The people here live in alleys two yards wide, which have a smell about them which is peculiar but not entertaining. It is well the alleys are not wider, because they hold as much smell now as a person can stand, and if they were wider they would hold more, and then the people would die. These alleys are paved in stone and carpeted with deceased cats and decayed rags and decomposed vegetable tops, and remnants of old boots, all soaked with dishwater. . . . All this country belongs to the Papal States. They do not appear to have any schools here, and only one billiard table. [Twain measured the cultural refinement of European cities in large part on the availability and quality of billiard tables in each.] Their education is at a very low stage. One portion of the men go into the military, another into the priesthood, and the rest into the shoemaking business." Civitavecchia, "ancient city" in Italian, had been a part of the Papal States for more than four centuries. It would remain so for barely four years longer.

Unlike the pope's spiritual authority, which waxed and waned over the centuries, by the mid-nineteenth century the pontiff's once-substantial temporal powers had been in more or less steady decline for two hundred years.[1] The tipping point came during the last few years of the eighteenth century. In early 1797 the Holy See had signed a peace treaty with France, the Treaty of Tolentino, which had been forced on it following Napoleon's victories at the head of the French republican army in Italy. The next year the city was occupied by French troops, Pius VI's army was disarmed, Rome's portable wealth was shipped off to Paris, church property was seized, and the pope was expelled to Siena (where the old, frail man died in 1799). The lopsided battle between Napoleon and the pope continued after Pius VII replaced Pius VI, and even after the new pope witnessed Napoleon's coronation of himself—a humiliation inflicted on the pontiff—in Notre Dame in 1804.

Decades of tag-team warfare by foreign armies followed. Amid all this lethal squabbling between foreigners and natives, earnest nationalists were attempting to construct a single Italian state while the papacy orbited overhead the excitement trying to preserve its power and wealth by ecclesiastical threats, diplomacy, and force of arms. The frenzy peaked during an outburst of republican revolutions that roiled Europe in 1848 but were soon suppressed.

By 1860 the various bits and pieces that once speckled the map of the Italian peninsula had been reduced to the Papal States plus ten: the Kingdom of the Two Sicilies to the south, the Kingdom of Sardinia offshore and in the Piedmont, and all the others lying to the north. This cluster of competitors would soon be distilled down to just one survivor on the boot of Italy. For that process to move to its conclusion, however, it was not enough for Italians finally to overcome centrifugal forces and to see an end to the armed intervention of France and Austria, for whom Italy was a convenient southern theater for their ambition. The Papal States, a swath of land across central Italy from the Tyrrhenian Sea over the Apennines to the shores of the Adriatic, also had to be absorbed into the new country lest these substantial holdings—once the modest "patrimony of Saint Peter" but grown over a thousand years to some sixteen thousand square miles, about the size of Connecticut and Massachusetts together—continue to divide the northern and southern halves of the peninsula.

In retrospect Italian unification seems inevitable—a like process went on in Germany at about the same time and ended in 1871 with Prussia at the head of a German confederation—but it could have been delayed, and hindsight has a way of eliminating alternative outcomes. Its timing was inadvertently paced by Louis Napoleon, Emperor Napoleon III, whose bungling triggered the Franco-Prussian War in 1870 and changed the future of Europe. Almost immediately hard-pressed after the fighting began in July, the French army was compelled quickly to deploy its formations from the Italian peninsula, where they had been the last prop supporting the pope against miscellaneous appetites and local ambition for change, back home to defend the Second Empire. Austria, the pope's other traditional defender, soon revealed that the Hapsburgs had no heart to take up the slack and take on the republicans of Italy. That left Pius IX alone.

Surratt stepped unwittingly into this ferment very near its end point, with little more than what he was wearing but carrying a passport with a visa for entry into the Papal States and probably also letters of introduction from his coreligionists in England to Rector Frederick Neve, head of the Venerable English College.

Not surprisingly, after a few days' delay at the port waiting for money that Neve generously sent him, Surratt went to ground in the "Venerable." His choice of hideout was perfect: a centuries-old enclave of English Roman Catholic priests and seminarians in the heart of Rome with ancient and close ties to the priesthood in the mother country.

Interior court of the Venerable English College, Rome. Still on Via di Monserrato (where it has been since 1361), the Venerable was Surratt's hideout in Rome until he joined the Zouaves. This college for seminarians proudly claims to be the oldest English overseas institution in the world. Until the mid-nineteenth century, Oxford's graduates were almost exclusively Anglican clergy, sent into the world to serve God and to combat the pernicious influence of the Venerable's priests. (Courtesy of the Venerable English College)

The Venerable was then one of four English-speaking pontifical colleges in the holy city. (The others were the Irish, Scottish, and North American Colleges, the last opened just a few years earlier in a former French army barracks on the Via Dell'Umilita.) Since the late 1840s foreign pontifical colleges in Rome had been considered national property, but as Italian republicanism and the drive toward unification grew more vigorous after the 1850s, Her Majesty's government in London looked at these schools with a historic connection to the United Kingdom increasingly as foreign institutions. This estrangement was accelerated by the First Vatican Council's declaration of papal infallibility, a document that signaled the terminal stage in the pope's metamorphosis from pre-1848 liberal to unyielding conservative in 1870 and enormously discomfited Christians elsewhere.

"Venerable" is an apt adjective. What began as a medieval pilgrims' hospice had by the 1860s a three-hundred-year history of church service as a teaching institution.[2] By then the college was on a reasonably firm financial footing, supported by rents from properties in Rome and the Alban Hills. Surratt's protector was Frederick Neve, fifty-seven, the rector of the Venerable in 1863–67. Neve was a graduate of Eton and Oxford and an alumnus of the college. As an adult convert from the Anglican Church, he was perhaps an odd choice for the post.[3]

Rector Frederick Neve. Neve, here about sixty years old, was the rector of the Venerable English College in Rome for only five years, 1863–67. He sent Surratt some money at Civitavecchia and sheltered him at the Venerable until Surratt joined the Zouaves. (Courtesy of the Venerable English College)

He was rector at a difficult time, but it was not international politics but rather church politics in Rome that had Neve out of his post at the school after such a relatively short stay.

There appears to have been no motive other than charity that accounted for Neve's hospitality to Surratt in November, between the latter's arrival in the city and his enlistment in the papal army in early December. Neve came to the Venerable from the post of vicar general of the diocese of Clifton in Bristol, England, where he had been since ordination in 1848. When he finally left Rome in 1868 it was to go first to the Franciscan Convent in Taunton and then five years later back to Clifton and his home diocese. Unlike Liverpool, the Bristol area had no special economic or other reasons for sympathy with the South in the war just past. Its days as a major slave port were long since past, and only four Bristol-registered steamers are recorded as having run the Union blockade, the *Calypso*, *Juno*, *Flora*, and *Old Dominion*, a tiny fraction of the roughly two hundred steamers from the United Kingdom in such service (something more than half of the total from all builders).

On December 9, 1865, Surratt enlisted in the Pontifical Zouaves. Zouaves, European and American light infantry uniformed to mimic the native garb of

Berber fighting men of the Zouaoua tribe (or what passed for that in foreign minds and at foreign tailors), came late to the pope's army but by a direct route. They had their origin in western North Africa (now northern Algeria) in the 1830s, when some fierce native warriors were first attached to the French army as auxiliary battalions.

The early successes of the French colonial adventure in Algeria, eventually under the command of Louis-Christophe-Leon Juchault de la Moricière, the same French general who would briefly lead the pope's army, and the brio and élan of French Zouave units fighting against Russian levees in the Crimean War, especially during the siege of Sevastapol in 1855, led to general recognition of the Zouave as "the *beau ideal* of a soldier."

General de la Moricière had commanded Zouaves in Algeria as a young captain. Between 1830 and 1847 de la Moricière served in Africa "as a pioneer of civilization, loved and esteemed by the Arabs as well as by his own soldiers," as the *Catholic Encyclopedia* loyally but improbably had it in 1910. When in 1860 he accepted his cousin's, the papal defense minister, offer to take command of the new army it was natural that de la Moricière turned to his military roots for an archetype. Although the general didn't last long—his badly outnumbered troops were overwhelmed by the Piedmontese at Castlefiardo in September, and the defeat shrank the Papal States by half, prompting his resignation and return to France—Zouaves remained the model for the pontifical army.

Loose trousers (*serouel*) bloused into laced canvas leggings (*guetres*, to keep sand out, or leather *jambieres*, to protect the lower legs), a generously cut shirt, sleeveless vest (*gilet*) or jacket, a long sash (*ceinture*), and a colorful fez (*chechia*) or turban (*cheche*) distinguished a Zouave from more mundane troops. In the decades just after midcentury, the outfit signaled the wearer was member of a bold elite in the army of any of several states.

Zouaves found their way into the American Civil War right at the start. The first two such units in the Union army, the famed 1st and 2nd Fire Zouaves, the 11th and 73rd New York Volunteer Infantry Regiments, respectively, were recruited from members of the city's volunteer fire companies and mustered into federal service in the spring of 1861. Their stylish uniforms and flashy manual of arms were adopted from a Chicago drill team, the Zouave Cadets, organized by Elmer Ellsworth. In full stride on public display, Ellsworth's cadets must have looked like a militarized Big Ten marching band pompom section at halftime.

Back in his home state from Illinois, Ellsworth raised the 11th New York and led it to Washington and to the preemptive seizure of Alexandria, Virginia.

He died there on May 24, 1861, eight weeks before the first battle of Bull Run in a scrap taking down Confederate colors flying above a building in the city. Ellsworth is remembered as the first noted Union casualty of the war (and the only one in the raid on Alexandria). He was a close personal friend and protégé of Lincoln's, and Ellsworth's sudden death might have been the new president's first intimation of the pain of loss that war would soon bring to families on both sides.

Other Union Zouave units included Duryea's and Hawkin's Zouaves (the 5th and 9th New York) and Collis's Zouaves d'Afrique, the 114th Pennsylvania. Zouave formations were less common in the South, although Louisiana and Virginia both raised such units; those from Company E of the 44th Virginia Infantry (the "Richmond Zouaves") looking especially sharp in blue jackets, orange *serouels*, and white *guetres*. Distinctive uniforms didn't last long in the Confederate army, where for many regiments uniforms of any sort after 1861 became an unsupportable expense. Some Union formations stayed in Zouave uniform throughout the war, the handsomest perhaps being that of Collis's Pennsylvanians, who on the march in full regalia (brick red trousers and caps, the latter with a golden tassel; dark blue jackets, vests, and shirts trimmed in red; a French blue *ceinture*; and white leggings) would have resembled a flock of tropical birds in mating display. For another few dozen years—until 1914, when the industrial strength slaughter of World War I forced soldiers into less conspicuous field gray and mustard brown—such attention-getting uniforms decorated battlefields from Asia to the New World. Compared to such martial splendor, the Pontifical Zouaves (officers in black trimmed with red, men in gray with red) would have appeared as dowdy as chimney swifts.

Once at the main Zouave encampment in Rome and after an indeterminate period of basic training Surratt would have been assigned to a line infantry company, one of twenty-four in the regiment of Zouaves. His basic training would sound familiar to any soldier of any army in any time: "At first the recruits form a depôt, to be drilled, and to learn the details of a soldier's life; as they advance they are drafted into companies." This is from a letter home by Joseph Powell in April 1868, but Surratt's experience two years earlier would have been the same. "In the depôts," Powell continued, "our time is divided between drill, duty such as picket, guard, keeping our clothes in order, cleaning our arms, belts, &c., making up our knapsacks; with our overcoats, tents, rug rolled round; then we march out with all our kit for inspection by the lieutenant, who remarks if even a

Surratt in the uniform of a private of the Pontifical Zouaves. Surratt wore this gray and red-trimmed uniform from the time of his escape from arrest in November 1866 to his incarceration in the Washington County Jail in February 1867. He appeared at his trials in civilian clothes. (Library of Congress, LC-DIG cwpbh-00483)

buckle is out of place. This morning our lieutenant and sub-lieutenant inspected all our effects in the barracks room. We had to brush up and arrange everything on our tent beds."

In the nineteenth century the safety of the pope's person and the security of his lands were provided largely by foreign military units, manned by Catholics from the European states where that faith was, or had been, the established religion. (The last vestige of this is found in the Swiss Guards, the pope's personal bodyguard and Vatican security force, whose blue and orange dress uniforms from another epoch charm tourists today.) "Foreign" because today in the West one thinks in terms of nationality rather than religion as the core of identity. Pius IX, however, would have seen young men in the uniforms of Pontifical Zouaves and Dragoons as his subjects and accepted their fealty as his due.

Among the armies of the nineteenth century the Zouaves were not uniquely multinational. The ranks of Zouave battalions were filled by young Catholic men from more than two dozen countries and five continents. Encouraged by their priests to see their service as a modern crusade, fully formed units and eager individuals headed off to Civitavecchia, most outfitted by public subscription, where once in the ranks they could expect to be fed and paid (according to an American consul in Rome, Edward Cushman) three cents per day. Cushman, in Rome during the last years of the Papal States, found the Pontifical Zouaves "well disciplined and zealous, being composed of young men of the best Catholic families of Europe. It is my observation that almost in no instance do these serve as mercenaries, as commonly reported, but almost entirely from a sense of religious duty."[4]

Early on the largest national contingent in the Pontifical Zouaves was French; consequently, the French language was (literally) the lingua franca of the force. The next largest volunteer bodies came from the Low Countries (three thousand), the Italian Peninsula, French Canada, the British Isles, and Spain and Portugal, finally tailing off into scant representation from South America and elsewhere.

In the spring of 1868, long after Surratt had fled through its sewer from the Zouave barracks prison at Veroli, there were only fourteen Americans in the Zouaves, one-tenth as many as there were from Canada, according to a count by the New York Herald's Rome correspondent. It is unlikely there were many more Americans in 1866–67. Despite a brief period through that summer, during which Pius IX mused about a thousand-man-strong contingent from the reunited United States funded by American bishops for three years, Americans were always scarce in the Pontifical Zouaves. A determined recruiting drive spearheaded by New York City's Freeman's Journal and Catholic Register produced few recruits and an embarrassingly small sum of money, some seven hundred dollars, to be contributed to the defense of the Holy Father's temporal crown. (Like many Catholic newspapers of the day, this one was known for its Southern sympathies during the Civil War. Its presses were shut down for a time because of the paper's virulent editorial posture.) A campaign to raise an all-American papal regiment by Lt. Col. C. Carrol Tevis, a Civil War veteran of the 4th Delaware Volunteer Infantry, quietly collapsed in July. Another such recruiting drive, by a former 78th Pennsylvania Infantry Regiment company commander named Capt. Charles Gillespie, a physician, also came to naught.

The pope's effort to raise and deploy his own army began in spring 1860 under Belgian general Xavier de Merode and his French subordinate, Gen. de la Moricière.

The pace picked up in autumn 1865 under de la Moricière's Swiss successor, Gen. Hermann Kanzler. Although reportedly the *Freeman's Journal* received "a great many" letters from putative American volunteers, in fact, very few materialized. Exhaustion rather than a lack of piety was the likely cause of the poor response. Because mobilization in Rome overlapped the American Civil War and the first few postwar years, there cannot have been much enthusiasm among the Civil War veterans left standing to go fight another war in a distant place for pennies per day.

Some otherwise willing few might have been dissuaded from joining by prohibitions in U.S. law against foreign military recruiting in the United States. Congress had prohibited such activity in its act of April 20, 1818, a codification of neutrality regulations that dated back to proclamations issued by President Washington in 1793–94. Captain Gillespie may have ceased his efforts to raise a Pontifical Zouave company because of this injunction.

Available records suggest that several hundred thousand Catholics fought on both sides of the Civil War, some in regiments of coreligionists—Louisiana, for example, fielded a number of essentially all-Catholic regiments, and so did New York, Massachusetts, and Pennsylvania—and others, especially later in the war after the bloodletting of the first great battles had drained ardor, imbedded in heterogeneous formations. Perhaps three-quarters of all Catholics in uniform came from Ireland.

In the early fighting Union regiments filled largely by Irish Catholics from the great cities of the North suffered losses in combat even above the horrific norms of the war. (The famous Irish Brigade finally returned home to New York with fewer than one thousand men. During the war some seven thousand had passed through its regimental muster rolls at one time or another. The missing six thousand had died of combat or disease, been captured or invalided out, or had deserted.) By 1863 what to American Roman Catholics had started a year and a half earlier as not only an adventure but also as an opportunity for a maligned minority to demonstrate its patriotism and manliness, had changed. With that change came an end to naïve zeal and to reckless volunteering.

One face of the change was the product of lethal reality. Well before Gettysburg the rate of slaughter—on the Peninsula, at Shiloh, in the second battle of Bull Run, and at Antietam—had shredded volunteer formations, halving entire regiments in a few minutes of terrible fighting. Recruiting drives to raise their replacements faltered. Deaths in combat, disabling wounds, and losses from disease and desertion soon forced both sides to introduce conscription, first by the less populous Confederacy (in April 1862) and then by the Union (in March the following year).

Its other face was a perceived change in war aims. In the North conscription came soon after Lincoln issued the Emancipation Proclamation, a manifesto the urban, immigrant poor read as a warning that at war's end free blacks would join the competition for unskilled jobs on a preferred basis. After violent antidraft, antiblack riots finally blew themselves out in New York and other northern cities, recruiting proceeded almost exclusively on a cash basis; enlistment bonuses and bounties paid to emigrants just off their ships made up for the decline in volunteers and patriotic zeal.

Throughout the war, generally following the lead of their bishops, the voices from Catholic pulpits on both sides of the lines deliberately left to individual congregants the decision on joining the fight. This posture reflected a careful profit and loss analysis on the part of the establishment. "The church took a stand in the war—to allow Catholics to follow their section," wrote one historian. "It thus continued the American Catholic policy of avoiding political involvement while holding Catholics to their faith and securing Catholic institutions. In short, the church tolerated disunity in political matters so that it could concentrate on achieving ethnic unity in religious ones."[5]

In French Canada, however, where warfare had been a spectator sport (if that) since the battle for Quebec in the French and Indian War, the response to recruiting pitches from the pulpit was enthusiastic. The goals swiftly became to raise a battalion of Canadians who would camp and mess together and fight for the pope under their own officers, and to amass $100,000 for the cause (at the rate of 25 cents from each of the 400,000 Roman Catholics in the diocese of Montreal).

Soon enough 503 stalwarts marched bravely off to Rome under a splendid banner:

The flag was attached to a maple pole, with a golden spearhead and tassels. It was of white silk, with the keys and miter in gold on the reverse. It bore an escutcheon azure, with a bar, argent, on which were the beaver and maple leaves, Canadian emblems. A cross surmounted the shield, behind which were crossed two silver battle axes. Beneath it was the word "Canada" in gold, and upon the blue of the shield was inscribed the motto of the corps, "Aime Dieu et va ton chemin," Love God and go thy way.[6]

As it happened, fault was quickly found in Rome with the monochromatic white of the flag's field and a replacement with the correct yellow and white background was swiftly sewn up.

The departure of the first detachment of Canadian Pontifical Zouaves from Montreal, one of the touchstones of French Canadian military history, was commemorated in 1969 by the National Film Board of Canada in a short, "humorous but sympathetic" film of its centennial reenactment, *With Drums and Trumpets*. After the fall of Rome to the Italian army in September 1870 the pope's army was disbanded, and soon thereafter the first of the young Canadians who had proudly marched through New York City on the way to Rome were now back in New York, but heading the other way, toward home.

Surratt, who saw the Civil War from its margins, might have had mixed motives for joining the Zouaves, in which piety, guilt, adventure, and the need for cover from pursuit all could have played a part. Ten weeks earlier, Surratt had told McMillan of his intention to go to Rome, information the doctor had swiftly passed to the U.S. consul in Montreal, who promptly relayed it to Secretary Seward in Washington.

The reasons for Henri Beaumont de Sainte Marie's enlistment are also unclear. If his story is believed, he probably had a more realistic sense of the realities of combat than did Surratt. For Sainte Marie, who joined and left the Pontifical Zouaves before the mass deployment of his enthusiastic countrymen, the zeal to serve the holy father in uniform quickly wore off. By the spring 1866 he had had enough of drums and trumpets and was writing, "I have been greatly disappointed with this Zouave Corps," as if the pope's army had somehow failed him personally.

Motives aside, both Surratt and Sainte Marie ended up in the Zouaves two years ahead of the big recruiting drive of 1868, and neither one was in the field in November 1867 at the Battle of Mentana, when the Zouaves defeated Garibaldi's irregulars in their only notable victory. The next time the Zouaves fought, in the defense of Rome, it was only to preserve their pride; the walls were swiftly breached and the city fell immediately thereafter.

Given the polyglot character of the Zouaves as the small army was assembled in the 1860s and the bare sprinkling of Americans in its ranks, very long odds had to be overcome before anyone could stumble on Surratt in uniform who knew him. But it happened.

Henri Beaumont ("Benjamin" in the trial record) de Sainte Marie, of the 9th Company of Pontifical Zouaves at Velletri, was a blowhard and storyteller. His résumé at the age of thirty-three was already decorated with so many whorls of fiction and fantasy that it is difficult to trust anything he said. Sainte Marie was Canadian, with swarthy skin, dark hair, and brown eyes, and he was fluent in three languages: English, French, and Italian. That much is probably true. It is likely that he was born in La Pierre, Canada. So said one trial witness, Louis Sicotte, who claimed to have met residents of the village who knew Sainte Marie from birth. Zouave records had Sainte Marie born on May 14, 1835, in Quebec. In June 1866, to establish his bona fides, Sainte Marie told Rufus King, the U.S. minister in Rome, that he had served briefly in the Union army, straggled behind the line of march and was captured by Maj. Gen. J. E. B. Stuart's cavalry near Orange Courthouse in Virginia, was jailed in Richmond's Castle Thunder prison and then released in gratitude by the warden for having exposed a gang of forgers, made his way to Nassau and then England aboard a blockade runner, and from there returned home to Canada.* Sainte Marie didn't lack cheek: One of

---

*   Gen. Rufus King (1814–1876), minister resident of the United States at Rome during 1863–67, was not the most determined American diplomat involved in the international pursuit of Surratt, but he was the most successful. After more than a year of waffling by cabinet department heads in Washington, King managed to extract their decision to seek either Surratt's arrest and delivery or his extradition from the Papal States.

In 1833 King graduated fourth in his class from West Point, and his high standing led to a commission in the Corps of Engineers, the army's elite officer cadre. Three years later, presumably bored in peacetime, he resigned and went to work in journalism, politics, and academia in New York and Wisconsin until the start of the Civil War. In 1861, instead of immediately accepting an appointment from President Lincoln to go to Rome as the fourth U.S. minister in the Papal States, King took a commission to raise a volunteer infantry regiment.

Between 1861 and 1863 Brevet Brigadier General King rose to brigade and then division command, but his military service ended midway through the war and somewhat mysteriously. Its abrupt termination has been variously attributed to epilepsy or alcoholism, even to poor tactical sense in command. The truth could be a combination of all three. As a division commander in Gen. Irvin McDowell's corps at Second Manassas, King withdrew his men from Gainesville without authority and a disaster soon followed. A court of inquiry found King guilty of "grave error." Rumors of drunkenness and health problems filled out the trifecta that ended King's military career. Naturally there is no hint of any reason in King's farewell letter to his division on October 17, 1863, at Fairfax Station, Virginia, in which he expressed "infinite reluctance" to leave his comrades in arms. King's resignation was effective three days later, and soon thereafter he left to replace Richard Blatchford in Rome, where he served for four years.

A native New Yorker like the secretary of state, King had served as Seward's adjutant general when the latter was governor of New York. Reflecting their early relationship, his personal correspondence to the secretary from Rome was addressed to "My Dear Governor." His official correspondence reveals an able diplomat and observant reporter of European politics in the 1860s.

All of the first American diplomats at the Holy See were Protestants. Immediately after King, U.S. diplomatic relations with the Papal States and later with the Vatican fell victim to anti-Catholicism in the United States. King's replacement arrived in Rome seventy-one years after he left. In December 1939 President Franklin Roosevelt appointed a "personal representative" to the Vatican, Myron Taylor, who presented his credentials to the pope two months later. In 1984 the personal representative's title was changed to reflect the reality that the incumbent truly was an ambassador.

the names he passed to King as a personal reference was that of Capt. George Alexander, CSA, the commander of the Confederate prison, née tobacco warehouse, in which he was allegedly jailed. He was also not above a little gentle extortion. When later his exposure of Surratt didn't bear fruit as swiftly as Sainte Marie had hoped, he pressed. "It appears the Washington Cabinet seems very indifferent on this important matter," he wrote King on September 12. "I know some papers in New York and Philadelphia who if they were in possession of this information would force the government to act upon it in justice to the memory of P. Lincoln."

Some of Sainte Marie's curriculum vitae, that he taught school in Ellengowan, Maryland, where he said he first met Surratt and William [sic] Weichmann, is certainly true. (At Surratt's trial Weichmann testified that he had introduced the two in Ellengowan on April 3, 1863.) So too were the essential points of what he told to King on Saturday, April 21, 1866, during their first meeting about a fellow Zouave. Surratt, Sainte Marie told King (and King promptly told Washington), "had recently enlisted in the Papal Zouaves, and was now stationed with his company, the 3rd, at Sezze" under the name John Watson. Sainte Marie was absolutely certain of the identification. He recognized the man he first met near Baltimore, Maryland, more than a year before. Moreover, at their accidental meeting two weeks ago, Surratt had confirmed who he was and asked for Sainte Marie's silence.

In late April and early May Sainte Marie followed up his personal call on King at the legation on Rome's Via Del Corse with two letters to put down his markers. Now at risk, he imagined, from Surratt's friends wherever they might be for having exposed the conspirator, Sainte Marie hoped the United States would buy out his enlistment in the Pontifical Zouaves so that he could leave Italy and "revisit his native land and the grey hair of his father and mother." Here followed a patriotic fillip, transparently intended to ingratiate him with the U.S. diplomat reading his note. "I . . . wish," Sainte Marie averred, "to make of the United States my last and permanent home."

Sainte Marie was one of the few in this story who got much of what they hoped was coming to them for services rendered in the pursuit of Booth and the Lincoln conspirators. King did pay the Zouaves to terminate Sainte Marie's enlistment, and then he put him aboard a U.S. Navy ship for transportation back to the United States, to the gray hair of his parents and, not incidentally, to identify Surratt and then testify at the trial. In the event, Sainte Marie was actually put ashore from the USS *Swatara* at Villefranche-sur-Mer, France, by the ship's exasperated captain, who explained later:

Rufus King in Union uniform. King resigned his commission and took up his civilian post in Rome in October 1863. Approached at the outset by Henri Beaumont de Sainte Marie, King soon became the U.S. diplomat in Europe most responsible for the successful pursuit and arrest of Surratt. He left Rome in August 1867, when Congress refused to fund the legation any longer. (Brady-Handy Photograph Collection, Library of Congress, LC BH82-4065)

I took him aboard at Rome, at the request of our minister, for the purpose of identifying Surratt, but he had not been aboard but a few hours before he had told everyone everything he had done, if not more. At Malta he wanted to go ashore; I refused permission because I did not want him to babble to the people there. At Alexandria I also refused him permission to go ashore. At Villa Franca he wrote me rather a sharp letter, complaining of not being allowed his liberty. . . . I did not consider him a prisoner at all; but at the same time I thought it proper to prevent him from going on shore and babbling to the people there in regard to persons on the ship and his own matters.

King then paid Sainte Marie's commercial passage back to the United States from State Department funds.

It's not clear that the United States got fair value at the trial for money spent. Although he was paid per diem for 143 days in the witness pool (and mileage for nearly five thousand miles of travel), Sainte Marie testified at Surratt's trial only for a few minutes late in the day on Tuesday, July 2, and said little more than Surratt had told him he escaped Washington on April 14 or 15 disguised as a Briton and wearing a shawl. The defense didn't even choose to cross-examine Surratt's former comrade in arms. It might have been a missed opportunity. What Sainte Marie said under oath made him the fourteenth prosecution witness to fix Surratt in Washington on the day Lincoln was slain, and the only one to do so purportedly quoting Surratt himself.

If he had repeated in court in 1867 what he had said in speech and letters to Rufus King in 1866, Sainte Marie's testimony would have been sensational. Sainte Marie had told King on April 21, during their first meeting, that Surratt had confessed to him participation in the assassination plot and Jefferson Davis's knowledge of it. The revelations got better. Surratt supposedly also told Sainte Marie that he was the instigator of the murder and had acted under instruction from parties in New York and London. Surratt then threatened the murder of "that coward, Weichman" and later confirmed that Davis's cabinet had approved the murder and financed it. So said Sainte Marie.

In early October 1867, in a letter that blended equal parts of paranoia and appeals to fair play, Sainte Marie formally asked for more than his modest requests presented in spring the year before. From Montreal (so much for his "last and permanent home" in the United States) he wrote Acting Secretary of War Gen. Ulysses Grant seeking the reward of twenty-five thousand dollars in exchange for information leading to the capture of Surratt that had been offered in April 1865 but withdrawn that November:

> I think General King too much of a gentleman not to have informed me of the revocation of [the reward] if he himself had been aware of the revocation. Surely the government of the United States cannot think that mileage and expenses from Italy here a sufficient remuneration for the dangers I have been and still am exposed to. I have been here now about six months, and it is impossible for me to get anything to do. I am surrounded by numerous enemies, and am liable to suffer at any moment from the vengeance of Surratt's sympathizers. My name has

been thrown to all the world, and there is no place on earth where I can go in my own name. . . .

[I]nform me if you would be disposed to pay that reward, or even part of it, as I am at present dependent on my brothers for support, and my position is far from agreeable.

Two weeks later Judge Advocate General Holt, with Sainte Marie's letter in hand and parsing the relevant general orders at the Bureau of Military Justice, pointed out that the twenty-five thousand dollars offered for the *arrest* of Surratt had been withdrawn but the promised "liberal reward" for *information* conducive to his arrest seemed to be on offer still. Holt concluded that such a reward should be paid. In November a three-man Army board concluded that in this case "liberal" equated to fifteen thousand dollars, but Sainte Marie was actually paid only ten thousand dollars.

The amount was a generous one. In his last job before the trial of the eight, Louis Weichmann had been clerk in the Office of the Commissary General of Prisoners at the War Department at an annual salary of $960. In 1867 the annual salary of the president of the United States was $25,000, that of one of his cabinet officers $8,000. A handsome two-story brick home in Washington City could be purchased for less than $4,000, and a good horse and its tack could be had for $200. Union enlisted men had fought the war and risked death for $16 per month. Ten thousand dollars was a small fortune in 1867.

Sainte Marie, however, was not satisfied. He eventually sued the United States for the difference between his expectations and receipts but lost in the court of claims during its December 1873 term. The presiding judge found that Sainte Marie had been rewarded for what he had done, provided valuable information, and properly not rewarded for what he hadn't done, accomplished the actual capture and arrest of Surratt.

Sainte Marie appealed. On September 8, 1874, while his appeal was still pending at the U.S. Supreme Court, Sainte Marie, then forty-one, collapsed on a Philadelphia street and died. William Shuey, his executor, pressed on with the suit and lost.

What looks like pure coincidence, two men who knew each other in Maryland bumping together again near Rome a year later, might have been something else. Henry Lipman, who claimed to have served with both men in the Zouaves, told his saloon acquaintances and newspaper reporters that Sainte Marie went to Rome and joined the Zouaves in deliberate pursuit of Surratt and of the reward offered for his capture and arrest. That's certainly possible. The timing of Sainte Marie's enlistment, on March 24, 1866, almost four months after Surratt's, fits Lipman's scenario, but there is no other evidence of this, and nothing whatever that even hints at a deal in place between Sainte Marie and Surratt's hunters before King became involved.

As to Sainte Marie's motive for the betrayal, that's much more certain: money. An Associated Press cable from Rome December 11, 1866 (printed in the *Elmira Advertiser* the next day) suggested something even more basic than love of money. It claimed, "Both [Sainte Marie] and Surratt were in love with the same lady in Washington, and Ste. Marie betrayed Surratt through jealousy." There is a candidate for the role, the mysterious Confederate courier Sarah Slater, but there's no evidence of such an unlikely triangle to support the *Advertiser* allegation, and Sainte Marie's determined pursuit of the reward speaks for itself.*

King himself applied for the reward for unearthing Surratt, granted somewhat obliquely. In August 1866, while Surratt was still with his company in Sezze and presumably unaware of what was swirling around him, in a private note to Secretary Seward, King allowed, "I don't know whether the government cares to pay the promised reward of $10,000 for Surratt, but the sum would not come amiss in the exchequer of the legation." There is no record that Seward replied.

Among the other claimants for rewards only one got as much as did Sainte Marie. The total of seventy-five thousand dollars for Booth's and Herold's capture was divided up among many claimants, but one, Everton Conger of the National Detective Police, got fifteen thousand dollars of it.

Five thousand dollars were awarded to the ten who played some part in the capture of Powell at Mary Surratt's rooming house on April 17. Another nine shared in twenty-five thousand dollars awarded by Congress for the arrest of Atzerodt.

---

* Sarah Slater was one of the more intriguing Confederate agents. Born in Connecticut as Sarah Antoinette Gilbert in January 1843 of French-speaking parents from the Caribbean, "Nettie" moved with her family to North Carolina in her teens. In June 1861, at eighteen, she married Rowan Slater, the black-sheep son of the Slaters of Salisbury, North Carolina. Six months after Rowan joined the army (and three months before he was captured in Virginia) Sarah left Richmond for Montreal on her first Confederate mission.

Pretty, daring, fluent in French, and behaving as if she were still single, Sarah Slater was the perfect courier to French Canada. In this role she made two round trips across the lower Potomac, one in February 1865 and one in March, always with a male escort. Each took about a month. During her April mission from Richmond, she left Washington by train with Surratt on April 4 heading for New York City and vanished.

This biographic information about Slater is drawn from an essay by James O. Hall, "The Lady in the Veil." Michael Kauffman (*American Brutus*, 327, 336) implies that Slater was caught up in Stanton's manhunt, jailed in the Old Capitol Prison, and then released.

Giacomo Cardinal Antonelli. Antonelli, the long-service sec-
retary of state to Pius IX, was wrongly suspected as having
been the chief reactionary in the pope's court. After 1848,
Pius IX needed no bolstering from the right. Antonelli repre-
sented the papacy in diplomatic discussions with U.S. Consul
Rufus King about Surratt's identity and fate. From the outset
Antonelli was cooperative about Surratt's surrender to the
Americans. (Library of Congress)

The papacy, in the person of its secretary of state, Cardinal Antonelli,
proved to be unexpectedly accommodating when approached by Rufus King on
the subject of Zouave No. 1857, "Giovanni Watson," a junior enlisted man in the
3rd Company at Sezze.

Between April and August 1866 King exchanged letters with Secretary of
State Seward about Sainte Marie's discovery. The thrust of detailed instructions
that went to Rome from Washington City in October was first confirm Surratt's
identity and then ask for his custody. The desired scenario was complicated by

the fact that the United States had no extradition treaty with the Papal States and hence no legal basis for asking that Surratt be delivered to King.

The first time the subject of Watson/Surratt came up between the two governments was August 7, 1866, when King recited to the cardinal the astonishing information he had learned from Sainte Marie: Surratt, a suspect in the assassination of the late president, was "Zouave Giovanni Watson" in the pope's army and had been there in hiding since early December. If King is believed, Antonelli took the news with impressive aplomb, because King reported that the cardinal "intimated" that there would be no difficulty in the surrender of Surratt to the United States.

On November 2 King, now accompanied by the legation's acting secretary, J. Clinton Hooker (who spoke Italian; King did not and had to converse with the cardinal in French), called on Cardinal Antonelli in private. (The visit came at an awkward time for the Vatican. Rumors were everywhere that the pope, under military pressure from Republicans, might abandon Rome and seek refuge in Malta. All premature but prescient.) King's mission was explicitly to ask whether the pope would agree to deliver Surratt absent an extradition treaty or whether such a treaty could be agreed to if one were required.

Antonelli, King reported to Seward the same day, was agreeable. According to King, the cardinal secretary of state took the nuanced position that "to surrender a criminal, where capital punishment was likely to ensue, was not exactly in accordance with the spirit of the Papal government; but that in so grave and exceptional a case, and with the understanding that the United States government, under parallel circumstances, would do as they desired to be done by . . . the request of the State department for the surrender of Surratt would be granted." In effect, Antonelli offered a de facto, one-time extradition treaty.

The Vatican moved swiftly. Four days later, on November 6, and even before any formal request for action came from the United States, the minister of war instructed Surratt's battalion commander to arrest him and take him to the military prison in Rome under secure escort.

A search for Surratt at Trisulti, his company's garrison, was unsuccessful, but he was quickly found nearby, in Veroli, where he had gone on leave. Surratt was arrested there on Wednesday, November 7, by Captain de Lambilly, commanding the local detachment, whose plan was to confine Surratt overnight and then take him under armed guard to the military prison in Rome early the next day.

A telegram sent by de Lambilly from Velletri at 4:30 AM on November 8 arrived in Rome at 8:50 AM. It announced that his prisoner was on the loose.

After Pope Pius IX's easy acquiescence to the American's surrender, the news that Surratt had escaped his guards, reportedly by recklessly plunging into a ravine more than one hundred feet deep to land safely on a garbage-strewn ledge, and evaded a subsequent pursuit by fifty armed Zouaves must have seemed incredible and raised American suspicions in Rome and Washington.

Amplification on Friday, after an on-site investigation by one Lieutenant de Farnel, made the feat even more impressive. "I am assured that the escape of Watson savors of a prodigy," Colonel Allet, the responsible commander, wrote to the minister that afternoon, almost certainly borrowing de Farnel's description. "He leaped from a height of twenty-three feet on a very narrow rock, beyond which is the precipice. The filth from the barracks accumulated on the rock and in this manner the fall of Watson was broken. Had he leaped a little further he would have fallen into an abyss."[7]

As detailed in copies of internal correspondence provided to King the same day, the order for Surratt's arrest had been issued the Tuesday before by Gen. Hermann Kanzler, the handsome Swiss who now commanded the pontifical army. Kanzler (sometimes Kausler) was to all outward signs the model nineteenth-century general officer; his tightly waxed moustaches, rigid as semaphore blades beneath his nose, and a uniform tunic ablaze with a constellation of medals and orders exuded military expertise. Sadly, from now on until the collapse of his army three years hence, he had little good to tell the pope.

King accepted the pope's explanation at face value. On November 10 he concluded his first report to the secretary of state about Surratt's improbable escape by saying, "I feel bound to add, incredible as the details of the story appear, the cardinal spoke of them as verified beyond all question and expressed very great and apparently sincere regret at Surratt's escape." Twice more during the next ten days King repeated this judgment, first to Consul Marsh in Florence on the thirteenth, after he had received more reports about investigation of the arrest and escape of Surratt. "They certainly show, on the surface, perfect good faith on the part of the Papal authorities, and an earnest desire to arrest the criminal, of whose guilt the cardinal expressed himself fully satisfied," he told Marsh. And again to Seward on the nineteenth: "I have no reason to doubt the entire good faith of the Papal government in the matter." King's report about the escape was briefed on November 30 to Johnson's Cabinet, where, according to Secretary Browning, the news was received without comment. (Four days later Seward was able to announce to the president and his colleagues that Surratt had been captured in Alexandria.)

The improbable explanation is that Surratt had been inadvertently fore-warned. A letter from King to Sainte Marie in English had been delivered to the wrong Zouave Sainte Marie—not to Henri, King's source, but to a certain trumpeter with the same last name, who, confused by the foreign language, had shown it to Surratt for translation. Yet another hard-to-believe coincidence.

There is another, very different story describing Surratt's escape from arrest, one that has the advantage of neither being susceptible to spin by senior Zouaves nor requiring faith in Surratt's near supernatural athleticism.[8] This other descrip-tion came years after the fact from a former Zouave, one Henry Lipman, who told his story in February 1881 to the *New York Tribune*. (And to the *Washington Post* the next year, and almost certainly to other newspapers as well. The impres-sion is that Lipman, "a strongly-built, low-sized truckman with a smooth shaven face and sharp features," as one reporter described him, drank for free many times on the strength of his entertaining story.)

According to his account, Lipman, twenty-one, joined the Zouaves in February 1866, three months after Surratt had signed up and the month before Sainte Marie did. "The Pope's emissaries and recruiting bureaus in Belgium were busy at the time," Lipman told a reporter in explanation, "promising all manner of advantages and the happiest of prospects, both in this world and the hereafter, to recruits." He promptly left his home in Deventer, "a little, out-of-the-way Dutch town" due east from Amsterdam, and soon found himself with the 6th Company, 1st Battalion at Velletri. Three weeks later he met "Watson," an American in the 3rd Company, when both were returning to base from leave in Rome. Not long after that, the 6th Company relocated to Veroli and Lipman found that his roommate now was the same American. "Sometimes in the middle of the night I would hear him sobbing and praying," Lipman said. "Then again he would be murmuring something about his 'poor mother,' and her 'terrible end,' and so go on till at last overcome with fatigue he would sink back on his pillow and fall asleep." Lipman's touching narrative included mention of another American Zouave, one "Sainte Mary," who was searching suspiciously for coun-trymen in the fourteen-hundred-man-strong 1st Battalion.

In Lipman's version Surratt went AWOL from a camp at Coli Pardo, but he was promptly pursued, captured, and jailed overnight in the barracks prison at Veroli pending delivery under arrest to Rome. But then,

> [Lieutenant] de Monsty detailed twelve of us . . . all tried friends of
> Watson to guard the dungeon and its inmate. . . . Soon night fell upon

us, and all around became as quiet as death. Next to the dungeon was a small compartment containing the entrance to the barrack sewer. As had been arranged between Surratt and ourselves, as soon as the clock struck twelve he was allowed to enter this compartment, as prisoners were in the habit of doing. Apparently we forgot him, but at ten minutes to 2 we all made a rush to the dungeon, and as several among us had expected, Surratt had disappeared. He had lowered himself into the sewer and had made his way out at an opening into the neighboring rivulet. The discovery led to a furious fusillade on our part, its object being naturally to divert suspicion and to make believe that we were trying to stop the fugitive. As soon as the Lieutenant heard of the escape, he ordered the entire party on watch to be put under arrest, but I remember that a smile of satisfaction seemed to play around his lips, and there is no doubt in my mind that he secretly rejoiced at what had occurred.

Not so the Captain. When the news was broken to him he exclaimed, "I am ruined forever!" and sent off a regiment of cavalry in pursuit of Surratt. . . . All twelve of us were put in irons and imprisoned on bread and water for an entire month.

It is easy to see why the Zouaves preferred to report the other escape story, one that featured a minute of sudden, astonishing derring-do by their prisoner, instead of a long night of stolid incompetence by officers and criminal conspiracy by enlisted guards, guards who saw no reason to turn over a comrade in arms to a distant, godless government.

Even as Surratt was on the way home in chains months after his "escape," a debate began in Congress ignited by a handful of nativists in the House of Representatives, the residue of the short-lived Know-Nothing Party, about the fiscal appropriation to maintain a U.S. legation in Rome. The trigger for this discussion was a false report roiling the House that the Protestant chapel in the legation had been relocated outside of the city's walls at the insistence of the pope and that Rufus King had agreed to this affront to Protestant faith and dignity.

King denied it all. In a long report to Seward on February 18 he described the recent history of Grace Church, the American Protestant congregation then meeting for worship in the central city. While this arrangement stretched a diplomat's personal right to private freedom of worship in his own home beyond its elastic limit under international law—on some occasions the Sunday assembly of the faithful exceeded several hundred expatriates and tourists—the papacy had not objected. Nor had most other outsized national congregations been molested, although two Scottish Presbyterian churches had been removed from the city to beyond its walls on Pius IX's instructions.

During the debate in the House after the New Year, Massachusetts congressman (and former Union general) Nathaniel Banks unsuccessfully argued for retention of the legation explicitly on the grounds of the papacy's cooperation in the arrest of Surratt among other reasons. Rome's status as the second most popular American tourist destination in Europe (only behind Paris) was a factor, too. Banks and other defenders of the status quo, however, lost the vote in the House by four to one.

The debate in Congress had been conducted against the backdrop of an emotional newspaper campaign that featured religious and secular arguments on both sides. The *New York Times* gave vent to one perspective, describing the papacy as a "feeble, corrupt, dying remnant of despotic rulership—the very caricature and ghostly counterfeit of impotent tyranny with its paralytic army of petticoated priests." Less scurrilously, other papers made their arguments for closure on economic or political grounds, or pretended to. Closing the legation would save the federal budget its annual cost, and the peninsula would soon be unified under Victor Emmanuel II, whose kingdom would absorb the Papal States.

The case for retention was simply overwhelmed, despite the fact that the underlying "cause" was soon known to be a fabrication. The Senate acceded in the cutoff, and funding for the legation was terminated effective June 30, 1867, as one of the last acts of the Thirty-ninth Congress, thus ending twenty years of diplomatic representation.

The defeat prompted another long letter from King to Seward again raising the fact of papal cooperation in the arrest and extradition of Surratt among other arguments against closing the legation. He knew his political essay would arrive after the issue was decided by Congress, so he wrote for the record only, in a tone that could be a model for the "more in sorrow than in anger" voice. King returned to the United States soon thereafter and formally resigned his position on January 1, 1868. He never was reimbursed for the cost of his passage back to the United States, despite pleading that his "circumstances were such, as to make every dollar count."

Even after King was stiffed for his return travel expenses, the savings from closure of the legation in Rome didn't amount to much. King's salary as minister was seventy-five hundred dollars a year, with another one thousand dollars in the

Pope Pius IX (1792–1878). Pius IX's increasingly conservative views formed the church's politics and policies during and after the violent European revolutions of 1848. In 1866 his quick agreement to permit the arrest and extradition of John Surratt to the United States launched Surratt on the last leg of his escape from arrest. Pius IX spent the last eight years of his life cloistered in the Vatican. (University of Texas Libraries)

budget annually to operate the legation. Payments in connection with the arrest and delivery of Surratt had come from a special five-hundred-dollar allocation from Washington for that purpose, half of which went directly to Sainte Marie in gold coin in exchange for his information.

If the pope thought that he held an American IOU for his assistance in the pursuit of Surratt, he never attempted to cash it in. It's just as well he didn't try. The subject had come up during one of President Johnson's cabinet meetings.

On December 11, 1866, Secretary Seward reminded the assembled group "how friendly the Pope and Cardinal Antonelli had been in the matter of arresting Surratt, the assassin." (The quotes are from Welles's diary for the day.) Seward, always happy to suggest things for the Navy to do, proposed that in view of "Italian troubles," a U.S. Navy ship should join the international fleet standing by at Civitavecchia. He added that "Mr. King had advised him that two of the Pope's confidants had inquired whether, if the Pope was compelled to flee the Papal dominions, he could find protection in the United States."

"Seward replied to all this affirmatively," Welles wrote, saying the secretary of state wanted to tell King that "the Pope could come to this country in a merchant ship, and there could be no objection to his coming in a naval vessel. He could have an asylum under our flag, would be secure on board of our public ship, and the naval officer who should bring him to this country would receive honorable consideration. The Pope himself would be welcomed here and treated as the nation's guest by the people."

In the cabinet Randall, Stanbery, and Browning were inclined to agree, but Welles and McCulloch were aghast at Seward's ideas. Stanton was too. He feared that "the intrigues of every court in Europe would follow" the pope to the United States. President Johnson apparently said nothing.

Three days later Seward had a change of mind, perhaps persuaded by Stanton's firm opposition. All the "exceptionable parts" in the letter to King were removed: no more transatlantic voyage in a Navy ship, no "national guest," no (in Welles's words) "transferring the Pontificate from Rome here."

Some have speculated that the pope and Antonelli accommodated the United States regarding Surratt because they wanted to keep their options for sanctuary open in the event that the military situation deteriorated enough to force yet another papal flight from the Vatican. The notion that Pius IX would decamp to the United States if forced out of Rome was always fantastic. The pope would never have considered a distant, Protestant republic as a suitable refuge for himself and his court. When he actually had to face the fall of Rome in September 1870, Pius IX didn't have many alternatives to hunkering down in St. Peter's. France proposed Corsica or Algeria, both unacceptable to the pope. Staunchly Catholic Malta had been considered several times as a possible refuge, but Great Britain quickly got goosey and withdrew its short-lived offer of refuge there. Austria offered no place. Without any real choice, Pius IX decided to lock himself up in the papal compound in lieu of foreign exile. He remained there until his death, casting excommunications at his tormentors.

Still, it's not strictly true that Pope Pius IX and his cardinal secretary of state, Giacomo Antonelli, got nothing in exchange for either their regular cordial discourse with King (given their continuing serious troubles, it's astonishing how accessible Antonelli was to the American minister) or for their agreeable response in the matter of Surratt. Their avowed willingness to extradite Surratt gave the Roman Catholic Church a powerful defense against charges of church complicity in the assassination and of abetting Surratt's flight from arrest.

Surratt's chief counsel, Catholic himself, made use of the papacy's cooperation just as Congressman Banks had tried to do. "To the honor of the Catholic Church be it said," defense counsel told the jury August 1, 1867, "that when this young man was accused of crime in the Papal dominions, and there was no extradition treaty between this country and that, and no power to compel the Pope to surrender him, the Pope and Cardinal Antonelli voluntarily, and without hesitation, gave him up. They said, 'Take him back to America and try him; if guilty, execute him.' The Catholic Church is on the side of virtue and mercy. She protects the fleeing criminal when she believes him to be innocent, but when the hand of power says, 'he is guilty, give him to me,' she gave him up without a word."

Merrick salved the church's reputation, but he did so at some risk to his client by implying that belief in Surratt's guilt had been the reason for Surratt's surrender by Rome to the United States.

The Roman Catholic Church in America needed defending. Xenophobia, the fear and loathing of strangers, had a very specific focus in the United States of the nineteenth century: the Catholic Church. It was prompted largely by the arrival of impoverished immigrants from Ireland, a tide beginning in the 1820s that swelled to a half-million-strong torrent during the famine years of 1845–51, when the staple potato crop failed repeatedly, turned to inedible mush by the plant pathogen *Phytophthora infestans*. The 1860 census recorded 1.611 million men, women, and children from this single, long-suffering country, by far the largest bloc of foreigners in the United States. In that year more than a quarter of Boston's residents were Irish born, as were a quarter of New York's. Other major cities fell in between Chicago's 18 percent from Ireland and Baltimore's 7 percent.

Accordingly, one root of anti-Catholic prejudice was economic, its close identification with an Irish urban underclass. Other roots, as Daniel Walker Howe recently observed in his *What Hath God Wrought*, were doctrinal and political:

Many American Protestants had an interpretation of their own for the Book of Revelation. The Antichrist whose downfall it seems to predict they identified with the Roman Catholic Church. The overthrow of the papacy would be one of the events heralding either a premillennial or postmillennial Second Coming. This vision of the Last Things, coupled with the identification of Roman Catholicism with royal absolutism in Anglo-American historical tradition, and reinforced by the very real hostility manifested by the nineteenth-century papacy toward political liberalism and 'modern' ideas of many kinds, combined to foster an ideological hostility toward Catholicism that went well beyond the interdenominational rivalry among Protestant sects. The growth of the Roman Catholic Church . . . seemed to some Protestants to threaten American democratic institutions. . . . conclusion: Catholicism could not be allowed to flourish in America if America were to fulfill her mission in the world. (320)

The Irish Catholic presence in the United States prompted a powerful reaction among native citizens almost from the beginning. In May 1844 and again that July, for example, Philadelphia and its suburbs exploded in days of sectarian rioting that saw the deaths of several dozen people and the destruction of some churches and homes. (Many German Catholics, escaping the political upheavals of midcentury in Europe, generally passed through eastern port cities and settled on farm country in the interior. Consequently, they were a much less visible target for hostility.)

One of the century's most outspoken and influential nativists was Samuel F. B. Morse, a middling professional painter of miniatures and professor of art, much better known to all as the inventor of the telegraph and of the eponymous Morse code.* In 1835, around the same time that Morse was perfecting

---

* Morse (1791–1872), the man and his myth, has been the subject of a number of books, the first written by Samuel I. Prime just three years after Morse's death. The second and weightiest of all these biographies is a two-volume compilation of his letters and journals by his fifth son, Edward Lind Morse, published in 1914. One reviewer charitably described his effort as "written from a filial point of view." A no less admiring biography by historian Carleton Mabee, *The American Leonardo: A Life of Samuel F. B. Morse*, was published in 1943. Mabee was awarded the Pulitzer Prize for it the next year. His book was followed fully sixty years later by what is today's definitive biography, also from Knopf but otherwise very different, *Lightning Man: the Accursed Life of Samuel F. B. Morse*, by a contemporary Pulitzer Prize–winning biographer, Kenneth Silverman.

Samuel Morse never moved away from his nativist views, even as his wealth and reputation grew as a result of the swift success of the telegraph. At midcentury, now prosperous and comfortably settled with his young second wife on a grand Hudson River estate near Poughkeepsie, New York, and embroiled in nearly endless litigation to defend his patents, his attention turned to the era's most divisive domestic issue.

Morse was an outspoken apologist for slavery. In 1863, midway through the Civil War and long after his failed attempts to be elected mayor of New York City and to Congress on an anti-Irish, nativist platform, he published *An Argument on the Ethical Position of Slavery*, in which his point of departure was the

his device (and roughly ten years before a telegraph line connected Washington to Baltimore, thanks to his efforts—the first such connection in the world) he published a small pamphlet, a compilation of separate articles printed the year before in the *New York Observer* under the pseudonym "Brutus." Morse's short book (132 pages, with a 55-page appendix), *Foreign Conspiracy Against the Liberties of the United States*, was a breathless screed against Catholicism and the papacy as well as their chief tools, Imperial Austria and the Jesuits. (Sample: "Yes, the rocks are in full view on which American liberty must invariably be wrecked, unless all hands are aroused to immediate action.") Throughout, this son of a Calvinist minister distinguished "Papists," Roman Catholics invariably committing "sacred treason" against the state, from "Christians," by which he meant fellow Protestants.

Morse's thesis was summarized in a manifesto he proposed in connection with floating the idea of an antipopery union among American Protestants. The italics and capitals are his.

> Popery is a *Political system, despotic* in its organization, *anti-democratic* and *anti-republican,* and cannot therefore co-exist with American republicanism.
>
> The ratio of *increase of Popery* is the exact ratio of the *decrease of civil liberty.*
>
> The *dominance of Popery* in the United States is the *certain destruction of our free institutions.*
>
> Popery, by its organization, is wholly under the control of a FOREIGN DESPOTIC SOVEREIGN. . . .
>
> Popery is more dangerous and more formidable than any power in the United States, on the ground that, through its *despotic organization* it can *concentrate its efforts* for any purpose with complete effect, and that organization being wholly under *foreign* control, it can have no real sympathy with anything American. (118–20)

---

conviction that "slavery or the servile relation is . . . divinely ordained for the discipline of the human race in this world." In slavery Morse found "some of the most beautiful examples of domestic happiness and contentment that this fallen world knows," leading him to the conclusion that "if the Bible is to be the umpire, as I hold it to be, then it is the Abolitionist that is denounced as worthy of excommunication; it is the Abolitionist from whom we are commanded to withdraw ourselves, while not a syllable of reproof do I find in the sacred volume administered to those who maintain, in the spirit of the Gospel, the relations of Masters and Slaves."[9] His views put him firmly in the mainstream of Southern opinion. They were indistinguishable, for example, from what J. B. D. DeBow was publishing in the columns of his *New Orleans Review*.

Morse's cramped views about immigrants (he recommended that U.S. naturalization laws be amended to deny the vote to the foreign born forever, arguing that such a restriction denied no one anything to which he was truly entitled) and specifically about Catholics put him among a substantial and influential company in midcentury. In 1849 a New Yorker, one Charles Allen, established the Order of the Star Spangled Banner, a Protestant men's secret society that morphed into a short-lived, national nativist political party whose candidates were successful in New England and the Midwest—and especially so in Massachusetts, Morse's home state. Members were instructed to reply they knew nothing in response to questions about their affiliation, hence the party's "Know-Nothing" moniker. In 1855 Henry Ward Beecher's brother and fellow churchman, Edward, published his *Papal Conspiracy Exposed*, not as twitchy as Morse's book but to the same point.[10] One year later the Know-Nothings nominated a candidate for president; two sometime Know-Nothings later rose to the vice presidency.

While the Know-Nothings soon came apart in divisions over slavery—the same tensions had pried apart the Whig Party, too, into proslavery "cotton Whigs" and antislavery "conscience Whigs," and then disassembled the party completely in the election of 1852—anti-Catholicism remained socially respectable and a powerful political plank well into the next century. It was, for example, a central element in the presidential campaign of 1928, when Al Smith ran unsuccessfully against Herbert Hoover, and was still clearly visible in 1961 during the election of John Fitzgerald Kennedy to be the nation's thirty-fifth president.

In the North, the Civil War heightened anti-Catholicism because the general view, with some justification, was that the Catholic Church's hierarchy was insufficiently zealous condemning slavery. In fact, few Catholic prelates spoke out against slavery, as did Archbishop John Purcell of Cincinnati. Most saw it as not inconsistent with Scripture and elected instead to represent the economic interests of their generally Irish parishioners (competing with blacks for unskilled jobs) from the pulpit rather than supporting abolition, which they associated with northern Protestants.

New York City's enormously influential Archbishop John Hughes, a friend of Governor William Seward and later Lincoln's emissary to the Catholic courts of Europe and to the pope in Rome, managed to be pro-Union and anti-abolition all at once. He took the pragmatic (if evasive) view that "slavery constituted no crime once it is an established institution" but supported the war and later the draft on the basis that the Union and the Constitution should be preserved. Some of this same ambiguity is found in the actions of his parishioners: some volunteered in huge numbers for the Union army and fought with great courage and horrific losses; later others rioted violently in the streets of the city in response to the implementation of the draft in 1863.

In fairness to Hughes, the archbishop's straddling stance on the geography of slavery in the United States was not perceptibly different from Lincoln's before the Civil War. Lincoln said at Cooper Union in February 1860, "Wrong as we think slavery is, we can yet afford to let it alone where it is, because that much is due to the necessity arising from its actual presence in the nation." (He then went on to ask rhetorically, "But can we, while our votes will prevent it, allow it to spread into the National Territories, and to over-run us here in these Free States?") Anyone, like Lincoln, whose convictions brought them up short of outright abolition ended in the same place: Slavery should not be permitted to expand its scope but could not constitutionally be rooted out from where it was entrenched. There the "peculiar institution" had to be permitted to atrophy and die.

Subtleties aside, Hughes's position, and the less nuanced postures of his fellows, had the result of aligning the Catholic Church in the North with Southern Protestants (and with Southern Catholics) on one of the chief questions of the war. The result was to infuriate congregants of "churches of the New England persuasion," meaning most northern Protestants. In part for this reason anti-Catholicism remained a palpable undercurrent in the nation's life even during the war, and its strains were visible in anything having to do with the Surratts, mother and son, after it.

Surratt's supposed crime was horrific, but his escape was a fascinating adventure in foreign places that most nineteenth-century Americans would never see. Once the story came out journalists moved quickly to satisfy public curiosity about it, even if that required imagination to be presented as fact. In early 1867 a veteran reporter for the *Cincinnati Daily Commercial* helped his paper's readers picture what the last days of Surratt's Zouave service had been like, salting pure fiction with occasional references to things they might have once read about:

> Forty-two miles from Rome stands Viterbo. Thither Surratt's battalion was ordered, and he crossed the Tiber on the ancient Ponte Mulvius [Milvio], the same to which the Roman sweethearts followed their soldier boys. There was no one to wave goodbye to Surratt from its parapet. He trudged in his new dress with a squad of adventurers along the

Flaminian Way, and at the end of two days arrived at Viterbo. It is a strange illustration of the murder of an American President, this banished boy crossing the vast Campagna, among the savage bulls, under the tinkle of wine carts, past the Roman milestones, treading the same hard blocks that Cataline and "False Sextus" trod. He found Viterbo a strange old town of 20,000 souls, lying across the ancient "turnpike" at the foot of Mount Ciraimo [Cimini?], an isolated volcanic rock.

It's easy to suspect the narrative thus far was cribbed practically whole from a guide book. Surratt now appears on the scene, barely recognizable in what could be the set for an opera by Pietro Mascagni or Ruggiero Leoncavallo:

Sometimes he was set on picket, watching the frontier that smugglers and patriots from Italy, or "Piedmont," as the Pope's government called it, might not enter. Here at midnight, as the diligence [a fast passenger stagecoach] came into Acquapendente and Montefiascone, Surratt, on guard, would see descend to take a cup of coffee or smoke a cheroot, a couple of young Americans, in smart gaiters and fob chains, traveling sacks of morocco swung about them, and the tones of voice, the phrases, and the stride of the land he knew so well. To them, he was only a foreigner—the soldier of the most illiberal government in the world—a uniformed impediment to travel and free thought. . . .

Whoever has ridden at night in the banquette of a diligence through the passes of the Appenines may gain some notion of the fugitive's flight across the Tiber and into the Saline mountains. He was in the region of the brigands, those marauders who haunt the Papal frontier, and crossing the boundary to and fro find easy escape in the mutual jealousy of the two governments. From such gentry, men who carry a crime like Surratt's have no visitations. The best they had done was to slit an ear, for tribute's sake, or violate some country gentleman's daughter. They look out from their dens upon this assassin and let him pass. Lean dogs of the cotters bayed as he approached; the fires of the charcoal-burners lit his path; the rushing streams half stilled; at dawn the sunrise lit a hundred capes and islands; he went southward begging his way.

In the beautiful city of Naples Surratt went boldly and declared himself to British Consul. The perfidious sympathy of the *attaches* of that country that wished us no success gave him relief, and dispatched him to Malta. Here he would probably have enlisted as a British soldier, the natural position for an American assassin. . . . British fear and gall could not shelter him but would not give him up. So he continued to Alexandria. . . .

Surratt's flight as it was reported or imagined (the two were often the same) by contemporary newspapermen was one thing. His flight as depicted in fine art is something else again. In 1976 Marcia Goldberg explained in the *Art Bulletin* (vol. 58, no. 2) that she had found just such a painting, William Rimmer's *Flight and Pursuit,* an oil painted in 1872 and now hanging in the Museum of Fine Arts in Boston. It was an allegory, she said, a murderer—Surratt, specifically, there in tunic, cape, and sandals with a knife at his waist—fleeing to asylum toward an altar in a Moorish-looking hall, paced by a ghostly pursuer to his right and chased by something unseen casting a shadow behind him. The news of Surratt's flight and capture, she pointed out as proof, was in the *New York Times* issue of December 11, 1866, soon after Rimmer arrived in New York. For the unpersuaded, Goldberg offered a clincher: Jean-Léon Gérôme's *Death of Caesar,* allegedly "the source Rimmer used for the setting of his painting." She noted that it, too, was about a political assassination.

Flight and Pursuit had been described very differently just three years earlier by one Charles Sarnoff in a rival periodical, the *American Art Journal* (vol. 5, no. 1). Sarnoff began by observing that there was "not in all of American art a painting that evokes as much reaction as 'Flight and Pursuit.' . . . Yet its actual meaning has evaded its audiences." He concluded that the painting was autobiographical, a reflection of Rimmer's and his father's weird conviction that the artist was the lost Dauphin and the rightful king of France and that their lives were in danger from assassins sent by the usurper, Louis XVIII.

Across the great divide that separated them, Goldberg and Sarnoff did manage to agree that the work's alternate title, *On the Horns of the Altar,* was a biblical reference to the right of sanctuary, and both cited the same chapters in the books of Exodus and Kings as authority. Sadly, no one had thought to ask Rimmer before he died in 1879 if he had John Surratt in mind when he painted it.

Two years after Neve's departure from the Venerable, the Republicans—"Piedmontese" is how the pope characterized them in denial that there was such a thing as an "Italian"—finally moved directly against Rome. On September 20, 1870,

Flight and Pursuit (1872). William Rimmer's mysterious oil painting has been improbably interpreted by one twentieth-century art critic as an allegory of Surratt's flight from arrest. Rimmer, born in Liverpool in 1816, moved as a child with his family to Boston, where the self-taught physician, artist, and anatomist sculpted, painted, and taught until his death in 1879. (Museum of Fine Arts, Boston)

four days after the fall of Civitavecchia, the capital came under direct attack. Given that the pope had commanded a purely symbolic defense, the fighting was quickly over. Soon after Gen. Rafaelle Cadorna's gunners started shelling the city's ancient walls, Rome's outnumbered defenders, Zouaves, Swiss Carbineers, and others, followed orders passed down through the military chain of command from the pope to cease fire, and the first of King Victor Emmanuel's sixty thousand troops began their march into the city through a fifty-foot gap in the wall near the Porta Pia gate.

"On calm reflection," Powell, who was there, later wrote, "everyone will see that the Holy Father was guided in his decision in this affair, by the greatest prudence,"

for had he not made any resistance to the superior forces of the Italians, they might have distorted his conduct into an approval of their iniquitous spoliation; on the other hand, had he made a prolonged resistance, in the face of the immensely superior strength of the Italian army, the ultimate result must have been the same, and his enemies would have had the pretext for accusing him of sacrificing many valuable lives to no purpose. Thus in deciding to resist the forcible seizure of Rome, and at the same time issuing orders to General Kanzler, to capitulate should a breach in the walls be effected, we may conclude that Pius IX. chose the happy medium, and acted with the most consummate wisdom.

Only a handful of his troops died in the defense of Rome and the Papal States that day.

After many centuries, so ended the pope's temporal kingdom. Some among Pius IX's defeated Zouaves promptly made their way home. Others bounced from one defeat to another. They quickly joined the French army (no longer Napoleon III's, as he had been captured a few weeks earlier with eighty thousand of his troops at the Battle of Sedan, but that of the newly declared French Republic) fighting against the Prussians—just in time to participate in the last eight months or so of that debacle at arms.

5

"I BELIEVE YOUR NAME IS SURRATT"

On November 23, 1866, still dressed in his Pontifical Zouave uniform, Surratt stepped ashore at Alexandria, Egypt, from the gangplank of the British and North American Royal Mail Steamship Company's RMS *Tripoli*, a free man for the last time in a long time. He had no special affection for the garb, and certainly would have wished to have fled from the Papal States in something less distinctive and conspicuous, but the uniform was the only clothing he had. Surratt's civilian clothes had been confiscated when he enlisted, standard procedure for the armies of the day to prevent, or at least impede, desertion.

During all of Surratt's previous moves to sanctuary he had been equipped with letters of introduction to likely sympathizers or otherwise helped along the way. This time he was alone and improvising furiously. Until now, he'd managed well. Even detractors had to admire his elusiveness and determination. "Surratt is a man chiefly noticeable for his criminality," *Harper's Weekly* wrote a little later. The article went on grudgingly, "So obscure as to easily hide himself, by the aid of a few friends, from the eyes of the world; so ignorant that we almost wonder at the shrewdness of some of his devices. . . . [He] showed himself capable of the most desperate actions when these were necessary to his own safety."

In the ten days between November 8 and 18 Surratt had made his way on foot nearly one hundred miles cross-country from Veroli, in the Papal States, to Naples, in the Kingdom of Italy. The young man who had made a profession of passing across military lines did so again, for the last time. Not far from Veroli, just across the frontier, Surratt paused at a military hospital in the town of Sora for treatment of the bruises from his escape earlier in the day. He then spent several nights in jail in Naples (at his own request and where he was accommodated rent free, "not exactly as a prisoner"), persuaded a credulous British diplomat that he was a destitute Canadian deserter from the Zouaves, and finally talked his way aboard the steamship *Tripoli* with his fare paid (or perhaps just his meals) to Alexandria by a sympathetic "English gentleman."

The *Tripoli*, a little more than 2,050 gross tons, was another of the many Scottish-built steamers that dominated world trade by sea in the nineteenth century. Its home yard was the J. and G. Thompson Works at Govan, up river on the Clyde near Glasgow. The same shipyard was well known as the constructor of a small fleet of Civil War blockade runners, fast steamers that slipped high-value cargoes past Union navy pickets to the Confederacy and raced cotton exports from the South to Great Britain. Not enough moved outbound through the blockade to finance the war, and not enough cleared inbound to change its course.

The vessel was barely three years old when she served as Surratt's ride from pursuit. Sadly, but not unusually, the *Tripoli* had a short biography. It was launched in August 1863, spent its first year at sea in the Mediterranean, and then in August 1865 was shifted to British and North American's Atlantic schedule, carrying three hundred or so emigrants at a time (slowly, at something under eleven knots) from Liverpool to Halifax and New York. On October 19, 1866, the *Tripoli* finished a passage to Liverpool from New York via Queenstown, Ireland (now Cobh), through "very tempestuous weather." Still under Captain Martin's command on October 27, it headed back into the Mediterranean for a single voyage, filling in on the company's schedule for a ship with machinery problems. After stops in Genoa and Livorno, the *Tripoli* steamed into Naples on November 16 for an overnight port call, and that's where its story and Surratt's intersected.[1]

In good weather Captain Martin would have put the *Tripoli* through the narrow Strait of Messina on the way to Malta from Naples, 179 nautical miles port to port. Going east of Sicily heading for Alexandria would have saved Martin better than half a day's steaming and coal consumption. In poor weather, the low clouds, rain, and limited visibility typical of late autumn in the central Mediterranean, he would have steamed instead around Sicily's west coast, 329 miles, looking for sea room and avoiding the narrow, two-mile-wide strait that in classical times was believed to be a ship-wrecking passage between Scylla, the rock, and the whirlpool, Charybdis.

Passengers and cargo from Naples safely ashore in Alexandria—the former marking time uncomfortably in quarantine, the latter slowly passing through Ottoman customs and then via train or the Mahmoudiya Canal to Cairo and beyond—the steamship *Tripoli* hauled up its anchor and headed west, out of the Mediterranean.

Early the next year the *Tripoli* was back in the Atlantic permanently. Not yet ten years old on May 17, 1872, and barely out of Liverpool for Boston, the ship ran aground on Tuskar Rock in St. George's Channel near Wexford, Ireland, one of the deadliest ship traps in the southern Irish Sea. She lies there still, in some twenty-five feet of water, one of four vessels that sank in the same place that year.

Alexandria appears to have been Surratt's destination only because that's where the ship he boarded in Naples the night of November 18 was bound the next day. There was a Roman Catholic church in Alexandria (the Cathedral Church of St. Catherine, the seat of the Catholic vicar apostolic in Egypt, described decades later by E. M. Forster as "gaunt without and tawdry within"), in the tony international district between the eastern and western harbor basins just below the old Ottoman town, but nothing suggests that Surratt went to Egypt specifically intending to find refuge there. His goal had been to leave Naples ahead of certain pursuit, not necessarily to go to Alexandria.

Later William Winthrop told Charles Hale—both men were U.S. consuls in the eastern Mediterranean—he thought that Surratt had fled Italy with an escape to India in mind. Maybe. If that were his intention, Surratt would have had to make his way from Alexandria across the Nile Delta and almost ninety miles down the Sinai Peninsula to Port Suez at the head of the Red Sea. An overland mail and passenger route between Alexandria and the Red Sea, the inspiration of Lt. Thomas Waghorn, a former Royal Navy officer with an entrepreneurial turn of mind, had been operating for the past thirty years. The glib Surratt probably could have talked his way from end to end. Alternatively, he could have caught a ride on the Alexandria-Cairo railroad, opened in 1854, proceeded to Port Suez from Cairo, and there boarded a ship to India. (The Suez Canal, under construction since 1859, would not be finished for another three years, and that thanks only to the steam-powered equipment now at work supplementing the shovels and picks of Egyptian *fellahin* press gangs.) Once on the subcontinent, Surratt would again have been under the protection of British law, a regime very unlikely to give him up. Not impossible, but there is no other indication and no proof that this was his plan.

Now, fifteen days after and some fourteen hundred miles miles away from the site of his supposedly athletic "escape" from arrest, the usually fastidious Surratt must have looked bedraggled and smelled ripe. He had been wearing the same uniform since he escaped military arrest in Veroli, while he scampered across the border to the neighboring Kingdom of Italy, and from there to aboard ship and away. Still, he had eluded capture for more than a year and a half and had reason to believe he had gotten away clean from the gravest threats yet—from arrest by fellow Zouaves of Lieutenant Colonel Allet's battalion and from quick delivery into the custody of the senior U.S. diplomat in Rome, Rufus King.

But when he came ashore in Egypt Surratt unknowingly gave up legal protections that had, until then, kept him out of the hands of his pursuers several times. Months earlier the United States had not even approached Great Britain about arresting and extraditing Surratt when he was known to be in Liverpool because of an assumption that Her Majesty's government would never agree to do it. That untested conviction seemed to have been substantiated just a few days earlier in Valetta, when on November 19 Malta's government coolly stiff-armed an official U.S. request that Surratt be plucked from a ship in transit and handed over to the U.S. consul general. And it was not just the British who were sticklers about extradition. At about the same time the secretary general of foreign affairs of the Kingdom of Italy led the U.S. minister in Florence, Marsh, to understand that Surratt would not be turned over to him if discovered on its soil.

In Ottoman Egypt, however, there were no such niceties to insulate Surratt from capture and arrest. To the contrary, while the Ottoman Empire declined from its sixteenth-century heights, foreign diplomats gained more and more authority over their nationals and their coreligionists in its territory. The process had begun as an effort to encourage intracommunal trade by working around fundamental incompatibilities in legal codes derived from religious tradition. By the time this adjustment was substantially complete in the mid-nineteenth century, the citizens of the United States and fourteen other nations enjoyed extraterritoriality in the empire: a free pass from Turkish law. (The United States had joined this privileged group of scofflaws in 1830.) Until 1914, when Turkey unilaterally abrogated what had been a humiliating constriction on its sovereignty, extraterritoriality empowered ambassadors, ministers, and consuls general in the empire with almost complete legal authority over their resident citizens.

By landing in Alexandria, Surratt had unwittingly made himself subject to U.S. law as exercised there by American government officials.

Americans were uncommon but not unseen in Alexandria before the Civil War. On average, five had checked in each month with the consul during the preceding several decades (more in the cooler months, fewer in the warmer), some to vacation and some hoping to unearth business.[2] After the war American tourism in the Middle East surged, the sightseers funneling in and out of the region through the great ports of Istanbul and Alexandria. Moreover, the separatist province of Egypt under Pasha Ismail, the Ottoman viceroy from 1863 to 1879, became for the 1870s a haven and a business opportunity for a number of Civil War veterans who found themselves out of work after Appomattox.[3] Some fifty U.S. Army and Navy officers from both sides passed through Ismail's service, most of them from the second and third command levels and with unimpressive service records. Working for the despotic Ismail and his pashas could not have been easy.

Several didn't adjust to life and work in Egypt, performed poorly there, and left quickly. That group included David Essex Porter, son of Adm. David Dixon Porter, USN, the hero of the Union's successful brown-water war on the Mississippi River. Distinguished father notwithstanding, like other contract dropouts, young Porter lasted less than one year in Egypt as an assistant engineer. But Gen. Thaddeus Mott and Gen. William Loring, and a few dozen equally sturdy others, spent as long as ten years in the country, training, teaching, exploring, and occasionally even fighting. The collapse of the Egyptian economy and Ismail's subsequent ejection led to the end of their workshop in Egyptian military modernization.

Among the stampede of American tourists to Egypt after the war were some of the herd bulls. (The influx was so great that Michael Oren titled the relevant chapter in his encyclopedic *Power, Faith and Fantasy: America in the Middle East 1776 to the Present,* "American Onslaught.") These distinguished visitors included William Seward, the former secretary of state, in 1869, Gen. William Sherman in 1872, Gen. George McClellan in 1874, and President and Mrs. Ulysses S. Grant in 1878. They and most other tourists shared Mark Twain's dyspeptic assessment of the Muslim faith and Ottoman government, ventilated at length during the author's own travels in the region.

Ashore amid the ancient port's colorful swirl of national costumes, it's possible that anyone else dressed in Surratt's fashion, in laced white leggings and matching loose gray trousers, tunic, and long-tasseled fez, all once handsomely trimmed in the red cord frogging that denoted a Pontifical Zouave, would have attracted no particular attention in 1866. Mark Twain, touring Istanbul with a party of "innocents abroad" some months after Surratt landed in Egypt, described male fashions in the eastern Mediterranean: "The men were dressed in all the outrageous, outlandish, idolatrous, extravagant, thunder-and-lightning costumes that ever a tailor with the delirium tremens and seven devils could conceive of. There was no freak in dress too crazy to be indulged in, no absurdity too absurd to be tolerated, no frenzy in ragged diabolism too fantastic to be attempted."[4]

Alexandria wasn't Istanbul, but the smaller city's cosmopolitan waterfront boasted its own colorful flock that could have provided a background of protective coloration for the arriving Zouave deserter. Surratt, however, enjoyed no such anonymity. He had been closely tracked since leaving Veroli. The Neapolitan police, for example, were able to report in detail on Surratt's departure from their port just hours after an inquiry was made. (The *Giornale di Napoli* loyally but mistakenly credited a report from the Neapolitan prefect of police direct to the Egyptian authorities with prompting the arrest.)

Surratt had avoided capture when the *Tripoli* stopped briefly in Valetta to coal only thanks to local unwillingness to permit Consul William Winthrop to lift his prey from the ship. Winthrop, a Bostonian who had represented U.S. interests in Malta since October 1834 (and would die there still in diplomatic service in July 1869), knew his British hosts on the island well. He had gone so far as to marry the daughter of one. His frustration with their lack of cooperation in this case seethes out of a November 20 letter he sent to the U.S. consul in Naples, Frank Swan, a peripheral participant in the Surratt manhunt:

> I received your telegraph respecting Surratt on Sunday evening at eight o'clock, and before nine the next morning had written to the acting chief secretary, asking that this notorious criminal might be landed here and kept under guard until I could send him to the United States, where his crime was committed. Nothwithstanding I pressed for an immediate answer, both in my public dispatch and by a private note, still it did not reach me until 4:00 p.m., when the steamer Tripoli was ready to leave for Alexandria; and then, as I think, owing to literal quibbling, my request was not granted. This was most annoying, and I shall send all the correspondence to Hon. W. H. Seward, in the hope that he will give the officials in this neighborhood some knowledge of the treaty now existing for the arrest of criminals, which they would appear so much to require.

One day out of Naples the *Tripoli* had entered Valetta on November 19 and been subjected to a fifteen-day quarantine, under which without special permission no one would have been allowed on or off the ship for a fortnight, had it stayed in port that long. (The outbreak of the third global pandemic of cholera the previous year is the likely explanation for such a long quarantine being imposed on a ship arriving from Naples. In November 1865 King had told Seward that the disease had become "quite fatal" in Naples though not yet present in the Papal States. Eleven months later he reported that cholera had finally appeared in Rome, with some fifty to sixty cases authenticated in the first four weeks of contagion.) Isolated at the port's lazaretto anchorage while taking on three hundred tons of coal during a short stop, the *Tripoli* was out of Winthrop's reach. There was no opportunity for him to improvise around the intransigence of local authorities, but he did the best he could.

Bunkers filled, the *Tripoli* hauled up her anchor and steamed southeast over the horizon with Surratt aboard traveling as "John Agostini." The alias was enough to divert the Maltese, who unenthusiastically searched the ship looking for a Zouave named "Walter" or "Watson" and chose to overlook the only man in Papal States uniform aboard, who claimed to be Canadian. (The Maltese recorded "Agostini" as being not from Canada but from "Candia," meaning the city on Crete, adding a further layer of confusion to what should have been a simple arrest.) Winthrop now became furiously busy. Whether because of genuine anger that a criminal had escaped him or because he feared his failed efforts would be judged in Washington as insufficiently zealous, during the last ten days of November Winthrop launched a storm of letters and telegrams addressed to the state department and consulates across the Mediterranean telling everyone everything he knew about the status of the chase.

Later London might have been slightly conscience-stricken by Surratt's easy passage through Malta in the face of Winthrop's frantic importuning. The *Times* of London published a sober and generally misleading defense of the island government's inaction in a December 1866 postarrest recap of the Surratt story.

It will not be thought surprising that evidence which had been owned at every point of the case to be insufficient for immediate action by American Ministers themselves should have been found inadequate by our own authorities at Malta. These authorities could not be expected to do in a few minutes' notice, and on the warrant of a consul's telegram, what the representatives of the United States in London, Rome, and Florence had not been prepared to demand. Had SURRATT actually landed at Malta, and time been given, the capture might have been effected . . . but the Maltese authorities had not even as much information as had been given to the Papal or Italian government, and in an hour the Tripoli was on her way to Alexandria. There SURRATT came under the jurisdiction of the Egyptian government, which, after eighteen days consideration of the evidence, at length decided that extradition was justifiable, and surrendered the fugitive to the captain of the Swatara.

The new telegraph cables connecting principal cities accelerated the pursuit in ways that would have been unimaginable just a few years earlier. It was now possible for the first time in history to move information across oceanic distances faster than a man could travel. Despite its unreliability (for example, cables to Alexandria from the north and west, Syria and Benghazi respectively, and from Malta were all inoperative in November 1866 while Surratt was steaming to Egypt), the telegraph changed international police work forever, to Surratt's disadvantage. Until early December, when the Malta-Alexandria break was repaired, two-way communications between Washington and Alexandria took only ten days, even though one thousand of the six thousand miles in each direction had to be covered by mail steamer. This was many weeks faster than had been possible before the cables were laid.

What had not yet changed was the science of identification. The same *Times* reporter explained to his readers, "It appears representatives of the United States were put upon his track almost as soon as he effected his escape to Europe, but the difficulties in the way of identification were so great that, though every Government in turn was willing enough to promote the ends of justice in his case, more than a year elapsed before the arrest was actually accomplished."

Months later one of Surratt's lawyers told the jury that "there is nothing more unreliable than proof of identity." That was true outside of the courtroom, too. Surratt moved around easily in part because establishing his identity to skeptical foreign officials in the thicket of aliases in which he concealed himself was so difficult. In an era before picture identification cards, drivers' licenses, photos on passports, and the like, in general you were who you said you were and the burden fell on someone else to prove otherwise. Thus in April 1865, during the heat of the first manhunt, two detectives were sent to Canada with Lou Weichmann and John Holohan. Weichmann and Holohan's sole function was to identify the man when found. Similarly, when the USS *Swatara* left Civitavecchia for Alexandria nineteen months later to collect Surratt and bring him home, she carried former Zouave No. 2730, Henri Beaumont de Sainte Marie, Surratt's one-time boon companion, onboard to provide positive identification. As it turned out, Sainte Marie's services weren't necessary in Alexandria—in any case the *Swatara* arrived in Egypt after Surratt had been apprehended—but everyone thought they would be and reluctantly put up with Sainte Marie's increasingly self-important posturing for that reason.

After the 1830s, and especially after midcentury when cameras and image processing became, albeit awkwardly, truly portable, photographs showed what someone really looked like, but unless a recent image was available where required, the problem remained. And then there was the matter of identifying the figure in the photo. Two of the nine witnesses before the Judiciary Committee investigating the Johnson administration's pursuit of Surratt, Marshal Gooding and Reverend Wiget (one of the priests who had consoled Mary Surratt on the gallows during the last moments of her life), were there only to testify to Surratt's resemblance to his own photographs.

Forensic identification, identification in support of police work, went down a number of dead ends at first. These included an effort by a French anthropologist named Alphonse Bertillon, who in 1870 developed a set of specialized calipers used to establish identity through "anthropometry," a series of body part measurements that combined into a supposedly unique formula for each person. The Bertillon system collapsed in ambiguity after the turn of the century. Other ideas based on even more exotic, not to say crackpot, identification concepts failed too. Finally, in 1880 an English medical doctor in Tokyo, Henry Fauld, proposed a rival system, fingerprinting, that actually worked. Not long thereafter fingerprinting made it theoretically possible to connect someone with a crime or crime scene; it became practically possible to do that after 1890 or so, but this wasn't necessarily the same thing as establishing identity through fingerprinting. That had to await the general use of identity documents such as those mentioned above and the construction of huge fingerprint databases.

The first and best verbal description of Surratt was probably the one printed on the wanted poster published by the secretary of war April 20, 1865. It credited Surratt with a pale and clear complexion with color in his cheeks; prominent cheekbones and a narrow chin; a broad, low, and square forehead; and firmly set lips, among other things. (That poster, one of the first to feature pictures from photographs, wisely augmented its description of Surratt with his portrait.)

Between the issue date of that poster and November 1868, when the last legal action against Surratt came to its conclusion, describing him grew into something of a cottage industry.[5] The most revealing description, less for what it said about Surratt than for what it said about its author, came after the mid-point of the period and appeared in the *New York Times'* reporting about the trial. "The idea of calling him a gentleman is apt to shock loyal notions of right and wrong," the *Times* opined, warming up to the subject. Its reporter then went on to describe the prisoner for his readers:

> A pale, student like face about twenty-five or six years old is seen, with a broad forehead, prominent nose, and cheeks receding from high cheek-bones toward the jaw, which terminates in a sharp, pointed chin. The eyes are bluish gray, hair light brown, moustache and long goatee a shade lighter, and the lips are thin though fresh and full, and are generally compressed tightly together, with an air of determination, which, however, taken into consideration with the rest of his physique, leads to the impression that he would do no one any harm unless certain that he could escape the consequences. He has a cold, selfish, calculating, face.

The thumbnail psychiatric evaluation was a bonus.[6]

Discovering that the undersea cable between Valetta and Alexandria was inoperative (it was not repaired until December 9), Winthrop sent a telegram to Alexandria via Istanbul expecting that even with the extra handling his alert would arrive at least one day ahead of the ship. And there, he knew, things would be very different. In Muslim Egypt there would be no interfering legal-isms nor any special sympathy for an American Catholic being pursued by his government as there might have been in Valetta. On December 1 Winthrop was pleased to report—his sigh of relief was probably audible in the capital—to Assistant Secretary Seward that Surratt had been arrested. By then all of official Washington knew that the last of the Lincoln conspirators had finally been run to ground.

Surratt had come ashore in a city that for a while at least had held a fair claim to being the intellectual capital of the world, then fallen on very hard times, and only recently recovered its place of importance on the North African littoral and the Eastern Mediterranean.

By the end of the eighteenth century Alexandria—Alexander the Great's heritage in Egypt and the capital of his heirs and their successors for a thousand years, the site of one of antiquity's greatest libraries and first university, and the home of two of the seven wonders of the ancient world—had been a backwater for many centuries. In August 1798, when Adm. Horatio Nelson shattered Adm. François-Paul Brueys's French fleet at the Battle of the Nile in Aboukir Bay fifteen miles east of Alexandria, the population of the once-grand city was down to four or five thousand, including fewer than one hundred expatriate Europeans. In better times just one month earlier, Dominque-Vivant Denon, one of the French *savants* who accompanied Napoleon on the general's catastrophic Egyptian adventure, had peered at Alexandria from the deck of his ship in the harbor and saw nothing, not "a single tree, or a single house." A colleague with better vision spotted more, seeing there "ruins, barbarism, poverty, and degradation."

Only three generations later sleepy Alexandria had become the fourth largest port in the Mediterranean Sea, ranked after Istanbul, Marseilles, and Genoa. A demotion still, as in her prime, Alexandria had been the Roman Empire's second city, behind only the imperial capital. (Alexandria shared with Istanbul another special distinction. It was, together with the Ottoman seat, one of two great transshipment points for the annual spread westward of cholera and other epidemic diseases brewed up in the great petri dish that was each year's pilgrimage to Mecca.)

In the mid-1860s Alexandria was home to nearly two hundred thousand, roughly twice the population of Washington City at war. Its residents included a vibrant expatriate population of Greeks and Italians and smaller numbers from elsewhere in Europe, among whom French and British bankers and merchants stood, sweating, in the first ranks of society. Flush with the wealth of shipping long staple Egyptian cotton, a substitute for the blockaded American product, to the starved looms of Manchester and Leeds, and Egyptian wheat, barley, and beans to the hungry of Europe and Anatolia, Alexandria boomed.

Its success and resemblance to other great cities seem to be the reasons why Mark Twain, who landed there in the SS *Quaker City* very near the end of his famous luxury cruise and less than a year after Surratt left the place, sounded uninterested by what he saw. First came a promising start: "Out of the mellowest of sunsets we saw the domes and minarets of Alexandria rise into view. . . . When we reached the pier we found an army of Egyptian boys with donkeys no larger than themselves—for donkeys are the omnibuses of Egypt." But then Twain stumbled into end-of-trip ennui: "We went abroad through the town then and found it a city of huge commercial buildings and broad, handsome streets brilliant with gaslight. By night it was a sort of reminiscence of Paris. . . .

Alexandria was too much like a European city to be novel and we soon tired of it." A reminiscence of Paris with rental donkey transport; still, by the standards of Twain's other municipal critiques in the Levant, this was high praise.

Every since the Albanian soldier of fortune Muhammad Ali took charge of the province in 1805, the Ottoman viceroys in Egypt had been insubordinate. In 1882, fifteen years after Twain's visit there and a few years after Ismail was deposed for profligacy, patience with them finally ran out. Not Turkish patience, English. Just before 7 AM on July 11, the Royal Navy began to shell Alexandria. The punishing, daylong bombardment softened up the port and the country, triggered violent xenophobic rioting in the city, and marked the beginning of Great Britain's long imperial presence on the ground in Egypt and the Sudan. A century of anticolonial battles followed, shaking North Africa from end to end. When Surratt arrived there in 1866, however, Alexandria was full of promise. None of it for him.

Something about Alexandria makes its best archivists writers of fiction rather than the Egyptologists and historians, archaeologists, or veteran tourists of the exotic that one might expect. In part, of course, it was precisely the exotic, and especially the erotic, that powerfully attracted Europeans to the Levant and Alexandria. Gustav Flaubert visited Alexandria in November 1849 in his late twenties, unknown, unpublished, and still years away from writing his first great triumph, *Madame Bovary* (1856). Disembarking from the sidewheel steamer that had struggled to bring him from Marseilles, Flaubert instantly "gobbled up a bellyful of colour, like a donkey filling himself with oats."[7] Ten days later and not yet sated, he left for a trip up the Nile, soon to write an account of mid-nineteenth-century Egypt that can be read in part as a record of sexual adventures in the Orient. (Athens appealed to a different appetite. There Flaubert "inhaled antiquity in great brainfuls.")

Not surprisingly, in view of Alexandria's colonial history, both of the city's best known memorialists are twentieth-century British authors. E. M. Forster wrote two loosely autobiographical monographs about the city where he lived for a time during World War I, *Alexandria: A History and a Guide* (1922) and *Pharos and Pharillon* (1923). Lawrence Durrell wrote only a novel, but his was the four-volume *Alexandria Quartet* (1957–60), which drew its imagery and languid prose from four years of his life in the city during World War II.

Forster's masterwork is generally agreed to be *Passage to India*, written in 1924 and based on his experiences on the subcontinent in 1912–13 and again in 1921–22. In between were his years in Alexandria working for the Red Cross, and from this time came his Alexandria books. He admired the city, the site of an intense love affair with a young tram driver, but both his books about it, although workman-like, are of no particular merit. They occupy a shaded corner in the Forster canon, barely visible beside *Howard's End* (1910), *Passage to India*, or his other works of fiction, commentary, and criticism. In *Pharos and Pharillon* Forster managed no better than this dry, voiceover narrative description of the city:

> Such is the scene where the following actions and meditations take place; that limestone ridge, with alluvial country on one side of it and harbours on the other, jutting from the desert, pointing towards the Nile; a scene unique in Egypt, nor have the Alexandrians ever been truly Egyptian. Here Africans, Greeks and Jews combined to make a city; here a thousand years later the Arabs set faintly but durably the impress of the Orient; here after secular decay rose another city.

For the generations after Forster, Durrell described twentieth-century Alexandria anew to English speakers. The city was the setting and a major character in his tetralogy—four views of the same narrative, "a sort of prism-sightedness" as he had one of his characters describe the approach—of interlocked love affairs, each a novel itself. Not until television's *Seinfeld* series would one meet a more self-absorbed cast of characters than those Durrell borrowed from his own life, animated, and then set adrift to couple and uncouple in the city.

In *Justine*, the first of the four volumes, Alexandria in the 1930s appears first as atmosphere ("Light filtered through the essence of lemons. An air full of brick-dust—sweet-smelling brick dust and the odour of hot pavements slaked with water . . . the deep camphor-scented afternoon"), and later as architecture ("Stores that run back from the docks with their tattered, rotten supercargo of houses. . . . Peeling walls leaning drunkenly to east and west of their true centre of gravity"). *The Alexandria Quartet* was an immediate critical and commercial success in the 1960s; its only detractors seemed to be Marcel Proust's admirers, who ungenerously thought Durrell's tetralogy was a failed and foreshortened attempt at the genius contained in their master's seven-volume *Remembrance of Things Past*.[8]

During the four weeks Surratt was held in Alexandria, he experienced none of its graces. No "essence of lemons" or "sweet-smelling brick dust" for him, no "sea-gleaming milk-white Alexandrian midnight," no "heady perfume of jasmine" hanging in the air.

On November 23, after a five-day ocean passage, Surratt disembarked from the RMS *Tripoli* amid a gaggle of seventy-seven other third-class passengers and was swept with them directly into a scheduled six days of quarantine. He was intercepted in the quarantine hall, perhaps on the grounds of the military hospital on the Ras el Tin headland, four days later by Consul General Charles Hale.* "It was easy to distinguish him," Consul Hale reported to Secretary Seward in a cable, "by his Zouave uniform and scarcely less easy by his almost unmistakable American type of countenance."[9] Identification had been further facilitated by a physical description wired to Consul Hale quoting Louis Weichmann's May 12, 1865, testimony at the trial in the Arsenal. "John Surratt is about six feet high," Weichmann had then said in court, giving Surratt the benefit of several extra inches, "with very prominent forehead, very large nose, and sunken eyes; he has a goatee, and very long hair of a light color." Hale accosted Surratt on sight.

Hale: "You are the man I want; you are an American?"

Surratt: "Yes, sir."

"You doubtless know why I want you. What is your name?"

"Walters."

"I believe your name is Surratt."

Consul Hale then identified himself and "gave him the usual magisterial caution, that he was not obliged to say anything, and that anything he said would be taken down in writing." It was all very easy. As Hale later explained to the secretary of state,

---

* Charles Hale (1831–1882) was one of eight children of Nathan and Sarah Everett Hale of Boston, Massachusetts. Hale, a Harvard graduate, was a sometime journalist and politician in his youth. He served in the Massachusetts House of Representatives for several years and as its speaker from 1859 to 1861. Poor health soon forced his retirement from state politics.

In October 1864 he replaced William Thayer, who had died in his post after less than three years on the job, as U.S. consul general in Alexandria. As such Hale was the senior American diplomat in Egypt, an important assignment in that for the past fifteen years at least the United States had treated with Egypt as if it were an independent state, neglecting its nominal subservience to Istanbul. The arrest of John Harrison Surratt was the highlight of Hale's tour of duty.

Hale's five years of service in Egypt were marred by unsubstantiated charges and unsuccessful lawsuits against him by Francis Dainese, an erstwhile acting consul general in Istanbul who had served briefly as temporary consul in Alexandria after the death of his mentor, Thayer. In 1866 Dainese published *The History of Mr. Seward's Pet in Egypt: His Acts Denounced, and His Usurpations Condemned by the Courts*, a book-length abuse of Hale. Dainese's continuing allegations and embarrassments finally provoked a request for Hale's resignation in May 1870. He was replaced by a Grant nominee, George Butler.

Hale's youngest sister, Susan, visited him on post in 1867–68, and her published letters offer a charming glimpse into an American diplomat's life-style in midcentury Egypt. See Caroline P. Atkinson, ed., *Letters of Susan Hale* (Boston: Marshall Jones, 1918), 22–61.

According to the well established public law of this place, as the prisoner avowed himself to be an American, and submitted, without objection, to arrest by me on my statement that I acted for the United States, and especially as he has no paper to suggest even a prima facie claim for belonging to any other jurisdiction, there is no other authority that can rightfully interfere here with his present custody; and I have good reason for saying that no attempt at interference will be set on foot by any authority, whatever pretensions he may make. The prisoner's quarantine will expire on the 29th; he will then be received into the prison of the local government, which cordially gives me every assistance.

Hale had been briefly concerned by the possibility that Her Majesty's government might interfere in the arrest of someone who had until then claimed British citizenship at every stop. He told Seward, "I took care to inform Mr. Francis, her Britannic Majesty's legal vice-consul and judge, that [Surratt] was in the custody of this consulate general, which would not admit his right to any other jurisdiction, but that meanwhile he might be visited by her Britannic Majesty's authorities to hear any claims or pretensions he might choose to put forward." He was relieved when Francis "found no occasion for any proceedings, and, in point of fact, Surratt never claimed British protection."

Later, in early August 1867 as Surratt's first trial drew to a close, an obviously overheated Edwards Pierrepont, the government's lead counsel, described the moment of arrest to the jury as part of his interminable closing speech for the prosecution. Surratt, he said, helping them imagine an event he seems to have known nothing about, "flies into Egypt. Was he not safe then?" And now, counsel's prose, always feverish, practically lifted Pierrepont from the ground. Surratt, he said,

had got into that "ancient land of mystery and of eld [antiquity]," where the Pharaohs dwelt; where Joseph was a slave; where Moses lived; where by the power of devils and the power of God such miracles were wrought. Up to the wondrous Nile he goes, on whose banks are the grandest ruins of forgotten empires; where are the pyramids; and there, even, the colossal Sphynx looking at him with stony eyes seemed to say, "What scourge for treason and for murder can this dark monarchy afford this traitor"; and he fled no more. His knees smote together, and his arms fell nerveless at his side. He resisted not at all; He gave himself up without a struggle, was placed upon a ship of war of the United States, and came over the long sea and up the broad river to the scene of his crime.[10]

The jury, filling the same seats in Judge George Fisher's stuffy courtroom ever since mid-June with time off only on Sundays and the Fourth of July, sequestered at the Seaton House on Louisiana Avenue every night for the past six weeks, denied even the comfort of a professional shave (the judge thought that barbers were gossips second only to old maids), and required to go to church en masse, must have absorbed this flourish with numb resignation.

On November 16, while the international pursuit of Surratt very slowly approached its climax, Rufus King wired the minister resident in Lisbon, James Harvey, his counterpart in Portugal, to pass to the commander of the U.S. Navy's European Squadron that "very important matters render the immediate presence of one of our ships-of-war necessary at Vecchia." The plan was that a Navy ship would take Surratt and Sainte Marie home from the port of Rome, the former to his trial and the latter to be a material witness, but by mid-November Surratt had been at large for a week. On November 17 Harvey confirmed that the screw sloop of war USS *Swatara*, then in the western Mediterranean at Marseilles, France, was being diverted to Civitavecchia in response to King's request. Her backup was the tidy, two-stacked, side-wheel steamer USS *Frolic*, a former civilian packet boat whose speed made her an ideal dispatch boat and suitable for special service.

While King and Harvey scrambled to put something together, the *Swatara*, ten guns, Cdr. William Jeffers in command, was a little less than five months out of Hampton Roads, Virginia, into the usual three-year cruise with one of the Navy's squadrons deployed on foreign station.* Rear Adm. Lewis Goldsborough,

---

* The ship's name, from a creek and township in central Pennsylvania, is supposed to be a word in the Iroquois language that translates to "where we feed on eels."

The *Swatara's* commanding officer in 1866–67, William Nicholson Jeffers (1824–1883), was a veteran of twenty-six years of Navy service when he brought Surratt back in her to the United States for trial. The *Swatara* was Jeffers's fifth of six ship commands during a forty-three-year career.

After graduating from the Naval Academy fourth in its first class in 1846, Jeffers served at sea during the Mexican-American War and Civil War. For six months in 1862 he commanded what was the Union navy's arguably most famous ship, the USS *Monitor*, the pioneering ironclad, much of which was recently put on display at the Mariners' Museum in Newport News, Virginia. Jeffers took command immediately after her historic battle with the CSS *Virginia* in Hampton Roads and was aboard during the *Monitor's*

USN, was in command of the European Squadron, riding in the USS *Colorado*, forty-eight guns, his flagship. The rest of his ten-ship squadron spanned the steam sloop of war USS *Ticonderoga*, eleven guns, to the former merchantman USS *Ino*, with only three guns. After the *Swatara*'s midsummer Atlantic crossing the ship joined his squadron and spent the next several months showing the flag in Southampton, England, and continental ports from Germany south, with an extended stop in Vigo, a sleepy fishing port on Spain's Atlantic Coast, where it cleared quarantine for the Mediterranean.

The small steamer (216 feet long, 1,113 tons displacement) had been commissioned the November before, and so it had missed the Civil War entirely, but the *Swatara*'s brief history before sailing for Europe had been a colorful one. While fitting out at the Washington Navy Yard, the ship's steam engine fell to the deck during installation when some lifting tackle parted. The chief of the Bureau of Steam Engineering insisted on a formal investigation. To his disappointment the inquiry subsequently exonerated all concerned. Some months later, after returning from the West Indies at the end of its first cruise, at the request of Treasury Secretary Hugh McCulloch the ship was searched for smuggled goods and its officers interrogated. A second exoneration followed.[11]

On June 27, 1866, the ship steamed out of Hampton Roads for the passage to Fayal in the Azores and thence to Europe with 16 officers (including 10 watchstanding midshipmen), 126 enlisted sailors, and 15 Marines aboard. Below in the hold along with everything else it carried two hundred tons of coal (two or three weeks' worth of steaming at something less than ten knots) and two thousand gallons of drinking water, a supply lasting ten days to two weeks. Once in the Mediterranean, the *Swatara* would stop often to take on coal and water, and meat, vegetables, and bread.

Pursuing Surratt, the *Swatara* sped from Civitavecchia on December 14 to Malta, roughly 325 nautical miles in two days, and from Malta (where it quickly took on nine hundred gallons of water) to Alexandria, approximately 835 miles,

---

unsuccessful attempt in May to force the James River past Drewry's Bluff to Richmond. In 1873 he became chief of the Bureau of Ordnance.

The photograph of Jeffers as a lieutenant commander that appears on his carte de visite shows him confidently staring at the camera, his full, round face elongated by a sharply receding hairline and framed by dark, brushy sideburns and a trim moustache. He shows, too, the beginnings of a paunch that would become more impressive in later life. A kewpie doll in dress blue uniform.

Commodore Jeffers's namesake, the USS *Jeffers* (DD-621), a *Gleaves*-class destroyer, participated in the invasions of North Africa, Normandy, and Okinawa and was present at the surrender ceremony in Tokyo Bay at the end of World War II.

The USS *Swatara*. The *Swatara* was launched and commissioned in 1865. After cruising with the West Indies, European, and North Atlantic squadrons, it was laid up for overhaul in 1872 at the navy yard in Brooklyn. What was presented to Congress as a ship's overhaul was really a comprehensive reconstruction, the product of which, shown here, was a larger and more powerful ship, effectively an entirely new vessel. The ruse was meant to get around limitations on new ship construction after the Civil War. No picture exists of the first, Surratt's, *Swatara*. (Library of Congress, Lot 3000-V, no. 020974)

in four more days. Just after noon on Thursday, December 20, the *Swatara* anchored off Alexandria and exchanged a salute of twenty-one guns with the fort guarding the port. The shots, alternating from ship and shore, boomed out across the harbor like rolling thunder. Her gun crews were exercised again the next morning when Consul Hale came aboard and was honored by the deep reports of a nine-gun salute.

That same day, Friday, December 21, the *Swatara* took aboard 145 pounds fresh beef, 145 pounds of vegetables, and 116 pounds of bread. These deliveries were duly noted in the deck log by the midshipman on watch, Leonard Chenery. Surratt was brought aboard the ship early in the afternoon, prepared for the experience to come by three weeks in an Egyptian jail. His arrival was also recorded in the log in Midshipman Chenery's loose, open script, just as the beef, vegetables, and bread had been: "At 1 PM received on board a person delivered by the U.S. Consul General, Mr. Charles Hale, supposed to be John H. Surratt, one of the conspirators implicated in the assassination of the late President Lincoln."

Surratt's time aboard was governed by Jeffers's written standing orders to officers and sentries, orders Jeffers proudly told Congressman George Boutwell of the Judiciary Committee in Washington two months later so strict and complete that Admiral Goldsborough had thought of nothing to add to them. During the passage to Washington Surratt was to be kept in single irons (manacles) in a locked compartment furnished with a mattress and two blankets, allowed out under guard only "when necessary to use the captain's water closet," and fed from the officers' wardroom, his food diced up and served with a spoon. Surratt was to speak with no one and was not allowed to overhear anything but conversations about routine ship's work. If Surratt grew violent, he was to be placed in double irons with his hands locked behind him. (Double irons, manacles and fetters, in confinement was the usual punishment for infractions of ship's regulations by crew members.)

"It is to be carefully borne in mind," Jeffers instructed his crew, "that the prisoner is put on board for safe-keeping and transportation to the United States, and that his death is preferable to his escape." Loaded carbines, the stubby Sharps and Hankins 1861 Navy model with its distinctive leather-wrapped barrel, were kept in ready issue lockers on deck, to be used should Surratt attempt to escape. Curiously, no provision in Jeffers's otherwise comprehensive standing orders addressed care of the prisoner in the event of an emergency on board.[12]

Accompanied by Consul Hale, Captain Jeffers now went to Cairo with a small group of officers for a formal visit. Before he left the port Hale introduced him to Alexandria's governor, Zulfikar Pasha, and on arrival in Cairo Jeffers was presented to his highness at Ghazereh Palace, "who exhibited the most cordial courtesy at his reception." These formalities done, the party of commissioned tourists returned to the ship late Christmas Eve.

Shortly after noon on December 26, with Surratt chained below, coal and water topped up, and the holiday observance over, the *Swatara* started home from Egypt. (On the way west it must have passed a disappointed USS *Canadaigua* hovering around Malta, whose officers had mistakenly told King a week earlier that they expected to take Surratt on board for the ocean crossing.) A few days later, while the *Swatara* was steaming through the central Mediterranean, Consul Hale telegraphed the news to Secretary Seward. He thriftily limited his report to the essential minimum: "I delivered Surratt aboard Corvette Swatara twenty-first December. No trouble." The telegram was received at the War Department's Military Telegraph Office on December 29.

Surratt wasn't the only man leaving Egypt in chains in the *Swatara*. George Brown, the second coxswain, who had insulted a Royal Navy officer ashore, was, pending summary court-martial for the offense, confined below in double irons on bread and water. Brown had company. Another sailor was held with him for having been drunk and disorderly ashore, and two others for fighting. Brown was released four days later after the court found him guilty, derated him, and fined him two months' pay, forty dollars.

To keep Surratt in more perfect isolation, Welles had wanted the *Swatara* to sail nonstop Alexandria to Washington, but as the secretary ought to have known, no small steamer in the 1860s had that kind of endurance. The ship's first stop for coal and water on her long passage west was in the quarantine anchorage at Port Mahon, Minorca, on January 2, 1867. Out of Port Mahon on the fourth after one day's steaming, the *Swatara* then arrived in Villefranche sur Mer on January 5, 1867, so that Captain Jeffers could report to Admiral Goldsborough in port in the *Colorado*. Here former Zouave Sainte Marie was put ashore, either at his own request because of ill treatment (his version of the story) or because he had finally exhausted Captain Jeffers's patience (the captain's).

Camped out with Asa Aldis, the U.S. consul in Nice, and with no money or good ideas, Sainte Marie promptly wrote his mentor in Rome for help. After a flurry of correspondence (all copied to Seward in Washington), those concerned, Aldis in Nice, King in Rome, and Gen. John Dix, the U.S. minister in Paris (of the Dix-Hill cartel), managed to get Sainte Marie aboard a French steamer to New York on February 2. After several weeks spent improvising a solution, the three American diplomats must have been elated to have this important and tiresome young man at sea, irreversibly heading toward a distant continent.

The *Swatara* was at sea too. Stores topped up and Surratt still confined below, it had departed Villefranche at 2:50 PM on January 8 for what turned out to be a slow, fifteen-day passage to Funchal, Madeira, in the eastern Atlantic Ocean. (In a letter that was read to the cabinet by Secretary Welles on January 25, Admiral Goldsborough reported to Welles that the *Swatara* had sailed on the eighth with Surratt aboard and, according to Interior Secretary Browning's diary entry that day, described the ship's prisoner as "a handsome, cultivated, well behaved young man, perfectly self possessed, about 23 years old, and who conducted himself with great propriety.")

Three deserters from the *Swatara* were left behind, ashore somewhere in France. Their clothes and kits were sold to the crew at auction the next day. On January 25, after loading coal, water, and victuals for the last time in Europe, the

Swatara got underway from Funchal for Washington. She carried five civilians in addition to Surratt, three of them "distressed seamen" embarked in Madeira for passage to the United States at the request of the resident U.S. consul.

On January 23, 1867, while Surratt was on the Atlantic in the *Swatara*, Secretary Seward wrote Consul Hale to say that "the President of the United States has been highly gratified by the considerate and friendly disposition which the Egyptian government has manifested in permitting and aiding the arrest and delivery of John H. Surratt, who is charged as an accomplice in the assassination of the late President Abraham Lincoln." As an expression of national gratitude, a portrait of Lincoln was presented to the pasha in due course. His highness was pleased to learn of all this, but one wonders what Egyptian officials made of the framed engraving of an unfamiliar seamed, sad face with dark hair and heavy-lidded eyes.

In Washington on the last day of January, Johnson and Welles talked about Surratt during a private meeting. "The President remarked," Welles wrote that evening in his diary, that

> no good could result from any communication with Surratt, and that the more reckless Radicals, if they could have access to him, would be ready to tamper with and suborn him. The man's life was at stake, he was desperate and resentful. Such a person and in such a condition might, if approached, make almost any statement. He, therefore, thought [Surratt] should not be allowed to communicate with others, nor should unauthorized persons be permitted to see him.

Welles agreed. Surratt was to be held incommunicado as long as possible.

The two might have had Toledo, Ohio's Representative James Ashley in mind when speaking about "reckless Radicals." Ashley, one of the House of Representatives' committed abolitionists, had been a key player in getting passage of the Thirteenth Amendment to the Constitution outlawing slavery passed in Congress while Lincoln was alive. (The amendment was ratified that December.) He had graduated from that to leadership of the campaign to impeach Johnson. On January 7 Ashley introduced a resolution, one of three submitted and the one chosen for action, to impeach Andrew Johnson, whom he styled "Vice-president and acting President of the United States." The high crimes and misdemeanors alleged included interference in elections and corruption in the use of the appointing, pardoning, and veto powers and in the disposal of public property.

Ashley's resolution passed 107 to 38, with 45 abstentions. With this on his plate Johnson didn't need any complications from whatever Surratt might say to an unfriendly ear.

Speaking to the House of Representatives several weeks after Johnson and Welles had this meeting of their minds, Ashley delivered a speech describing the president as a "moral incubus," guilty of complicity in Lincoln's assassination. Ashley's search for proof would lead him down dark passages.

Aboard the *Swatara* such hermetic isolation was possible, but once the prisoner was brought ashore it would not be. (In this instance, at least, Johnson proved not to be paranoid. Carmen Cumming says in *Devil's Game* that Surratt was later approached in prison several times by different people—among them agents of the irrepressible scamster Charles Dunham, locked in a cell not far away—soliciting his testimony implicating Johnson in Lincoln's murder in exchange for pardon. Surratt reportedly declined, confident that he would not be convicted.)

The early winter crossing was through remarkably good weather, allowing the *Swatara* to stay under sail, pushed along by the prevailing easterlies through mid-ocean while burning only a few hundred pounds of coal each day. The ship arrived in Hampton Roads, Virginia, on February 16 and was at the mouth of the Potomac River by three o'clock the next afternoon.

Monday, February 18, was a pleasant day on the Potomac, clear and 40 degrees in the afternoon, although a large and brilliant halo around the moon later that night promised a change to come. When the *Swatara* steamed past Mount Vernon on her port side, Jeffers had the ship's bell tolled and the flag lowered to half staff, the usual passing salute honoring the memory of President George Washington. When at 4:15 PM the ship finally dropped anchor in three fathoms of water off the Washington Navy Yard, Surratt had been below in solitary confinement and in chains for sixty days.

Nine weeks later, in a petition to the court for a speedy trial that would be ignored, Surratt's counsel wrote that

in the month of October [really November; the three petitioners erred] last he was arrested in Egypt and placed on board of an armed vessel of the United States, and from that time forth was kept in close confinement; heavily ironed; allowed only a brief time occasionally to breath the fresh air; wholly excluded from all intercourse with any human being but those who were employed to administer to his absolute needs; without change of external raiment, obliged to wear the very dress in which he was arrested, and thus kept in prison until the month of February.

That said, counsel concluded, "He has no complaint to make of the severity of his confinement on board ship where he was treated with as much levity [?] as the officer in command deemed consistent with his duty, and where he was not subjected to any indignity or personal injury." Had he known of it, Captain Jeffers would have been pleased by this unsolicited confirmation that his orders to the *Swatara*'s crew had been obeyed so scrupulously.

Ocean passage over, Surratt's delivery into custody in Washington went much more quickly and easily than feared initially. The winter of 1866–67 along the eastern seaboard was a frigid one. Well through January pack ice closed many Chesapeake Bay ports. Baltimore at the head of the bay was closed by ice, as were the ports of Annapolis, Georgetown, Washington, and Alexandria, and so too were the small put-ins on both banks of the Potomac for forty miles south of the capital.[13]

Such winters were unusual, but not unheard of. The harsh winter of 1866–67 wasn't unprecedented. Eleven years earlier, in 1855–56, the upper Chesapeake Bay had also been frozen hard. That winter steam packet companies operating from Baltimore hired tugs to break through the ice so that they could move their ships from place to place. Both years were moderate El Niño years, a warming of the eastern Pacific Ocean's surface temperature that manifests itself in a distinctive weather pattern over North America, often including nasty weather on the East Coast of the United States. It's possible that El Niño's perturbations caused the icing on the bay.

Hampton Roads, at the bottom of the bay, however, was actually ice free and open during the last week of January 1867, when the subject of Surratt's return came up in the cabinet, and Johnson, Seward, Stanton, and Welles agreed that the *Swatara* would be held in the roadstead incommunicado with the shore until she could pass to Washington.

On February 18, some eight weeks out of Alexandria, the *Swatara* dropped anchor in the Potomac off the Washington Navy Yard. When the ship was reported in the stream, Secretary Welles issued clear instructions to the yard commandant:

> You [Commo. William Radford] will direct the *Swatara* to anchor in the stream, off the yard; and you will permit no one to go aboard or

Bench warrant for Surratt's arrest issued on February 19, 1867. (National Archives)

hold communication with the vessel without a written permit from the Department. Put a sufficient guard on the wharf to enforce this order.

You will also direct the officers and men of the *Swatara* to give no information concerning the prisoner, his conduct, or conversation during the voyage, or upon any other matter pertaining to him.

The next day Surratt was delivered in manacles to Acting U.S. Marshal David Gooding, then handed over to the warden of the Washington County jail, Thomas Brown, who would be his keeper in the months to come. As luck had it, Midshipman Chenery had the deck watch on the *Swatara* that afternoon, too. "At 4:40," he wrote, "delivered the state prisoner John H. Surratt to D. S. Gooding, U.S. Marshal, by order of the Navy Department. Weather overcast & cool. Wind light at ENE. Sea smooth."

A drawing of the prisoner turnover from the navy to civil authority appeared as an engraving in *Harper's Weekly* March 9, 1867. In artist Andrew McCallum's sketch, Surratt, hands chained, is just stepping from the *Swatara*'s cutter into a crowd of forty or fifty people standing on the pier. Behind the assembled observers rises one end of the yard's three-hundred-foot-long, seventy-foot-high western shiphouse, a Washington landmark since its construction in the 1820s. To the right of the image stands a small mountain of stacked solid shot, a reminder of the war. Everyone in the scene looks appropriately serious, as if aware there is an artist present recording the moment. Remarkably, the reception party on shore includes three Sioux in feathered headdresses. (An accompanying text explained that the three were members of a tribal delegation visiting the city who had been given permission to observe the historic event. The United States was then midway through losing its war with Chief Red Cloud's Oglala Sioux in the Montana Territory, and presumably this impromptu civics lesson played some part in Washington's negotiating strategy with the tribe.)

The turnover of the prisoner to Marshal Gooding formally marked the transfer of custody from the federal executive to the Supreme Court of the District of Columbia and from Navy to civilian control. Once in Gooding's hands Surratt would never again fall under military incarceration or military judgment.

Warden Brown had just finished construction of three special "iron clad" cells in his jail for the use of "murderers and desperate characters," and Surratt was locked in one of these escape-proof vaults, into which no one but his counsel and his guards were to be admitted, the same strict regime under which the eight had been jailed in the penitentiary at the Arsenal.[14] At least that was the original plan. In fact, a number of prospective witnesses were practically chivied into his cell to see Surratt. General interest in observing the prisoner was so high before the trial that defense counsel petitioned the court to control such informal visitations "because there were certain members of Congress prowling around the jail desirous to see the prisoner for bad purposes, and the counsel did not wish them or other persons who desired to see him for bad purposes go there."

In January, while the *Swatara,* Surratt aboard, was still steaming home, the House of Representatives turned its attention to the prisoner's remarkable flight. The trigger seems to have been Executive Documents No. 9 and No. 25, "messages" from President Johnson dated December 10, 1866, and January 3, 1867, which responded to a request from the House of Representatives for documents "relating to the discovery and arrest of John H. Surratt." In these two submissions Johnson forwarded to the House a total of fifty-six letters about Surratt, all of them exchanged between officials in Washington, U.S. diplomats abroad, or consuls and the secretary of state from September 1865 to December 1866 as the hunt drew slowly toward its conclusion. It says something about the immutability of Washington practices that a complete copy of Executive Document No. 9 appeared in the *New York Times* on December 11 under the headline "Full Official History of the Affair." Subheads cascaded down the column, ticking off the exciting phases of the hunt for Surratt.

The House of Representatives' Judiciary Committee then conducted an investigation of the pursuit and arrest and published its findings on March 2 in Report No. 33 of the Thirty-ninth Congress, second session. Because the same nine congressmen, eight of them Republicans, had been since the New Year involved in considering the impeachment of the president, the Surratt investigation necessarily was done in the margins of the greater issue. The next day the two-year-old Thirty-ninth Congress gave way to the Fortieth, and it fell to this new group of men representing twenty-seven states and eight territories to conclude both matters.

As part of its investigation of the pursuit of Surratt the Judiciary Committee interviewed a mixed bag of nine sworn witnesses during late January and February before drawing its conclusions and publishing its report. The nine included Secretary Seward (twice); Secretary Stanton (three times); William Hunter, the second assistant secretary of state; Brigadier General Holt, judge advocate general of the War Department; Robert Chew, chief clerk of the State Department; Captain Jeffers of the *Swatara*; L. J. McMillan, the RMS *Peruvian*'s doctor and the original whistle blower; U.S. Marshal David Gooding; and Father B. F. Wiget, who had testified briefly as a character witness at Mary Surratt's trial.

Predictably, the committee's finished report was highly critical of the executive branch. The committee (at least its majority Republicans, led by Chairman James Wilson of Iowa) loathed the president and approved of nothing he was doing or had done. Not long thereafter Wilson was appointed to be one of the House of Representatives' impeachment managers, the several members responsible for taking the charges to the Senate for adjudication. If anyone on the committee defended the administration's conduct of the hunt for Surratt during its hearings, it is possible that Congressman Sydenham Ancona, Democrat of Pennsylvania, did; he was the only one to find fault with the committee's concurrent impeachment hearings, and Ancona's sympathy for Johnson might have spilled over into this detail.

The committee dutifully reported to the House it had concluded that "due diligence in the arrest of John H. Surratt was not exercised by the Executive Department of the government," after finding first that "the testimony of the Secretary of State, the Secretary of War, and others . . . tending to justify the acts of the government in the premises, does not, in the opinion of your committee, excuse the great delay in arresting a person charged with complicity in the assassination of the late President Abraham Lincoln."

Surratt's passage from North America to Europe and from one place to another on the Continent seemed so inexplicably swift and effortless that suspicions arose in Washington he had assistance from unknown persons abroad. In January 1867, as part of the administration's preparations for Surratt's arrival and trial, George Sharpe, a former brevet brigadier general, was sent by the secretary of state to Europe to investigate the possibility that as-yet-unidentified Americans had been involved in the assassination.

Sharpe began his investigation in England but got nowhere with his inquiries there. Surratt appeared to have traveled to London on September 30, soon after he arrived in England, but there was no evidence of his meeting with "rebels known to be in London at that time." No evidence of anything, really, despite the fact that Sharpe claimed to have tracked down Surratt's London cab driver ("an old man, prostrated by serious and lingering disease . . . and incapacitated from recalling incidents to promote the inquiries") and to have confirmed the identity of the five "John Watsons" of Edinburgh, men whose name Surratt's current alias shared, one of whom had coincidently applied for a passport in October 1865 while Surratt was in London.

Sharpe next examined how Surratt had entered the Papal States. In Rome Sharpe managed to recover Surratt's original passport from the Ministry of War and discovered that it had been issued in Canada and held an American visa as well as a free-of-charge entry permit to the Papal States issued by the papal nuncio in Paris, Monseignor Flavio Chigi. Sharpe pursued this lead, noting that

inquiries were made at his [Chigi's]office to ascertain under what circumstances [the visa] had been procured.

These steps, although taken with great care, and after permission for the interview had been asked, were met with rudeness and discourtesy on the part of the nuncio himself and his secretary; but I was subsequently informed, through our legation in Paris, that the nuncio stated his visé had been obtained, not through any letter or special recommendation, but upon the personal presentation of the passport by Surratt, whom the official remembers to have seen, and upon the former's statement that he was going to Rome for the purpose of enlistment.

Sharpe's uncooperative interlocutor in Paris sprang from an ancient and powerful Italian family from Siena, one that counted a pope (Alexander VII) among three earlier churchmen also named Flavio Chigi. Midway through his ten years at the nunciature and given his roots, it's not surprising that Chigi viewed Sharpe's attempt at interrogation as an unwelcome interruption to the more important business of his office.

Other than establishing the route by which Surratt traveled from England to the Papal States (overland, rather than by sea), Sharpe's six-month investigation led to one conclusion: There was no evidence in Europe that among the former citizens of the United States living there were any "loathsome instigators" of the great crime against Lincoln.[15]

6

"SEDUCED BY THE INSTIGATION OF THE DEVIL"

On February 4, 1867, two weeks to the day before the USS *Swatara* with its infamous passenger on board anchored in the Potomac River abeam the Washington Navy Yard, Surratt's indictment on four counts in connection with the murder of Abraham Lincoln emerged from the grand jury. Months later, on July 26, defense counsel summarized the indictment, noting that "the first count in the indictment was against Surratt for having killed with his own hand; the second against Surratt and Booth for having killed; and the third and fourth against all of them for having killed." In the records of the Supreme Court of the District of Columbia, Surratt's 1867 trial is Criminal Docket No. 4,731.

Looking back, Surratt's grand jury seems to have been unduly generous. The indictment of President Lincoln's accused assassins had included only a single charge—"combining, confederating, and conspiring to kill and murder" Lincoln, Johnson, Seward, and Grant, and then murdering Lincoln, assaulting Seward, and lying in wait with intent to kill Johnson and Grant—not four charges, and only a single specification.

In the ritual language of an eighteenth- or nineteenth-century indictment, "the jurors of the United States of America for the County of Washington" charged first that John H. Surratt, "not having the fear of God before his eyes but being moved and seduced by the instigation of the devil . . . did kill and murder" Abraham Lincoln. He did this, in the words of the text, by "discharging and setting off" a pistol against the "left and posterior side" of Lincoln's head. Its leaden bullet then caused "one mortal wound of the depth of six inches and of the breadth of half an inch, from which said Abraham Lincoln first languished living and then died."

In fact, this is the murder that John Wilkes Booth committed in sight of hundreds of witnesses at Ford's New Theatre, and so a second count in the same language charged Booth with the actual attack on Lincoln but added that Surratt was present there, "aiding, helping, and abetting, comforting, assisting and maintaining" Booth to commit the crime. The third count of the indictment charged Surratt together with the four condemned and executed at the Arsenal by name, and with unnamed "others to the jurors unknown," with being "present, aiding, helping, and abetting, comforting, assisting and maintaining the said John Wilkes Booth, the said felony and murder aforesaid, in manner and form aforesaid, to do and commit."

The last count said the same all over again, adding the phrase "wicked and unlawful conspiracy" and so enlarging the offense charged. Assistant District Attorney Nathaniel Wilson's opening for the prosecution described Surratt's role in the assassination of Lincoln, in the simultaneous attack on Seward, and in the aborted one on Johnson in a more emotional way. Surratt, Wilson said, "was the contriver of that villainy . . . the butchery that ensued was the ripe result of a long premeditated plot, in which [Surratt] was the chief conspirator."

The murder weapon, "then and there charged with gunpowder and one leaden bullet," is mentioned in every count of the indictment. Throughout the indictment, regardless in whose hand it is described as being, Booth's derringer is referred to as "a certain pistol of the value of ten dollars." This is descriptive, not dismissive; Booth's weapon was no Saturday night special. Henry Deringer's fine muzzle-loading pocket pistols, the gentleman's self-defense weapon of choice, sold for twenty to twenty-five dollars the pair during the period. In the 1860s a plain one such as Booth's, of high mechanical quality but without any precious metal decoration, could certainly be had for half that amount or less.

Later Joseph Bradley Sr., the lead defense counsel, made much of the fact that Surratt was charged with the murder and conspiracy to murder Lincoln, the man, with the "well-known, common law offense of killing," not explicitly with assassination of the president of the United States in time of war. He argued, therefore, that no special rules applied in this case: One murder was the same as the next. Government counsel, of course, rejected that. Edwards Pierrepont, the ex officio lead prosecution attorney, told the jury, "It is a far more heinous crime to conspire against the Government of the United States and to murder its President for the purpose of bringing anarchy and confusion on the land than it is to murder a single individual."

On some level he may have been correct, but Bradley was right, too. Surratt's indictment didn't describe the slain Lincoln as president and commander in chief of the Army and Navy, as had the charge against the eight. The distinction wasn't trivial. Under law it was possible to be found an accessory in an ordinary murder, but in the case of regicide (or, here, the murder of the president) Pierrepont pointed out that English common law held this crime was so heinous that *all* participants were principals and tried to extend this concept to the republican United States as well.

The two trials, that of the eight in the Arsenal in 1865 and Surratt's almost exactly two years later in Washington City's Supreme Court, were alike in many important respects. The same crime was at the core of both trials, both necessarily shared many witnesses, and both attracted huge crowds of observers. Their outcomes, however, were stunningly different.

Inevitably the shade of Mary Surratt hovered over her son's trial, occasionally summoned to appear by counsel for one or the other side, other times present there unbidden. She was "one of the ghosts brought before the trial," Pierrepont said poetically while inexplicably seeing double or counting by twos, "trailing their calico dresses and making them rustle over the chairs." (The phrase was vintage Pierrepont; he got the imagery exactly right, but the substance all wrong.) Later, in the first few sentences of the defense's opening statement on July 6, Bradley explicitly paired Surratt's defense to that of his late mother's. "We have at last arrived at the stage of this case," he said, "when an opportunity is afforded to the prisoner to say something by way of defense, not only of his own character, his own reputation, of his life and of his honor, but also, as it shall arise incidentally in the discussion of the evidence before you, something to vindicate the pure fame of his departed mother."

Later still, District Attorney Edward Carrington called Mary forth out of the morning rain on July 29 during the second day of his closing statement. (There would be two such statements by the prosecution, Carrington's and an even longer one by Pierrepont.) "He regretted," Carrington said piously to the jury while putting Mary Surratt in nasty company, "that an American tribunal ever found it necessary to find a woman guilty of murder, but when the daughter of Herodius murdered John the Baptist she deserved hanging; when Lucretia Borgia shed blood she deserved hanging, and when Mary E. Surratt compassed this murder of President Lincoln, and permitted her house to become the headquarters of the conspirators, public safety demanded that she should be condemned when found guilty."

During the defense's summation on August 1, attorney Richard Merrick conjured her up in response. "And now will the prosecution try the dead as well as the living?" he asked rhetorically. Reminding the jury of the trial two years ago and of the ongoing debate about her execution in the face of a recommendation for clemency, Merrick continued dramatically:

> A priest [Reverend Jacob Walter] was put upon the stand, and he said he gave Mrs. Surratt the consolation of religion. He was not permitted to say what Mrs. Surratt said. Tottering to the scaffold between two priests, with the world behind her and eternity before her, and her load of guilt laid at the feet of her Savior, why was not her declaration [of innocence] admitted? Did they fear she would lie? No! But hardness of heart. Reckless of guilt and indifferent of justice, they would not let her voice be heard. But still it falls upon their ears; that voice of the woman in a nameless grave, whose very body has been refused to a pleading daughter.

The next day Surratt's mother was metaphorically exhumed again, this time by Joseph Bradley Sr. following a brief tirade about John Wilkes Booth's "diary." The so-called diary had been found on Booth's body after death. It was, in fact, a pocket appointment book that Booth had pressed into use in mid-April 1865, during the height of the pursuit, to record a last defense of his character and motives. In a few dozen sentences he managed to write "I" forty times. That and text fragments ("Until today nothing was ever thought. . . . For six months we had worked to capture") made it easy for readers so inclined to believe Booth had acted alone and impulsively. The diary had not been introduced into evidence during the Arsenal trial, and the "suppression" of this text was widely believed to have proved that Mary Surratt was railroaded into her grave.

"A woman—," Bradley said after making just that accusation, "not a man; not a hard vigorous nature; not a wild, reckless man, not a foe to society; but a pious mother; a loving woman, kind and gentle . . . who had gathered around her a circle of friends who loved and respected her; who had two orphan sons."

Earlier, defense counsel had referred to Mary Surratt in even more emotional terms, as a "murdered" woman and even as a "butchered" one, prompting Carrington's emphatic rejection. No slouch he in the business of over-the-top appeals to the jury. Despite his repeated avowals of "love of woman," there is a streak of misogyny that rises to the surface occasionally in Carrington's prose. "There is no man who has a heart more capable for love of woman than myself," he averred. "But when she unsexes herself, when she conceives, when she encourages, when she urges on, and is instrumental in committing, the crime of murder, she places herself beyond the pale of protection." Carrington was speaking of Mary Surratt, but he was describing Lady Macbeth.

All the while, Mary's earthly remains lay in her ersatz coffin in the ground inside the walls encompassing Greenleaf Point, some twenty city blocks south of the courtroom.

Both sides had good tactical reasons to allude to the previous trial. The prosecution wanted to bind Surratt as closely as possible to the murder of Lincoln, to the despised assassin Booth—whose guilt no one doubted—and to Booth's eight accomplices, every one of whom had famously been found guilty. In mid-July, during an attorneys' debate before Judge George Fisher on the admissibility of certain evidence, District Attorney Carrington offered his capsule view of both trials, the finished one and the one still underway. He told the court, "All who were condemned by the military commission met a deserved murderer's death. The prosecution would show the country that Surratt was the armor-bearer of Booth, a man who was false to his country, false to his government, and who deserted his mother, and by flight had admitted his guilt."

Much later the New York Times, in characterizing the government's strategy, noted that "the energy of the prosecution was directed to revive the terrible national excitement that hung about the former trial, and to borrow the grand scenery of that tragedy to decorate their smaller stage." For its part, the defense sought to benefit from growing public uncertainty about the quality of justice dispensed by the military commission, an uncertainty sharpened barely one year earlier by the Supreme Court's decision in Ex parte Mulligan (71 U.S. 2, 1866).

In that case the court found a military commission sitting in Indiana had no jurisdiction to try a civilian, one Lambden Milligan, "upon any charges whatever" because during the war "in Indiana the Federal authority was always unopposed, and its courts always open to hear criminal accusations and redress grievances; and no usage of war could sanction a military trial there for any offence whatever of a citizen in civil life, in nowise connected with the military service." This was precisely the argument that Reverdy Johnson had made unsuccessfully at Mary's trial. The court's opinion, written by Justice David Davis of Illinois, granted that circumstances could require that habeas corpus be suspended and martial law imposed but nothing more. To many in 1867 even a quick reading of *Ex parte Mulligan* said that the Arsenal trial had been a miscarriage of justice.

A new controversy that suddenly flared up in August, as Surratt's trial moved toward its own conclusion, lent more weight to the suspicion that Mary Surratt had been wrongly convicted and then hustled into her grave—and that the same fate threatened her son. On June 30, 1865, five of the nine commissioners sitting in judgment had recommended clemency in her case. Whether or not Johnson ever saw their recommendation, or saw it in time to consider it, became the subject of a vicious political battle two years later between the president and his increasingly embittered opponents in Congress and the Department of War. Inevitably counsel on both sides in Surratt's trial found ammunition in the dispute then churning Washington.

Joseph Holt, the judge advocate general of the War Department, aware of the need in 1865 to justify a military commission in lieu of a criminal trial in open court, had ensured that the assassinated president was identified in the indictment as "the commander in chief" and the site of the crime was described as "within the Military Department of Washington and within the fortified and entrenched lines thereof." His intent was to give an unmistakably military character to the crimes committed, so that a tribunal rather than a court would be the logical forum for trial.

The resulting trial was something of a hybrid. The Arsenal trial was not a court-martial, although an observer could easily have confused it for one. Its defendants were not in uniformed service. They were, however, tried on the grounds of an army installation thick with armed men and judged by combat veterans in uniform for violation not of the criminal code but of the laws of war.

Surratt's trial was very different. The courthouse in which Surratt's fate was decided stood, instead, in the heart of the city, and his was a criminal trial conducted under common-law procedures. All its principal figures were civilians. The court, the Supreme Court for the District of Columbia, was a new one, established only two years earlier after the District's existing circuit and district courts had been abolished by Congress suspicious of their judges' loyalty to the Union. Under its rules, any of the new court's four judges could sit alone as a criminal court. Although relatively new, the court was the clear, lineal descendant of the District of Columbia's court system, not some improvised tribunal based on an Army general order about the laws of war.

The *New York Times*'s correspondent set the scene of Surratt's trial for his newspaper's largely Yankee readership, an audience still inclined, approaching two years after the last shots in the great war were fired, to view its national capital as an irredeemably southern city populated by men of doubtful loyalty to the Union. Later Edwards Pierrepont tried to get some leverage from this sentiment. "A great many men from interested motives, some from political motives, and some possibly from patriotic motives, are very anxious to remove this capital from its present place," he warned the jury, hoping to manipulate their deliberations. "They say it does not belong here; that the people are not in sympathy and in harmony with this great government; that it is full of people who hate the government, and therefore they would like to see it removed. They would like any excuse in order to get it removed." He was right; there was talk in some circles of relocating the capital to the American heartland, west "on the other side of the mountains."

"At the head of Four-and-a-Half Street, in this city," the *Times* man wrote,

> surrounded by a dilapidated park, in which sickly, half-grown maple saplings struggle for life, with their roots tangled and smothered in a rank growth of matted clover and dog-weed, stands a building remarkable in appearance for its straggling style of architecture. It bears every indication of Southern energy and progress, for its foundation is imposing, and promises more than the building itself realizes, and the gravel composition which covers the bricks has disappeared from the outer walls in many places, and the bricks protrude, giving the entire structure an air of cheap and shabby pretension. It is called City Hall, and is known to the country at large as the building . . . where JOHN HARRISON SURRATT, the last of the assassination conspirators, is on trial.

Anthony Trollope at his best could not have been any more dismissive.

Every morning Surratt was marched south three city blocks from the Washington Jail at Fourth Street and G Street, past the neighboring hospital, to the courtroom in City Hall. He was escorted there and back each evening by Marshal Gooding and probably one or more of the guards among the eight on Warden Brown's small staff. The jail, a three-story Gothic revival building with a faintly bluish cast (the tint was a well-intentioned effort to make cheap scored plaster over brick look like expensive granite, and the reason for the building's nickname, the "Blue Jug"), was just twenty-five years old when Surratt was locked inside. Those had been hard years. Talk of replacing the building began in the mid-1850s, but it stood on the northeast corner of Judiciary Square, surrounded by an eighteen- to twenty-foot brick wall, chronically overcrowded—the inmate population peaked at 240—until 1874. In 1864, three years before Surratt's incarceration, the architect of the Capitol identified a number of remedial construction projects to correct the jail's security, sanitary, and other deficiencies, but none appears to have been implemented before Surratt moved into his cell on the second floor. Once inside, he shared the place with a mixed bag of criminals, debtors, and mental cases.

Sister Anna came to see her brother in jail, the first time on February 20 for more than an hour with Merrick and a guard watching, again the next day, and probably other times as well. He had thought her dead. The *Baltimore Sun* on the twenty-first reported about their reunion: "Both sister and brother were much affected, and gave way to tears. The conversation was carried on between them in low tones, and principally related to personal matters. No allusion whatever was made to the exciting affairs of the spring of 1865 [Lincoln's murder and the trial of the eight], not to the arrest of the accused; and no questions were asked as to his wanderings."

Compared to confinement in the USS *Swatara* conditions in the Blue Jug must have quickly seemed baronial, despite Warden Brown's advertised escape-proof, metal-sided cells. Perhaps because Surratt told Brown he intended to cause no trouble the warden permitted Surratt to smoke a pipe and to exercise regularly in the main corridor of the jail's second floor. At least one enterprising reporter was granted permission to interview Surratt, and to his surprise he found his subject ensconced comfortably in the watchman's shanty in the jail yard, reading peacefully in a chair by an open window.

By the time Surratt's case came to court President Johnson had less reason to fear that the young defendant was going to be bent by Radical Republicans into a weapon against him than he once had. If Surratt had not been suborned during the four months since he was first sent into the Blue Jug, it was improbable that he would be now. This danger apparently past, Surratt seemingly receded in Johnson's mind. Elsewhere in Washington, however, the late Mary Surratt's second son was still a headliner.

Surratt's trial was summer in the city's great free attraction. Judge George Fisher, one of the District of Columbia's three Supreme Court associate justices, presided over a courtroom in City Hall's eastern wing, room 222, that could contain snugly as many as three hundred people and apparently often did. Even

A portion of Johnson's 1862, 1:26,000-scale "Georgetown & the City of Washington" map showing the capital's center as Surratt would have known it early in the Civil War. The arrows mark (*top to bottom*) the Blue Jug, City Hall, the western half of Washington Navy Yard, and the penitentiary at the Arsenal. (New York, Johnson & Ward, Library of Congress)

Center city Washington from Capitol Hill, looking northwest, ca. 1863. The Washington County Jail is the light-colored three-story building at the center top of this detail. On the master photograph several other buildings can be identified, including Aldrich's flour, grain, and feed warehouse, the Shamokin and Lykins wood and coal yard, and Boyle's door, sash, and blind millworks. (Library of Congress)

before Surratt, Fisher's courtroom, an "oblong, plain, rather dingy-looking apartment," enjoyed a certain notoriety on the Washington scene. During the past ten years Washington's residents had become accustomed to dropping in at the court for prime, no-cost entertainment.

In mid-1856 the same courtroom with Thomas Crawford, judge of the Criminal Court of the District of Columbia, on the bench was the venue of the trials of Congressman Philemon Herbert, Democrat of California, who in early May that year had shot to death a waiter at Willard's Hotel for the affront of failing to serve him breakfast after hours. The midmorning killing was the climax of a raucous scene that began with Herbert calling the waiter, Thomas Keating, "a damned Irish son of a bitch" and progressed through a violent pas de deux during which Herbert and Keating circled a dining room table hurling furniture, dishes, and oaths at each other while Dutch ambassador Dubois and other witnesses crouching near the floor watched in horror. Herbert's subsequent acquittal on a charge of manslaughter—his first trial on a murder charge ended in a hung jury with seven of twelve voting for acquittal; the second freed him—stunned Washington's Hibernians. Herbert's release moved fifty-seven "Irishmen of Washington City" to publish a long address "to the Citizens of the United States" bewailing this proof of American anti-Irish, anti-Catholic prejudice. In their address the Hibernians took the opportunity in passing to criticize the anemic prosecutorial zeal of the U.S. district attorney in the case, Phillip Barton Key, whose own fate three years later proved that what went around came around, even in the nineteenth century.[1]

In 1859 Crawford's courtroom became the site of the trial of New York congressman Dan Sickles, in the dock for the sensational murder of the same Barton Key, his wife Teresa's late lover. Sickles's subsequent acquittal of murder charges, for a pistol shot killing observed by half a dozen or more pedestrians on the city's streets, was the first successful insanity defense in a U.S. court.* In 1882 President James Garfield's assassin, Charles Guiteau, was tried and condemned in the same room, proving that the insanity defense was no sure thing, not even in room 222.

Privileged observers at the Surratt trial, including ladies and those with some special status or holding a pass from the judge, had seats inside the bar, the wooden railing that divided the room. Commoners sat on the other side

---

*   The eight lawyers on Sickle's defense team included Edwin Stanton, who two years later joined Lincoln's cabinet.

Daniel Edgar Sickles (1819–1914) was one of the great American rogues of the second half of the nineteenth century. By turns, and beginning at a young age, he was a lawyer, a successful New York City Tammany politician, diplomat in Europe, U.S. congressman, friend of presidents, crypto-Republican and major general of Union volunteers during the Civil War (on July 2, 1863, he famously misdeployed his 3rd Corps at Gettysburg ahead of line and nearly caused a disaster), military governor of South Carolina, and throughout a model for congenital marital infidelity.

For a man of such choleric temper and bad habits, Sickles had a remarkably long life. He died at age ninety-five, having spent the last fifty years on only one leg, the left. His right one had been lost to a cannonball at Gettysburg. (The amputated limb is enshrined in the National Museum of Health and Medicine in Washington, once the Army Medical Museum.)

Years later, in 1872, John Surratt married Mary Victorine Hunter, a second cousin of Francis Scott Key, the father of Barton Key, the man who had cuckolded Dan Sickles and died for that transgression in

of the division, farther away from the defendant, counsel, judge, and jury. Both classes of people often clustered in Judiciary Square outside of City Hall's door an hour or more before court opened waiting for admission. Once inside they sweltered so much on especially hot days that their palm-leaf fans failed them. On at least one occasion Fisher called a recess as an act of mercy to the densely packed multitude.

Some real celebrities came, some to testify and others only to observe. Among the former were General Grant, who testified about an inconsequential meeting with Jacob Thompson on the Mississippi in early 1863; Secretary Seward's son, who had bravely defended his injured father from Powell's attack; and Thaddeus Lincoln, the late president's younger son, who swore that someone who looked very much like Surratt twice tried to call on his father aboard a steamboat at City Point. The latter included Robert Lincoln (Lincoln's elder son) and Speaker of the House Schuyler Colfax, on his way to disgrace a few years later as Grant's first vice president. Underemployed senators and other congressmen occasionally dropped in, too, looking for distraction during Congress's long summer recess. At least one author joined the audience, possibly looking for material for her next book. Isaac Surratt was in the courtroom often, seated inside the bar next to his brother. Interestingly, sister Anna never appeared there, evidently unwilling to sit through another relative's trial on capital charges.

The *Times* had the measure of the less distinguished half of the crowd, from which, the newspaper wrote, rose "such an undertone of comment and expression as [leads one] to believe that he is in the house of the prisoner's friends. . . . These seats are monopolized by rank rebels and secessionists who got there partly out of curiosity doubtless, but chiefly to manifest sympathy and encouragement for the prisoner."

By the end of July spectators were massed in such numbers in the courtroom every day that they not only obstructed the progress of the trial but also "prevented, to some extent, the free flow of air throughout the room." To limit

---

February 1859, which suggests how remarkably small a place the nineteenth century was.

Barton was murdered long after his father's death in 1843, but even in life Francis Scott Key, the father of ten and a three-time U.S. district attorney himself, had troubles with members of his brood stepping in front of loaded and cocked pistols. Young son Daniel Key, then barely out of his teens, died in a duel at Bladensburg, Maryland, in 1836. Reportedly the fight grew from a quarrel he and another navy midshipman had over the speed of a steamship.

Sickles is the subject of a recent biography by Thomas Keneally, *America's Scoundrel: The Life of the Notorious Civil War General Dan Sickles* (New York: Doubleday, 2002).

Judge George Fisher. Lincoln appointed Fisher to a seat on the Supreme Court of the District of Columbia after the latter's failed reelection campaign for Congress in 1862. The climax of Fisher's years on the bench was the trial of John Harrison Surratt in 1867, during which he revealed clear bias against the defendant. (Library of Congress)

their number inside the bar, Judge Fisher withdrew most admission tickets on Saturday, July 27, and issued a smaller number of new ones.

Judge George Fisher owed his seat on the Supreme Court of the District of Columbia directly to President Lincoln, who appointed him to its bench in 1863 after Fisher failed the year before to be reelected to the House of Representatives from his home state, Delaware.* Fisher's performance through Surratt's trial led

---

* Delaware mirrored in microcosm Maryland's divided loyalties as the Civil War approached. Republicans were especially unpopular among the dwarf state's many farmers, whose strong southern sympathies were out of proportion to Delaware's relatively small slave population; fully half the state's blacks were freemen, not slaves. Not surprisingly, Lincoln ran third in Delaware in 1860; only Stephen Douglas got fewer votes than Lincoln's 3,815. Lincoln lost the state to a Democrat again in 1864.

Predictably, Delaware's 1862 midterm election was hard on both of the state's Democrats-turned-Republicans, William Cannon and George Fisher, despite a corps of twelve hundred Union army poll

some to believe that he was repaying an obligation to his late mentor, but it's at least possible that it was not remembered debts to the late president, or Fisher's friendship with Secretary of War Stanton, but the actions of Surratt's combative chief counsel, Joseph Bradley Sr., that provoked the judge into the appearance of bias if not its reality. Seemingly, the two just didn't like each other.

Fisher and Bradley waited only one day, until June 18, to begin poking at each other like urchins in a playground. It happened at the end of Bradley's cross-examination of Susan Johnson, the Surratts' new housemaid at the time of the assassination, just after her inventive testimony about seeing Surratt at the family's boardinghouse the night Lincoln was shot. The *Times* summarized their childish exchange:

> "The Court said the same answer had been given at least a dozen times."
>
> "Mr. Bradley said he wanted no reflections from the Court."
>
> "The Court said anyone of the dullest comprehension could have understood the answer."
>
> "Mr. Bradley said his comprehension was as sharp as that of the Court and he wanted no reflections."

On June 20 Bradley overheated again, once during a discussion about the recall of prosecution witnesses and later during the examination of William Cleaver, one of the prosecution's soiled witnesses. This time Bradley thuggishly threatened to teach Pierrepont some courtesy.

Push almost came to shove again two weeks later, on July 1, when Fisher and Bradley nearly got into a brawl after court adjourned for the day. According to the *Washington Evening* Star on July 2, bystanders had to pull the sputtering

---

watchers sent there to prevent Democratic chicanery. Cannon won his race for governor by 111 votes but suffered a miserably unproductive term and died in office in March 1865 having accomplished little else. Fisher expected an election squeaker and got one: He lost his only reelection race for U.S. representative by 37 votes.

Lincoln's consolation—he knew Fisher well; inter alia the two had cooperated closely on an unsuccessful cash compensation plan for the emancipation of Delaware's seventeen hundred slaves, a first step toward resettlement of the freedmen in Africa—was to appoint him a justice on the Supreme Court of the District of Columbia. But Fisher's salary of three thousand dollars a year fell short of his expectations, and he unsuccessfully sought one of three seats on the better-paying court of claims instead.

Fisher (1817–1899) spent seven years on the District of Columbia Supreme Court, from March 1863 to 1870, when he was appointed district attorney to replace Edward Carrington, Surratt's prosecutor. Fisher went on to serve as the federal government's chief prosecutor in the District for the next five years.

judge and senior defense counsel apart. Another account described the encounter as follows:

> Those who witnessed the difficulty say that harsh language was used, and that Mr. Bradley informed the judge that if he (Fisher) were not sick he would thrash him. Judge Fisher replied that he did not claim immunity from the threatened castigation on account of illness. The combatants were about to come to close quarters when Deputy Marshal Philipps placed himself between them, and endeavored to force the Judge into the Marshal's room . . . but before the door could be closed, Mr. Bradley made his appearance, and Judge Fisher turned and grappled with him. The parties were then separated again, and Judge Fisher was locked in the Marshal's room. . . . [He] was eventually induced to go to his home in Georgetown.

Had Fisher and Bradley come to fisticuffs, it is unlikely much damage would have been done to either combatant. Fisher was fifty, "portly," and feeling poorly during the trial. He had been absent from the bench two days during jury selection in June and looked so wan during the first few days of July that the *Washington Evening Star* commented on his peaked appearance in its accounts of the trial on July 1 and 2. Fisher was under doctor's orders not to overwork and occasionally recessed court for the day early citing his health in explanation. Bradley, then sixty-five, was described as "fleshy," a "full-faced, side-whiskered, double-chinned, rotund man," an unpromising form for a successful corridor grappler, despite all his fulminating.

Fisher and Bradley's spat came to its climax just after the end of the trial, when the judge accused the lawyer of challenging him to a duel on August 10. Reportedly Bradley had followed Fisher onto a streetcar and handed the judge a letter containing the challenge. Offering or accepting such challenges had been illegal in the District of Columbia since 1839, and in so doing—if he actually did, there's some confusion about what really happened—Bradley exposed himself to five years in prison for the crime of "incitement." (Although dueling was illegal in the District of Columbia and in many states after 1840, the law was not enforced in Maryland. Until well past midcentury the District of Columbia's offended gentlemen could retire to a semiofficial dueling ground in a ravine near Bladensburg, where their honor could be satisfied by shooting at one another.)

To someone gaming the sides, Surratt's defense team would have appeared less capable than did his mother's because it lacked anyone with Senator Reverdy Johnson's candlepower, but that was misleading. Bradley, the son of President Washington's postmaster general, had more than forty years' experience in the practice of law in Washington City when he took Surratt's case, fifteen more than did Judge Fisher, and the pushy self-assurance to match.* One commentator described him as "the bully of the courthouse," a characterization that would be substantiated later. Moreover, Bradley was deeply engaged in Surratt's defense, something that Johnson never was on behalf of his client.

Surratt's defense team also included Joseph Bradley Jr. (age thirty-six, Bradley Sr.'s second son) and another midcareer attorney, Richard Merrick. Both were very much in the older man's shadow until the defense's closing argument during the first week of August, when Merrick gave that address.

War correspondent George Townsend unkindly described him as "good looking Merrick . . . with his affected Virginia dialect, three-fourth negro, one-fourth boarding school," making him out to be at once effete and mongrel. Townsend's grotesque slur may have had its roots in simple prejudice. Merrick was Catholic, like his client, and was suspected for it. (The Bradleys were Episcopalians.) That said, Merrick held remarkably ecumenical views, as he revealed later. "My views and my feelings on this subject may be peculiar," he told the court, "but they are my own. I believe that churches differ more in form than in substance, and that the true conscientious Christian in one Church

---

* Bradley's death in April 1887, at eighty-five and after sixty years lawyering in Washington, prompted an appropriately long and generally admiring obituary in the *Washington Post* on April 4, but its author couldn't resist reminding his readers that at age eighty Bradley had married a former client, one Mary Harris, whom he had defended in a sensational murder case in July 1865 when she was nineteen. Bradley's commitment to Harris's defense prevented him from playing any part in the Arsenal trial. His dedication to Harris, forty-four years his junior, paid off: The jury took just five minutes to find his client not guilty.

Harris's victim was her fiancé, one Adoniram J. Burroughs. "Wishing to break off with Miss Harris," the *Post* reported, "he set a trap for her and had her decoyed to a house in Chicago, which proved to be a disreputable resort. . . . She learned the whole plot and his motive for getting rid of her, and then came on to Washington. One day she quietly went to the Treasury Department . . . near the room where he was employed. When he came out of the room, she shot him dead."

"She was acquitted on the ground that the killing was the result of paroxysmal [temporary] insanity. After her acquittal she was in the asylum from time to time for several years. Mr. Bradley kept up his interest in her, and finally to the surprise of all his friends . . . he married her." The most impetuous act in a life and career marked by many of them.

A contemporary account of Harris's crime and trial is in James E. Clephane, *Official Report of the Trial of Mary Harris . . . for the Murder of Adoniram J. Burroughs . . . July 3, 1865* (Washington, D.C.: W. H & O. H. Morrison, 1865). A more recent retelling is in Michael A. Bellesiles, ed., *Lethal Imaginations: Violence and Brutality in American History* (New York: New York University Press, 1999).

serves his God if his conviction be there, as faithfully as he does in any other
... [of] these various churches. They are but the different branches of one great
stream, whose source is in Calvary, at the foot of the Cross."

None of the three had been involved in the trial of the eight in 1865. Although
invited, Bradley Sr. had declined to team with Frederick Stone in David Herold's
defense just as Merrick had passed up the chance to join Stone and Brig. Gen.
Thomas Ewing in Samuel Mudd's defense.

The three put forth an energetic defense of Surratt on a pro bono basis,
"professional charity" as Merrick described it. Bradley Sr. knew, he later said
in court, when he accepted the case that the Surratts were not able to pay
for his team's services or even reimburse its expenses. On June 17 Bradley
Sr. petitioned the court, telling Judge Fisher that Surratt "has exhausted all
his means," including contributions from friends, and asking that the cost
of bringing defense witnesses to Washington be borne by the United States.
Fisher agreed. Even so, Surratt's impoverishment might have had a real impact
on the quality of his defense. His side didn't have the money to buy the daily
transcript of trial recorded by court reporters and the government refused to
provide a copy for free. Consequently, the defense had to make do with its own
hand-written notes of the testimony.[2] The junior Bradley was charged with
taking notes in longhand for his side, and that resulted in frequent requests for
testimony to be suspended while he laboriously wrote out with pen and ink
what had just been said.

Even before Anna Surratt first approached Bradley Sr. to recruit him to lead
her younger brother's defense, young Bradley had a weird, personal connection
to the case. Immediately after the assassination he had been misidentified as John
Wilkes Booth by some of Secretary Stanton's agents and held by them under
arrest until his identity was established.[3]

The United States was represented by four lawyers: District Attorney Edward
Carrington, a native Virginian promoted to the post by President Johnson at
the end of 1865 from within the same office; Nathaniel Wilson, Carrington's
assistant; former Ohio congressman Albert Riddle; and a ringer brought in from
New York to strengthen the team, Judge Edwards Pierrepont.*

Edward Carrington's elevation to the position of United States attorney for
the District of Columbia might have been a surprise to contemporary court

---

* Riddle (1816–1902), a one-term Republican congressman from Ohio, spent much of the Civil War as
the U.S. consul in Matanzas, Cuba. He had lost his campaign for reelection in 1862 because of charges
in Cleveland newspapers that he had exhibited cowardice amid the flight of panicked civilian sightseers

watchers. Early in Lincoln's administration, in July 1861, he had been denied the same post when Senator Henry Wilson (Massachusetts) and Senator Kinsley Bingham (Michigan) objected to his nomination because a few years earlier in private practice he had allegedly pocketed the fees paid to him for the legal defense of a black man and instead "allowed him to be taken to New Orleans and sold into bondage."[4]

The presence of outside counsel, in a time when which state one came from meant a great deal, prompted curiosity. Pierrepont explained in court, not completely accurately, that Attorney General Henry Stanbery (whom he had known for decades) and Secretary of State William Seward (a fellow New Yorker) had solicited him to assist Carrington after the district attorney had first asked for reinforcement. The New York Herald, perhaps playing favorites for a local boy, handicapped the field for its readers this way. Pierrepont, "a quiet, painstaking, business looking lawyer," appeared to be the lead prosecutor. Youthful Wilson looked to know quite as much as Pierrepont and considerably more than his chief, Carrington, who the reporter thought "evidently regards himself as more picturesque than useful in making up the group." Poor Riddle didn't even merit offhand mention.

The Herald reporter's wisecrack must have discomfited the district attorney. At trial's end Carrington made a special point of explaining that this was neither the first nor the only time outside counsel had been invited in to carry

---

from the battlefield after First Bull Run. Riddle returned to Washington from Cuba and entered the private practice of law in the city in 1864.

Like both Bradleys, Pierrepont (1813–1892) was a graduate of Yale and the New Haven Law School. Unlike them, Pierrepont, scion of an old and wealthy Connecticut family, could trace his ancestors in America back to one of the founders of his alma mater, the Reverend James Pierrepont. The trial record suggests that his was the kind of preening, self-important personality that induces claustrophobia even in very large spaces.

In his prime Pierrepont was a confident and imposing figure. In an era when extravagant facial hair was commonplace on men, his face was adorned with the dark, tightly curled beard of an ancient Assyrian god. By the time he led the prosecution of Surratt in 1867 Pierrepont had been a lawyer for almost thirty years and had served as a judge of the New York State Supreme Court for three, hence the honorific title. In the future Pierrepont would become a U.S. district attorney in New York, very briefly one of President Grant's five attorneys general, and finally for eighteen months minister to the United Kingdom five years after Reverdy Johnson held the same post. (He had earlier declined appointment as minister to the Russian Imperial Court in St. Petersburg.) Both appointments were rewards for his strong support of the presidential campaigns of General Grant.

After that public service he returned to New York and the law. Pierrepont died in March 1892 at his home on Fifth Avenue in New York City of a cerebral hemorrhage. He had been the victim of "a nervous affliction" that had left him paralyzed for the last two years of life. His only son, Edwin, predeceased him, dying in Rome in 1885, where he had been the U.S. chargé d'affaires at the American mission to the Kingdom of Italy.

the government's water in an important case. He reminded the audience that even Judge Fisher ("who presides over this tribunal with so much courtesy and dignity," Carrington added greasily) as Delaware's attorney general once drew on such outside help. Carrington then went on to speak for several days, giving the government a double-barreled shot at the jury; Carrington and Pierrepont sandwiched the closing statements of both defense counsels between their two perorations. His role over several days was to explain to the jury how the law defined an "accessory," a "conspiracy," "evidence," and an "alibi"; to confirm that the facts necessary for a conviction had been established by the testimony presented beyond a reasonable doubt; and to ask the jury for Surratt's execution.

Edwards Pierrepont was the government's closer. With all the heavy lifting—examinations and cross-examinations of hundreds of witnesses—nominally done in advance by others, his role was to bring the work of weeks together and order it, to convince the jury of the essential correctness of the case against Surratt by the clarity of his logic and force of his language. Reflecting Pierrepont's special status as the prosecution's headliner and his own sense of worth, however, he interrupted freely, almost obsessively, throughout the trial and then gave his side's final closing statement. His was a marathon oration extending over the better part of four hot summer days that must have stupefied the judge, jury, opposing counsel, defendant, and observers alike.

The officers who sat as judges on the military commission that tried the eight conspirators in 1865 were detailed to their assignment by name in War Department special orders. There was no discussion in court as to their fitness or willingness to serve. With the possible exception of Maj. Gen. Lewis Wallace, U.S. Volunteers, who sketched and chatted during testimony, they apparently took their responsibilities seriously.* Years later, however, one of the former

---

* Maj. Gen. Lew Wallace (1827–1903) is best known as the author of the novel *Ben Hur: A Tale of the Christ*, an enormously successful book and Broadway stage play in the nineteenth century and movie in the twentieth. In his other life Wallace was a soldier in two wars and later a territorial governor and diplomat. He represented the United States in Istanbul at Ottoman Sultan Abdul Hamid II's court from 1881 to 1885.

Wallace's service in the war against Mexico was undistinguished, but until the Battle of Shiloh during the Civil War he enjoyed a brilliant reputation and quick promotions, rising to major general by thirty-four years of age. At Shiloh, in April 1862, his division marched inexplicably in a huge circle instead of relieving Sherman's division, then under terrific attack. Grant, commanding the Army of the Tennessee, relieved Wallace of command and never forgave him. Later in the war, on July 9, 1864, it was Major General Wallace at the head of fifty-eight hundred men on the east bank of the Monocacy River near Frederick, Maryland, who held up Gen. Jubal Early in what was the last Confederate march on Washington

commissioners, Brig. Gen. Thomas Harris, U.S. Volunteers, published a pamphlet, *Rome's Responsibility for the Assassination of Lincoln* (1897), which revealed that he at least might have taken a seat on the commission carrying some very heavy baggage.[5] In it, twenty years after a trial that had revealed nothing of the sort, Harris identified the "Roman Hierarchy," working closely with Confederate officials in Richmond and Montreal, as "most likely the original source of the inspiration of the assassination plot."

Jury selection for John Surratt's trial proved to be a week-long effort. The twelve finally seated on June 17 were the products of a selection process that began just after 11:00 AM, Monday, June 10, with the prosecution's surprise motion to reject the entire twenty-six-man pool from which the jury originally was to be drawn. The basis of the petition, eventually granted by the judge, was that governing law ("An act for the selection of jurors to serve in the several courts of the District of Columbia," passed in June 1862) had not been followed by responsible officers. Jurors on the panel offered had been summoned illegally. The three registrars had selected jurors independently rather than collectively and one of the registrars, not the circuit court clerk, made the final draw from the pool of candidates. Interrogation of the senior registrar revealed yet another technical flaw: No check had been made to ensure prospective jurors were taxpayers, as required. Pierrepont made much of this. He argued that the law explicitly required white, male taxpayers and that any variance, such as the selection of nontaxpayers or equally of "wooly-headed Africans," was unlawful. The example passed for a quip, and he was rewarded by laughter.

The *New York Herald* speculated that the real reason for this government maneuver was not procedural irregularities in establishing the first pool of talesmen as claimed, but that the pool selected, a carry-over from a criminal trial two months before, was known to include fully sixteen Catholics among twenty-six candidates from whom twelve jurors were to be selected. These, the prosecution expected, would be naturally sympathetic to the young, former seminarian. (The *Times* thought so too. Its correspondent mused that Surratt would do better relying on the "ignorance and prejudices of fellow Catholics

---

of the war. Wallace slowed Early's fifteen thousand enough that Grant had time to reinforce the Union fortifications north of the capital. Early was repulsed. He had, however, managed to get within five miles of the White House.

Immediately after the trial of the Lincoln conspirators Wallace presided over the military tribunal that tried Capt. Henry Wirz, CSA, the former commandant of Andersonville Prison, and sentenced him to death.

than on the intelligence of another jury selected from leading citizens by the Marshal.") In explanation to the press, the prosecution denied any desire to manipulate the jury's composition but passed on an opportunity to correct suspicions that it was doing exactly that. Carrington went only so far as to declaim that "no one more earnestly and sincerely deprecated appeals to religious prejudice than himself." So ended two days of arm wrestling.

Below the surface something much more interesting than overt rejiggering of the jury pool had been going on invisibly. Pierrepont, and especially Riddle, had been working covertly in Congress to get legislation that would permit either importing jurors from other jurisdictions or changing the venue from the District of Columbia to one more likely to produce a more accommodating jury. "Such a bill was matured in the House," Riddle told Secretary Seward wistfully in his final report, "and could have been passed through that body; but it received none [sic] or very little support in the Senate, although Judge Pierrepont and other gentlemen of eminence urged the measure upon the attention of leading Senators with much earnestness. We failed to secure the needed legislation."[6] Instead, the responsible registrars summoned hundreds of new men from the rolls of taxpaying residents of the District's three jurisdictions, and the winnowing process began anew on June 12. It instantly triggered a flurry of requests to be excused, just like those heard in courtrooms today.

Most among the talesmen who showed up thought they had the usual good reasons not to serve—health problems, business concerns, family matters, or a firm opinion as to guilt or innocence already formed and publicly aired. Judge Fisher heard them out and excused a few. He recognized, too, that a number in the pool likely held "conscientious scruples on the subject of capital punishment as would preclude them from rendering a verdict of guilty if the law and the evidence justified it." Fisher went on to opine that "there are many persons opposed to capital punishment, and think hanging is the worst use to which a man can be put." And in fact a few talesmen, not only Daniel Breed, the single Quaker called up, were spared jury service for exactly this reason. Much later the district attorney attempted to ease any consciences still troubled by the idea of capital punishment by citing St. Paul (Romans 14:4) and explaining that the first object of punishment was to "execute wrath upon him that doeth evil." Purposes such as deterrence of crime and criminal reform came after vengeance.

From the twenty-six finalists the defense could challenge and remove ten, the prosecution four. The remaining twelve were to sit in judgment on Surratt.

Each juror received two dollars per day for his services, hotel accommodations, and transportation to and from court every day.

Those finally selected to serve as jurors were William Todd, Robert Ball, J. Russell Barr, Thomas Berry, George Bohrer, Christian Schneider, James Davis, Columbus Alexander, William McLean, Benjamin Morsell, Benjamin Gittings, and William Birth. The twelve swore "to well and truly try, and true deliverance make between the United States of America and John H. Surratt, the prisoner at the bar, whom you have in charge and a true verdict give according to your evidence."[7]

McLean was born in Kilmarnock, Scotland, and Schneider was a native of Württemburg, Germany. The other ten were native-born Americans. Beyond their birthplaces, not much else is known about the jurors, other than all were white, taxpaying residents of Washington, Georgetown, or the rural places in the District of Columbia outside of its two cities; that none was under twenty-one or over sixty-five; and that none claimed "conscientious scruples." Not about the death penalty in any case. Todd was selected by them to be the jury's foreman.

When all the machinations of jury rejection and jury selection were complete, government counsel and the press began describing the twelve jurors in flattering terms, for example, as a "remarkably intelligent body of men, with a dignified sprinkling of bald and gray heads . . . which adds to the favorable impression created at a single glance by their generally sound and substantial appearance." On July 6 counsel for the defense, the younger Bradley, announced that his side, too, was well satisfied with the twelve jurors. He told them that they represented "the social interests of this District, its material wealth, its intelligence, and its honesty—men who in this case have a double duty to perform, not only to stand between the innocent and the accuser, but also to vindicate the reputation of this district, whose loyalty has been so much defamed." Men, he said moreover, who "cannot be charged with having the taint of any religious or any other bias, for you represent different preferences in modes of worship and opposite opinions upon the political questions of the day." Anticipating a congenial outcome, the *New York Herald* wrote a few weeks later, "If at the close of the case these men should come into the box with a verdict of guilty, no one would think of saying that such a verdict was wrung from the ignorance, the stupidity, the weakness, or the unfairness of the jury." The unthinkable, that the majority would conclude on the basis of evidence that Surratt was not guilty, was left unsaid.

Counsel continued to stroke the jury practically to the end. District Attorney Carrington spoke for the last time on July 27 and began by expressing his "sincere and cordial acknowledgments for the becoming manner in which you have generally borne yourselves during this long, tedious, and painful investigation. Your courteous, benignant and solemn bearing is a proper and eloquent rebuke to the spirit of levity which, I regret to say, has sometimes pervaded the audience; and is alike worthy of imitation, and of the highest commendation."

All this seduction, of course, came before the jury reported out of its deliberations on August 10, at the end of the trial.

Much later, in October when he presented his fifteen-hundred-dollar invoice for four months of professional services, Riddle casually glossed over the "moral certainty that no conviction could be had in the District," but in June when the trial began, everyone acted as if he believed one could.

On May 13, 1867, roughly one month before jury selection in Surratt's trial began, Jefferson Davis was released from prison on $100,000 bail, a huge sum at the time. The Davises' Mississippi plantation, Brierfield, and their great wealth were long since gone. With Davis in jail, management of the family's dwindling accounts had fallen to his wife, Varina. She had been living since the end of the war and supporting her family on loans and gifts from friends and admirers.

Soon after his capture but before their conviction Jefferson Davis and Booth's eight familiars had been reviled as "Uncle Sam's menagerie" in a savage political cartoon by G. Querner, who unaccountably left John Surratt out of his lineup. The cartoonist's message, however, was clear. All of them deserved hanging for their crime, not just the eight "gallow's birds" perched in a line on individual gibbets at the top of the sketch. Below them, top-hatted Uncle Sam pointed happily at Booth's skull lying on the ground between Mary Surratt and Samuel Arnold, a raven pecking at its vacant eye sockets. In the busy center of the sketch, "Hyena Jeff Davis" stood caged, clawing what must have been Lincoln's bones, with a noose around his neck being ratcheted slowly tighter while an organ grinder belted out "Yankee Doodle." (Gibbets and nooses enjoyed a prominent place in Querner's oeuvre. His "John Brown Visiting his Hangman" cartoon features one of each, together with another image of a caged Davis.)

Jefferson Davis's noose never did get as tight as Querner hoped. In May 1867, when Davis emerged from his cell at Fort Monroe, he was already past the halfway point to amnesty, although he didn't know it. The former Confederate president's trial on a charge of treason was scheduled and rescheduled several times between 1865 and 1868, while Andrew Johnson and his cabinet fumbled around trying to agree on a scenario (charges, a court, and a trial judge) that would produce the desired outcome and not risk an embarrassing surprise. Meanwhile, once Davis was out on bail the Davises followed Surratt's escape track most of the way, a groove worn into the ocean by other former Confederates looking for sanctuary. A quick relocation to Montreal, followed a year later with an ocean crossing from there to Liverpool, and then time in London and Paris before returning to the United States. In December 1868, Johnson's general amnesty made it all moot.

Davis's two years in jail awaiting trial turned out to be all the punishment inflicted on him. The president of the Confederate States of America never went to trial, but one of his lowly couriers did.

7

"A NEW TRIAL WILL DOUBTLESS FOLLOW"

In 1865 witness testimony during the trial of the eight in the Arsenal took forty-nine days in court. Two years later the trial of Mary Surratt's son alone took fifty-three days, between Monday, June 10, and Saturday, August 10. John Surratt's trial proceeded slowly, even ponderously: usually two hours in court every morning followed by two and a half more every afternoon, Monday through Saturday. Observers filled Judge George Fisher's courtroom day after day, while witnesses followed one another in a procession punctuated only by the legal arguments counsel threw back and forth through the midsummer heat.[1]

Although Surratt's trial lasted only a few days longer than did the eight's, it produced a verbatim transcript more than twice the length of theirs. During its course nearly three hundred witnesses took the stand, were sworn, and testified. One, the familiar Louis Weichmann, was examined and cross-examined for the better part of three days. Others appeared for only several minutes to answer a few questions. Some watched opposing counsel spar and were allowed by Judge Fisher to say practically nothing.

The criminal trial of John Harrison Surratt appears superficially to have been a modern judicial proceeding, an event familiar to any jury veteran or fan of producer Dick Wolf's long-running *Law and Order* TV show on NBC. Judge, jury, accused, counsel, and witnesses all filled familiar roles. Those with speaking parts, meaning everyone but Surratt, came in on cue and talked earnestly in the usual courtroom vocabulary. The verbatim record of the trial described a careful process following time-honored forms. Defense counsel raised more than 150 objections, and almost all were overruled.

Despite appearances there were several important differences between procedures then and now that biased the trial heavily in favor of the prosecution.

There was no pretrial "discovery" associated with Surratt's trial, no formal process outside of the courtroom through which defense counsel could obtain from the prosecution documents or other evidence in advance in order to better prepare for the trial. Nor was the prosecution obliged to provide its list of witnesses to the defense ahead of time. Each witness called by the government, consequently, represented a potential ambush for the defense. Moreover, Judge Fisher's disinclination to permit the recall of prosecution witnesses meant that defense cross-examinations were often improvised on the fly with little chance to construct and execute a deliberate attack against previous testimony. Moreover, the defense was not allowed to introduce new material and was restricted to responding to what had been first put into the record by the prosecution

There was another difference. The atmosphere in Fisher's courtroom was absolutely poisonous. While some recent trials have dipped into farce, none has been steeped in the vitriol that daily washed over those proceedings in 1867. Counsels took turns abusing one another, witnesses, and the judge with vigor and vocabulary. Their mutual hostility reflected more than just the stakes in a capital case, professional competition, personal antipathy, and party politics. (In the first trial and also in this one, and in general, government lawyers were Republicans, defense lawyers were Democrats.) Fisher's courtroom during Surratt's trial appeared to be one of the small, last battlefields of the Civil War; its clash between North and South would become even more apparent for what it was in mid-August, when Foreman William Todd reported the results of his jury's deliberations.

The atmosphere was poisonous and palpably unfair, or so Merrick thought and told the jury at trial's end: "Whenever any technical rule of law could by any constraint whatever exclude a piece of testimony calculated to enlighten your [the jury's] judgment, it has been invoked to exclude that testimony; has been bent from its uniform application and its generally understood principle for that purpose . . . there is nothing that has fallen from his honor in the adjudication upon these questions of testimony that has changed my opinion that the testimony should be allowed to go to the jury."

Like the eight in 1865, Surratt was prohibited by law from testifying in his own defense in 1867, but counsel might have elected to keep him off the stand anyway, as criminal defense attorneys do today for many reasons, so this prohibition probably didn't affect Bradley's case.

With a new jury finally in place, examination of witnesses for the prosecution began June 17, immediately after Deputy District Attorney Nathaniel

Wilson's short opening statement, when Maj. Gen. Joseph Barnes was sworn and took the stand. On April 14, 1865, Barnes, the army's surgeon general, had attended Lincoln in Petersen's townhouse on Tenth Street, across from Ford's Theatre, during the comatose president's last hours alive. Later Barnes was the supervising physician at Lincoln's autopsy and at Booth's, too. Doctor Barnes's testimony about Lincoln's wound and death began a parade of government witnesses that eventually included eighty-four others before their testimony finally ended on July 5 with the examination of Frederick Hall, a War Department cryptographer.

District Attorney Edward Carrington, or perhaps his associate counsel, Judge Edwards Pierrepont, scripted the prosecution's case in chief in three acts. The first was a brief flashback to the president's assassination—a blink, only six witnesses, including General Barnes and Maj. Henry Rathbone, who with his fiancée, Clara Harris, had shared the theater box with the Lincolns that terrible night.* A few reminders of the attack: a glance at the pistol, the fatal ball, and

---

* Some physicians now believe Lincoln could have survived his wound had modern shock trauma care been available in 1865. If so, the president would have been "partially blind, unsteady on his feet, numb in certain regions of his body and inarticulate. Nevertheless, he might have been able to think [the ball did not penetrate into the brain's frontal lobes] and, after much rehabilitation, communicate." These conclusions were presented to the thirteenth Historical Clinicopathological Conference in May 2007 in Baltimore by Dr. Thomas Scalea (David Brown, "Could Modern Medicine Have Saved Lincoln?" *Washington Post*, May 21, 2007, A6).

How, one hundred years before the Twenty-fifth Amendment, the executive branch of the federal government would have continued to operate with a president in such condition absent any constitutional provision for presidential disability or incapacity is unknowable. Given the issues facing Washington at war's end and the profound partisan divisions in the capital, the ensuing legitimacy crisis could have been even more divisive than was the battle between President Johnson and Congress that followed Lincoln's death.

The night Rathbone shared the Lincolns' box at the theater was the apogee of the young officer's life. Several other couples had declined the honor before late on Friday the Lincolns invited Rathbone and Harris to join them that evening at Ford's Theatre to see *Our American Cousin*. At least one did so because of discomfort with the idea of enjoying frivolous entertainment on a holy day. After shooting Lincoln, Booth stabbed Rathbone, seriously wounded him and spraying Clara Harris with her fiancé's blood. For Rathbone, everything that followed tracked along a downward spiral that ended in his confinement in a German asylum for the criminally insane at Hildesheim in Prussia, where he died twenty-eight years later in 1911.

Henry Rathbone and Clara Harris were married in July 1867, while Surratt was on trial, the same year that Clara's father finished his only term as a senator from New York. (He had replaced Seward when the latter left the U.S. Senate to join Lincoln's cabinet.) The Rathbone and Harris families came from upstate New York. His late father had been mayor of Albany. Curiously, her father, Judge Ira Harris, was also Rathbone's stepfather. A widower, he had married Rathbone's widowed mother, Pauline, some years earlier.

In December 1870, and then a colonel, Rathbone resigned from the Army. Soon thereafter he began a fruitless hunt for medical care and relief from incipient madness. Just before Christmas 1883, in rented

a bit of the president's skull, all to move the jury mentally back in time to April 1865. Next, a lengthy reprise of the trial of the eight, built largely around the testimony of Weichmann, Mary Surratt's tenant and John Surratt's roommate on the third floor of the house on H Street, to refresh the jurors' indignation about the crime and to remind them of the wicked cabal that had conceived and executed it. Finally, a detailed reconstruction of the week from April 12, when Surratt left Montreal for Elmira, through April 18, by which time he was back in Canada. Witnesses were generally heard as available, and not in chronological or other logical order, so it fell to counsel in the prosecution's closing statements to tie the narrative together for the jurors in some coherent form.

Between April 12 and April 18, 1865, Pierrepont told the jury on August 5, "all these things of which we have spoken relating to this murder were done. Where was John Surratt all this while?" That would prove to be the central question. The prosecution granted that Surratt was in Elmira early on April 13, but its focus, of course, was on April 14, and Pierrepont was determined to prove him in Washington that day. Beginning on the first afternoon of testimony Carrington and his co-counsel brought to the stand thirteen witnesses to substantiate the prosecution's essential assertion: Surratt had been present with Booth at Ford's Theatre the night of the assassination, present at the scene of the crime. One after the other each of these witnesses testified under oath that he (or in one case, she) had seen Surratt downtown in Washington City sometime on April 14, 1865. When the last left the stand, if they were believed, Surratt had not just passed through Washington on Good Friday two years earlier but he had a very busy day moving about the city in company with the assassin beginning around 10:30 AM, just after a train from Baltimore arrived at the Baltimore and Ohio depot, until roughly twelve hours later, when Lincoln was shot.

Charles Wood, a barber who had a chair in Brooker and Stewart's parlor on E Street, began the reconstruction of Surratt's schedule of April 14. John Wilkes Booth, John Surratt, Michael O'Laughlen, and someone who sounded a lot like George Atzerodt in Wood's description, came into Brooker and Stewart's together before midmorning, he said, not long after Wood himself got to the

---

accommodations in Hanover, Germany, to which place he had been appointed U.S. consul by President Grover Cleveland, Rathbone shot his wife, the mother of their three children, to death and then unsuccessfully attempted suicide with a knife.

The spattered evening dress Clara wore the night of Lincoln's assassination, and reportedly preserved soiled but intact for many years thereafter, has since taken on a life of its own in ghostly legend. In 1930 the dress was the subject of Mary Raymond Shipman Andrews's short novella, *The White Satin Dress* (New York: Charles Scribners' Sons).

shop after shaving the convalescent Secretary Seward in his bed at home a few blocks away. "Mr. Surratt," Wood continued, "took my chair immediately on Mr. Booth's getting out. . . . This time Mr. Surratt said to me, 'Give me a nice shave and clean me up nicely; I am going away in a day or two.' He seemed to be a little dusty, as though he had been traveling some little distance and wanted a little cleaning and dressing up, as I am frequently called upon by gentlemen coming in after a short travel."

"This time . . . ," "I am going away . . . ," "A little dusty . . . ," "Traveling some little distance . . ." Here again, as at the trial in the Arsenal, a witness testifying added just the right detail to lend fine grain texture to his story, and coincidently to fit it into the narrative arc of the prosecution's case. "I then went on and completed the shaving operation," Wood said. "I shaved him clean all around the face, with the exception of where the moustache was. He had a slight moustache at the time. After I was done shaving I washed him off in the usual way, dressed his hair, and put on the usual tonics and pomade."

Surratt's long day in Washington approached its climax, according to three other witnesses, with him and Booth mingling suspiciously among the passersby in front of Ford's New Theatre—Satan and Beelzebub at the scene of the crime—between eight and ten o'clock in the evening. That's where Frank Heaton, a clerk at the General Land Office (helpfully described by counsel as having "an honest face"), Sgt. Joseph Dye, and former sergeant Robert Cooper placed him.

In 1867 Sergeant Dye was an army recruiter in Philadelphia, a job that seems like a sinecure at a time when the U.S. Army had just finished deliberately shedding hundreds of thousands of men, but those had been volunteers and conscripts. Now Dye was enlisting regulars for the Indian wars. Two years earlier he had been a company first sergeant assigned to Thompson's Battery (Battery C) of the Independent Pennsylvania Light Artillery, stationed at Camp Barry, north of the city center on the Baltimore Pike.

Dye testified that on the evening of April 14, 1865, he had been downtown, away from camp without an officer's permission and with Cooper to see the city's torchlight parade celebrating the coming end of the war. He was certain of what he saw that night in front of Ford's Theatre. Booth was there, Dye said, "conversing with a low, villainous looking person" when a "neatly dressed person" joined the conversation. The latter soon

stepped up in front of the theater and called the time . . . and called the time again . . . and seemed excited. It was not long before he appeared again, going on a fast walk from the direction of H Street. He placed himself in front of the theater, where the light shone clear on his face. There was a picture on that countenance of great excitement, exceedingly nervous and very pale. . . . It was ten minutes past ten o'clock.

By implication, Ned Spangler was the second of the three lurking about the theater with Booth. Dye identified Surratt as the third, the neatly dressed man.

Pierrepont [pointing at Surratt]: "Is that the man?"
Dye: "It is. I have seen his face often since, while I have been sleeping—it was so exceedingly pale. . . ."
"You say he was the prisoner at the bar?"
"Yes sir, and I say I have seen him since, while I have been sleeping."

During cross-examination Dye told defense counsel that he believed Surratt was "regulating the time for Booth, Payne, and the whole of them to strike."

Merrick: "He was a general commander [of the plot]?"
Dye: "Yes, sir."
"Did you dream that?"
"No, sir."

Dye's volunteering the curious detail that he saw Surratt's face in his dreams opened a line of questioning by the defense seeking to discredit Dye by exploring a possible connection with the occult. Spiritualism and séances were in high fashion at the time in the U.S. and Europe—among many others, Queen Victoria and Mary Lincoln enthusiastically attempted to communicate with the other side, the queen hoping to hear from her beloved Albert and the first lady from her dead sons, Edward and Willie—so it's possible that Bradley thought he was approaching a rich vein with this line of questioning. He came up empty-handed.

Bradley: "Have you ever had any communication with spiritual mediums?"
Dye: No , sir. I don't believe in foolishness such as that. I cannot say that I am a firm believer in dreams, but I have often seen things in my dreams that I have seen before."

Bradley didn't give up right away. He next asked if Dye was a Swedenborgian but then quickly withdrew the question about religion when it prompted an objection from opposing counsel.[2] Bradley continued, asking,

"Then there are some of your dreams which tell of the future as well as the past?"
"Yes, sir. But I never put confidence in them or allow them bother me."
"But they obtrude themselves upon you sometimes, do they not?"
"Not materially."
"But they do to some extent."
"That is the only case."

After all the testimony was over, Merrick reviewed Dye's for the jury, calling him "a dreamer, a speculative dreamer," and worse, suggesting he was a perjurer to boot.

Ten other witnesses testified about the in-between hours of Surratt's day downtown, those that fell after his morning shave and before Dye's reported clock-watching incident in front of the theater. The group included a clock repairman named Theodore Rhodes; a New York lawyer, Maj. Benjamin Vanderpoel (occasionally "Vanderpool"); Walter Coleman and George Cushing, civil servants in the Treasury Department; Peter Taltavul, who owned a restaurant next to the theater; a "tall, brawny" tailor named David Reed with a shop at 617 H Street; William Cleaver, the hostler and horse doctor who owned the stable at Sixth Street where Booth had boarded his horse; Deputy U.S. Marshal John Lee; Scipriano Grillo, a former musician and owner of the Star Saloon next to Ford's Theatre; and a new servant in the Surratt house on H Street at the time of the assassination, a young black woman named Susan Ann Jackson. (She and her husband, Samuel, were two of only three blacks who testified at the trial, although the barber, Wood, was evidently of mixed race and would have been counted then as a fourth. After the Civil War black witnesses at trials became more common. White control over the process was retained, however, by continuing to deny blacks a presence on the jury.)

Rhodes said he saw Surratt before noon inside of the presidential box at Ford's Theatre, just after play rehearsal was over, whittling the peg (out of North Carolina pine, he thought) that would jam its door closed later that night with Booth inside. Reed repeated his testimony from the Arsenal trial and said that he saw Surratt at half past two walking on Pennsylvania Avenue looking "remarkably genteel . . . very pretty" and wearing new brass spurs with uncommonly large blue rowels. Vanderpoel came upon Booth and Surratt in a saloon during the afternoon, perhaps in Teutonia Hall on Pennsylvania Avenue, sitting together amid fifty or sixty others at tables while a woman on stage did "a sort of ballet dance." (Later Vanderpoel got a laugh from the cheap seats when he told Merrick, "I did not pay much attention to her face. I paid more attention to her legs.")

Cleaver said he saw Surratt near his stable at four, riding a "chestnut-sorrel," he recalled, or in any case "a rather darkish horse." Lee saw Surratt between Stinemetz's hat store and Franklin's spectacle store, moving at an ordinary gait. Grillo thought he saw someone who looked like him with Davey Herold in Willard's Hotel that afternoon. Coleman and Cushing saw him at six, standing in the street on Pennsylvania Avenue next to Booth, who was mounted "on a very nice little horse." Coleman was certain of the identification, Cushing less so. According to her testimony Susan Jackson must have been the last to see Surratt just before he joined Booth at the theater. She said that she had brought a pot of tea to him while he was at home that night between eight and nine o'clock.

In retrospect, the prosecution's determination to prove Surratt in Washington on Good Friday appears curious, because both Carrington and Pierrepont later insisted that whether or not Surratt was physically present in the capital wasn't relevant. As a member of the conspiracy he was "constructively present" at the scene of the crime, even if miles away committed to some other aspect of the plot. But in getting Surratt out of Elmira and into Washington, Carrington and Pierrepont were anticipating that their "constructive presence" argument wasn't going to get past the defense. Physical presence, Merrick would, and did, argue constituted the distinction between accessory and principal. If Surratt were not at the scene, the law held that he could not be a principal in the crime of murder. In fact, Surratt had to be in the city as charged for conviction.

Judge Pierrepont assured the jury repeatedly that the government's witnesses were testifying truthfully: All were honest, and none, he said, had the motivation (Lee), inclination (Heaton), or wit (Jackson) to lie. More than that, what they swore to formed a seamless web of veracity. "I pledge you my word, my honor and my eternal hope of salvation," Pierrepont told the jury, "that there is not a word of this evidence upon which the Government have relied that is not in perfect harmony with every other word, as you will see as we proceed; for I repeat, every truth is in perfect harmony with every other truth. So God has ordered it."

In a mid-nineteenth-century courtroom operating under principles of common law the sworn testimony of an eyewitness was the gold standard of truthfulness. That this was so grew from bold innovation. Its evolution required first setting aside the medieval faith that, if asked, God would helpfully sift the guilty from the innocent in combat or through some ordeal, and then rejecting reliance on confession that inevitably came from horrific torture meant to hurry jurisprudence along. Witness testimony, documents and unambiguous physical evidence, and (still) the occasional volunteered confession were about all the raw materials counsel at the time had to make his case. The near-magical products of science that would forever change the pursuit of crime and trial by jury were still a century away. Also a century away was the idea that eyewitnesses were hardly infallible, that good faith errors in reporting observed events and identifying persons were common, perhaps even very common, and that consequently too much weight was credited to their testimony.

Good faith errors aside, no one doubted that a witness could lie. For recent proof of the possibility, the trial at the Arsenal had produced at least one master liar (the convicted perjurer, Charles Dunham, a.k.a. Sanford Conover) and several journeyman and apprentice fabricators of facts.* Much of the testimony during Surratt's trial was an exploration of the truthfulness of a witness based on his community reputation as described by other witnesses. The result was

---

* Judge George Fisher presided over Charles Dunham's week-long trial for perjury, held February 5–11, 1867, two weeks before Surratt stepped out of the *Swatara*'s small boat and into Marshall Gooding's custody. District Attorney Carrington was the government's counsel in the case against Dunham.

   Dunham and Surratt shared more than a courtroom, judge, and prosecutor; they also shared an afternoon in court. Just after noon on February 23 Dunham was brought before Fisher to hear his sentence, where he discovered Surratt—now four days off the *Swatara* and in civilian clothes for the first time in months: a black suit, white shirt, and holding a black hat of "Resorts style"—in the dock for arraignment. According to the *New York Herald*, the two sitting side by side appeared not to recognize each other. There is no reason why they should have. Surratt was only in the courtroom long enough to answer two questions, a reporter wrote the next day:

   "The clerk of the court proceeded to read the indictment, at the close of which he asked the prisoner: What say you, are you guilty as indicted, or not guilty?"
   The prisoner: Not guilty.
   The clerk: How will you be tried?
   The prisoner: By my country. [Meaning by judge and jury rather than by ordeal. The original response to the question reflected an accused's choice between "God," and trial by ordeal, or "country," and trial in court.]
   The clerk: May God send you safe deliverance.

   Dunham's biographer makes one other connection between the two, who had cells in the Blue Jug for a while. Cumming says that Dunham later attempted to "urge Surratt to name [President] Johnson as one

not clarification but confusion. "Another special feature which aided to perplex the case and lengthen it inordinately," the *New York Times* wrote retrospectively in mid-August 1867, "was the controversy over the character of witnesses. At one time, indeed, it seemed as if a whole county would become ranged on the side of attack or defense over the body of some writhing occupant of the stand. This building up one day of a stainless character, to be dashed on the next into the ruins of profligate disrepute,—this every-widening array of impeachment and rehabilitation—weakened the strength of both sides, and threw grave doubts upon the genuineness of most of the testimony."

In a July 2007 *New Yorker* essay on lie-detection technology, Margaret Talbot wrote about efforts over nearly three centuries directed at finding a sure way to discern truth from falsehood. "A liar's testimony is often more persuasive than a truthteller's," she observed, after first noting that extensive research indicated that subjects in experiments could accurately separate the truth from lies only about half the time. That statistic suggests that the jury system is a highly imperfect method of determining the truth. The search for possible alternatives to it has been a long one.

Talbot's chronology began in 1730 with Daniel Defoe's notion that lying is inevitably revealed by an irregular pulse, and then passed through later centuries with the history of various weird or complicated devices that measured pulse and other physiological indicia supposedly associated with the stress of lying (including the modern polygraph). "In the late nineteenth century," she wrote, "The Italian criminologist Cesare Lombroso invented his own version of a lie detector, based on the physiology of emotion. A suspect was told to plunge his hand into a tank filled with water, and the subject's pulse would cause the level of liquid to rise and fall slightly; the greater the fluctuation, the more dishonest the subject was judged to be."

Talbot concluded with a look at how one entrepreneur is trying to apply functional magnetic resonance imaging technology to lie detection. This technology measures the flow of oxygenated blood in areas of the cerebral cortex, on the theory that lying takes more cognitive effort than does telling the truth and that a magnetic resonance image scan makes this difference apparent.

---

of the assassins, promising in return a pardon from the Radicals." Surratt's refusal was the prompt for Dunham to coach the jailed William Cleaver to testify that Surratt was in Washington April 14.

In the end, all of his remarkable machinations were forgiven: President Johnson pardoned Dunham in February 1869, the same month that saw Samuel Mudd, Samuel Arnold, and Edman Spangler released from Fort Jefferson.

Of course, nothing like any of this was used in the courtroom facing 4½ Street. In Judge Fisher's courtroom, like all the others in the country, jurors were entirely on their own in sifting fact from falsehood.

Few believed that a drunk in his cups could tell the truth or even distinguish it from falsehood. John Lloyd, Mary Surratt's tippling tenant, testified at both trials. What he said should have been difficult to evaluate given Lloyd's ready acknowledgment that liquor "oftentimes made me forget things that I do not wish to forget." Still, his confession about stupors from regular binge drinking and liquor's power as a mental eraser didn't impress Pierrepont. As a man of the world, counsel's experience was "not that a man's getting drunk affected his truthfulness. A man may have a passion for liquor, a passion for other things. [The reference here is apparently to William Cleaver.] I have known some men, entirely truthful men, who were drunk three times a week, and whose truthfulness, whether everything or anything was at stake, nothing could shake."

Surratt's jury listened to hundreds of witnesses giving sworn testimony about what had happened nearly two years earlier. But how memory worked and the influences on memory of preconceptions or later events were almost entirely unknown. Witnesses who had no obvious motive to lie were generally believed to be telling the truth. Not until the publication of Harvard professor Hugo Münsterberg's short collection of essays on psychology and crime, *On the Witness Stand*, in 1908 did eyewitness reliability begin to get anything like scientific scrutiny in the United States. By the 1970s doubts about police lineup procedures had triggered serious academic study of eyewitnesses and identification. The scale of the potential problem of misidentification in good faith wasn't fully appreciated, however, until nuclear DNA evidence became available beginning in the mid-1990s and confirmed how common eyewitness and victim identification errors were.

How memory worked and where it resided in the human brain were mysteries in the nineteenth century and for the most part still are today. Only very recently has it become clear that there are many kinds of memory ("semantic," "episodic," "emotional," and "implicit" memory are among those mentioned in the literature of neuroscience) and that memory in its different manifestations probably rests in several different structures in the brain. None of that was known then, but how to manipulate or fabricate what we now call "episodic memory," how to coach a witness to tell a story, that was reasonably well understood.

In March, three months before Surratt's trial, Sgt. Joseph Dye was admitted into the District's jail by order of District Attorney Carrington, expressly to see Surratt in what amounted to a single-suspect police lineup. "When I spoke to him," Dye told the court on June 18, "I saw the same excited and pale countenance that I had after the assassination in my dreams. The man I saw in prison I can positively say was the owner of the face I saw in front of Ford's theater on the night of the 14th of April; and this is the man here. There is no doubt about it. . . . If I had met him on the street I would have recognized him at once."

Bradley: "Why, then, did you deem it necessary to go to his cell if you could have recognized him so readily among others?"
Dye: "I went there by request."
"Did not you ask to go?"
"No, sir."
"Did not you request to see him?"
"No, sir. They told me I had better go there and see whether I would recognize him."
"What did you say?"
"I told them I would go."

Other prospective witnesses were also sent to the prison by the prosecution to see Surratt in his cell, and to refresh their memories of what they had seen or not seen that day.

The core of the prosecution's case against Surratt was built around the testimony of three men: Louis Weichmann, Sgt. Joseph Dye, and Dr. Lewis McMillan. The first two had appeared in the trial of the eight; only McMillan's was a new face. Weichmann's purpose was to embed Surratt firmly into Booth's plot, where the defendant was cast as second in command of the band that found haven in his mother's house and emerged from there to murder the President. Dye's role was to put Surratt at the scene of the crime as an active participant, acting in some mysterious way as the terrible deed's master clock, its "regulator." And it was McMillan's place to condemn Surratt by his own words, offered up on the deck of the RMS *Peruvian* as the ship neared landfall in Europe.

Weichmann's testimony two years earlier in May sent Surratt's mother to the gallows. Beginning on June 27 and running through July 1 he repeated much of it in Fisher's courtroom, first recounting how from March 1863 to February 1865 he was introduced through the Surratts to Booth and to each of the other conspirators. Early on the second day of his testimony, Weichmann revealed Mary Surratt knew what was coming later and welcomed it. Sitting with her in a buggy on the heights across the river east of Washington the evening of April 14, looking at the illuminated city two miles away, he had Mary saying presciently, "I am afraid that all this rejoicing will be turned into mourning and all this gladness into sorrow." A few minutes later he quoted her making another revealing observation: "I think John Wilkes Booth was only an instrument in the hands of the Almighty to punish this proud and licentious people."

The Booth–Mary Surratt relationship intrigued Pierrepont.

Pierrepont: "How often was Booth at Mrs. Surratt's house two or three months prior to the murder?"

Weichmann: "He came very frequently. It was a very common thing for me to see him in the parlor with Surratt, when Booth was in town after 4 o'clock. They appeared like brothers.

"Was there any term by which Booth was called?"

"Mrs. Surratt appeared to like him very much."

"What term did she use in speaking of him?"

"I heard her once when Booth had stayed two or three hours in the parlor call him 'Pet,' saying, 'Pet stayed two or three hours in the parlor last evening.' I am positive she used the word 'Pet.' She named the hours from 10 at night until 1 in the morning."

But if Pierrepont had hoped for something more suggestive, more salacious, he was quickly disappointed, even after trying hard to elicit it.

Pierrepont: "What was the character of his intimacy there?"

Weichmann: "I think he was nothing more than a friend."

"State the character of his intimacy. . . ."

"He was just as intimate there as I was."

With that disappointing answer Pierrepont gave up his line of questioning, but the entirely unsubstantiated notion that there must have been more to the Mary Surratt–John Wilkes Booth relationship than simply politics or logistics has endured. In 1978 Pamela Redford Russell wrote and Putnam published a sappy romance novel, *The Woman Who Loved John Wilkes Booth*, based on this idea and an imagined diary.

Part way through Russell's story Booth and Mary are riding through south-ern Maryland together in a carriage, beneath "a crystalline blue sky which looked almost hard and brittle enough to crack." They stop to take a walk. "He helped me from the carriage," Mary said. "His hand rested on my arm for a moment longer than was needed. I could feel him looking down at me, but I could not lift my eyes. He took my hand and raised it to his lips." And soon,

Booth: "I hate the suspicion in your eyes. It is from you that I am hiding. I am concealing my impossible love for a woman."

Mary: "What woman?"

"A woman, beautiful and sad, a widow."

I could hardly bear to listen. "What has that to do with me? Why should you want to keep this from me?"

Booth: "Because you are the woman of whom I speak."

Mary: I felt faint. "It cannot be. . . . This is impossible."

"Don't." He raised a beautiful hand to my lips. "Please don't say that. I love you."

"This is a dream. A mad dream. It cannot be that you have wanted me as I have wanted you. Why me, old and ugly, while you are so young and beautiful? There is no reason for you to desire me."

"There can be only one. I love you."

Not exactly bodice-ripping, but not the usual portrayal of the sexless matron Mary Surratt either. Booth, on the other hand, had the morals of a tomcat, if not the manners of one. Michael Kauffman, Booth's biographer, names half a dozen women in his *American Brutus* with whom Booth was romantically, or at least physically, coupled and mentions two unnamed others. A search of Booth's body after he was shot at Garrett's farm supposedly revealed photographs of several young women in his pockets, presumably his roster of current interests. Whatever Mary, just old enough to have been Booth's mother, might have felt or thought, it's absurd to imagine it was reciprocated.

Nevertheless, some entrepreneur has decided that Booth and Mary Surratt cast as star-crossed lovers is good business, if not good history. Russell's thirty-year-old book has been resurrected from hard-cover obscurity by the Internet and print-on-demand technology.

Weichmann's testimony in 1865 had been lethal. Pierrepont meant it to be again in 1867. If left unchallenged, Weichmann's smoothly recited account of the plotters who, having failed March 16 to kidnap Lincoln, went on to kill him April 14, might have convicted Surratt. In response, Bradley attacked the witness on two fronts, charging that what Weichmann said was a lie, and that his motive for perjury was self-preservation.

"I want to know if," Bradley asked Weichmann during cross-examination Friday afternoon, June 28, "in your communication with any officer of the government, you have been told if you did not testify to more than you had stated, they would hang you too?"

"No sir," was the reply.

Bradley didn't let go. Twice on July 1 he came back to the subject: "I ask you whether you did not tell Mr. Maddox and Mr. Gifford that you were told by Mr. Bingham that if you did not state more fully than you had done, all you know, you would be treated as one of the conspirators?" Weichmann denied it. Bradley, boring down hard, said,

> I want you to state whether, after the conspiracy trials, you had a conversation with Mr. Carland in reference to testimony you had given on that trial. . . . Do you remember stating to him that the testimony you had given was prepared for you, written out for you, and that . . . you were told that you must swear to the substance of that paper. . . .
>
> Do you remember telling him that you were obliged to swear to that statement or you would be threatened with prosecution for perjury, or threatened to be charged as one of the conspirators?
>
> Weichmann: "No, sir. . . . I do not remember anything of the kind. These questions look so silly to me that I almost hate to answer them; I never heard of such things before."

Bradley called four defense witnesses whose testimony was meant to prove that Weichmann's testimony had been suborned, John Ford and three of his former employees at Ford's New Theatre: James Maddox, the theater's property man; James Gifford, the stage carpenter (he was credited with building the theater); and Louis Carland, its costumer and a sometime actor. After the assassination all but Carland had been confined in Carroll Prison—Ford recalled, bitterly, he had been held there for "thirty-nine days and a half." Weichmann had also been held in Carroll Prison, and Ford's, Maddox's, and Gifford's terms there overlapped his thirty-day stay.

Carland's testimony on Tuesday, July 16, was the most damaging. He spoke of a walk he took with Weichmann during the trial in 1865 and confirmed the conversation that Weichmann denied had ever happened.

Carland: "He said if he had been let alone, and had been allowed to give his statement as he had wanted to, it would have been quite a different affair with Mrs. Surratt than what it was. . . ."

Merrick: "Did he say who troubled him?"

"Yes, sir; he said the parties who had charge of the military commission."

"Did he say to you that he had been obliged to swear to the statement that had been prepared for him, and that he was threatened with prosecution for perjury—threatened with being charged as one of the conspirators unless he did?"

"Yes, sir; he did; that it was written out for him and that he was threatened with prosecution as one of the conspirators if he did not swear to it."

"Did he say to you anything about his having been told by a man that he had made the confessions or statements in his sleep?"

"Yes, sir. He said that a detective had been put in Carroll Prison with him, and that this man had written out a statement which he had said he had made in his sleep; and that he had to swear to that statement. I asked him why he swore to it when he knew it was not true. He said part of it was true."

Lewis McMillan's role was also to get Mary's son convicted, in his case by reciting to the court a lengthy catalogue of criminal confessions Surratt evidently volunteered during the week and a half they rode in the RMS *Peruvian* together to Ireland.

After leaving the *Peruvian* in Liverpool—a mechanical problem forced the ship to remain in port one month for repairs and McMillan sailed in a different Allan Line vessel westbound—the doctor then served as physician in three, perhaps four, other company ships. Since September 1866, however, he had been unemployed. By the time McMillan finally took the stand in Fisher's courtroom on Monday afternoon, July 1, right after Weichmann was excused, he had been camped out in Washington City with his wife for almost six months, living on an allowance from the State Department and patiently "doing nothing" while waiting to testify.

McMillan was on the stand three times during Surratt's trial. The first session began on the afternoon of Monday, July 1, and continued through to noon the next day. If the *Peruvian*'s doctor's testimony then were to be believed, as their ship steamed slowly east Surratt had incautiously, perhaps even proudly, volunteered that he had participated in wartime atrocities. According to McMillan, while Surratt and a female agent (allegedly Sarah Slater) were on a courier mission behind Confederate lines just south of Fredericksburg they came upon half a dozen emaciated Union prisoners or prison escapees, coolly shot them to death, then rode on, the bodies "left to rot in the roadside." McMillan's apparent reference to Slater later pushed Carrington into another hyperventilated bit of misogyny:

O, that it were not so, that an American woman should be found in such company, giving her countenance and support to the cruel and bloody purposes of this infernal conspiracy. But there she is. Yes, there is Mrs. Slater. I know no infernal deity whom she could properly personate; for it has been truly said that hell hath no fury like that of a depraved and wicked woman. I hope I will not be understood by these remarks as casting any reflection upon the fairer sex, for I yield to no living man in admiration for true female character. Gentle, virtuous, pious woman is the most beautiful object in all creation; but when she yields herself to the devil, she becomes, of all objects, the most offensive and revolting . . . when she casts aside her womanly nature and enters into a hell-inspired plot, she is of all objects then most offensive and disgusting.

During a second incident, McMillan averred, Surratt escaped capture on the Potomac by firing from under a flag of truce at the crew of a Union boat, and during a third he participated in the summary execution of a Union telegrapher discovered in the field.

On Tuesday morning Pierrepont's questioning led McMillan away from lurid accounts of war crimes and dishonor in Virginia to Surratt's flight from Elmira to Canada (leaving a convenient few days open for a quick trip to Washington to kill Lincoln) and his flight through a succession of hideouts to Liverpool. During cross-examination McMillan salted his account of the ocean crossing with another damning quotation from Surratt. Standing on deck behind the *Peruvian*'s wheelhouse and waving a pistol for emphasis, Surratt supposedly told McMillan, "I hope to God I may live another two years longer, in order that I may serve Andrew Johnson as Abraham Lincoln has been served."

And so during several hours of testimony on both days McMillan had Surratt confessing to war crimes and to participating in plots to abduct and murder Lincoln, exulting in the slain president's death, and threatening his successor with murder.

McMillan was recalled by Merrick the next morning. Counsel's purpose was to set up the appearance of one of his defense witnesses to come, Stephen Cameron, a former Confederate army Roman Catholic chaplain, who would tell a different story about what McMillan heard from Surratt and what the doctor had concluded from it.

Two weeks later, on July 16, the defense called Cameron, who had ridden in the RMS *Nova Scotian* with McMillan eastbound to Liverpool at the end of October 1865. In quick answers to one leading question from Merrick after another, astonishingly without objection by Pierrepont, Cameron quickly eviscerated McMillan's testimony. The thrust of Cameron's responses to Merrick was he had heard from McMillan that Surratt had told the doctor he had been in Elmira when the president was assassinated, that Surratt had gone from there directly to Canada, and that McMillan then believed Surratt could not have been a participant in the murder.

When his turn came to cross-examine Cameron, Pierrepont jumped on the witness. The focus of his interrogation was not to cast everything Cameron said as hearsay but to tarnish the witness by prying out details of his "detached service" in Canada after the Confederate cross-border bank robberies in the village of St. Albans, Vermont, in October 1864. It was Cameron who, after the raid, had smuggled military commissions from Richmond to the raiders, formalizing their status as regulars in the Confederate army and enabling their escape from the unlikely threat of extradition to the United States.

McMillan was back in the courtroom on July 23, recalled this time by the prosecution for the purpose of exploring his feud with Abbé Boucher.

At least in theory, Surratt, the courier between Richmond, Washington, and Montreal, could also have served as a bridge between the assassination plot and the Confederate senior leadership, a connection the government had tried to make at the Arsenal and that would become the central issue if or when Jefferson Davis finally was brought to trial. Oddly, Judge Fisher dismissed this connection, so important to Judge Advocate General Joseph Holt, in an almost offhand way on July 18, when in response to counsels' heated discussion about Weichmann, Fisher opined that if Weichmann had passed military intelligence to Richmond he could be counted an accomplice, but only if it could then be proved "that

the confederate government was the principal in the murder of Mr. Lincoln."
That a Supreme Court judge of the District of Columbia unprompted sounded
doubtful about Richmond's role in the assassination was a bad omen for any
Davis prosecution to come.

When its turn came, the defense first discredited the prosecution's chief
witnesses to the conspiracy and then moved immediately to assail the credibility
of those who had testified that Surratt was in Washington on April 14, beginning
with the most damaging, that of Sgt. Joseph Dye.

Among the other witnesses for the prosecution, John Lloyd was a confessed,
unapologetic drunk. The jury's challenge was to decide how much of what he
said to believe in view of his mind's great blank spaces. Weichmann posed a
different problem. The suspicion then (and now) was that he, a tenant for nearly
six months in Mary Surratt's boardinghouse, had at very least known of Booth's
aborted kidnapping plot and testified to save himself after being threatened.
Some went further and believed Weichmann had passed military intelligence
to Richmond about the locations and numbers of Confederate prisoners held
by the Union. Merrick tried to get at this during examination of John Ford, who
spent nearly six weeks in Carroll Prison with Weichmann, and of a third inmate,
James Maddox. His questions were disallowed.

Dye's testimony was demolished on July 8. That's when James Gifford, the
carpenter at Ford's; C. B. Hess, a singer from Philadelphia; and Louis Carland,
the costumer, testified they had been standing on Tenth Street outside of Ford's
the night Lincoln was murdered and had not seen Surratt there. According to
them, it was Carland, not Surratt acting as the master clock for the plot, who had
announced the hour aloud during the third act of *My American Cousin*. He did it
innocently, to alert Hess, one of a trio scheduled to sing an homage to Lincoln
after the play ended, of the time. Later Pierrepont would dismissively describe
Hess as "little Hess . . . blue-black hair, very heavy moustache, very dark, swarthy
face," as having been brought forward by the defense to "personate" Surratt and
so to vitiate Dye's testimony.

Contradictory testimony was not the only blemish on Dye's credibility.
A possibly murky personal history was another. Dye had been charged in
Pennsylvania with passing forged banknotes, but the charge was subsequently
dismissed. The defense later conceded the charge should not have been raised,
but the dismissal could have been in exchange for testimony.

Next came the impeachment of David Reed ("a notorious gambler . . .
indictment in this court of a penitentiary offense yet to be answered"), of William

Cleaver ("just fresh from the jail . . . committed there originally for murder by the most foul and cruel means that could be applied"), and of the "utterly infamous" William Vanderpoel. Then glancing blows struck at all the others who imagined they saw, or lied that they saw, Surratt in Washington that day.

William E. Cleaver was a veterinarian and former government horse buyer who beginning in 1865 kept a livery stable on Sixth Street, between B Street and Missouri Avenue, several blocks from Ford's Theatre. On May 22, 1865, Cleaver was a minor prosecution witness during the trial at the Arsenal. He testified much more extensively June 20, 1867, for the prosecution in the Surratt trial.

In 1867 Cleaver swore that midafternoon on January 25, 1865, Surratt had described to him some "bloody work" he and Booth had to do, that they were going to kill the "damned old scoundrel" Lincoln. He went on to say he saw Surratt midafternoon the day of the assassination in Washington City, on horseback on H Street between the Printing Office and the railroad.

The defense attacked the testimony of most prosecution witnesses either directly through the conflicting statements of others or by making them out to be known, practiced liars. Detective John Lee, for example, was the target of a parade of defense witnesses, all swearing to his reputation for dishonesty. Cleaver, however, merited a special approach. Several months earlier, Cleaver had been tried and convicted during the March term of the same court of the rape and murder of a young girl and sentenced to five years' imprisonment in the penitentiary at Albany.

The defense suspected, rightly as it turned out, that Cleaver's testimony against Surratt was part of a scruffy deal that got Cleaver out of jail on bail and a new trial. During testimony the prosecution argued that evidence of Cleaver's criminal history was either inadmissible or offered too late, relevant only to Cleaver's admissibility as a witness and not to his credibility as one. Fisher took the prosecution's position a step further: The prospect of a second trial meant that the first trial (and conviction) carried no weight at all, he said.[3]

The closest the prosecution came to acknowledging their witness's criminal history was to describe him euphemistically as "a man of violent passion in a certain way" and then to assert this did not impair his ability to tell the truth. Well, perhaps the prosecution came closer than that: Carrington did concede "frankly" during closing argument that he "would not convict any living man upon the uncorroborated testimony of William E. Cleaver."

Five weeks into testimony, Bradley offered an alternate reality: On April 14, 1865, Surratt was nowhere near Ford's Theatre. He was, in fact, four hundred miles away from the city performing a legitimate—even a daring, although vain—military mission. The conspiracy to murder the president, to which the prosecution had worked so hard to attach their client, Bradley believed, included just four men: Booth, Powell, Herold, and Atzerodt—now all conveniently dead. No one else. Surratt, Bradley would grant, had joined a kidnapping plot, abandoned a month before the President's death, but he had participated in and was guilty of nothing else.

Beginning late in the morning on Monday, July 15, Brig. Gen. Edwin Lee, CSA, testified for the defense. This was not Lee's first attempt at a public defense of his side during the late war. That had been in a letter published in the *Montreal Gazette* on April 26, 1865, in response to Secretary Edwin Stanton's charge that "the President's murder was organized in Canada and approved at Richmond." Lee's letter to the paper, dated the day before publication, called Stanton's accusation "preposterous for its littleness and meanness" and denied the charge "indignantly, contemptuously." "I aver," he wrote to the *Gazette*'s editor, "upon the faith of a Christian, and the honor of a gentleman, my belief that [members of the Confederate States government] were as little the promoters of this murder as Secretary Stanton or Vice President Johnson." Now, twenty-six months later, Lee was to have been among the few most important defense witnesses at Surratt's trial.

Bradley wanted Lee's testimony to establish that Surratt
- left Washington on March 25, arrived in Richmond on the twenty-ninth, then left Richmond for Montreal two days later, carrying a dispatch from Secretary of State Benjamin to Brigadier General Lee;
- arrived in Montreal on April 6 with instructions from Secretary Benjamin regarding the disposition of the Confederacy's funds in Canada, until then managed by Jacob Thompson;
- left Montreal the afternoon of April 12 for Elmira, New York, where he was to "ascertain the position and condition of the confederate prisoners confined at or near said town . . . and to make sketches of the stations of the guards and approaches to said prison, and also the number of the arms and troops there"; and
- returned to Montreal on April 17 or 18 to report to Lee on his mission, delivering "rude sketches of the said prison and its approaches," for which he was paid for expenses and services rendered.

Lee was potentially among the few most important defense witnesses. Seven questions into his testimony, barely past establishing who the unhealthy man on the stand was, Pierrepont began objecting to Bradley's follow-on questions. Every one of his objections was sustained by Judge Fisher. The defense examination of this witness started, and practically finished, with General Lee's explanation that he was in Canada in April 1865 while on a six-month sick furlough and that he saw Surratt there on April 6, 1865.

Consequently, when Lee left the stand shortly after noon, he had played only a minor walk-on part. All that the defense had been able to establish by his presence was that Surratt had a very light moustache ("like one of a man who had never shaved—a boy's moustache; and he had a very light goatee") and that between April 6 and April 17 or 18 Surratt was absent from Montreal for "an interval of several days." The impact of what General Lee said was so slight that when Bradley turned over the witness for cross-examination by the prosecution, Pierrepont didn't even deign to stand up to release him.

Poor Lee. The man was in frail health. He would die in several years' time, consumed in the end by the same disease that had forced medical retirement from the Confederate army before his assignment to Canada. Lee had managed to escape one great killer, the Civil War, only to die victim of an even more voracious one, tuberculosis.

In 1867 Lee spent sixty-one days in Washington awaiting the court's pleasure. He was paid $1.25 for every day, the usual witness per diem rate, and 5 cents for each of his 1,541 miles of travel between Texas and Washington. Lee's trip from a sanitarium in Texas to the trial must have been exhausting, but his long presence in Washington was to no purpose. Bradley had been neatly finessed by Pierrepont and the judge. Neither side in the trial got anything in exchange for two months of Lee's life.

Surratt's mission to Elmira's prison camp formed half the heart of his alibi. Although not substantiated by General Lee, his presence in the small western New York city around the time of the assassination was confirmed by the testimony of several city clothiers and merchant tailors—Charles Stuart, John Cass, and Joseph Carroll, the latter described as the "world-famous" menswear cutter at Stuart and Ufford's shops at 20–22 Lake Street—as well as by Frank Atkinson, Stuart's bookkeeper and a city alderman. All these substantial citizens were positive they saw Surratt shopping at their stores in Elmira April 13–15. Each one remembered his distinctive, foreign-looking attire (a type of belted jacket) and personal appearance, and each had since seen Surratt in jail and confirmed him as the clothing shopper they clearly remembered. Their testimony, substantiated by that of Augustus Bissell, a New York City physician who passed through Elmira on April 14, prompted Pierrepont into forceful and repetitive cross-examinations, in the face of which the defense's witnesses stood their ground.

The other half of Surratt's alibi lay buried in an elaborate analysis presented to the jury by lawyers from both sides, complete with a large-scale map of rail lines between Montreal and Washington. The issue had to do with a possible southbound trip from Elmira to Washington City on Thursday, April 13—not withstanding Stuart's, Cass's, and Carroll's contradictory testimony—that would have put Surratt through Harrisburg, Pennsylvania, about 3:00 AM Friday, in Baltimore at 7:25 AM, out from there at 8:50 AM for Washington, and in Washington before 11:00 AM, albeit not really in time for Charles Wood's morning cleanup and all that supposedly followed, but maybe close enough. If the prosecution were correct, after the killing and between Saturday, April 15, and Tuesday, April 18, northbound trains then took Surratt to New York and via Albany, Burlington, St. Albans, and Rouse's Point back into his Canadian sanctuary, a movement attested to by another six prosecution witnesses.

Railroad routes and schedules were central to the case both sides had to make. The prosecution needed to prove he could have made this 292-mile trip on their schedule, a preliminary to proving that he actually did so. The defense wished to prove that Surratt had gone north, not south, from Elmira, and, moreover, that one couldn't get from there to Washington City on the schedule posited by Pierrepont et al.

The essential threads of what decades later would become a virtual cobweb of rails across the northeastern United States were already substantially in place in 1865, following a construction boom in the 1850s that connected (for example, and very indirectly) Boston to New Orleans and La Crosse to Savannah. Fully seventeen lines crossed the international border between Canada and the United States.[4] (The dense network of rails made relatively swift overland travel possible, but it did not make it easy. Just five years before, Lincoln took three full days to ride the twelve hundred miles from Springfield, Illinois, to New York City. He had to change trains five times en route and finally ended his trip with a ferry boat crossing of the Hudson River from New Jersey.)

Along the mid-Atlantic seaboard the key transportation node was Baltimore. More than just a major seaport, the city was the home of American railroading after 1827, when the Baltimore and Ohio Railroad was chartered. In 1865 a traveler in Baltimore could leave by rail in any compass direction. North on the Northern Central Railroad to the rail hub at Harrisburg, Pennsylvania, and from there outbound on the Pennsylvania Railroad or any of several other lines to other places. East on the Baltimore and Philadelphia, or the Philadelphia, Wilmington and Baltimore, toward New York and New England, or west on the Baltimore and Ohio through the Allegheny Mountains and beyond into the great open spaces of the Midwest. South eleven stops on the Washington Railroad to the national capital, and from there across the Long Bridge over the Potomac by omnibus and then onto the rails of the Loudoun and Hampshire, the Manassas Gap, or the Orange and Alexandria into what had been, until the month before, the Confederate States of America.

By the end of the Civil War the United States' railroad infrastructure, excepting that of the battered South, equaled—perhaps exceeded—the best in Europe. Although inefficiencies, among them seven different rail gauges and the absence of standard time zones, impeded flow, passengers were moved day and night at an average speed of twenty miles per hour for a fare of a few cents per mile. Farmers and manufacturers saw their produce and products travel only two-thirds as fast, but that was still much more quickly than by freight wagon or canal barge.

Along these tracks, and down the tendrils of branch and connecting lines, many communities once isolated by dirt roads were being tied into the larger society and economy just over the horizon. There were more than seventy stations laced together along the right of way of the three railroad companies that constituted "the direct route" between Elmira, New York, and Washington City, the route that Pierrepont insisted Surratt had traveled immediately before the assassination.

J. N. Dubarry, the general superintendent of the Northern Central Railroad, was the senior railroad executive who testified at the trial, first on July 15 and then again on the twenty-fifth. In 1865 Dubarry's Northern Central ran nearly due north out of Baltimore to Harrisburg, Pennsylvania, connecting there to the Pennsylvania Railroad and several other east-west lines. Past Harrisburg the Northern Central followed the Susquehanna River to Sunbury, Pennsylvania, some forty miles south of Williamsport. Out of Sunbury, through passengers for destinations in north-central Pennsylvania or western New York State rode the Philadelphia and Erie (the P&E) to the ferry crossing over the Susquehanna River at Williamsport, and then the Williamsport and Elmira to Elmira. Although there were three other routes connecting Elmira to Baltimore and Washington (through Philadelphia, Scranton, and even out-of-the-way New York City), this was the most direct and counsel for both sides concentrated on it.

Referring to company records, Dubarry testified with authority and confidence, and at first his words seemed to provide proof that Surratt could not have left Elmira on April 13 for Washington or left Washington April 14 after the assassination and arrived back in Elmira the following night. Ten days after his first appearance, however, Dubarry was recalled to the stand by the prosecution and testified then that on April 13 passenger trains had indeed run between Elmira and Williamsport and between Sunbury and Baltimore, with one arriving in Baltimore at 7:25 the next morning, Good Friday.

Dubarry was joined by witnesses representing his and several other railroads carrying passengers and hauling freight north of Washington City. They included Francis Fitch, train master (dispatcher) at Williamsport; George Strayer and George Hambright, a Northern Central train engineer and conductor, respectively; Charles Hepburn, acting superintendent of the P&E's eastern division; Ezra Westfall, the P&E's dispatcher at Williamsport; Joseph Guppy, assistant superintendent of the Erie Railroad; George Koontz, general agent of the Baltimore and Ohio railroad; and John George, who described himself on July 25 as "through baggage master between Washington and New York." The goal was a reconstruction of train movements over the three critical days, April 13, 14, and 15. By weaving together the movement of "special trains, construction trains, gravel trains," to get around the fact that flooded bridges prevented the running of the usual night schedule from Elmira, the prosecution made the case that Surratt could have left the St. Lawrence Hotel at 3:30 PM April 12 and arrived in Washington City a day and a half later.

That Surratt was in Washington on April 14 became one of Carrington's summary points to the jury. He asserted to them that although the prosecution had established this "beyond controversy" by means of thirteen witnesses, it was under no obligation to prove how he got there or how he got away. It was the burden of the opposite side, he said, to show that it was impossible for Surratt to get to Washington and impossible for him to get away.

Passing 140 years later, the answer to the key question—where Surratt was the night Lincoln was shot—is not more certain than it was in 1867, although the defense's witnesses from Elmira sound persuasive today. The fact that he was not caught in Stanton's fast-moving dragnet is evidence of a sort that Surratt was not in Washington City that night. But that hunt's focus was to the south and east of the city, toward supposed safe haven in Virginia and elsewhere in the dying Confederacy, roughly along the established Secret Service "lines" that connected the two belligerents during the war. If Surratt were in the city the night of Good Friday 1865, if only a few of the government's witnesses actually saw what they swore to, then his decision to flee north to Canada kept him out ahead of the expanding circle of searches, drawn in the opposite direction by the pursuit of Booth.

If Surratt had been permitted to testify he would have likely recounted a story very like the one he recited to an admission-paying audience in the Rockville, Maryland, courthouse on December 6, 1870. The lecture was arranged to make him money. "Its impetus," as Surratt frankly confessed at the outset, was "pecuniary necessity." Fifty cents' admission for each adult and twenty-five cents for every child for an after-dinner talk an hour and a quarter in length (twice as much as adults had paid to hear Lincoln speak in New York ten years earlier). His audience was likely respectful and sympathetic, perhaps even admiring as suggested by the fact that the evening ended with a brass band concert led off with a spirited playing by cornets of the Confederacy's informal national anthem, "Dixie."

Three days after appearing in Rockville, Surratt was in New York City, lecturing at the Cooper Institute's Great Hall to an audience of 150 sprinkled among 1,650 empty seats. From the account in the *New York Times* the next day, the small house in New York was much less enthusiastic than the one in Maryland had been. "The lecture was read from a manuscript," the paper reported, "and was, with one or two occasions of applause, listened to quietly by the small audience." No rousing rendition of "Dixie" at the end of the talk here.

If his story is to be believed, one man in Surratt's New York audience found the lecture especially interesting. He was Henry Lipman, the same "little red-faced, thick-set Hollander" who claimed that as a Pontifical Zouave in November 1866 he had been one of the twelve guards who had conspired to let their American comrade in arms escape arrest from the barracks dungeon in Veroli. "When I attended a lecture he gave in this city [New York]," Lipman told a *Tribune* reporter in 1881, "he singled me out among the audience and embraced me with gratitude."

"Pecuniary necessity" aside, Surratt's lectures were meant to recover his honor by explaining his apparent indifference to the execution of his mother. "It has been asserted over and over again, and for the purposes of damning me in the estimation of every honest man that I deserted her who gave me birth in the direst hour of her need. . . . But such was not the case," he said in Rockville. His mother's true situation was concealed from him at the end of June by a friend in Washington and by the messenger he had sent there "to see how matters stood." He learned of her execution from a newspaper after the fact. "That paper informed me that on a day which was then present, and at an hour which had then come and gone, the most hellish of deeds was to be enacted. It had been determined upon and carried out even before I had any intimation that there was any danger."

Taking the few in the audience who had followed him through that convoluted syntax, Surratt moved briskly ahead. He charged the prosecution with deliberately concealing evidence (the Brainard House's hotel register) that would have freed him, and the "unprincipled and vindictive" Judge Fisher with bias. Surratt then went on to pillory Weichmann: "I proclaim it here and before the world that Louis J. Weichmann was a party to the plan to abduct President Lincoln. He had been told all about it. . . . I have very little to say of Louis J. Weichmann, but I do pronounce him a base-born perjurer; a murderer of the meanest hue." Surratt continued, "Hell possesses no worse fiend than a character of that kind. Away with such a character. I leave him in the pit of infamy, which he has dug for himself, a prey to the lights of his guilty conscience."

There is no reason to disbelieve the essential elements of what Surratt told his audience about his movements that April more than five years before. "I left Richmond on Saturday morning," he said about his last cross-border mission (and likely one of the last intelligence courier missions) of the war, "and reached Washington the following Monday, at 4:00 o'clock PM, April 3rd, 1865." Surratt said he then departed Washington on the early train for New York the next morning heading for Canada, having easily evaded the detectives looking for him, "and that was the last time I was ever in Washington until brought there by the U.S. Government a captive in irons, all reports to the contrary notwithstanding."

On Thursday, April 6, Surratt registered at the St. Lawrence Hotel, and soon thereafter he delivered Secretary Benjamin's dispatches to Gen. Edwin Lee. The next Wednesday, April 12, following what appears to have been a generally idle week in Montreal, Surratt was back in the United States at the Brainard House hotel in Elmira on General Lee's intelligence collection assignment.

"I slept [Friday] night through and came down the next morning, little dreaming of the storm then brewing around my head," Surratt told his lecture audiences. "When I took a seat at the table around 9 o'clock AM, a gentleman to my left remarked: 'Have you heard the news?' No, I've not, I replied, what is it? 'Why President Lincoln and Secretary Steward have been assassinated.' I really put so little faith in what the man said that I made a remark it was too early in the morning to get off such jokes as that. 'It's so,' he said, at the same time drawing out a paper and showing it to me." Intelligence collection mission suddenly pushed aside, Surratt immediately left Elmira for Canandaigua, New York, heading for home and knowing only that Lincoln had been attacked the day before. He spent the rest of Saturday and Sunday there, at the northern end of the Finger Lake of the same name, waiting for the start of the week and the first train out of town.

In Canandaigua on Monday he read in New York newspapers that he was now suspected of the assault on Seward: "'The assassin of Secretary Seward is said to be John H. Surratt, a notorious secessionist of Southern Maryland. His name, with that of J. Wilkes Booth will forever lead the infamous role [*sic*] of assassins.' I could scarcely believe my senses," he recited to the crowd. "I gazed upon my name, the letters of which seemed sometimes to grow as large as mountains and then to dwindle away to nothing. So much for my former connection with him I thought. After fully realizing the state of the case, I concluded to change my course and go direct to Canada."

What had started as a train trip home via Baltimore became instead a flight for refuge in Canada: first through Albany, New York (roughly two hundred miles), and St. Albans, Vermont (a little less than two hundred miles more), and finally to Montreal (another seventy-five or so), where he arrived, safe for the moment, at midafternoon on Tuesday, April 18.

So said Surratt.

Passing midcentury, entertainment in the United States outside of the home often meant attending public lectures like John Surratt's. Among the legion of itinerant speakers after the Civil War was one fast making a reputation for knee-slapping wit, Mark Twain. Twain's fabulously successful first book, *The Innocents Abroad or the New Pilgrim's Progress*, stitched together acerbic newspaper columns about the pleasure cruise of the SS *Quaker City* to Europe, Russia, and the Ottoman Empire in 1867. It catapulted the humorist to celebrity status as the first authentic American literary voice, where he would remain forever.

Twain lectured when he wasn't absorbed in writing. By the time *Innocents Abroad* was published Twain was already an acknowledged expert in the business of entertaining a paying audience. His first speaking tour in 1866–67 was a triumph; audiences throughout California and Nevada ended each sold-out appearance with applause and ear-splitting approval.

Twain quickly learned of Surratt's foray into his business. On January 4, 1871, a few weeks after what turned out to be Surratt's last lecture, a *Brooklyn Eagle* correspondent reported what the great American wit thought of Surratt and his new career. "Mark Twain thinks that John H. Surratt's manager understands his business," the *Eagle*'s reporter wrote, or else Surratt is fortunate above the average of snubbed and struggling would-be lecturers—for every day the newspapers reveal to the people that the gentleman is being persecuted. He [Twain] says that there are other ways to get before the public and crowd his houses, but this is the cheapest and surest. . . . The kind of public interest excited in Mr. Surratt's case will cram the largest halls in America, and his sly manager knows this and keeps up the excitement. The talks of Surratt's arrest—the story that Attorney General Holt offered to save Mrs. Surratt, and set her free, if the son would take her place, which the son refused to do—the announcement that his Baltimore lecture was interfered with by his arrest for a nonpayment of a tobacco tax years ago—and now, the announcement that the Mayor of Washington has warned Surratt against driving the people of the Capital to extremities [sic] are the crowning triumphs of this manager's inventive genius. Mr. Surratt, [Twain] says, is on the high road to success and an income for $25,000 a year, and the only way to stop it is for the newspapers to let him alone. Then his little candle would straightway begin to burn weaker and weaker, and presently the poor thing would flicker out and pass away in a film of smoke, leaving nothing behind but an evanescent stench.

With its witnesses swearing they saw Surratt in Washington on Good Friday, the prosecution wanted to prove that it was possible for Surratt to have left Montreal on Wednesday, April 12, passed through Elmira on Thursday, and disembarked at the railroad depot on North Capitol Street Friday morning in time to be in Wood's barber chair and present in the city for all that followed. The defense needed to prove that was impossible.

"It is understood," the *Chicago Tribune*'s reporter wrote on February 23, the day Surratt was arraigned in court, "that he will attempt to prove an *alibi*." "Alibi" from the Latin meaning "elsewhere": The defendant wasn't at a particular place at a particular time.

"Alibi" was a very suspect concept in the 1860s. Pierrepont and his team wanted the jury to believe that an alibi was an inferior form of courtroom defense, the desperate resort of a prisoner who concedes everything charged is true but true of someone else, a defense "easily concocted and frequently resorted to falsely."

To government counsel, and the several learned sources they quoted at length, the weakness of alibi as a criminal defense had two roots, uncertainty as to the facts ("a witness is always liable to be mistaken") and about the time. This latter flaw was a nineteenth-century mechanical problem. "There is always room for the difference of time to be explained," Carrington explained to the jury, "owing to the difference of time-pieces, which sometimes vary from five to ten minutes."

"You know," Pierrepont added on August 3, "that when a man has great motives, such as the desire to save his life, he will take any means to save it, and you know that he will swear to any falsehood, that he will make up any evidence, and you know that one of the most common things, if you have ever read much of proceedings in courts, is to attempt to prove an *alibi*." An alibi, he said, "is one of those things most easily forged of any defense."

The judge on the bench held a similar view. An "honest and sensible jury," Fisher said, "cannot fail to regard it [an alibi] with suspicion." It was

> a line of defense always held in little favor by courts and juries, not only because it is one which common sense teaches us may be most easily supported by perjury, but because it is one involving identity of time, as to which mistakes are very easily made, so that it is by no means difficult to support this plea frequently (and especially after the lapse of months or years) by the testimony of honest and truthful witnesses, who, on account of the great liability of the human mind, particularly when influenced by the promptings of pity or sympathy, to be mistaken in the precise time.

Nothing in this trial swung on a ten-minute difference between pocket watches, but Fisher, Pierrepont, and Carrington were all agreed: Anyone who would resort to defense by alibi would stoop to anything. Besides, as Carrington pointed out later, thirteen swore Surratt was in Washington on April 14. Only five (three really, as two were uncertain of the exact date) proved his presence in Elmira. Even allowing for the possibility of a few liars in the mix, "the weight of evidence," Carrington said, speaking literally about the weight of witnesses, "is on our side."

A midcentury religious revival in the United States, the Great Awakening sharply reversed the creeping secularism that until then had accompanied the migration of landless peoples westward. By 1850 roughly one-third of all Americans claimed membership in a church, fully twice as many as had belonged to a congregation at the end of the colonial era. Many Americans in the later nineteenth century, including and perhaps especially those in the social class from which the population in Fisher's courtroom came, believed devoutly in God and his heavenly host, in Satan and his imps, and in heaven and hell, not as metaphors and symbols but as palpable presences and as real places.

When government counsel at John Surratt's trial described John Wilkes Booth as "Satan" and Surratt as the demon "Beelzebub," partners in an infernal conspiracy, he meant exactly that: The two were the chief devils of hell and their plot was hatched there. Merrick, speaking for the defense, took a secular stance, criticizing District Attorney Carrington's equation of crime with overarching evil:

> He [Carrington] said he could show that the heart was generally wicked; that the party was possessed by the devil and this in order to prove malice. He could do no such thing. . . . Malice in criminal law means willfulness, intention.

Carrington was not persuaded. "The Satan in this infernal conspiracy has gone to hell," he later explained, "there to atone in penal fires forever and ever for his horrid crime."

> But the Beelzebub still lives and moves upon the face of this green earth, as the dramatist says, "there to mock the name of man." In John H. Surratt, the prisoner at the bar, you behold the Beelzebub of this infernal conspiracy. Second he may be in rank and power, but none the less in hatred, malice, and revenge, and to those red and bloody demons lurking in every wicked, base, depraved heart, and prompting to the commission of those crimes which shock and outrage human nature.

Carrington found the answer to this "shock and outrage" in the Bible. Not for him some "milder penalty . . . in place of the death penalty" proposed by "certain modern philanthropists. . . . Jails and penitentiaries were not intended to be boarding-houses for the instruction of criminals. The Bible contains the best code of laws that was ever promulgated for the government of man; and whenever statesmen depart from its teachings they run either into despotism on the one hand or anarchy on the other."

Religiosity and the equation of crime to sin permeated the trial. Thus Surratt (and Booth, posthumously) were indicted by the grand jurors in each charge with committing crimes while "not having the fear of God before their eyes but being moved and seduced by the instigation of the devil." A popular political cartoon of the period illustrated the seduction alleged. In it a dapper Booth is holding his pistol at the ready outside of the presidential box at Ford's Theatre while a beady-eyed and be-fanged Lucifer (pridefully crowned between his horns with a peacock feather symbolizing eternal life) stands behind the assassin-to-be, pointing helpfully at the back of the doomed president.

God, or in this case God made manifest in the form of "the mysterious means by which omniscient and omnipotent justice reveals and punishes the doers of evil," got credit for Surratt's capture, too, a work that inexplicably took the Almighty many months to accomplish.

Pierrepont began his summation with a text that can only be described as a sermon. "In the arrangements of Divine Providence in this world, things are so ordered that every truth is in perfect harmony with every other truth," he said.

> It is always so. From that there is no variation. God is a god of truth, and all the sin and woe on earth come from a divergency from that line of truth that proceeds from His heavenly throne. If everything was truth, there would be no crime. If all was truth, there would be no wrong. All wrong comes from a violation of that great principle. The moment you violate the truth, everything is out of joint. Every truth being in harmony with every other truth, every falsehood that is interposed dislocates it, and breeds mischief and injury to the community. It is so in the physical life. It is so in nature in every form. It is so in the moral world. . . . You cannot violate a law of God without punishment even on this earth. No man ever did do it; no man ever went to his grave, having violated a law of God, without having been punished for it, and no man ever will, even in this world.

Further along in his near endless oration, Judge Pierrepont moved from theology and politics to outright mystery. "Gentlemen," he addressed the jury, hoping to focus attention, "I now come to an act in this dark drama, which, though strange, is not new."

> So wonderful is it, that it seems to us to come from beyond the veil which separates us from death. As I have already said, "all government is of God." The powers that be are ordained of God, and for some wise

purpose which we do not understand the great Ruler of all, by present-ments, by portents, by bodings, and by dreams, sends some shadowy warning of the coming doom when some great disaster is to befall a nation. So it was in the days of Saul, so it was when the great Julius Caesar fell; so it was when Brutus fell at Philippi; so it was when Christ was crucified, [and on the judge went, spinning out examples in a roll call of slain rulers and the portents that foreshadowed their murders] . . . never in the whole history with which we have been familiar has there been a single instance of the assassination of the head of a government in which the assassins have not been brought to justice. It is a terrible thing to fight against God. Government being of God, any attempt to throw a people into confusion and anarchy is fighting against God, and in no instance has he ever suffered a man guilty of such a crime to go unpunished. Though he may have taken unto himself the wings of the morning, and fled to the uttermost parts of the earth, yet the eye of God has watched him and the hand of justice has brought him back to give a rendition of his bloody account.

Finally, on August 6, in the last of his very many words to the jury, Judge Pierrepont asked them to consult God for guidance in their deliberations, the same divinity who never before had let an assassin escape justice:

If, when you are doubting, you will go before your God on bended knees, asking for that light which comes alone from heaven, to enlighten your minds to a knowledge of the truth, and will rise from your knees, I know that God will give you light, and I will say that your verdict is of God and is right, whatever it shall be. Take that test, and you will have not trouble; take that test, and your consciences will be at ease. You will feel that you have done your duty to yourselves, to your country, to your holy faith, to the God before whom you and I shall soon appear.

Soon after court convened on Wednesday morning, August 7, Judge Fisher read his charge to the jury. Fisher began by quoting Genesis 9:6, "Whoso sheddeth man's blood, by man shall his blood be shed" (not necessarily a good start for young Surratt), then segued into a defense of the legitimacy of the military commission that in 1865 had hanged the defendant's mother (another bad sign for Surratt). Prologue over, the judge moved on.

The question the jury had to answer, Fisher told them, was "whether the prisoner at the bar participated with John Wilkes Booth and the others named in the indictment, or either or any of them, in this diabolical crime." Fisher's charge, especially his summary of the evidence, clearly favored the prosecution's case, an imbalance that some commentators would remark about later. Helpfully, nearing the end, Fisher recited numbered key points he wanted the jury to take with them when they withdrew to deliberate:

First. That a conspiracy formed in time of war, to take the life of the President and Vice-President of the republic and the heads of the executive departments, for the purpose of aiding the enemies of the federal government, by throwing it into anarchy and confusion, is treason as heinous and hurtful to the people of this country as the compassing the death of the king or queen of Great Britain is to the subjects of that realm.

Second. That every person engaged in such conspiracy, as long as he continues a member of it, is responsible not only for the act of treason, but for any murder or less crime which may flow from it in its prosecution.

Third. That the government may waive the charge of treason against any or all the conspirators and proceed against them for the smaller crime of murder, included in the greater crime of treason.

Fourth. That under an indictment for a murder resulting from the prosecution, evidence of the entire scope of the conspiracy may be considered in estimating the heinous character of the offense laid in the indictment.

Fifth. That it was not necessary to aver in the indictment the fact that Abraham Lincoln, the victim of the murder, was at the time of its commission President of the United States, or to prove it in order to allow the jury to take that fact into account in determining the heinous character of the crime, it being a fact of which courts will take judicial cognizance.

Sixth. That he who does an act by another does it by himself, and is responsible for its consequences in criminal as well as civil cases.

Seventh. That although an *alibi*, when clearly established, forms a complete and unanswerable defense, the mere absence from the immediate scene of a crime resulting from a conspiracy unrepented of and unabandoned by the party charged, will not avail him if he were at some other place assigned him performing his part in that conspiracy.

Eighth. That this plea is, unless clearly made out, always regarded with suspicion, and a circumstance weighed against him who attempts it, because it implies an admission of the truth of the facts alleged against him, and the correctness of the inferences drawn from the evidence.

Ninth. That flight from the scene of crime, the fabrication of false accounts, the concealment of instruments of violence, are circumstances indicating guilt for the consideration of the jury.

Tenth. Although a confession in the slightest degree tainted with the promise of favor, or by duress or fear, is not admitted as evidence against him who makes it, yet, if made freely and voluntarily, is one of the surest proofs of guilt.

Surratt had made no confession. Fisher was referring to, and accepting at face value, what Surratt had allegedly told Lewis McMillan about his reasons for being aboard the RMS *Peruvian* and to Henri Beaumont de Sainte Marie when both were in camp with the Zouaves. (The judge had an almost poetic vision of confession. It was, he said, "the testimony of the Omniscient speaking through the conscience of the culprit.")

Eight of Fisher's points closely supported the prosecution's theory of the case. The second and third, however, sounded as if he had consulted with Judge Advocate General Holt when he wrote them. The crime of treason, not mentioned until now directly, would soon come up again.

Fisher spoke without pause until about 11:30, and then the jury retired to begin its deliberations a few minutes later. At not much over an hour in length, Fisher's was one of the shorter orations of the trial. It's possible that the prosecution had some hint of what the judge was going to say, because Carrington made a special point of warning its members beforehand that "a juror who swears to decide according to the law, and departs but a hair's breadth from the instructions of the court, and decides according to his own abstract notions of right and wrong—pardon me for saying so, I do it in no offensive sense—commits the awful and Heaven-daring crime of perjury." Were Fisher's instructions observed as strictly as Carrington's standard required, Surratt was short days away from being a dead man. At 10:00 that evening, with no news from the jury, the court recessed. On Thursday, still waiting for a verdict, the court recessed at 6:00 PM, and on Friday Judge Fisher left shortly after noon.

At 1:08 PM on Saturday, August 10, after three days of deliberations, the jury returned to the courtroom, now filled again with officers of the court and an audience and surrounded by armed policemen. Earlier in the day Foreman Todd had told Judge Fisher that they were "nearly equally divided" and had been since their first ballot.

Hours later they were still unable to agree. Surratt must have already heard this good news, because he came into the room smiling. Todd's report was brief: "We deem it our duty to the court, to the country, and in view of the condition of our private affairs and situation of our families, and in view of the fact that the health of several of our number is becoming seriously impaired under protracted confinement, and to make this statement, and to ask your honor to dismiss us at once."

At the outset, some on the jury had optimistically expected the trial to last two to three weeks; others thought perhaps three or four. In late spring they had been praised as experienced and wise, obviously capable. Now, nearly two months later in midsummer, they were frustrated and tired, and some claimed to be unwell. Bradley, facing a retrial, immediately and probably reflexively protested their dismissal. "The prisoner," he said, "gave no consent. . . . If they were discharged . . . it was against his will and protest." Carrington flinched; he told Fisher that the government left the decision to the discretion of the court. With that, Fisher sent this remarkably intelligent body of men home.

And then, with the court still in session, the judge fired off a final shot at the defense's senior counsel. "I now have," Fisher said to everyone who remained in the room, "a very unpleasant duty to discharge, but one I cannot forego."

On the 2d day of July last . . . as the presiding justice was descending from the bench, Joseph H. Bradley, Esquire, accosted him in a rude and insulting manner, charging the judge with having offered him a series of insults from the bench from the commencement of the trial. . . . Mr. Bradley . . . threatened the judge with personal chastisement [as Fisher understood it]. No court can administer justice or live if its judges are to be threatened with personal violence on all occasions whenever the irascibility of counsel may be excited by an imaginary insult. The offense of Mr. Bradley is one which even his years will not palliate. It cannot be overlooked or go unpunished as a contempt of court. It is therefore ordered that his name be stricken from the rolls of attorneys practicing in this court.

With Bradley ignited in fury behind him, Fisher left the courtroom, throwing over his shoulder the suggestion that Bradley appeal to the U.S. Supreme Court if that was his wont.

Fisher's summary disbarment of Bradley was a catastrophe for the man. It powerfully threatened both his income and his ego. Litigating was how Bradley made his living, and being one of the giants of the Washington City bar was who he was. The judge's act was, as well, a potential disaster for Surratt's legal defense. Fisher's action decapitated the team that so far had successfully fought off the government attack on their client's life.

Their feud festered for years. Bradley soon sued Fisher twice, once "for trespass in expelling him, the other for libel in the order of expulsion." Fisher's successful defense against both claims, by Washington lawyers Riddle and Cooke, ended up in the U.S. Supreme Court. The legal victory cost the judge $576.25 in fees and expenses. In 1874, with Fisher no longer on the bench but now the U.S. district attorney for Washington, Congress agreed that he should be reimbursed this sum, and he was.

Foreman Todd's assessment that the jury was "nearly equally divided" might have been a sop to the prosecution, but it seems not to have been an accurate description of the final vote in the jury room on City Hall's top floor. Later newspaper reports had the jury split seven to four to acquit on its first ballot with one abstention, then eight to four to acquit on all later caucuses in their private, locked room. Reportedly the four for conviction were all Yankees, and seven of the eight who voted to acquit came from the District of Columbia, Virginia, or Maryland.[5] That's how the *Philadelphia Press* tallied the result in its August 11, 1867, issue. Todd, Burr, McLean, and Schneider voted for conviction, the *Press* wrote. Among the eight voting for acquittal was one New York native (Berry), two citizens of Virginia (Alexander and Davis), two from Maryland (Gittings and Morsell), and three from the District of Columbia (Ball, Birth, and Bohrer). Given New York City's close commercial ties with the cotton-growing South before the Civil War and the influence of antiwar, anti-abolition Copperheads in the city, that Surratt won Berry's sympathy is not necessarily remarkable.

The jury did not vote on entirely sectional lines, but it very nearly did so. It's also possible to conclude that the testimony the twelve heard was so contradictory and the truthfulness of the many witnesses so difficult to judge that partisan sentiment aside, a hung jury was the logical outcome, given that the triers of fact were hard pressed to define exactly what the facts in the case were. That was the conclusion of the *Times* on August 13, when it chided, "The endeavor of Washington correspondents to explain the result of the Surratt trial by a reference to the geographical origin of the jurors, is puerile . . . the great body of the public recognize wide room for doubt in the testimony adduced."

The outcome, a hung jury, was not a complete surprise to political players in Washington. One of the most savvy (and opinionated) insiders was the secretary of the Navy, Gideon Welles. Welles shared his views with his diary later that day: "The jury did not agree. This was expected. I have not read all the evidence. That Surratt was in the conspiracy to kidnap I have always believed, but I have had the impression that when the conclusion was to kill, he flinched, and his mother favored his absence in order that he should not be under the influence of Booth. But this may be all a mistake on my part." In the same entry for August 10 Welles continued: "The judge was disgracefully partial and unjust, I thought, and his charge highly improper. The senior Bradley was irascible, violent, and indiscreet,— some difficulty brought him and the judge in collision almost,—and the judge, at the conclusion of the trial, ordered his name stricken from the roll of attorneys, an arbitrary act."

The *New York Times* told its readers on August 11 pretty much what Welles had recorded privately in his diary the day before. "The result of the trial of SURRATT is not unexpected," the paper wrote on page 4:

> More than one attempt has been made to ascribe the difference among the jurors to personal and partisan considerations. But there is no necessity and perhaps no excuse for these imputations. There is quite enough in the conflict of evidence, in the doubtful character of witnesses, and the conjectural character of many of the more positive statements, to suggest doubts and explain the grounds of disagreement. . . .
>
> Of the conduct of the trial, as well for the prosecution as for the defense, the impartial observer will not be inclined to speak very highly. The unseemly violence of Mr. Bradley must have been of but slight service to the prisoner, while upon himself it brought discredit. On the other hand, the excess of zeal which has been observable throughout Judge Pierrepont's management of the prosecution, has tended to excite misgivings as to the real strength of his cause. He has done over-much, both in the line of evidence and argument; introducing irrelevant matters continually, and parading issues not properly involved in the trial. Judge Fisher's bias, too, has been as evident as the bad taste and feeble logic of his final charge.

Welles's judgment and that of the unnamed *Times* reporter that Fisher's charge was partisan were consistent with what Fisher himself wrote about the trial years later in a text that seems to have been the script for his public commentary on the trial. As his note reveals, Fisher believed that Surratt had been in Washington the night of the assassination, that he had confessed to McMillan and Sainte Marie, and that his international flight was further proof of his guilt.[6]

If Welles truly believed that Surratt knew about the planned assassination but "flinched" and didn't participate actively, then he was remarkably sanguine about Surratt's escape from justice.* Others in Washington and elsewhere took the news much less coolly.

Harper's Weekly believed in the defendant's guilt, "so ably developed by Mr. Pierrepont," and its opinion was that "testimony for the defense was not so voluminous nor so positive; the lawyers of the prisoner appear to have based their hopes on proving an alibi." Still, granted the article's author, "that [Surratt] was in Washington at the time of the murder, as charged in the indictment, appears to have been doubted by the majority of the jury, and hence the disagreement." His conclusion was philosophical: "A new trial will doubtless follow at the next term of the court, and will doubtless result as all new trials do—in nothing."

Frustrated Union sentiment aside, the *Harper's Weekly* columnist got the essentials right: The proof the prosecution presented of Surratt's presence in Washington the day Lincoln was murdered, the hinge around which much else in its case for conviction swung, was unconvincing, and follow-on legal proceedings did not accomplish what many wanted.

---

* Welles's long (more than eighteen hundred pages in three volumes, spanning 1861–69) and very readable dairy reflects his education in the law and experience as a newspaper journalist. It was published in 1911 by Houghton Mifflin.

Gideon Welles (1802–1878), a former Democrat, journalist, and state legislator from Hartford, Connecticut, held what amounted to New England's seat in Lincoln's carefully geographically balanced cabinet. His immediate predecessor in Buchanan's cabinet, Isaac Toucey, had been the first navy secretary from that state. Appropriately, Welles had prior experience in the department. He had been the civilian chief of the navy's Bureau of Provisions and Clothing in the late 1840s, one of the five bureaus established by Congress in 1842 to manage the shore establishment.

Welles served Lincoln and Johnson as the secretary of the navy for eight years, half of them during wartime. Largely under his leadership the Union navy afloat grew nearly tenfold in just four years, peaking in 1865 at 671 ships and 58,300 officers and men, up from fewer than 10,000 in 1860. Navy personnel strength declined just as swiftly after the war to just under 10,600 in 1870.

8

"PRESIDENT JOHNSON WAS A DRUNKARD"

The international hunt for Surratt in 1865–66 and his criminal court appearances in 1867–68 played out against the backdrop of the strangely amorphous prosecution of Jefferson Davis and an increasingly evil-spirited battle between President Andrew Johnson and the Thirty-ninth and Fortieth Congresses over exactly how and by whom the defeated states were to be woven back into the political fabric of the country.

Although curious Washingtonians thronged the courtroom every day Surratt appeared before Judge George Fisher, history moved very quickly in the years after Lincoln was shot, and by mid-1867 the trial of the last conspirator already had a faint aroma of yesterday's news about it, even as it began. The assassination of the revered president had receded into the past, eased there first by a tidal wave of cathartic public grief (two hundred thousand Union army men marched in memorial procession through Washington; perhaps a million mourners stood at trackside during his funeral train's 1,650-mile meander from the capital to Springfield or passed by his open casket when the body lay in state in eleven cities en route) and then by the swift conviction and punishment of the eight accused conspirators.

The high stakes dramas of Reconstruction and Johnson's impeachment put further distance between the past and the present. By the time Surratt stood in Fisher's courtroom, Lincoln was part of the firmament and both regions of the nation had moved on to grope with the great open questions of the day. Who in Washington would define the terms under which the eleven former Confederate states would be reintegrated into the Union? How was the defunct Confederacy's political and military leadership to be treated? What was to be the future status of four million "freedmen," former slaves now adrift in the South without voice or the means to sustain themselves?

In the slow and imperfect resolution of these political uncertainties lie hints that may explain the intermittent pursuit of a man identified during the immediate post-assassination frenzy as John Wilkes Booth's principal assistant and chief recruiter and the outcome of Surratt's trials.

It is one of the great ironies of American history that in the aftermath of the Civil War the president of the defeated Confederate States of America escaped judgment in court for leading the rebellion but his counterpart in Washington, the new commander in chief of the victorious Union armies, stood trial for "high crimes and misdemeanors."

The pursuit of Davis was quickly successful, thanks to near-ubiquitous Union cavalry riding unfettered through Virginia, the Carolinas, and Georgia at war's end. The only senior Confederates who escaped were those few who made it to the coast and fled overseas. All who stayed on land north of the Rio Grande were nabbed sooner or later.

Once Jefferson Davis was locked in Fort Monroe, his captors turned to the question of what to do with their prisoner. Soon caught in the political maelstrom that was spinning around Andrew Johnson and his critics in Congress, and tugged at by an undertow of the private agendas of powerful men, the case against Jefferson Davis moved forward very slowly, its progress further impeded by a lack of focus and inept performance at all levels in the Department of Justice. Formal charges against Booth's eight had been drawn up and delivered several weeks after the assassination. The first grand jury indictment against John Surratt was presented even before he was returned to U.S. soil. Two others followed. (The last, as we will see, too late.) In comparison the government did not have an indictment against Davis together with a case it was willing to take to trial until March 1868, nearly three years after Davis was arrested and just one month ahead of an absolute legal deadline. By then the hot outrage that had fueled the trial of the eight three years earlier had largely dissipated, and universal amnesty, Johnson's preferred outcome, was being spoken of in cabinet meetings and openly in the press.

Even while Lincoln was alive indications of an impending brawl over Reconstruction between the chief executive and Congress were visible. An early clue appeared during the summer of 1864, when Congress sent the Wade-Davis bill to Lincoln for signature. In addition to grafting military governors atop southern state governments, the bill's provisions required fully half the electorate of a southern state to swear loyalty to the Union before civil government could be reestablished there and its representation restored in Congress. Lincoln, who in a proclamation the previous December had set the standard at 10 percent, not 50, allowed the bill to die unsigned in July while Congress was in recess.

Newly sworn into office, President Johnson appeared to Radical Republicans to be in their camp, as stern and unyielding in his determination to punish the chief Confederates and to reform the South as they were, indeed, much more so than Lincoln had revealed himself to be before his death. For example, Johnson's May 1865 amnesty proclamation excluded the South's political, military, and economic leadership from its offer of pardon, beginning with the first class exempted, those "who are or shall have been pretended civil or diplomatic officers . . . of the pretended Confederate government," and running to a fourteenth class, comprised of all those who previously took an oath of amnesty or allegiance but had not "thenceforward kept and maintained the same inviolate." These outliers, including essentially all the survivors who had governed the South and led its armies for the past four years, were required to apply individually for pardon.[1]

After a short springtime honeymoon with recessed members of Congress, however, as 1865 unfolded, the president soon stood increasingly exposed as what he was: a conservative southern Democrat with his own agenda.

Surratt might have been the dead John Wilkes Booth's principal accomplice, but that still made him pretty small beer compared to the living archvillain in the piece, Jefferson Davis. Davis's conflicted legacy is nowhere better represented than in Richmond, Virginia, the second Confederate capital and the site of his office and family residence during four war years. The small city is still uncomfortable with its past. (Approaching a population of 200,000 today, Richmond was roughly 38,000 at the start of the Civil War and rose to some two and a half times as many at its wartime peak.) For years that discomfort was reflected in debates about statuary along leafy Memorial Avenue, where tennis champion Arthur Ashe now stands ennobled in granite, incongruously near statues of five of the Confederacy's greats: Davis, Lee, Jackson, Stuart, and Maury. (A similar press-to-fit coupling was once found in the celebration of Lee-Jackson-King Day, a state holiday that awkwardly bundled homage to two Confederate generals and the 1960s civil rights movement's martyr into a single day of commemoration near their birthdays in mid-January.)

It is apparent also in the status of two of Richmond's oldest downtown attractions: the restored White House of the Confederacy at Twelfth Street and Clay Street and the adjacent Museum of the Confederacy, both nestled in a canyon of tall Virginia Commonwealth University medical buildings. The two are presented to the public modestly, even apologetically, appropriately so in a city that is more than 50 percent African American and in a state that is increasingly more mid-Atlantic than southern. The museum, a one-time shrine believed to hold "sacred relics" rather than mere historical artifacts, competes unsuccessfully today with the new American Civil War Center on the expansive grounds of the old Tredegar gun foundry that carries none of the baggage (supporters would call it "heritage") of "the Lost Cause."

This ambivalence accurately reflects not only modern sensibilities but also Virginia history. Secession and the Confederacy sprang from the Deep South, the seven states that grew cotton and where slaves amounted to almost half of the population. As one moved north, the "peculiar institution" of legalized human bondage in a democratic country lost traction. Agriculture and industry outside of Tidewater Virginia and in the other three states of the mid-South rested on a different base, obviating the need for the armies of field hands that cotton cultivation required. Before the war came, slavery in the four border states, none of which withdrew from the Union, was already moving toward remission. It took time for Virginia to take sides against the Union. Before Fort Sumter its decision to do so was not a sure thing, and Virginia's secession when it came failed to carry its separatist Appalachian counties, which bolted to become the State of West Virginia officially in June 1863.

When Dixie, the Deep South, struck out on its own in early February 1861, delegates from the first six states to secede met in Montgomery, Alabama, and self-consciously began the business of creating a new country. Their template, naturally, came from their experience, so the new constitution and the form of government it described were a great deal like the ones they had just rejected, as filtered through the eyes of men who believed cotton culture and slavery were the foundations of economic and social order.

The convention considered several men for the post of provisional president, all from the relatively moderate political center of secession sentiment, meaning that firebrands at one pole and Johnny-come-latelies at the other were ineligible. Jefferson Davis, of Mississippi, quickly emerged as the convention's choice. Alternatives to him either eliminated themselves (Robert Toombs of Georgia by his incipient alcoholism, William Yancey of Alabama by his radicalism, Howell Cobb by his lack of conviction) or lost out in the political logrolling that preceded the vote (Alexander Stephens of Georgia).

Davis, fifty-three in 1861 and not present in Montgomery, had the perfect résumé to become president of the Confederacy: twenty-third among thirty-three in his graduating class at West Point in 1828; military service on the Indian frontier and in the Mexican-American War; political experience in Washington as a congressman, senator, and cabinet officer; ownership of a thriving cotton plantation and many slaves in Mississippi; and outspoken, inflexible views supporting states' rights. Moreover, he was as handsome as Lincoln was not. In a modern televised campaign debate it is difficult to tell which attribute would put its man on top: Lincoln's eloquence or Davis's luster.

Jefferson Davis had deflected talk the year before proposing him as the Democrats' presidential candidate, and he didn't seek to be the Confederacy's chief executive now. He did, however, accept the unsolicited post among his own kind graciously when it was offered. On February 18, 1861, two weeks before Lincoln's inauguration day, Davis was sworn into office as the provisional president of the Confederate States of America on the steps of the Alabama state capitol.

In late May, Davis and his government relocated from Alabama to the new capital in Virginia, moving there by train but propelled to Richmond on a wave of optimism spun up by the Union's recent surrender of Fort Sumter in Charleston, South Carolina's harbor. The following November the convention's selection of Davis was ratified in a presidential election in which he ran unopposed. When the electoral votes were counted in February 1862 Davis and his vice president, Alexander Stephens, each received all 109 votes. Their six-year term was to extend until the next inauguration day in February 1868.

Lincoln's nomination had fractured his Democratic opposition. In response to it northern Democrats nominated Stephen Douglas of Illinois, secessionists picked John C. Breckinridge of Kentucky, and Southern unionists named John Bell of Tennessee. The three Democrats split 123 electoral votes, with Breckinridge, Buchanan's vice president, getting most of what was left, 72. Lincoln entered office in March 1861 with the remaining 180 electoral votes, not quite 60 percent of the 303 total and none from the South, where he had not appeared on the ballot.

The apparent difference, Davis getting all possible votes, Lincoln managing something over half, turned out to be deceptive. What seemed to be an impossibly divided Union was not, and the South was less monolithic than the unanimous vote for Davis suggested. The Confederacy carried within it, moreover, a powerful centrifugal force: a commitment to states' rights—the theme of Davis's inauguration address—that enormously complicated governing the new country and fighting the coming war.

Gracious Richmond was the natural choice for the Southern capital, after tropical heat and malarial mosquitoes teamed up to chase the infant Confederate government from Montgomery, but the once-lovely city on the James River eventually proved to be indefensible. Richmond had been selected for its role entirely on the basis of political, not military, considerations. Much later Davis would boast bravely that "it has been a source of national pride that for four years of unequaled warfare we have been able, in close proximity to the center of the enemy's power, to maintain the seat of our chosen Government free from the pollution of his presence," but that same "close proximity" made Richmond an exceptionally unwise choice for a capital at war.

By early February 1865 General Lee recognized that the defenses of Richmond and Petersburg would soon be crushed between the armies of Lieutenant General Grant on the north and those of two major generals, Sherman and Schofield, moving up from the south. In the face of Union pressure, on April 2 Lee finally abandoned the defense of the capital along a line connecting Petersburg and Richmond. His army's withdrawal west toward Amelia Court House triggered a general flight from the Confederate capital.

Despite Lee's earlier warnings, there had been few preparations in Richmond for such an evacuation, so in the usual response of weak government to crisis, generalized frenzy now substituted for execution of a plan. It was near midnight that same Sunday before members of Jefferson Davis's cabinet rode out toward their future packed together on the first of eight hastily improvised night trains for Danville, Virginia, near the North Carolina border. When the flight out of the city began, those eight comprised all of the company's rolling stock in the yard at the Richmond and Danville Railway's northern terminal. (That same night Surratt, oblivious to the turmoil far behind him, was riding the rails also. He was on the way from Richmond to New York via Washington in company with Sarah Slater, whom he would drop off in the big city before continuing on to Montreal.)

All but two of Davis's principal government officers were also aboard the first evacuation express: Secretary of State Judah P. Benjamin, Secretary of the Treasury George A. Trenholm, Secretary of the Navy Stephen Mallory, Attorney General George Davis, and Postmaster General John H. Reagan. The essential files of their cabinet departments were hastily boxed and jammed into the same rail cars, already full of people and their baggage. Only Vice President Stephens and the newly appointed (and sixth) secretary of war, General Breckinridge—the same Breckinridge who had been Buchanan's vice president and who had run against Lincoln as one of his three Democratic opponents—were not there.

The elfin Stephens (he weighed less than one hundred pounds) had led the Confederate delegation to the February 3, 1865, peace conference on the steamer *River Queen* offshore Fort Monroe in Hampton Roads. After this quick, failed mission—the Union's representatives were Lincoln and Secretary of State William Seward, and the sides talked past each other for four hours—Stephens gave up day-to-day participation in the business of government. He then left Richmond for his home in Crawfordville, Georgia, and was arrested there by federal cavalry on May 11, 1865, the day after Davis was seized. (Stephens's petition to President Johnson for clemency, submitted a few weeks later from a granite cell in Boston's Fort Warren, claimed that he had never supported secession and did not feel himself "morally responsible or accountable in any way for the appalling evils attending [the war].") Breckinridge organized the flight by train from the capital but then left Richmond on horseback with his aides and two senior supply officers hoping to meet Lee in the field, join up with Gen. Joseph Johnston in North Carolina, and, in so doing, somehow to wrest tolerable surrender terms from Grant and Lincoln.

Davis's train finally pulled out of the Richmond and Danville Railroad terminal at the foot of Fourteenth Street on the James River just before midnight. Usually an eight-hour trip, that night the president's special took seventeen hours to cross the James to Manchester and to steam the 141 miles between the capital and the city on the Dan River that had been an important Confederate supply center when hopes were still bright.

Behind the first train out of Richmond that night, described wryly by a young soldier who watched as "a government on wheels," was another, guarded by fifty Confederate navy midshipmen from the CSS *Patrick Henry*, the training ship tied up on the James River. In sealed casks aboard that train was some $450,000 in coin from the vaults of six Richmond banks and what was left of the Confederate treasury.[2] Behind the treasure train slowly came the others, full of refugees from the battered city and their scant belongings. The eighth didn't leave Manchester on the south bank of the James until nearly noon on Monday, just after the bridge across the river behind it was destroyed.

Behind the last train, Richmond burned uncontrollably. The conflagration mingled fires set to deny the Yankees stockpiled war materiel with others ignited by looters and arsonists. When the wind-blown flames finally died out, the city's downtown looked like Dresden in February 1945, as if it had been bombed from the sky. "At sunrise Monday morning," the *Richmond Whig* wrote mournfully on April 4,

Richmond presented a spectacle that we hope never to witness again. The last of the Confederate officials had gone; the air was lurid with the smoke and flame of hundreds of houses sweltering in a sea of fire. . . . Next to the river, the destruction of property has been fearfully complete. The Danville and Petersburg Railroad depots, and the buildings and shedding attached thereto. For the distance of half a mile from the north side of Main street to the river, and between 8th and 15th streets, embracing upwards of twenty blocks, presents one waste of smoking ruins, blackened walls and broken chimneys. . . . Of course, we cannot be expected at this time to enter into an estimate of the losses, but they are immense, and will amount to hundreds of millions of dollars.

Danville, the refugees' destination, was a significant metropolitan center by the countrified standards of the Confederacy. In 1860, the year of the last prewar federal census, what was to become the new southern nation boasted only one city, New Orleans, with a population as large as 170,000. Its next-largest city, Charleston, was less than one-quarter the size of New Orleans. The rest of the "big" cities of the South tailed off quickly into the 30,000–20,000 range. Most county seats mustered only 500 or so souls.

Davis's initial plan, such as it was, was to reconstitute the government in Danville, there to await what would come of Lee's attempt to join forces with Johnston. On April 4 (the same day the *Richmond Whig* published its city's obituary), now settled in Danville, Davis issued a proclamation "To the People of the Confederate States of America," which sounded exactly the right notes of resolution and confidence in the face of "the great moral as well as material injury to our cause that must result from the occupation of Richmond by the enemy." Necessarily his text rested firmly on fantasy. Two days after Richmond had fallen, and five before Lee would surrender his army at Appomattox, Davis managed to construe some reasons for optimism:

Relieved from the necessity of guarding cities and particular points, important but not vital to our defense, with an army free to move from point to point and strike in detail the detachments and garrisons of the enemy, operating on the interior of our own country, where supplies are more accessible, and where the foe will be far removed from his own base and cut off from all succor in case of reverse, nothing is now needed to render our triumph certain but the exhibition of our own unquenchable resolve. . . .

I announce to you, fellow-countrymen, that it is my purpose to maintain your cause with my whole heart and soul. . . . Let us not, then, despond, my countrymen; but, relying on the never-failing mercies and protecting care of our God, let us meet the foe with fresh defiance, with unconquered and unconquerable hearts.

It is possible he believed the optimistic tone. Davis later explained what he had in mind: Lee was to redeploy his army from Richmond and Petersburg to the south, into positions along a new defensive line on the Dan and Roanoke Rivers (roughly east-west along the western Virginia–North Carolina border), where he would join forces with Johnston. Together they would then attack Sherman. Success would cause other Confederate units to rally to Lee, and this revitalized force would then turn north and eject Grant from Virginia.

It's unlikely that many others believed as did their president, who later conceded that in "the light of subsequent events," his proclamation "was over-sanguine." In any event, the Confederacy's collapsing infrastructure meant that few beyond Danville's nine thousand residents ever had any knowledge of their chief's defiant message.

Few in the greater South, moreover, could have known that the day before Union troops took possession of Richmond, or that even while Davis's proclamation was being promulgated, Lincoln was sitting at what had been Davis's desk on the second floor of the executive mansion, savoring a tranquil moment during his short victory lap through the occupied Southern capital.

On April 10, while Davis was having dinner with his hosts in Danville, Maj. and Mrs. William Sutherlin in their home on Main Street (later the city's public library and now its Museum of Fine Arts and History), he learned the terrible news that Lee had surrendered, exposing Danville to Grant's army. Now an even more hasty decision was made to relocate the capital forty-eight miles farther south to the village of Greensboro, North Carolina. A twelve-car train was slowly coupled together, loaded, and sent out for the Virginia border on the tracks of the Piedmont Railroad just before midnight.

Danville had taken some satisfaction, some pride in its unexpected status as the new national capital. The welcome just across the Virginia–North Carolina border in Greensboro (the teeming Guilford County seat, population two thousand) was not nearly so warm, and it cooled perceptibly during the five days of the Davis visitation. The stop in Greensboro was, literally, the end of the line for Davis and his cabinet, now reunited with Breckinridge. In Greensboro most of what was left of the Confederate government seemingly seeped into the ground, leaving behind a little more than a gaggle of refugees.

In better times the North Carolina Railway ran trains from Greensboro south to Charlotte (and east to Goldsboro), but no longer. Here the desperate party abandoned their train and most of their files and on horseback or in horse-drawn ambulance wagons (the only available rolling stock) left late April 15 for Charlotte, North Carolina, by road, escorted by remnants of a cavalry division. That same night Surratt arrived by train from Elmira at Canandaigua, New York, on the way to Montreal. He spent the weekend at the Webster House, a hotel in that lakeside city, and took the first train out of town toward Montreal early Monday, April 17.

None with Davis on Saturday knew that Abraham Lincoln had died that morning, soon after sunrise in the back room of Petersen's townhouse on Tenth Street in Washington City, some three hundred miles north. Not until four days later in Charlotte—April 19, the day that the ranks of Lincoln's funeral procession slow-marched behind a horse-drawn catafalque down Pennsylvania Avenue toward the Capitol—did Davis learn in a telegram from Breckinridge that Lincoln had been assassinated.

By then Surratt was safely back in Montreal, temporarily hiding in John Porterfield's house. Of the eight who would stand trial in the Arsenal the next month, only George Atzerodt, Samuel Mudd, and Davey Herold were still at liberty on April 19. Atzerodt had just one day of freedom left, Mudd only six. Herold was in midflight with Booth, but their escape had slowed fatally. The pair was still in southern Maryland, concealed in a copse waiting for Thomas Jones, a sympathizer, to tell them it was safe to row across the Potomac. Mary and the other four were already in jail.

While Jefferson Davis and his party slowly moved south through their disintegrating country, first by train and then by horse and wagon, their destination and their purpose changed from week to week. Davis, famously inflexible, was perhaps the last of the shrinking group to recognize that reality was inexorably reshaping his plans, forcing their unwelcome evolution.

At first, the goal of the flight from Richmond had been merely (or not so merely) to relocate the national government to a new capital and then to continue the war as before from a new and more secure place. This move acknowledged that Grant's pressure on the city's defenses had finally become irresistible, but it yielded to nothing else.

However, the surrender of the Army of Northern Virginia on April 9 forced a change because Danville was now no longer tenable. The flight to Greensboro was a flight from Grant, nothing more. The new strategic objective was to head west to where Confederate armies were still capable of maneuvering and to lead the fight from there. Under this scenario Davis would substantially shed his civil functions and become less a chief of state than a generalissimo in the field with his army. (Mississippi had a role something like this in mind for him right after secession and before the convention picked him to be president.)

Finally, General Johnston's surrender to General Sherman on April 26 at Greensboro, coupled to the impossibly great distance to General Kirby and pursuit by federal cavalry, made even that fantasy impossible. Now all that was left was escape from retribution, from punishment for having led the rebellion and for the death of Lincoln at the hands of assassins.

With Lincoln dead, a victim allegedly of Davis and his coterie, an enraged federal government resolved on swift justice for the criminals in Richmond and Montreal who had unleashed Booth on the president and attempted to decapitate the Union near the moment of its victory. The search for Davis was formally launched on Tuesday, May 2, 1865, by President Johnson with the issue of a proclamation:

> Whereas it appears from evidence in the Bureau of Military Justice, that the atrocious murder of the late President, Abraham Lincoln, and the attempted assassination of the Honorable William A. Seward, Secretary of State, were incited, concerted and procured by and between Jefferson Davis, late of Richmond, Virginia, and Jacob Thompson, Clement C. Clay, Beverly Tucker, George N. Saunders, William C. Cleary, and other rebels and traitors against the Government of the United States, harbored in Canada;
>
> Now, therefore, to the end that justice may be done.

The proclamation and implementing wanted posters that soon slid off the presses offered a $100,000 reward for Davis's capture—a fortune then, and as much was offered for the gunman himself, John Wilkes Booth—and $25,000 each for the four other principal "rebels and traitors." (Cleary, Clay's clerk, was priced out at a still generous $10,000.)

The hunt for Davis was quickly successful. Early on Wednesday, May 10, he was captured some seventy-five miles north of the Florida border near Irwinville, Georgia, by a detachment of the 4th Michigan Cavalry. Davis's hastily improvised and quickly unsuccessful attempted escape covered in Varina Davis's raincoat and shawl led to the accusation that he had tried to flee from the troopers who discovered his party disgracefully disguised as a woman. (Another report had him in a man's dressing gown.)

The Civil War began with a shortage of prison space; it ended with a surfeit of it. Nearly all of the Union coastal defense fortifications that had been built, or rebuilt, to deflect Confederate assaults (or Royal Navy blockade busting) that never happened were now war surplus. Many were quickly converted into prison blocks. On May 22 Jefferson Davis was locked up in an improvised cell in one of the casemates (gun vaults) of Fort Monroe, Virginia, on Old Point Comfort. When the cell door first closed behind him, seven days of testimony had already been heard in the Arsenal's courtroom in Washington and Surratt had been in St. Liboire in Canada for one month.

Davis's new home was built between 1819 and 1834 to protect Hampton Roads and the James River estuary to the west and the approach to the capital via the Chesapeake Bay and the Potomac River to the east, a vulnerability embarrassingly exposed during the War of 1812. From where the fort squatted heavily on a tongue of land facing Willoughby Spit on the opposite shore, its batteries commanded uninterrupted sight lines over Horseshoe Flat, the lower Chesapeake Bay, and the Virginia Tidewater.

When constructed in the 1830s, the huge, hexagonal stone structure surrounded by a moat was an example of the period's standard practice in fortification design. Quick reinforcement during early 1861 and the powerful Union navy kept the stout fort in Union hands despite its location on enemy ground. A cartographer scanning charts in the 1860s could have reasonably concluded that Fort Monroe, lying at the throat of Hampton Roads and near the mouth of the James River, was one of the most strategically important places on the American Atlantic littoral. And so it might have been in Confederate hands, but the fort never turned into a focal point in the war. Immediately after April 1865 it was valuable chiefly as a military prison.

Davis was held in Casemate 2 under tight security for two years: bars on the cell's door and across the embrasure, armed guards all around, a lamp lit inside around the clock, and in manacles for part of that time. During the second year

Fortress Monroe, Old Point Comfort, and the Hygeia Hotel as they appeared in 1861. The Hygeia was one of the popular Virginia Tidewater resorts of midcentury. Behind it loom the walls of Fort Monroe, where Jefferson Davis was imprisoned. The sidewheel steamer in the foreground is the Old Bay Line's *Adelaide*, one of six ships the company owned. Excepting the war years, the *Adelaide* stayed on the schedule between Baltimore and Norfolk until 1879, when she was sold. One year later she was rammed in New York Harbor and sank. (Lithograph by E. Sachse and Company, 1861; Harry T. Peters "America on Stone" Collection, National Museum of American History, Smithsonian Institution)

Varina Davis lived in Fort Monroe also, not comfortably but not under confinement. Brig. Gen. Nelson Miles, the fort's commander, had first rudely proposed that she stay with the laundresses and prostitutes. She was able to visit her husband almost daily.

The question of what to do with and to Davis bedeviled Johnson, his cabinet, and Congress from the date of his capture in early May (while Surratt was hiding out in Father Boucher's rectory in St. Liboire, Quebec) until February nearly four years later (by which time Surratt had been a free man for several months and was traveling in South America).

President Johnson, Secretary of War Edwin Stanton, Attorney General James Speed, and Judge Advocate General Joseph Holt, in common with most Union leaders, were convinced that Davis had led the plot to assassinate Lincoln and that the murder had been done with the full knowledge of Davis's cabinet in Richmond and what was somewhat grandly called his "Canadian cabinet" in

Montreal, meaning the several men whose names appeared in Johnson's May 2 proclamation.* Holt's initial objective in the Arsenal trial had been to establish the existence of just such a general conspiracy and the guilt of the absent senior conspirators, Davis—then en route by sea under military escort from Savannah to Fort Monroe—and his Canadian minions. Only later, after his view of this context had been put into the record, did Holt shift the tribunal's focus from the alleged criminal masterminds who were not in the dock to the eight prisoners who actually were there.

Johnson's May 2 proclamation had announced that it "appears from evidence" that Jefferson Davis and company were guilty of an atrocious crime. There was no such evidence. That appearance, substantiated initially by generalized hatred of the defeated chief enemies and what soon was exposed as testimony based largely on facts manufactured to fit, turned out to be impossible to prove and, eventually, impossible even to present to a jury.

Holt's attempt to prove the existence of a general conspiracy to kill Lincoln during the trial at the Arsenal rested in large part on the testimony of three witnesses—Richard Montgomery, James Merritt, and Sanford Conover—although dozens of others were called to tell their bits and pieces of the same story. Montgomery and Merritt were War Department employees. Conover described himself as an absconded Confederate conscript and a freelance correspondent for the *New York Tribune* in Washington and Montreal. As we saw in chapter 2, he was a New York lawyer named Charles Dunham and "Sanford Conover" was one of many noms de guerre.

Montgomery, whose testimony opened the trial, was identified for the record as being "acquainted" with the Confederate leadership in Canada and its complicity in the assassination. Merritt, who testified the day after Montgomery, was said to be "intimate with the rebels in Canada" and knowledgeable about the assassination and other plots they had discussed and agreed among themselves. Conover, however, was the most important of the three, as evidenced by the fact that he was recalled twice by the prosecution after his first appearance in court on May 20. Just as Holt planned, Conover's sworn testimony over the three days appeared to bind the pieces together: Davis and his cabinet to Booth and his conspirators, and in turn to Lincoln and the assassins.

---

* Among whom Clement C. Clay (1816–1882) was something of an anomaly; he was the only one who willingly surrendered himself to the Union. Clay, from Huntsville, Alabama, whose father was also a U.S. senator from Alabama, served in the U.S. Senate between 1853 and 1861 and then in the Confederate Senate until defeated for reelection in 1864. In May 1865 he joined Davis in confinement at Fort Monroe but was pardoned and released in April 1866, only weeks after the *Ex parte Milligan* decision.

Unfortunately for the prosecution, after his testimony as "Sanford Conover" in Washington had been compared to his testimony as "James Watson Wallace" in Montreal, Conover, née Dunham, stood revealed by the press as an imaginative but unconvincing liar. With this exposure the legal attack on Davis might have run aground as early as midsummer 1865, but Holt couldn't let go of either his thesis or his discredited chief witness. Incredibly, after the trial of the eight was over Conover was hired by Holt to find new witnesses for the pending case against Davis. He dutifully managed to produce eight between August 1865 and February 1866, including two women who later turned out to be his masquerading wife and sister-in-law. All were carefully coached to swear to lies, the purpose of which was to link Jefferson Davis to the crime. Conover's fiction masterpiece started to come apart beginning in May during hearings before the House of Representatives' Committee on the Judiciary, when first Merritt and then several of Conover's recruits confessed to lying under oath. Eventually Conover was indicted for perjury, tried, found guilty, and imprisoned in Albany under a ten-year sentence. He served barely one before being pardoned.

Even before this imbroglio played itself out, the impetus to try Davis for murder had lost momentum. The first time the subject of his trial came up in the cabinet, on July 18, Johnson asked his department heads for their opinions. Seward counseled trial by military commission to hear charges of murder and treason but wanted to delay until an examination of Confederate government records could be finished. Presumably he expected such a review would reveal proof of suspected crimes. Stanton agreed. Secretary of the Navy Gideon Welles held exactly the opposite view, recommending a speedy civil trial. Hugh McCulloch, the treasury secretary, was noncommittal. No consensus was reached.

Davis's fate came up again three days later. This time everyone (the group now included Postmaster General William Dennison, Secretary of the Interior James Harlan, and Attorney General James Speed) agreed that the crime charged should be treason. Most opted for trial in a civil court, but Seward continued to favor the more reliable (or more malleable) military tribunal. Seward's consistently hard-line stance throughout these discussions—according to Welles, even more uncompromising than Stanton's—isn't surprising given that he and one son had barely survived the plot against Lincoln. Secretary Harlan wanted a tribunal, too, if there were any doubt a civil court would not convict on the basis of whatever evidence was available.

The question of what to do with Davis bounced around the cabinet five more times between late August and mid-October 1865, producing no explicit agreement but almost by default ending up with a decision to proceed in civil court in Virginia. (That conclusion meant that an indictment "found" in Washington against Davis was allowed to languish and finally to die in 1868.) About the same time as the last of these cabinet meetings, on October 16, Henri Beaumont de Sainte Marie's letter to Minister Rufus King uncovering Surratt was read to the cabinet by Seward, who expressed his personal conviction, unsupported by any evidence, that Booth, Surratt, and Confederate Secretary of State Benjamin had planned the assassination together but that Benjamin aside, Davis's cabinet in Richmond was unaware of the plot to kill Lincoln.[3]

Paradoxically the decision, meant to move toward Davis's trial and conviction, resulted in a game of legal kick-the-can, long ago described in high resolution detail by Roy Franklin Nichols in the *American Historical Review*. The game's players included three successive U.S. attorneys general (Speed, Henry Stanbery, and William Evarts), Justices Salmon Chase and John Underwood of the Supreme and Virginia Circuit Courts, respectively, District Attorney Chandler, a covey of counsel from both sides, and even Congress, which by scrambling court districts gave Supreme Court Chief Justice Chase yet another excuse for delay.* The cabinet's decision also cast Justice John Underwood, the U.S. circuit court judge in the District of Virginia, into a leading role. Underwood, an adopted Virginian with Radical Republican convictions, was notorious for his poor judgment, a man no official in Washington would confess to respecting. Some of the bizarre maneuvering to come was an effort to prevent Underwood from judging the sensitive case heading toward his court.

---

*   Chief Justice Chase, one-time rival to Lincoln for the Republican presidential nomination and erstwhile cabinet officer, complicated everything about the run up to the Davis trial that he touched. He, as much as anyone, was responsible for the series of delays that eventually morphed into abandonment of the effort to bring Davis to trial, although the list of the culpable also includes Attorney General Stanbery, who resisted playing any part in the proceedings.

Salmon Chase (1808–1873), Ohio's former governor and U.S. senator, was one of the four political rivals whom Lincoln successfully co-opted into his cabinet. He was, however, notable as the only one of the four who continued to campaign for the office even while he was serving the incumbent. Welles was merciless in his appraisal of the man, who he thought was "cowardly and aspiring, shirking and presumptuous, forward and evasive; . . . an ambitious politician; possessed of mental resources yet afraid to use them, irresolute as well as ambitious; intriguing, selfish, cold, grasping, and unreliable when he fancies his personal advancement is concerned."

Before Chase took his seat on the court he had served Lincoln (on balance, not badly) as secretary of the treasury until June 1864. That's when he overplayed his hand by presenting Lincoln with a fourth resignation letter, thinking the president would once again conclude he was irreplaceable. This time Lincoln called his bluff and accepted. Six months later Lincoln nominated Chase, still unemployed, to be the late Chief Justice Roger Taney's replacement on the Supreme Court. The appointment put Chase, who still craved the presidency, at the center of the legal spindrift blown ashore at the end of the Civil War.

The first date scheduled for Davis's trial was in autumn 1866 in district court in Richmond. Chase, under whose overarching authority such proceedings would have been conducted, refused to consent to a trial while Virginia was still under direct military control. Davis's trial was rescheduled for May 1867, then for November, and again for March 1868, for June, and finally for that November. Early delays flowed from a combination of events that left the government unprepared to proceed. Later ones were forced by events of Johnson's impeachment trial. Very early during this cascade of postponements, in mid-May 1867, with Surratt still confined in his specially secured cell in the District jail awaiting trial, Davis was released from Fort Monroe under bond to appear when summoned. His future appearance was guaranteed by three prominent Yankees, Horace Greeley, Cornelius Vanderbilt, and Gerrit Smith, and a group of southern businessmen who together had put up a $100,000 assurance bond.

More important than the procedural delays it prompted, the cabinet's decision for trial in court rather than before a tribunal meant, as Seward feared and Surratt's trial soon confirmed, that in so doing the administration would cede control of the outcome to a jury at least in theory capable of anything. The technical problems that forced trial delays were annoying but they fell one by one. What could not be overcome was the persistent fear that a jury in Virginia would find Davis innocent and that such a verdict would challenge the legitimacy of everything that had gone before. No less an authority than the maladroit Judge Underwood had said, audibly and unwisely, that only a hand-picked jury in his district could be trusted to judge a treason trial rightly.[4] Others made the same point more delicately.

The best expression of this concern was in an August 1868 letter from an outside associate counsel, Richard Dana, to the new (Johnson's third and last) attorney general, William Evarts. Dana pointed out that there was no possible upside for the government in such a trial, a conviction would only reaffirm what had already been settled, but the downside risk was very great: A "jury drawn from the region of the rebellion" would have an "opportunity to ignore the fact that Jefferson Davis took any part in the late Civil War."

Putting Jefferson Davis on trial, everyone finally agreed, was just too hard.

In late July 1868 Jefferson Davis, Varina, and their children sailed in the RMS *Adriatic* from Quebec for Liverpool and a new life abroad along the same ocean track that Surratt had followed three years earlier. The Davises arrived in England on August 4 to an excited greeting by the city's colony of Confederate exiles, who must have been disappointed when their former first family elected to move on the next January, ultimately back to the United States, leaving their sons behind in school.

In the end it was President Johnson's fourth and last amnesty proclamation, the universal amnesty he issued Christmas Day 1868, that settled Davis's fate. The Department of Justice fully implemented the Christmas 1868 proclamation in February 1869, one month before Johnson left office, by terminating the prosecution of Davis and thus releasing him from the threat of any future legal action. Former Confederate president Davis was now a free man, albeit not and never again a U.S. citizen. Unlike Judah Benjamin, who reinvented himself as a British barrister and then never looked back, Jefferson Davis never successfully made a new life for himself.

Davis returned alone to the United States in October 1869. During the next twelve years he went back to Europe through Liverpool four more times, in 1870 to collect his family, again in 1874 and 1876, and finally in 1881. Job searches each time were futile, a succession of failures that must have been painful for this very proud man.

After 1865 conspiracy theorists had some half a dozen candidates to choose among for the role of chief villain in the murder of Abraham Lincoln. The three most popular were Jefferson Davis and his cabinet, the pope and his church, and Andrew Johnson, who had much personally to gain from the death of the president. John Wilkes Booth, inescapably, had a leading role in all three scenarios, but in the fermenting imaginations of these contemporary students of the crime Booth was the instrument of murder and not its architect.

Davis was the choice of official Washington. Nativists, however, chose the pope, persuaded of the Roman Catholic Church's culpability by a need to believe the lurid worst about Catholic immigrants and by news that priests had spirited Surratt along a sort of Catholic conduit to Rome, where finally he sought refuge among the Pontifical Zouaves. One enduring, clear expression of their conviction is found in *Fifty Years in the Church of Rome*, a first book written in 1885 by Charles P. T. Chiniquy, a defrocked Canadian priest who claimed to have been a client of Lincoln's law practice and to have warned him about Jesuit plots against his life. Chiniquy spent the rest of his life libeling the Catholic Church.

His fables were the inspiration for a number of copycats, one of whom, Burke McCarty, a self-described "ex-Romanist," wrote *The Suppressed Truth about the Assassination of Abraham Lincoln* in 1924, another staple of this loopy group.[5] In *The Suppressed Truth* McCarty charged that the Vatican had fomented the

Civil War, arranged the assassination of Lincoln, and then protected Surratt, the president's last assassin at large. "I feel safe in stating," McCarty wrote in one place, "that nowhere else can be found in one book the connected presentation of the story leading up to the death of Abraham Lincoln, which was instigated by the 'Black' pope, the general of the Jesuit Order, camouflaged by the 'White' pope, Pius IX, aided, abetted and financed by other 'Divine Righters' of Europe, and finally consummated by the Roman Hierarchy and their paid agents in this country and French Canada on 'Good Friday' night, April 14th, 1865, at Ford's Theater."

Johnson's fierce political enemies, the Radical Republicans, would have agreed with McCarty's next accusation, this one in his chapter 10:

President Johnson was a drunkard. He came from a disloyal state. His revocation of a reward for the arrest of John H. Surratt is a conclusive proof to the mind of the writer, to say the least he was playing politics, which under the gravity of the circumstances would make his conduct criminal. Andrew Johnson, the drunkard, had nothing in common with Abraham Lincoln. Lincoln's pure, sober, honorable life was a rebuke to a man such as Johnson. At the first opportunity the latter dared to take advantage of, to show his dislike, which amounted to downright disrespect to the memory of Lincoln. It was President Johnson that paralyzed the arm of the Department of State in regard to Surratt's arrest. The whole official inertness amounting to treason it should seem, should be laid at Johnson's door.

Even a very hasty tour of the Internet reveals that the late Burke McCarty is not camped out alone in the distant marches of make-believe history, but putting aside the more bizarre, and unproven, charges against Andrew Johnson, he remains the model failed president.

Johnson's term was, almost from start to finish, a political train wreck. He competes with James Buchanan for the top position on most lists of the worst American chief executives, this notwithstanding an oddly anodyne biographical sketch on the Web site of the White House that suggests Johnson's problems arose from a combination of bad luck and good character. ("Although an honest and honorable man, Andrew Johnson was one of the most unfortunate of presidents. Arrayed against him were the Radical Republicans in Congress, brilliantly led and ruthless in their tactics. Johnson was no match for them.")

In fact, Johnson was a match for them. The Radical Republicans managed to deny Johnson a second term as president, but their goal had been to eject him from the current one, and it was his vision of the South and not theirs that formed the blueprint for the section's future. His reputation enjoyed a relatively brief uptick early in the last century, but eventually it fell and has remained near its nadir since.

In 1864, however, Johnson's selection by the nominating convention in Baltimore to be Lincoln's running mate seemed inspired. Adding a southern Democrat loyal to the Union to the Republican ticket gave it an extra dimension and a way for the party (renamed the National Union Party for purposes of this contest) to display proof of its claim to broad electoral support.

Lincoln's first vice president had been Hannibal Hamlin, and Hamlin was one of several men considered by the Republican Party's nominating convention in Baltimore to be Lincoln's running mate during a second campaign and his partner in a second term. Hamlin was from Maine, a former congressman and senator. He lost his chance at a reprise when the convention focused on considerations of political and geographical balance for the top of the ticket and in the cabinet to come.

Hamlin aside, the other prospective vice presidential candidates were two Democrats, Daniel Dickenson from New York and Andrew Johnson of Tennessee. Johnson was the only senator from the South who remained in his seat in the Senate when his home state seceded. In her *Team of Rivals* Doris Kearns Goodwin says a major factor in putting Johnson on the slate was not this distinction, however, but New York political boss Thurlow Weed's determination to keep his friend and fellow New Yorker, William Seward, in the cabinet. (Because of an unwritten political rule, selection of another New Yorker as vice president might have forced Seward to resign.) In retrospect, as part of a package deal that also included Johnson, Seward's second term as secretary of state came at a high price.

On election day, November 8, Lincoln outpolled his opponent, Gen. George McClellan, by more than 400,000 votes of 4 million cast and beat him ten to one in the electoral college, 212 to 21. Union soldiers favored Lincoln over the former general by a large margin. McClellan managed to carry only his home state of New Jersey, Delaware (still nursing a grudge against Lincoln), and Kentucky. Lincoln swept all the others. The number two candidate on the new National Union Party ticket made no obvious contribution to Lincoln's victory at the ballot box. From this far away, however, it's difficult to tell how big a part the votes of Johnson's natural constituency, War Democrats (as distinct from Peace Democrats, McClellan's electorate), played in the outcome.

Andrew Johnson started to earn his sad distinction as one of U.S. history's worst presidents even before he was sworn into office the day after Booth struck. Six weeks earlier, on March 4, Johnson had begun his truncated stint as Lincoln's vice president with a twenty-minute inaugural speech in the well of the Senate that many in the audience were happy to conclude was the product of drunkenness and that a biographer has attributed to his unwisely medicating typhoid fever with three quick tumblers of whiskey, swallowed neat.

The alternative and much less welcome explanation for Johnson's rambling, nearly incoherent monologue was that at some time during the ten months between his nomination and the inauguration the new man had lost his mind. Welles described the speech in his diary as "a rambling and strange harangue" that was "listened to with pain and mortification by all his friends." Welles, Attorney General Speed, and Secretary of War Stanton speculated among themselves at the inauguration that the possible causes included alcohol, other drugs, mental derangement, or disease.

Whatever its cause, Johnson's "strange harangue" produced equally strange echoes. When Lincoln's murder became known in European capitals, the news was generally met with the same combination of shock, horror, and uncertainty about the future course of U.S. politics that characterized the domestic response to the assassination . . . everywhere but in France. Suspicion of boisterous republicans came naturally to monarchical Frenchmen, an attitude heightened by Emperor Napoleon III's ambitions in Mexico. "The news of the murder of President Lincoln has created more sensation in Paris that any event I can remember since the death of Emperor Nicholas of Russia," wrote the *Evening Herald*'s correspondent on April 26 in a report quoted in the *Liverpool Mercury* two days later:

> Even now as I write the public can hardly make up their minds to believe that it is true, as no details have come to hand, and there appears to be no motive for so heinous and unnecessary a crime. The consequences of a drunken fanatic being placed by the machinery of the United States Constitution at the head of an unbridled democracy, whose passions are excited to fever height by the intoxication of their late triumph will, it is feared, be very serious, not only as regards the United States themselves, but Canada and Mexico. As for Mr. Lincoln, it is generally

considered that he is *felix opportunitate mortis*. He dies on the morrow of victory, and leaves to his successors the task of carrying out his plan for reconstructing the edifice he laboured so successfully to demolish. The work would require a sage, a philosopher, and a statesman, and it falls to the hands of a grotesque caricature on the atrocious miscreants of the French revolution. Americans in Paris express a hope that the new president will drink himself to death, or that Grant will take possession of the Government.

Although Grant did take possession of the government as those unnamed expatriates hoped, he did not become president until March 1869. Meanwhile, Johnson disappointed them also, by living through all of what would have been Lincoln's second term and for another six years after that, just long enough to be reelected to the Senate from Tennessee.

As president, Johnson's mantra, "The Union as it was, the Constitution as it is," summed up the man precisely. His principal goal after the war was to set the clock back, to restore the Union essentially as it had been before Fort Sumter, a house still divided into halves with sharply different societies and economies but now with its polity somehow spliced back together as if the great bloodletting just past had never happened. Otherwise, as little else changed as possible: White men, southerners, still in total control; black men still frozen in place in a mute and land-less underclass, providing the manual labor to make a plantation economy oper-ate; and slavery gone but its essential practices still in place. The policies Johnson implemented early in his presidency, first unilaterally in the form of amnesty dec-larations and patronage appointments and then through his vetoes, flowed directly from this retrograde vision and from his determination to prevent what he believed Republicans intended, "Africanizing the southern part of our territory."[6]

The leadership of the Radical Republicans defined its goal differently: a reconstruction of the former states of the Confederacy practically from the ground up, beginning with demotion to territorial status. Reconstruction in their eyes, to Senators Charles Sumner, Benjamin Wade, and Henry Wilson, and to Congressmen Thaddeus Stephens, James Ashley, and George Julian, among others, was to be done in deliberate stages: first punishment, then reformation, and finally, readmission. And that only after the South's former slaves were admitted to full citizenship, including the franchise.

Although Congress later wrested control of Reconstruction from the president, his model, not its, tragically, shaped the future. The battle over

Reconstruction threatened to cost Johnson the presidency, and it certainly cost him a term of his own, but by deliberately spurning fleeting opportunities to take history in a different direction, Johnson succeeded in establishing the preconditions that legitimized racism for nearly one hundred years.

That battle began in early December 1865, a few days after Surratt joined the Zouaves, when the new Thirty-ninth Congress finally convened on schedule to begin its long session, astonishingly the first time either house had met since before President Lincoln's assassination. The session not yet underway, the House refused to seat state delegations arriving from the South that had been voted into office by exclusively white electorates, delegations that included nine former Confederate congressmen, eight senior army officers, and seven state government officials among them. Georgia's boasted Alexander Stephens, no longer the Confederacy's vice president but now regrooved as one of the state's new senators.

Stephens's reappearance in Washington (he had represented Georgia's eighth congressional district in the House from 1843 to 1859) must have been especially galling. On March 21, 1861, in a widely reported speech, Stephens had defended slavery as the natural and normal condition of the black man. Speaking in the evening to a crowd that filled Savannah's Athenaeum and spilled out in huge numbers onto its grounds, he was reported to have said,

> The new constitution has put at rest, forever, all the agitating questions relating to our peculiar institution—African slavery as it exists amongst us—the proper status of the negro in our form of civilization. This was the immediate cause of the late rupture and present revolution. Jefferson in his forecast, had anticipated this, as the "rock upon which the old Union would split." He was right. What was conjecture with him, is now a realized fact. But whether he fully comprehended the great truth upon which that rock stood and stands, may be doubted. The prevailing ideas entertained by him and most of the leading statesmen at the time of the formation of the old constitution, were that the enslavement of the African was in violation of the laws of nature; that it was wrong in principle, socially, morally, and politically. It was an evil they knew not well how to deal with, but the general opinion of the men of that day was that, somehow or other in the order of Providence, the institution would be evanescent and pass away. This idea, though not incorporated in the constitution, was the prevailing

idea at that time. . . . Those ideas, however, were fundamentally wrong. They rested upon the assumption of the equality of races. This was an error. It was a sandy foundation, and the government built upon it fell when the "storm came and the wind blew."

Our new government is founded upon exactly the opposite idea; its foundations are laid, its corner-stone rests upon the great truth, that the negro is not equal to the white man; that slavery—subordination to the superior race—is his natural and normal condition. This, our new government, is the first, in the history of the world, based upon this great physical, philosophical, and moral truth. . . .

Those at the North, who still cling to these errors, with a zeal above knowledge, we justly denominate fanatics. All fanaticism springs from an aberration of the mind—from a defect in reasoning. It is a species of insanity. One of the most striking characteristics of insanity, in many instances, is forming correct conclusions from fancied or erroneous premises; so with the anti-slavery fanatics; their conclusions are right if their premises were. They assume that the negro is equal, and hence conclude that he is entitled to equal privileges and rights with the white man. If their premises were correct, their conclusions would be logical and just—but their premise being wrong, their whole argument fails.[7]

Two weeks later, the man who would become Mary Surratt's junior counsel, Frederick Aiken, explicitly endorsed Stephens's thesis of white supremacy in the letter soliciting employment that he mailed to Jefferson Davis.

Those whom Stephens had described four years ago as "insane fanatics" now guarded the door to Congress. Months later Tennessee's delegation was finally seated in the Thirty-ninth Congress. The other ten states waited to be represented until the Fortieth.

Taking the bit into their teeth, members of Congress promptly formed the Joint Committee on Reconstruction to capture control of the process from the president, a process already so far advanced during the recess that most Confederates had been pardoned; their property, except slaves, had been restored to them and land reform initiatives terminated; state constitutional conventions had met; and ten of the eleven former Confederate states had been readmitted to the Union—all under Johnson's executive authority.

This had been Lincoln's plan, too, to get all the big, postwar changes done during the long congressional summer recess. Had he lived, Lincoln might have had the wit and the agility to keep doing what he thought was "necessary to restoring the proper practical relations between [seceded] States and the Union," to have shaped near universal American racism into something more liberal and generous. Certainly his instincts would have led his administration and Congress in that direction. Johnson's didn't. As he revealed to Senator John Conness of California, Johnson believed, as Stephens did, that blacks were happiest as slaves.[8]

After December 1865, following its refusal to seat southern delegations and establishment of the Joint Committee on Reconstruction, Congress's trajectory toward impeaching and trying the president under Article 2, Section 4 of the Constitution can be roughly traced through several waypoints beginning early in 1866: first, Johnson's vetoes of Reconstruction legislation, including two Freedmen's Bureau bills (the first vetoed in February, the second veto overridden in July) and bills to grant former slaves citizenship and the franchise in the states and the District of Columbia; second, his efforts to create a new "National Union" political party combining Democrats and conservative Republicans and his "swing around the circle" speaking tour to market this party to the electorate; third, his opposition to the Fourteenth Amendment, an attempt by Congress to insert civil rights into the organic law of the land; fourth, the congressional elections in autumn 1866, in which Republicans increased their majorities in both houses (and so gained control of Reconstruction); and fifth, the ultimate provocation, Johnson's insistence on firing Secretary of War Stanton in the face of the Tenure of Office Act, a probably unconstitutional law passed over his veto that forbad the president from removing anyone from government office to whose appointment the Senate had consented. The act was passed in March 1867. Johnson suspended Stanton over the summer and appointed a replacement in February 1868.

Johnson's vetoes of legislation and his obstruction of the Fourteenth Amendment threatened achievement of the Radical Republicans' war aims, which foresaw the re-creation of the South on the basis of fundamentally different legal and economic models. His campaign to create a new fusion party in U.S. politics with himself as its chief and next presidential candidate challenged the Republican majority in Congress directly, a threat strengthened by restricting the franchise exclusively to whites. Continued black disenfranchisement guaranteed Democratic majorities throughout the South at every level of government.

The trigger for impeachment was Johnson's attempt to replace Stanton with the adjutant general of the army, Bvt. Maj. Gen. Lorenzo Thomas, but the decisive event in the accelerating march to put the president on trial had come months earlier in the midterm election that gave the Republicans 57 of 68 seats in the Senate and 173 of 226 seats in the House. With such majorities in place, anything looked possible to members who had come to despise Johnson.

On Saturday, March 7, 1868, a notice of impeachment was delivered to the White House. Receipt of the document was no surprise. The indictment had been bouncing around Capitol Hill for several days. The articles of impeachment were agreed by the House on Monday and presented to the Senate on Wednesday before finally being served on the president midway through the weekend.

More than a year earlier, in January, *Harper's Weekly* had summarized the assessment of the president that underlay everything that followed. "The President is in open political alliance with those who denounced and opposed the war," *Harper's* editorialized. "He steadily resists every effort to secure its just results. He is the great impediment in the path of a swift and prosperous national settlement."

In these three characterizations lay the philosophical basis for the Radical Republican opposition to Johnson. From them the House's impeachment managers had to fashion explicit charges that Johnson had committed "high crimes and misdemeanors," offenses nowhere described or defined under U.S. law.

The House of Representatives charged Johnson with eleven criminal counts. Eight of the eleven dealt with his violation of the Tenure in Office Act: the firing of Secretary Stanton and his temporary replacement by General Thomas. A ninth charge had to do with passing orders to the army directly rather than through the senior general officer. A tenth concerned attempts to "excite the odium and resentment of all good people of the United States against Congress and the laws by it duly and constitutionally enacted" in various public statements, a reference to Johnson's recent speeches. The eleventh contained a miscellany of other allegations in case none of the above stuck.

In May 1868 Johnson was tried in the Senate on these charges. Spared expulsion from office by the slimmest possible margin, the vote of Kansas's new Republican senator, Edmund Ross, the impossibility of his reelection and the (very remote) possibility of new charges and another trial shaped Johnson's behavior through the rest of his last year in office.

Anthony Trollope might have slept in the Senate gallery through parts of Johnson's impeachment trial, as an amused press reported, but he got the essence of the proceedings right and captured the natives' mood accurately. "Yesterday," he wrote to his publisher on May 27, 1868, "the impeachment of the President of the United States was brought to an end by a vote of acquittal on the 2nd and 3rd articles, and by a further vote of adjournment *sine die* on the eight articles as to which the senators have not voted." He continued with an observation that would have its own echoes:

There is hardly a man or woman in Washington who does not believe that in this great constitutional proceeding against the highest officer of the United States the foulest motives have been in operation on one side or the other. . . . It is a matter of deep moment that in a country possessed of endless natural resources, in which commerce has led to great wealth, the political institutions of which are continually held up to ourselves for admiration and imitation, no professional politician dreams of trusting an adversary for the commonest honesty, and none who are not politicians will trust any politician at all.

9

"A VERDICT OF ACQUITTAL"

Early on Saturday, July 17, 1867, near the beginning of what had slowly
unfolded into his three-day oral summation, District Attorney Edward
Carrington shared with the jury his view of what remained to be done:
"The scene before us is as solemn as the grave. You behold in the person of the
prisoner of the bar a dying man. He has forfeited his life to society by a deed of
blood and horror almost unprecedented in the annals of ancient or of modern
history. The voice of reason and of public justice alike demand this satisfaction
to an outraged and violated law. We must be cruel only to be kind. We must punish the guilty only to protect the innocent." Carrington concluded, "I charge you
then, gentlemen of the jury, assign to the prisoner at the bar, the blood stained
prisoner at the bar, that punishment which he deserves by the laws of God and
man, for the great crime which he has committed in the face of heaven and
earth. He is a murderer, and deserves a murderer's doom."

But Carrington was denied. The outcome of Surratt's trial before Judge
Fisher was, instead, something of a triumph for Bradley, Bradley, and Merrick.
Not so welcome as an outright acquittal, but as near to it—considering Fisher's
evident bias and everything else—as could have been expected. Surratt's connection to Booth's botched March 17 kidnapping plot was clear, readily acknowledged by his counsel, but his tie to the assassination was not and his presence in
Washington on April 14 had not been convincingly established.

Carrington had been successful at first, but his early legal triumph proved
to be temporary. Knowing that the outcome of the trial hinged entirely on the
jury, the prosecution had moved swiftly to supplant one, certain to be comprised
mostly of Roman Catholics presumed sympathetic to Surratt, with another,
while working surreptitiously for clearance either to export the trial to a more

congenial venue than Washington City or to import a jury of more trustworthy outsiders to the District of Columbia. A week into the trial the first jury pool was exchanged for a new one that, inevitably, contained a majority of southerners. Any random canvass of the District's white, adult male, taxpaying population would have produced the same result. In a case clouded by uncertainties, these jurors were unwilling to find Surratt guilty of murder and so to condemn him to death.

The trial was over, but for Surratt nothing seemed to have changed. After watching his lead counsel summarily disbarred, the prisoner was once again led off in chains back to solitary confinement in his iron-walled cell in the Blue Jug, to face another trial and a still uncertain future.

There was no such uncertainty eleven hundred miles south at Fort Jefferson Prison in the Dry Tortugas, where Mary Surratt's four surviving codefendants were now beginning their third year as denizens of a subtropical cage. Samuel Mudd, Samuel Arnold, and Michael O'Laughlen were still confined on Garden Key serving out life sentences at hard labor. Ned Spangler was one-third of the way through his six-year sentence. By local standards, Mudd (assigned to the prison's carpentry shop after a failed escape attempt but later responsible for nothing more arduous than sweeping out the casemates several hours a day) was a lucky man. He had dodged a death sentence at the Arsenal trial and swift execution by only a single commissioner's vote.

Their home there, Fort Jefferson, was the largest and most heavily armed coastal defense fort in the United States. Originally designed to house 450 guns and a complement of fifteen hundred when building began atop the tiny key in December 1846, Fort Jefferson was still unfinished when the Arsenal trial's four state prisoners arrived on July 24, 1865, aboard the USS *Florida*. When work was finally abandoned in the 1870s, the fort had been under more or less continuous construction for twenty-five years and was still not completed. It was, instead, a sump for bricks and labor and the archetype of some later defense programs: huge, hugely expensive, never truly operational, and obsolescent long before the money appropriated by Congress ran out.

Despite agitation for his pardon by Mudd's large and influential family, in 1867 only Spangler could have expected that he would live out his punishment and return to Washington as a free man. The sudden reappearance of yellow fever in the Florida Keys, however, must have changed everyone's survival calculus, prisoners and guards alike.[1] In those decades of the nineteenth century as many as half of all those whom the virus attacked died. Like other epidemics—cholera is the best-known nineteenth-century example—yellow fever traveled around the world by ship. In mid-August 1867 the disease came to Garden Key from Havana, across the Florida Strait in a vessel bringing an officer back to the fort after several days in Cuba.

Yellow fever's attack at Fort Jefferson fell hardest on the prison's guards, among them soldiers of the 82nd U.S. Colored Infantry. The belief, proved false yet again, had been that black troops were naturally immune to the disease. Curiously, yellow fever appears not to have culled the white prisoners at the fort. Thirty-five among the prison staff died, but only two of the remaining fifty-two inmates fell. A mercifully low mortality rate, all things considered. Among the thirty-five was the prison's only staff doctor, Bvt. Maj. Joseph Smith. Smith fell ill on September 5 and was dead three days later. His death turned out to be a macabre career opportunity for Mudd, who stepped in to assist Smith's civilian replacement, Dr. Daniel Whitehurst, himself bravely returned to the prison from Key West on September 9, the day after Smith died.

Michael O'Laughlen died on September 23. As the tribunal originally intended, his had turned out to be a life sentence at Fort Jefferson. Two weeks later Mudd caught yellow fever himself, or it caught him, but he was lucky once again and recovered after several weeks.

The ministrations of physicians Whitehurst and Mudd—there was no preventive or palliative and no cure for yellow fever—could not have been medically effective, but Mudd's visible attentiveness earned him the admiration of the survivors. On February 8, 1869, their appreciation of his emergency medical service earned the doctor two long paragraphs in President Johnson's "full and unconditional pardon."

"And whereas," Johnson wrote,

> upon occasion of the prevalence of the Yellow Fever at that military station, and the death by that pestilence of the medical officer of the Post [Mudd] devoted himself to the care and cure of the sick, and interposed his courage and his skill to protect the garrison, otherwise without adequate medical aid, from peril and alarm, and this, as the officers and men unite in testifying, saved many valuable lives and earned the admiration and gratitude of all who observed or experienced his generous and faithful service to humanity."

For that, and "diverse other good and sufficient reasons," Johnson granted Mudd "a full and unconditional pardon." He, Arnold, and Spangler (the latter two also the beneficiaries of pardons from the president) were free and off Garden Key before the next attack of yellow fever and the next hurricane hit.

As 1868 began, the start of Washington's "gay season," weeks of private receptions and public entertainments immediately after celebration of the New Year, suggested that the "passionate agitations" of two years ago had calmed, that the city had moved beyond mourning for the late chief executive. In January President Johnson's daughters, Martha and Mary, presided over social events at the White House that the local press described as "very agreeable." Elsewhere in Washington members of the cabinet and Congress received their guests at grand dinner parties rivaled in elegance only by the highlights of that festive time, namely, Mrs. Senator Edwin Morgan's weekly *soirées dansantes*. During the New York senator's single term in office, the wonderfully wealthy Morgans opened their home in the capital to the city's elite by invitation. Others, commoners who paid for their amusement, also had much from which to choose. Ford's Theatre, naturally, had remained dark since that dreadful night, but the National Theater (reopened in 1862 after its third serious fire in thirty years; nineteenth-century theaters were like ships at sea—full of inflammables and lit by oil lanterns or gas lamps, they often caught fire), Wall's Opera House, and Metzerott Hall offered cultivated entertainments. In the short days of winter these glittering private distractions competed for attention with the principal public one: the increasingly grim brawl between Johnson and Congress.

While Johnson and Congress fought out their differences from opposite ends of Pennsylvania Avenue, on Monday, January 20, 1868, Surratt's retrial for murder was placed on the criminal docket of the Supreme Court of the District of Columbia for February 24. (Purely by coincidence, that trial date four weeks hence would turn out to be the day that the House of Representatives voted the impeachment of the president on the basis of the resolution Congressman James Ashley had first presented to the body January 7.)

Judge Fisher was not to be on the bench for this case. As the District of Columbia's Supreme Court schedule first had it, he was to be replaced by the court's chief justice, David Cartter, later by an associate justice, Judge Andrew Wylie. But otherwise, most of the players in the trial to come had familiar faces. The government's trio of prosecutors was unchanged: Edward Carrington, Edwards Pierrepont, and Albert Riddle.[2] The latter's principal function appeared to be acting as Secretary Stanton's mole and a liaison to Radical Republicans. Surratt's team of lawyers was expected to feature a new senior counsel for the defense in the place of the choleric, disbarred Joseph Bradley Sr., now stewing in his office at number 1, 4½ Street over the wreckage of his practice. As it turned out, none of the three mentioned in the press as candidates to replace him, William Groesbeck, an Ohioan, and two Pennsylvanians named Black, took up the challenge, and so Merrick and Bradley Junior very reluctantly soldiered on alone. (One of the Pennsylvania Blacks was Jeremiah S., President Buchanan's attorney general and secretary of state, who drafted the reactionary veto message for Johnson's response to the first Reconstruction bill. He went on to serve on the team of five lawyers defending the president during the impeachment trial.)

A succession of delays pushed the start of Surratt's new trial from late winter to the spring, and in fact nothing noteworthy happened in court until Monday, June 22. These lost four months in 1868 are usually attributed to the wake turbulence of the Johnson impeachment proceedings moving through first one then the other house of Congress during roughly the same period. The president's trial began in the Senate on February 25, the day after Surratt's was supposed to start, and moved haltingly toward its climax on May 16. That's when Johnson was found not guilty on the eleventh article, the catch-all charge that Radical Republicans thought was most likely to bring the president down and consequently the first one brought to a vote. In an anticlimax ten days later Johnson was found not guilty on the second and third articles, and with this second rebuff his congressional tormentors finally gave up.

During these eleven weeks the trial of the president was public entertainment nonpareil, even more compelling than the trial of the eight in the Arsenal and Surratt's in City Hall had been. All Washington was consumed by the drama in the Senate. President Johnson was the only Washingtonian who didn't want to be there, and he never was. Setting a precedent that would be observed later, Johnson was tried by the Senate in absentia.

But there were two contributory reasons for the delay of Surratt's retrial. The hard-pressed and unpaid defense didn't want to move forward until a new lead counsel had been recruited to its cause, and down one to nothing already, the prosecution was uncertain about timing and the best way to proceed.

By mid-May 1868 all three prosecutors (Carrington, Pierrepont, and Riddle) were in agreement with defense counsel that a continuation, several months' delay to the autumn term, was wise despite the judge's determination to hear Surratt's case during the court's summer term. Pierrepont spoke for his colleagues yet again in his letter to Secretary Seward on May 18 explaining why. "Another hurried trial now with witnesses absent would result in an acquittal and in a *judgment* that an innocent had been persecuted," he wrote. "In my judgment it would be far wiser to have the case continued even if the prisoner was bailed, than to have such a verdict. A verdict of acquittal for one of Mr. Lincoln's assassins would just at this time have an ugly look. . . . I think an acquittal on a trial now more than probable."

Looking back on 1867, Carrington could share his failure to obtain a conviction with Judge Pierrepont and spread the blame that way. Pierrepont, Carrington would have recalled, had not been his first choice for "an eminent and special counsel" to assist him during the trial. At best, Pierrepont had been third in line for the job. When he asked the attorney general for outside help on January 17, Carrington proposed former congressman John Bingham of Ohio, who, he said, had "a more thorough knowledge of the case than any other person." Bingham, after all, as special judge advocate, had delivered the government's final argument in 1865. His speech to the tribunal, one of the trial's most impassioned events, ran for more than fifty two-column pages in Pittman's transcript. Bingham immediately and brusquely refused to participate, however, and offered no explanation for the rebuff.

The government's second choice as counsel was another Radical Republican, former Massachusetts governor and committed abolitionist John Andrews, age fifty, who also promptly declined, pleading other business and an unwillingness to "undertake a task involving indefinite absence [from Boston] as well as severe toil."

Edwards Pierrepont was ready and willing to take up the job, but in a letter dated May 20 to Secretary Seward he posed some conditions on his acceptance. "The trial of Surratt is very important in many respects," he reminded the secretary, who had been the one to approach him and whose department was to pay any outside counsel's legal fees.

> The impression made by the release of Davis is not entirely satisfactory to the public. If Surratt is now to be tried and the evidence fails to convince the public that he is guilty, the hasty conclusion will be drawn that his mother was unjustly executed. . . . Just at this time it would be very unfortunate to have him acquitted by twelve men, *if guilty*, and not well to put him on trial if innocent.

If I embark in the trial it will be on conviction [*sic*] that he is guilty & with an earnest purpose to prove the guilt. If the Government has any idea that the trial is to resemble the trial of Davis, my services would not be useful.

(When Pierrepont wrote this letter there had been no trial of Davis. But some days before, on May 11, the former Confederate president had been suddenly prised out of Fort Monroe by a writ of habeas corpus, brought to Richmond, and two days later freed on bail by Judge Underwood.) In case Seward missed his point, Pierrepont then repeated himself. "If there is to be a trial," he concluded, "it is *very important* that a conviction follows. The belief here is that which the [New York] Herald of to-day suggests, namely that this is also to be a farce."

Evidently reassured the government intended the trial of Surratt to be serious business, Pierrepont then signed on in the role of "eminent and special counsel." The outcome several months later, however, would be exactly what he had feared in May.

That he was not the only one responsible for the midsummer debacle might have consoled Carrington somewhat; even so, to lose a case that had national attention must have rankled. The district attorney didn't give up easily. Through what remained of 1867 and into the first months of the new year Carrington worked to craft another indictment against Surratt. This charge became Docket No. 5,920 on the District of Columbia's Supreme Court calendar. (There would eventually be a third case, Docket No. 6,954.) As the second case went forward, Pierrepont receded into the background. Carrington became the chief prosecutor in fact, and he carried the government's water during all the legal wrangles of 1868. Chastened by experience and informed by intelligence on the new presiding judge's views, Carrington now was finally ready to go for a solid double, a conviction for conspiracy, instead of again swinging for a home run, a murder conviction and capital punishment.

His idea wasn't new. The summer before the *New York Times* had told its readers that an anonymous "respectable authority" was the source of the paper's information that members of the just-dismissed jury "were entirely agreed upon the point that had [Surratt] been indicted for conspiracy he would have been convicted immediately upon retirement to their room." An unnamed juror had told Pierrepont as much in private, an insight the judge probably leaked to the newspaper, then passed on to the Department of Justice on December 31.[3] What was new months later was Carrington's willingness to scale down his ambition better to match the temper of the times, and the administration's readiness to agree. The great engine of revenge and loathing that had powered the trial in the Arsenal was by now running at low pressure. The new quest in court was less for vindication than for a face-saving outcome palatable to public opinion.

On June 9, 1868, Carrington wrote the interim attorney general, Orville Browning, to get advice on—more accurately, high level confirmation of—the approach he now intended to follow in court. (Confusingly, his letter was written on the attorney general's letterhead stationery. Perhaps it was penned while Carrington was in Browning's temporary office.)[4] Carrington proposed to terminate prosecution of the indictment for murder and to charge Surratt with conspiracy instead. The new strategy reflected a new reality: Judge Wylie was no Judge Fisher, as Carrington explained to Browning:

> Judge Fisher held during the former trial that actual presence was not necessary to convict the prisoner of murder—that if he was a member of the unlawful conspiracy which resulted in the death of the President and performed the part assigned to him, he was guilty no matter how far he may have been from the scene of the murder at the time it was committed. Judge Wylie, I am well satisfied, will rule that in order to convict the prisoner of murder the jury must be satisfied from the evidence that at the time the murder was committed the prisoner was near enough to render physical assistance if called upon.

Moreover, Carrington added, "I have received bad news in regard to the only witness who would testify that he saw the prisoner in front of Ford's Theatre the night of the murder. I allude to Sergeant Dye. I have no hope of securing his assistance." For some unknown reason, Dye, who had twice fixed Surratt at the scene of the crime, was not willing to commit himself a third time. Under the hot wind of Wylie's skepticism and in Dye's absence, Carrington's case for murder was evaporating.

Browning, Johnson's secretary of the interior, was a part-time placeholder between Henry Stanbery and William Evarts in the attorney general's office. Stanbery's resignation from the cabinet in March to lead Johnson's impeachment defense and the Senate's spiteful refusal to reconfirm him in June left the chief post in the Department of Justice vacant for several months. Browning was wedged into this gap, temporarily wearing a second hat from March 13 to July 19. (In mid-July Evarts, another impeachment defense counsel, became attorney general for the last eight months of Johnson's administration.) Browning, a one-time aspirant to a seat on the Supreme Court, trod cautiously in what was obviously a part-time job. Cautiously and lightly, too: Browning devoted only the weekday hours between 11 AM and 2 PM to his new responsibilities as head of the Department of Justice.

"This course, you believe," Browning replied to Carrington the same day, reciting the district attorney's evolving strategy back to him, "would avoid a long, tedious, and expensive trial, terminating, probably, in a discharge without verdict, or in an acquittal, and would [instead] secure a conviction, tending to vindicate the cause of public justice. . . . I have no such knowledge, official or otherwise, as would warrant me in forming an opinion of the expediency of the course you propose, but I perceive no ground for withholding my approbation." With this permission of a sort in hand, Carrington moved forward. On Thursday, June 18, he obtained an indictment for conspiracy. Once again the grand jury was led by the district attorney to issue a five-count indictment, this time for engaging in the rebellion by conspiring to murder and abduct the president of the United States.

The crimes alleged sounded like the familiar ones. Surratt was again accused of murder and of conspiracy to kidnap and murder, but the explicit connection of the crimes to the goals of the secession changed the offenses charged entirely. Carrington was now charging Surratt with crimes that had not existed before July 17, 1862, when Congress passed and Lincoln signed "An Act to suppress Insurrection, to punish Treason and Rebellion, to seize and confiscate the Property of Rebels, and for other Purposes." Specifically, Section 2 of that act defined a new crime in U.S. law—giving aid and comfort to the existing rebellion or insurrection—and provided for as much as ten years' imprisonment or a $10,000 fine and liberation of any slaves owned on conviction. Inexplicably, the crime described by the act, aiding and abetting the rebellion, was not defined as a felony but as a misdemeanor. Carrington had, in effect, flipped the first indictment upside down. Surratt was now accused of giving aid and comfort to the enemy in rebellion by conspiring to kidnap and murder the president. Aid and comfort was the crime; kidnap and murder were its method.

The district attorney intended to proceed with this trial on the basis of an indictment for conspiracy, the second indictment against Surratt found by the grand jury just a week earlier, and to get a continuance of the first. In doing so, as Riddle explained later in the letter to Seward that forwarded his invoice for services rendered, the district attorney had "decided not to abandon the indictment for murder, but to keep it alive, if possible, for any new developments that might occur." That new development almost certainly was the hoped-for return of Sergeant Dye to the prosecution's stable of witnesses.

On Monday, June 22, 1868, after having been rescheduled several times, the second trial of John Surratt was finally convened, with Judge Wylie presiding. Wylie moved quickly to distinguish these proceedings from those held the year before by his colleague on the bench, George Fisher: first superficially, and then, as Carrington had correctly anticipated, substantively.

Judge Fisher, Wylie implied, had erred in permitting spectators "promiscuous admission" beyond the bar and in so doing had not only inconvenienced officers of the court but also endangered their health. Henceforth, Wylie ruled, only distinguished visitors would be allowed within the bar. The "privileged parties" included members of Congress, officials of cabinet departments, the mayors and council members of Washington and Georgetown, and local judges. Presumably these stalwarts of the capital district's political elite presented none of the risks to public health posed by their constituents.

Merrick came to court intending to defend again against a charge of murder, the case scheduled on the court's docket. He was not, he said, prepared to defend against any other charge the government might raise. The two lawyers batted the issue back and forth until Judge Wylie impatiently intervened. As reported by the *New York Times*, Wylie finally announced, "The prisoner had not been convicted, and [Wylie] could not, therefore, presume him to be guilty; under the circumstances he was entitled to the same rights as any other prisoner would have, and he should have them. He directed that the prisoner be discharged under the indictment for murder, which was accordingly entered."

Most observers understood that the case against Surratt had just jumped into a new phase. Speaking for these people, on June 23 the *Times* editorialized:

Notwithstanding the refusal of the District Attorney to enter a *nolle prosequi* on the original indictment against Surratt for murder, we take it that his discharge under that indictment virtually ends it. Judge Wylie's reasoning in support of his decision will obtain general acquiescence. The failure of the government to convict on the capital charge, entitles the prisoner to the benefit of the belief that he cannot be convicted; and on this opinion the judge acted. The time for the accumulation of evidence has been ample; and it were wrong to keep even Surratt all his life in jail awaiting a conviction which the former trial proved to be unattainable.

"Even Surratt." The newspaper had come a long way since its reflexive scourging of the defendant at the start of his first trial, but change aside there was still the sense out there that Surratt was guilty of something and that the district attorney's challenge was not to prove he had committed a crime but to discover precisely what that crime had been and to couch it in the appropriate legal language for an indictment that could lead to a conviction.

Responding to a defense request for bail, Wylie explained that the new crime charged was very serious, as evidenced by the maximum sentence of ten years' imprisonment, and consequently a large amount of surety was appropriate. Bail was accordingly set at twenty thousand dollars. Four bondsmen immediately put up the required amount, each guaranteeing five thousand dollars with "their lands, tenements, goods, and chattels . . . should the defendant fail to appear." And with that, after eighteen months in a cell afloat and ashore, Surratt was released from jail.

He was not yet, however, a free man.

Bradley Sr. gone, Richard Merrick now found himself reluctantly, and he hoped temporarily, leading the defense in a case that threatened to continue into the indefinite future with a client who was unable to pay. The situation—a lawyer's nightmare, many billable hours but no one to bill—tested Merrick's southern sympathies very hard, and in response he wriggled unsuccessfully to get free.*

---

* Merrick was born in Charles County, Maryland, in 1828, a son of William Merrick, one of Maryland's U.S. senators at the time. The Merricks, father and sons William and Richard, were all graduates of Georgetown University, all lawyers, all Democrats, and all overt Confederate sympathizers. In her *Mary Surratt: An American Tragedy*, Elizabeth Trindal says that Mary attempted to get William Merrick, one of two well-known Catholic lawyers in Washington, as her defense counsel in 1865, but he declined under pressure from his father, who thought it a poor career move in postwar Washington.

Richard Merrick was well known as a "brilliant boy" in his home county, and after returning from the Mexican-American War, where he served in command of a company of the 3rd Regiment of Dragoons, he earned a reputation as an able and tireless lawyer. His legal career peaked in 1882–83, during two high-visibility trials meant to unearth corruption in the award of postal rural route contracts. Merrick was senior counsel on the government's side in the second of these "Star Route" trials and famously spoke at trial's end for more than a week straight, conspicuously backed up, like a marathon cyclist, by a physician "with medicines to stimulate Mr. Merrick in case he should swoon" in mid-oration. All nine defendants, including the assistant postmaster general, were ultimately acquitted, but counsel's bravura closing performance earned him the admiration of the judge, the now familiar Andrew Wylie.

Merrick's death in 1885 was preceded by several weeks of something diagnosed as "congestion of the brain," a condition first revealed by his inability to concentrate and a lack of vigor. He was suffering too, acquaintances believed, from knowledge of the grave medical misfortunes of his wife and two daughters.

One week later, on June 29, when the parties met again in court, he peti-
tioned Judge Wylie for yet another continuance of the case.* He and the junior
Bradley, Merrick told the court, were too busy to take the case on until mid-
September, and Surratt's lack of money meant that substitute counsel had not
yet been found. Merrick was hopeful, however, that William Groesbeck or
Jeremiah Black would soon take over. (Groesbeck, another one of President
Johnson's defense attorneys, might have had time on his hands since Johnson
had escaped conviction the month before. Black had failed in February 1861 to
gain the Senate's consent to a seat on the U.S. Supreme Court and was back in
the private practice of law in 1868.)

Merrick probably thought he had a deal when court finally adjourned around
noon on Monday, June 29. Wylie had set September 21 as a trial date, honoring
Merrick's personal schedule. Fixing that date and extending Surratt's freedom on
bail until then (the bond was good until the end of the year) were the only things
actually agreed, but Carrington had at least implied that in exchange for fixing a
date for the next round in the bout, he would *nolle prosequi* the first indictment.[5]

Near summer's end, on Monday, September 14, the court issued witness sub-
poenas for the trial scheduled to begin the following week. Merrick and Bradley
Jr. called ninety-six defense witnesses, all familiar names from the 1865 and 1867
trials. Carrington and company summoned roughly two-thirds as many, sixty-
nine, a list that included not only the government's headliners from the year
before (Weichmann, Sainte Marie, and McMillan) but also several new names.
None, however, would ever make it to the stand.

---

* Andrew Wylie (1814–1905) was on the bench June 14–15, 1867, during jury selection for Surratt's first
trial. He substituted for Judge Fisher, who was then sick at home, ill with attacks of "cholera morbus,"
summer gastroenteritis—a common ailment in hot weather during the days before refrigeration.

Judge Wylie was also on the bench in July 1865, during the two-week trial when Joseph Bradley Sr.'s
client and future wife, Mary Harris, was tried for murder. More significantly, earlier that month Wylie
had been the pajama-clad judge at whose house Mary Surratt's desperate counsel, Frederick Aiken, had
appeared the night before her execution, petition in hand for a writ of habeas corpus. Wylie's decision to
issue the writ was based on his view that "habeas corpus was indispensable to the protection of citizens,"
but some later could have seen in his decisions a more general sympathy for the Surratts and their treatment before the bar.

Wylie had been a lawyer in Pennsylvania (his home state) and Virginia for more than twenty-five years
before he took a seat on the Supreme Court of the District of Columbia in 1863, where he remained until
retirement in 1885 at age seventy-one. The *Washington Post* published his obituary August 3, 1905, neglecting mention of his role in John Surratt's second trial but recalling Mary's unsuccessful habeas corpus
petition. His biographies invariably note that Wylie's vote for Abraham Lincoln in 1860 was the only one
the Republican presidential candidate received in Alexandria, Virginia. Wylie's papers are held in the law
library of Harvard University.

Through the week leading up to the first day in court, chatter in Washington and Baltimore worried about an apparent impending disconnect. Over the summer recess the contending sides seemed to have changed strategies. As their witness lists suggested, the defense was now preparing for—indeed, insisting on—a retrial on the murder charge (Docket No. 4,731), but the prosecution expected a trial on the conspiracy charges alleged in its new indictment (Docket No. 5,920).

Carrington's motive for the change of mind is clear. Neither the Department of Justice nor public opinion was insisting on another capital trial. The presiding judge, for his part, had already revealed his skepticism about a simple "do-over." A new trial on the basis of the new indictment offered Carrington a chance for conviction that a rerun of the first trial, with the same plot line but minus Sergeant Dye in the box, did not. His interim boss had agreed. Accordingly, on September 21 Carrington entered a *nolle prosequi*, telling the judge the government no longer wished to proceed with the February 4, 1867, indictment for murder.

Merrick wanted a different outcome also. With trial on a murder charge now no longer threatening, on September 22 Merrick and Bradley Jr. told the court that their client should be freed. Earlier they had filed a "not guilty" plea in response to the second indictment. That was soon somewhat mysteriously withdrawn. Now, in a two-page special plea full of lawyerly jargon and dotted with enough Old Testament verbs to sound convincing, the two had their client "saith" over his signature that the president had issued an amnesty proclamation on July 4, 1868; that he (Surratt) had been indicted on February 4, 1867, but the U.S. district attorney had "nol prossed" that indictment on September 21; and that on the day of the proclamation he was not under any other indictment charging that he had committed a disqualifying crime. Therefore, the plea concluded in the third person, "he prays judgment, and that by the court he may be dismissed and discharged from said premises in the said indictment" under the terms of Johnson's amnesty.

Surratt's, really Merrick's, formal plea for discharge stretched Johnson's proclamation to its elastic limit, but its underlying logic was not inconsistent with the president's views. Johnson had expressed these on July 1, when the draft proclamation was being discussed during a cabinet meeting. "The President has read to us a form of proclamation prepared by Seward for general amnesty," Welles noted in his diary that day.

Exception was made of such persons as are under indictment. The President, I saw, was not pleased with that part of the document; asked how many were under indictment, why prolong this unhappy controversy by such a clause. Seward thought that was as restricted as we could make it. There were but two men, Davis and Surratt. I asked if exceptions were to be made, and there were but two, why not name them. I thought, however, Surratt was arraigned for a criminal, personal matter, rather than treason. The President said that was so, and there is really but one man, Davis. . . .

[Johnson] said he should revise the document and wished us [Welles and Browning, still interim attorney general] to reflect upon it and make suggestions. He particularly desired we should consider the subject of an unqualified amnesty to all, without any exception.

Johnson might have wanted to offer an unqualified amnesty to all comers, those few who were still out in the cold after the 1863, 1864, 1865, and 1867 amnesties, but what he actually proclaimed on July 4 was a little different. "I hereby proclaim and declare," Johnson wrote, "unconditionally and without reservation, to all and every person who directly or indirectly participated in the late insurrection or rebellion, excepting such person or persons as may be under presentment or indictment in any court of the United States having competent jurisdiction, upon a charge of treason or other felony, a full pardon and amnesty for the offense of treason against the United States, or of adhering to their enemies during the late civil war."

With language like that it was difficult to see how Merrick's plea could get past Carrington unscathed and persuade Wylie, and it didn't.

Amnesty (clemency granted to a class of people, as opposed to a pardon, which is granted to a single person) had been an arena in the battle between the president and Congress well before it was raised as a legal issue in Wylie's courtroom during 1868. Lincoln issued two amnesty proclamations even while troops were still fighting in the field, the first in December 1863 and a clarification in March 1864. Johnson published four more, the first in May 1865, soon after his assumption of office, and the last in December 1868, just months before the end of his term. Congress was restive with all these exercises of executive authority almost from the outset. Midway through Johnson's term radicals in both houses were in open revolt, furiously drafting legislation meant to constrain a presidential power granted remarkably broad scope by the Constitution.[6]

Johnson's first three amnesty proclamations (May 1865, September 1867, and July 1868) had progressively extended forgiveness to most former citizens of the

Confederacy, exempting its civil and military leadership from this automatic clemency and requiring individual petitions, which were swiftly approved. As Johnson personally redrafted the July 1868 proclamation—Seward was its original author—it would have granted "unqualified amnesty for all," but despite cabinet talk that suggested the president's instincts took him in a different direction, he was persuaded to make two exceptions: Jefferson Davis and John Surratt. Merrick was attempting to argue that wasn't so.

Carrington immediately filed a hastily scribbled motion to dismiss Merrick's plea. He must have been gratified, and perhaps even surprised, when the next afternoon Judge Wylie agreed completely with the prosecution's demurrer on a narrow technicality. The *Chicago Tribune* quoted Wylie's explanation to the court. "As it has been presented," Wylie said, "the offense as charged in the indictment amounted to giving aid and comfort to the enemy, by entering into a conspiracy to abduct and murder the late President Lincoln. The offense was a misdemeanor, and not a felony at common law. It was not treason, according to the definition, and therefore not covered by the President's pardon and amnesty of July last." The idea that engaging in such a conspiracy then was a misdemeanor seems astonishing now, when conviction for such a middling crime usually results in no more than one year in a local jail, but so it was.

Surratt was not going to be freed on the basis of President Johnson's July pardon. This was Carrington's second apparently important victory in sixteen months, but it lasted only twenty-four hours. Wylie, and Carrington, too, agreed to a defense request for a day in which to revise its plea, "to put it in better shape to meet the technical objections of the court." One day later Merrick returned to court with a revised plea, but also with something very different. Standing once again in front of Judge Wylie, Merrick observed, "by way of suggestion, but *not* by way of any motion," that the District of Columbia's statute of limitations had been exceeded: The indictment was found more than two years after the crime charged had been committed. The statute Merrick cited read:

> That no person or persons shall be persecuted, tried, or punished for treason or other capital offense aforesaid, willful murder or forgery excepted, unless the indictment for the same shall be found by a grand jury three years next after the treason or capital offense aforesaid shall be done or committed, nor shall any person be persecuted, tried, or punished for any offense not capital, nor for any fine or forfeiture under

any penal statute, unless the indictment or information for the same shall be found or instituted within two years from the time of committing the offense or incurring the fine or forfeiture aforesaid: *Provided, That nothing herein contained shall be extended to any person or persons fleeing from justice.*

Carrington's new indictment charging Surratt with aiding and abetting was dated June 18, 1868. The offenses it described occurred between March 6, 1865, "and long before that time," until April 15, 1865. If the statute Merrick was quoting governed, something Wylie had to decide, Carrington had missed the window for filing the second indictment against Surratt by fully fourteen months.

If spectators in the courtroom fully understood what Merrick was saying they now would have leaned forward in unison. Finally, the trial of John Harrison Surratt was at its climax. Merrick's dangerous "suggestion" was a mortal threat to Carrington's case, and the district attorney threw everything he had at it. In an indictment, he argued somewhat dubiously, the government was not obliged to "anticipate and avoid" the statue of limitations. No precedent (well, just a single shaky one, he conceded) required that. The government was, likewise, not bound to prove the time of the crime, but it could prove that Surratt had fled justice. Furthermore, Carrington claimed, Surratt had waived his right to any other defense when he filed a special plea citing the amnesty proclamation. This time, despite the fact that Carrington's new approach reflected Pierrepont's recommendations exactly, the former judge from New York was conspicuously absent from the well of the court. Nothing Carrington said persuaded Judge Wylie, who swiftly found the indictment to be defective, quashed it, and discharged Surratt from custody. And with that, the trial of John Harrison Surratt vaporized.

The next day, September 26, an exasperated *New York Times* correspondent (in a column entitled "Minor Topics") surveyed the wreckage of the government's case and uttered his judgment: "The Surratt business ended as might have been expected from the way the prosecution conducted the case. . . . The district attorney attempted to talk about an appeal, but this was evidently only intended as a means of keeping up the farce of a prosecution." Farce—exactly what Pierrepont had feared when he had joined the prosecution one year ago.

Before he appealed, Carrington first asked Judge Wylie to refer the case to the court in general term. Wylie refused, explaining that was not his habit but that Carrington could appeal if he wished. The district attorney then filed an appeal to the full court, Judges Cartter, Abram Olin, and Wylie sitting en banc. On the afternoon of November 6, 1868, the three found, in Cartter's words, that "this matter has no business here," and the government's appeal in the case of the *United States v. John H. Surratt* was dismissed. At about the same time the foreman of the grand jury, J. S. Blackford, scratched out the words "true bill" on the indictment for Criminal Docket No. 6,594 and inked in "Ignoramus." With that, Surratt was truly free.

But Carrington couldn't let go. The next day the *Chicago Tribune* told its readers that "the Surratt case has made one more step. The Supreme Court of the District of Columbia has to-day decided that under the law the new [sic] District Attorney could not appeal from the judgment of Justice Wylie in dismissing the case, as he did some weeks ago. The whole thing is therefore now out of court. The Attorney proposes, however, to bring it forward again by submitting a new indictment to the grand jury, which will probably result in nothing."

Carrington must have brooded about the case through November and December, because the *Tribune* reported on the first page of its first issue of the new year, 1869, that the "Surratt case is again before the grand jury of Washington. The district attorney is not at all satisfied with the manner in which his last suit was shoved out of court, and is trying to get up a new indictment. Several witnesses have been examined."

10

"FREE AS AN INNOCENT CHILD"

SURRATT, one of the conspirators in one of the most hellish assassina-
tions in the world's history, now walks the streets of the city where the
deed was committed, as free as an innocent child.

New York Times, SEPTEMBER 25, 1868

T he end game of Edward Carrington's pursuit of Surratt was played out
in January 1869 against the backdrop of a letter from the new attorney
general, William Evarts, to all U.S. district attorneys dated the day after
Christmas 1868. The letter provided the text of President Johnson's last pardon
for implementation. Evarts's letter instructed the district attorneys

to make an examination of the indictments in your district against any
person or persons whomever for the offense of treason against the
United States or abetting their enemies during the late civil war in order
that as early as you shall have proper opportunity you may enter a *nolle
prosequi* for the government upon such indictments. If upon such examination you should find any case when from the tenor of the indictment
or the nature of the case as known to you it should be [illegible] falls
within the embrace of this general amnesty and pardon, will you be so
good as to report the same to me without delay such a statement of the
indictment and case as may enable me to give you further instructions.

On January 13 Carrington read Evarts's letter to Judge George Fisher, presiding over the new term of the criminal court, and explained that as instructed
he would be filing a *nolle prosequi* in two cases, those filed in May 1865 against

Jefferson Davis and Confederate secretary of war John Breckinridge, but that the Surratt indictment of June 18, 1866, "was somewhat different from the others" and so "his duty would be to report to the attorney general," presumably for further instructions. Fisher agreed, but by then no one else in Washington seemed to care.

Months earlier, Surratt's case on the government's side had become the exclusive business of its team of prosecutors, the district attorney and his career and contract assistants. As time went on and his frustration mounted, Carrington's efforts to engage his boss in what was happening at the trial were unsuccessful. This was so largely because the Department of Justice was on its third attorney general in twelve months, and each of these worthies was focused elsewhere. Moreover, those who had driven the prosecution of the eight on the Arsenal grounds (and who for that reason could have been expected to have wished Surratt ill) had also moved on.

Edwin Stanton, now—finally—out of the War Department, was exhausted by his fight with Johnson over the president's determination to replace him. He would be dead before the end of the year, cheated of his chance to sit as a justice on the Supreme Court by a heart attack. Judge Advocate General Joseph Holt had his own reputation to defend, trying to preserve it in the middle of a nasty, years-long squabble with Johnson over what had really happened to the commissioners' clemency appeal for Mary Surratt. Johnson continued to claim complete ignorance of the clemency recommendation, sticking to the story he first told his cabinet in early August 1867 that there was no such recommendation attached to the papers presented to him by Holt for approval of the tribunal's sentences. As already noted, John Bingham, Holt's chief assistant in 1865, had made it clear from the beginning that he wanted no part in a reprise starring Mary's son.

Carrington, holding the bag pretty much alone, finally and reluctantly put it down a few months before the fourth anniversary of Lincoln's assassination.

John Surratt left the United States soon after he was freed and went to South America, where he stayed for about six months. Where he went, how and why, and who paid for his trip are mysteries. It is possible that he lived somewhere there among the small community of former Confederates who fled south, thinking like them to restart his life free of Yankee oversight.

The trip might have been nothing more than an attempt to get away, but on his return he reported to friends he was back "much improved in health," so Surratt might instead have left the country to avoid the winter of 1868–69, hoping that a change in climate would lead to renewed vigor. Travel was a common medical prescription in an age that offered not much else in the way of cures for an undiagnosed malaise.

On his return Surratt started business as a produce and general commission merchant, with offices on Baltimore's waterfront at 80 Light Street Wharf. A letter-writing campaign during the summer of 1869 soliciting business from friends and supporters must not have been successful because eighteen months later, after a brief venture selling tobacco and other commodities, Surratt surfaced as a teacher in Rockville, Maryland. It was here, in the Montgomery County Court House on December 6, 1870, that Surratt delivered the first of what was intended to be a series of tell-all lectures in various cities. His audience of several hundred would have included most of the town's citizens and many from the county's nearby farms.

Posters advertising his talk summarized four years of Surratt's life in a cascade of arresting subheads that, minus the assortment of type fonts à la P. T. Barnum, could have served as Surratt's lecture notes. According to the posters, Surratt would give his audience

a full and truthful account of his
Thrilling Adventures during the Rebellion
His Introduction To
J. Wilkes Booth
And The Plan Arranged to
Kidnap, not Murder President Lincoln,
The Attempted Abduction and its Defeat, together with the
    Abandonment of the Plot, the Arrest! Trial! Acquittal!
Denunciation of Judge Fisher, Judge Pierrepont, Edward M. Stanton,
    and Louis Weichmann
This Lecture will include
Surratt's Account of Himself!
From the time of his leaving College; his active service during the
    War; his many perilous journeys from Richmond to Washington
His Introduction to J. Wilkes Booth
And what occurred at that and subsequent interviews; his defense to
    the world; no desire for self-glorification; you have heard
One Side of the Story now listen to the other; Booth's plan; its
    attempt and failure;

trip to Richmond thence to Canada
Interview with Gen'l Lee
Ordered to Elmira; what was done there;
A Plan to Release Confederate Prisoners,
The Storm Brewing; First news of the Death of Lincoln;
Louis J. Weichmann a party to the abduction; he could neither ride
    nor fire a pistol; Telegram To Booth. A hell hound in human shape;
Loss of the Hotel Register, Cash Book and Original Telegram
Who Stole Them?
Running the Gauntlett of Stupid Detectives
$20,000!
Offered to a Poor Man With A Family, for the Surrender of Surratt;
    a failure
The Friend Proved True as Steel.
Escape from Montreal, long concealment and
Life Among the Papal Zouaves in Rome!
Arrest and Return to the United States!
A Captive in Irons
Trial, Continuing Sixty-two Days and
Honorable Acquittal

The poster finally ended with "Admission, 50 Cents."

Supported by a manager and a press agent, Surratt strode off in early December 1870 to tell his story. First on his home court in Rockville and then in halls in New York, Baltimore, and Washington. After those appearances presumably Surratt planned to set out on the same domestic lecture circuit that was making others famous and rich. Writing in the *Washington Post* on December 25, 1932, sixty-two years after the fact, David Rankin Barbee described Surratt's triumphant talk in Rockville, his drubbing in the New York City press over the Cooper Union talk, his lecture in Baltimore's nearly new Concordia Opera House on December 29, and the pressures in Washington that forced the cancellation of his lecture in the Odd Fellows' Hall scheduled for the next evening and marked the end of Surratt's brief career as a public speaker.[1]

After his modest, not to say misleading, success in Rockville and before being gang-tackled in New York by the press, Surratt might have nourished hopes for a career in public speaking—at least until interest in his single story finally aged out. Public speaking, after all, was an obvious route to fame and fortune in nineteenth-century America. Lincoln's February 1860 Cooper Union speech in Manhattan, quickly followed by nine more through New England, had put him on the Republican ticket five months later, nudging front-running William Seward aside. Public speaking had enriched Henry Ward Beecher and Mark Twain, two whose personalities and words easily filled great halls. Surratt had no such personality, no such touch. (Beecher's fame as an orator was so great he was selected to give the principal address at Fort Sumter, celebrating its return to Union hands at the end of the war. He was there at the fort that weekend when he learned of the attack on the president.)

It is possible things would have gone differently in Washington City had Surratt's reviews in New York been raves or simply resembled the generally generous assessments of his Rockville performance in the *Washington Star* and the *Washington National Republican*. In that case he might have been allowed on stage in the hall at Seventh and D streets to speak for himself, and who knows what might have followed a well-received talk in the national capital. But in New York City both the Democratic *World* and the Republican *Tribune* shredded Surratt. The former savagely described him as "hawking his mother's corpse . . . the most flagrantly and deliberately indecent method of making money which ever occurred to the depraved human mind." Greeley's *Tribune*, aghast that a southern audience had assembled to hear him elsewhere, refused to attend the lecture at Cooper Union and contented itself by preempting it. "The story itself is old and absurd," the *Tribune* pronounced, "and will hardly repay perusal; the strangest part of it is that it should ever have found listeners in any respectable community." Even the much less judgmental *Herald* was moved to observe that some might question Surratt's good taste in the enterprise of turning his experience into money.

While Surratt's agent scrambled to find a venue in Washington—he approached three, the Lincoln Hall, Odd Fellows' Hall, and Carusi's Hall, and the last was finally selected—Mayor Matthew Emery of Washington City simultaneously threatened and prepared for a street riot to protest the appearance, arranging in late afternoon for armed police reserves to be standing by on call. Someone finally blinked (in his *Lincoln's Assassins* Roy Chamlee said it was Surratt), and the lecture was cancelled even as crowds milled around in front of the building waiting for admission.[2]

During the first few years after his return from South America Surratt failed as an entrepreneur, was hooked off the lecture stage, and then filled two unsatisfying jobs in Maryland, first as a teacher in Rockville then as a school principal in Emmitsburg.

But his life held more than that. On May 21, 1872, Father Peter Kroes of St. Mary's Catholic Church in Alexandria, Virginia, married John Surratt and Victorine Hunter in the presence of the requisite two witnesses, Messrs. Hale and Buckley. In time the Surratts had ten children; seven, three sons and four daughters, survived to become adults.

Surratt appears to have been deeply unhappy in Emmitsburg. In an April 1873 letter, unearthed by Father Isaacson, to his old protector in Liverpool, Surratt asked for Father Charles Jolivet's help again: "My greatest desire, Father Jolivet is to leave this abominable country and go to Europe there to spend the balance of my days in peace and quiet. If I could only feel secure of something to do in France or England that would assure me of a moderate living, I would leave here in less than a week. Ah! Father Jolivet if you could only secure me some kind of employment, you would confer a favor indeed."[3] Jolivet, who by this time had been gone from Liverpool and away from Europe for six years, either couldn't or didn't help.

Some time after 1873 Surratt left his job as principal of St. Vincent's Academy and joined the Baltimore Steam Packet Company. Its management was well known for southern sympathies, a stance made absolutely clear on April 19, 1861, when the line's then-president, Moor Falls, "declined" to transport Union sailors to Hampton Roads, where their mission would have been to secure Union men-o'-war in port from seizure by secession-bound Virginians. Postwar, his successor, John Moncure Robinson, and many of his senior staff were Confederate veterans, and this could account for Surratt's welcome into an unfamiliar business.

The Baltimore Steam Packet Company, where Surratt spent almost his entire working life, was just over twenty years old when the Civil War began. Old enough, apparently, that it was soon to qualify for the nickname the "Old Bay Line." Almost from the start in 1840 the line connected Baltimore and Norfolk with daily service and Baltimore with Petersburg and Richmond at least once each week.

The heart of the Baltimore Steam Packet Company's business plan throughout the line's history, its overnight Baltimore-Norfolk shuttle in both directions, was disrupted during the Civil War when Norfolk was held by the South, but not as much as might have been expected. What had been a half-hour stop at Old Point Comfort thirteen miles north of Norfolk became instead the line's southern terminal in wartime, cutting roughly an hour's steaming from the peacetime schedule. But military movements of men and materiel from the port of Baltimore to the Union's front on the lower Chesapeake Bay and Grant's

The Baltimore Steam Packet Company's dock at Pier 10, Light Street, Baltimore, as it appeared from streetside around 1905. These offices replaced those on the Union Dock at the foot of Concord Street, destroyed by a fire in May 1889. Fire damaged the Light Street offices in 1904 and again in 1911. After each blaze the building was rebuilt to the original plan. Three serious fires and a flood cost the Old Bay Line its office files, complicating Alexander Brown's research for the centennial history of the company published by the Mariner's Museum in 1940. (Mariner's Museum)

headquarters were substantial and very lucrative. These bonus revenues more than made up for the loss of passengers to and from Norfolk and of cargo from Norfolk (cotton, for the most part) bound for the North and overseas. After fighting stopped the line was quick to restore daily service through to Norfolk and from Old Point Comfort up the James River to Richmond, to reequip, to come to terms with its competition, and to establish relationships with railroads that fed passengers and freight into its system for nearly a century to come.

Surratt saw the company through nearly fifty years, during the line's best years in business. When he retired in August 1915 at seventy-one (one year before his death) he was the company's general freight agent and auditor. Remarkably, in 1915 retiring at seventy-one made him something of a slacker. In that decade, the average age of retirement was seventy-four. If you lived that long in the early twentieth century, by escaping childhood disease and accident along the way, at seventy-two you probably had another few years left.

The line kept running for many more years. The last Old Bay Line steamer tied up and doused her fires in April 1962, marking the end of the oldest American steamship company then in service.

Isaac kept the lowest profile of the children of Mary and John Surratt Sr., a trio that avidly sought the shadows after their exposed public lives. His childhood had been miserable: tension at home, scattered attendance at school, and a series of odd jobs. (When Isaac was seventeen, in January 1858, Mary sent an impassioned letter to her priest about him. "As Mr. Surratt will not send Isaac to school and I have sent him as long as I have any means," she wrote, "I must now put him to doing of something to get his living. . . . O, I hope, dear Father, you will try to get him something to do, as it will be much better for him to get out of the sight of his Pa as he is drunk almost every day and I fear there is little hope of his ever doing any better. Oh I could not tell you what I see on this earth. I try to keep it all from the world on the account of my poor children.)[4] With such a past Isaac might have welcomed the coming of the war. His army service in its most distant theater was apparently honorable if not obviously distinguished, but the Civil War in Texas was always something of a sideshow and distinction in an enlisted cavalry trooper there would have been difficult to notice.

After the war and after the trial of his brother he moved to Baltimore, where he lived with one relative and worked with another. In this small circle, Isaac, whom everyone thought looked most among the Surratt siblings like his mother, lived out the remaining years of his life. He died in Baltimore in November 1907, age sixty-six, and was buried next to her in Washington's Mount Olivet Cemetery. Isaac's death prompted a lengthy obituary in the November 5, 1907, issue of the *Washington Star* that knowingly mentioned several years abroad in Europe among other events in his life that never happened.

Anna Surratt emerged after four years from her posttrial silence, barely and briefly, on June 17, 1869, when she married William Tonry, a schoolmate of her brother's at St. Charles' College and a Georgetown graduate. Two Catholic priests, Fathers Walter and Kane, conducted the service of holy matrimony at St. Patrick's Church, on F Street near Tenth in Washington. (Father Jacob Walter had been the parish priest at St. Patrick's for the past fifteen years, only its fourth since the parish was established at the end of the eighteenth century. He had been at her mother's side during the terrible short walk between the Arsenal prison and its gallows four years earlier.) Walter and Kane, the brothers Surratt, "and a few intimate acquaintances of the bridal party" were the only ones in St. Patrick's at the ceremony. No bridesmaids, no ushers, no audience in the pews. The wedding was conducted with almost perfect stealth thanks to Baltimore archbishop Martin Spalding's agreement not to require announcement of the banns, the usual three-time public announcement in church of an impending marriage. Even so the *Baltimore Sun*, always interested in the doings of the Surratts, reported on the ceremony in a short story the next day.

Although she visited him in jail at least twice, Anna never appeared in the courtroom during her brother's trial. If her absence there reflected estrangement, Surratt's attendance at her wedding confirms that the two were reconciled.

Tonry, then four years out of Georgetown College and working in the Army surgeon general's office as an assistant chemist, was fired four days after the wedding. Collateral damage from his new family's notoriety. He went on to a successful career as an analytical and consulting chemist in Baltimore. The Tonrys had three sons and one daughter. Anna died in October 1904; she'd been in frail health for years. Her husband died one year later.

In early spring of 1898 in Baltimore, John Harrison Surratt sat for three interviews with Hanson Hiss, a freelance journalist and sometime author of magazine articles on fox hunting. The result was a long piece in the *Washington Post* on Saturday, April 2, that was picked up by the *Boston Post* the next day. Or perhaps the interviews never happened. Hiss might have made the whole thing up by filtering common knowledge through his imagination. The Surratt family, bachelor Isaac and Anna and John and their spouses, was determinedly closed-mouth about all that had gone on before, and most would-be interviewers came away with nothing but demurrals.

That had been their response in July 1880, when the nomination of Maj. Gen. Winfield Hancock by the Democrats as their candidate for the presidency sent newspaper reporters scurrying to the Surratts' homes in Baltimore looking for quotable reactions. Hancock, after all, had appeared with the attorney general before Judge Wylie on execution day fifteen years ago to deliver the message that President Johnson would not comply with the judge's writ of habeas corpus. At that moment just before noon, Mary Surratt's execution in a few hours, time became certain. As commander of the Union army's Middle Military Division, it had been Hancock's responsibility to carry out her execution order. The general's nomination gave the press an opportunity to try to lead the Surratts over that hot sand all over again.

The *Washington Post* managed to get little more than Anna's husband, William's, denial that other interviews were authentic. He added that the family held the Republican Party responsible for the murder of his mother-in-law. The Surratts would not, William concluded, provide Republicans any political ammunition by commenting about General Hancock's role in the last-minute quest for executive clemency. In due course Hancock lost to Garfield, permitting the family to ease back into the obscurity it sought.

The Hiss interviews nearly twenty years later, if they truly happened, were quite a "get" for Hiss, who claimed that over one thousand prior efforts had been made by prominent journalists to get "Captain Surratt" to talk but that only he succeeded. Hiss's historic interviews have since been judged by many students of the assassination as bogus, a conclusion bolstered by the many factual errors in the text, but at least one scholar, Michael Kauffman, thinks they might be genuine, noting that Surratt never denied them.

Nevertheless, the product of their "talks" was published across five columns of the *Washington Post*, illustrated with line drawings of the drama's three principals: Surratt garbed as a Zouave, Booth looking dapper in topcoat and suit, and Mary from the waist up, staring fixedly ahead, drawn from the familiar photograph.

Hiss described his interlocutor as "55 years old [actually fifty-three] but looking 70" and as "a trusted and honored official in the Old Bay Line of Chesapeake steamers, whose life-story from the time he ran away from school as a mere lad of sixteen [actually seventeen] and joined the Secret Service Bureau of the Confederacy until the last day of his lengthy and highly sensational trial, reads like a fairy tale." And in Hiss's account it was, in fact, a fairytale. This was Surratt's story as he wished it had been.

John Harrison Surratt died a little after nine in the evening, on April 21, 1916, at his home on Baltimore's West Lanvale Street after being sick abed since early March. He was just seventy-two when he died, the last to pass away among all those who had played a part in the dramas of his mother's trial and his. Henri Beaumont de Sainte Marie, who had exposed him in the Zouaves, had been dead for more than forty years, his mother's nemesis, Louis Weichmann, for more than fourteen. Victorine was at his bedside, as were his daughters Mary Eugenia and Susanna. Two others of his children, Mary Victorine and William, survived him. John, Leo, and Ella did not.

Surratt in old age. The photo appears in Brown's 1940 history, with the caption "Auditor of the Old Bay Line from 1870 to his death in 1916." In fact, Surratt began his long career with the company as freight claim agent a few years later, after two jobs teaching in Frederick County, Maryland. (Mariner's Museum)

Surratt managed to outlive everyone else in the story, a reflection less of his natural vigor than of his youth that spring day when he suddenly realized that Booth had assassinated Lincoln and he was in desperate trouble. His cause of death was described in his obituary in the *Baltimore Sun* the next day as "pleuro-pneumonia." It's difficult to tell from that mention exactly what killed Surratt, but pneumonia in its several forms was a common enough killer of the elderly in that decade. Today's diagnosis of Surratt's condition would possibly be bacterial pneumonia, empyema if the infection advanced to the creation of pockets of pus in the chest. The modern treatment would begin with a cocktail of antibiotics and proceed, if necessary, to opening the chest surgically to install drain tubes.

In 1916 doctors could have done little for Surratt other than see to his comfort. Had he survived pneumonia, it is almost certain that the great influenza epidemic of 1918 would have carried Surratt away, as it did 675,000 others in the United States and tens of millions worldwide.[5]

"He was in Elmira, N.Y., when Lincoln was assassinated," the *Sun*'s obituary explained, "and when he heard that a warrant had been issued for his arrest as one of the conspirators, he fled to Canada, and thence to Europe, Ireland, Egypt, and South America. Later he was arrested, brought back to the U.S. for trial, and was acquitted." True to the standards of newspaper journalism in those years, the *Sun* got about half of it right, in this case, the important half. Surratt *was* in Elmira when Lincoln was assassinated, and the rest of his life flowed from that single fact.

NOTES

CHAPTER I. "ON THE HONOR OF A LADY"

1. Fanny Trollope's take on her several years in the United States beginning in 1827 was *Domestic Manners of the Americans* (1832), a title that sounds almost anthropological. Charles Dickens's 1842 visit resulted in his *American Notes for General Circulation* (1842) and in passages in the serialized novel, *The Life and Adventures of Martin Chuzzlewit* (1843–44). Dickens's second trip to the United States was a hugely successful speaking tour after the Civil War. A confirming, contemporary view of Washington City's rustic state in 1861 ("unattractive, straggling, sodden") is in Albert G. Riddle's *Recollections of War Times: Reminiscences of Men and Events in Washington, 1860–1865* (New York: G. P. Putnam's Sons, 1893).

2. A count by the Smithsonian Institution found five hundred registered brothels in the city during the Civil War. In connection with construction of its National Museum of the American Indian, the Smithsonian excavated one of Washington's historic bawdy houses, that of Mary Ann Hall, on the corner of Maryland Avenue and Fourth Street SW. Her establishment was open for business by 1840 and didn't close until 1878.

3. Washington temperature data for May–July 1865 can be found in "Records of Observations Made at the Smithsonian Institution, 1858–74," M1379, RG 27.3, NA, and "Journal of Daily Observations at the Naval Observatory, Washington D.C. 1842–1913," T907, RG 27.5.7, NA.

4. Descriptions of the temporary courtroom in Washington's Arsenal come from the May 19, 1865, issue of the *New York World*, as quoted in the February 1999 *Surratt Courier*.

5. The old penitentiary building was completed at the end of the 1820s. The building, built of brick throughout, was large: three stories high, three hundred feet by fifty feet. Its western end (toward the Potomac River) originally contained administrative offices and apartments for wardens' families. As built the prison contained cells for 160 men and a smaller number for women. Theirs were twice the size of the men's cells, a difference explained by the *Washington Evening Star* as arising from "a proper courtesy to their sex."

6. On April 11 in his last public address, Lincoln explained the problem to a group clustered outside one of the White House windows: "Unlike a case of war between

275

independent nations, there is no authorized organ for us to treat with—no one man has authority to give up the rebellion for any other man. We simply must begin with and mold from disorganized and discordant elements." Philip Van Doren Stern, ed., *The Life and Writings of Abraham Lincoln* (New York: Modern Library, 1999), 847.

7. The war continued a little longer in the west. Lt. Gen. Kirby Smith, commander of the Trans-Mississippi Department, didn't surrender officially until June 2, but by then most of his assigned forces had already melted away after fighting, and winning, the last land battle of the war on May 12–13 at Palmito Ranch near Brownsville, Texas. The last Confederate general to surrender his forces was Brig. Gen. Stand Watie, a Cherokee chieftain and commander of the largest Confederate Indian unit, several hundred Indians from four tribes. He surrendered on June 23 at Doaksville, in the Indian Territory, an uninhabited archaeological site in southeastern Oklahoma today.

8. An 1865 map of "the Defenses of Washington . . . showing forts and roads" is reproduced in *The Official Military Atlas of the Civil War*, reprinted from the 1891–95 original by Barnes and Noble in 2003. The few defensive works standing today include Forts Stevens, Foote, and Ward. Fort Ward boasts the most complete reconstruction.

9. A reprint of the verbatim trial record by Benn Pittman, introduced with eleven scene-setting essays by Edward Steers and other scholars, is in Edward Steers Jr., ed., *The Trial: The Assassination of President Lincoln and the Trial of the Conspirators* (Lexington: University Press of Kentucky, 2003).

10. Michael W. Kauffman's scholarly *American Brutus: John Wilkes Booth and the Lincoln Conspiracies* (New York: Random House, 2004) reflects the author's thirty-year obsession with the story of Lincoln's assassin. James L. Swanson's *Manhunt: The 12-Day Chase for Lincoln's Killer* (New York: William Morrow, 2006) focuses more narrowly on Booth's escape from Washington on April 14, 1865, and his capture on April 26 in Virginia. The description of Booth's burial in the Arsenal comes from Kauffman, *American Brutus*.

11. The report of Corbett's commander, 1st Lt. Edward P. Doherty of the 16th New York Cavalry, filed on April 19, 1865, "called the attention of the commanding general to the efficiency of Sergt. Boston Corbett, Company I, 16th New York Cavalry, who was untiring in his efforts to bring the murders to justice. His soldierly qualifications have been tested on this occasion and, in my judgment, are second to none in the service."

12. Here and elsewhere descriptions of U.S. Navy ships come from the Dictionary of American Naval Fighting Ships (DANFS), on the web site of the Naval Historical Center, http://www.history.navy.mil/danfs/.

13. Margaret Leech, *Reveille in Washington, 1860–1865* (New York: Time, 1962), 510. Mary was only forty-two at the time of her trial and execution. Leech cites no source, but there are contemporaries who said the same thing. See William E. Doster, *Lincoln*

and Episodes of the Civil War (New York: G. P. Putnam's Sons, 1915), 276. "Her sickness was change of life, which weakened her greatly." Brevet Brigadier General Doster was the provost marshal of Washington and later observed the executions from a window on the second floor of the Arsenal.

14. What was then a small, eight-room house atop a basement has since been renumbered 604 and is today home to the Wok N' Roll Chinese restaurant, proudly advertising "Japanese N' Chinese Fine Cuisine." H Street is now part of Washington's small Chinatown, and the Wok N' Roll is one of thirteen such restaurants on H Street between the red and gold gate across Seventh Street that marks the start of the tourist precinct and its eastern edge four blocks away. A metal plaque near the door of number 604 tells passersby of the building's history.

15. The mule kick unbalanced his face on its left side, an injury confirmed by inspection when Powell's skull was returned to the family in 1994 for burial with the rest of the body in Geneva, Florida. The skull had been unaccountably separated from the body in 1869 and then spent the intervening years in the Army Medical Museum and at the Smithsonian Institution. The odd course of Powell's peripatetic head during more than a century has been traced by his biographer, Betty J. Owensbey, in *Alias Payne: Lewis Thornton Powell, the Mystery Man of the Lincoln Conspiracy* (Jefferson, N.C.: McFarland, 1993).

16. Census data for 1860 are available at http://www2.census.gov/prod2/decennial/documents/1860a-15.pdf and at the University of Virginia's Geospatial and Statistical Data Center at http://fisher.lib.virginia.edu/collections/stats/histcensus/index.html.

17. Maj. Gen. Philip Sheridan's description (in a telegram to Secretary Stanton sent in October 1865) was more descriptive. Isaac Surratt, Sheridan said quoting one of his subordinates, had an "olive complexion," stood five nine or ten, had a "full beard, dark eyes, black, curly hair," and was "good looking." Sheridan's enciphered telegram to his civilian master had a serious purpose. He was passing on chilling, and entirely bogus, intelligence from Maj. Gen. Frederick Steele that a "frantic" Isaac Surratt was riding from Mexico to Washington with the murder of President Johnson on his mind.

18. In midcentury easterners apparently took their Shakespeare seriously. The archetype New York City street riot was not the bloody draft protests of July 1863 but a violent, night-long brawl in May 1849 between fans of rival Shakespearian actors in front of an opera house—the famous Astor Place riot—that saw some twenty killed and many more injured when supporters of actor and native son Edwin Forrest went into lethal combat against English thespian William Macready's admirers, ostensibly over which man's Macbeth better served the bard.

In fact, New York City's Astor Place riot was a clash between working-class supporters of Forrest, then playing Macbeth at the Bowery Theater, and his rival's upper-class enthusiasts, who were assembled to see the Englishman act at the Astor

Place Theater. Nigel Cliff describes the brawl as a set-piece battle in the city's ongoing nineteenth-century class war.

But even if the American theater was not necessarily something to fight over and die for, thanks in part to its faint sheen of vice and dissipation, for some going to see a stage play was one of nineteenth-century life's guilty pleasures. A decade or so later the Booths, father and sons, were the beneficiaries of this passion. The youngest Booth, especially, was idolized as one of the age's great Shakespearian actors. His income, a princely twenty thousand dollars during his last year on the stage, matched his reputation.

19. Michael Kauffman has suggested that the immediate goal of Booth's escape was Gordonville, Virginia, an important rail junction in the Piedmont served by the Virginia Central (later the Chesapeake and Ohio) and the Orange and Alexandria (later the Orange, Alexandria and Manassas) railroads. Once there, Booth could have continued his escape westward by rail.

20. John Wilkes Booth died in pain with Mexico City still thousands of miles away, but he won after all, although his victory was posthumous. Lincoln's vision of the postwar Union, encapsulated in his second inaugural address on March 4, was buried with him. The Faustian bargain struck over the next ten years was reunion and domestic tranquility in exchange for restoration of the old segregated society led yet again by aristocratic planters. Reconstruction's history has been most recently examined by Nicholas Lemann, *Redemption: The Last Battle of the Civil War* (New York: Farrar, Straus & Giroux, 2006). The classic treatment of the subject is Eric Foner's *Reconstruction: America's Unfinished Revolution, 1863–1877* (New York: Harper and Row, 1988).

21. When the military commission convened that May, the first substantive issue was not the pace of the prosecution, even less the question of guilt or innocence (on the street guilt was a foregone conclusion), but rather if these nine officers and the special court they constituted had the legal jurisdiction to try a case against civilians. The presumption that they did was challenged both before and during the trial, and has been many times since. The question of the suitability of military tribunals has come up more recently, during World War II, when Nazi spies were caught in the United States, and most famously in this century in connection with "detainees" held in Cuba and prisons elsewhere who were captured in Afghanistan or Iraq. See Louis Fisher, *Military Tribunals and Presidential Power* (Lawrence: University Press of Kansas, 2005).

22. Edward Steers Jr., *Blood on the Moon: The Assassination of Abraham Lincoln* (Lexington: University Press of Kentucky, 2001), 201. Steers says that Aiken served on Maj. Gen. Winfield Scott Hancock's staff after first volunteering in April 1861 his "intellectual services" to the Confederacy. There is no record of Aiken's service to either side in the National Park Service's Civil War Soldiers and Sailors System

database of the names of veterans of that war. Clampitt spent only a few weeks in Company A, Fourth Battalion, District of Columbia Infantry.

23. On August 5, 1975, at the old Custis-Lee Mansion in Arlington, Virginia, President Gerald Ford signed Public Law 94-67, restoring the full rights of citizenship to General Lee. The usual explanation for the long delay is that Lee's oath of allegiance somehow got separated from his application and consequently the paperwork was not processed until the oath was discovered in the National Archives in 1970.

24. The reference to church bells tolling comes from Counsel Merrick's final argument to the Surratt jury, Thursday, August 1, 1867.

25. "The Removal of the Remains of Mrs. Mary Surratt," *New York Times*, February 10, 1869, 1.

26. Cpl. William Coxshall, twenty-two, a veteran of the 37th Volunteer Wisconsin Infantry, was one of the four "prop kickers," the army volunteers selected to spring the traps on the gallows at the Arsenal. Coxshall had lost a finger in the fight for Petersburg and thus been reassigned from a line infantry unit to Company F, 14th Veterans Reserve Corps. His company was detailed to the Arsenal on July 7. Coxhall's account is one source of information about the practice on Thursday and the execution on Friday. Harlow Randall Hoyt, *Town Hall Tonight!* (Englewood Cliffs, N.J.: Prentice-Hall, 1955), 148–52. Quoted in the September 1986 *Surratt Courier*.

Such practice drops are also a part of modern execution protocols, the short procedural guides that tell death row staff how to do it. Delaware's 1990 *Execution by Hanging Manual* (the First State was the last to hang a convict, in January 1996) reads as if it were written by Franz Kafka's penal colony officer. "It is the author's intent to make the execution as easy and painless as possible for both the Executee and those persons tasked with carrying out the execution," the manual intones solemnly, scattering capital letters for maximum persuasive effect. "Until very recently Execution was an Art employed only by the Executioner. It is only now becoming a Science with the Training and Certification of other types of Execution Technicians (i.e., Lethal Injection and Electrocution). Those persons carrying out the Protocol and Procedures in this Manual shall be Trained and Certified as Hanging Technicians."

Delaware's manual goes on to describe the duties of the warden, the executioner, and the "certified hanging technicians"; gallows' features; and how to prepare and lubricate the rope and tie the knot. Even notes on decor are included. Body and leg restraints, the collapse frame, and the hoods are to be black, with chrome fasteners where necessary. The Delaware manual also prescribes a minimum of twelve tests "to insure proper mechanical operation of the trap door and that the rope is secure and will not break."

The manual's author seems to have been Fred A. Leuchter, the chief executive and "chief engineer" of his eponymous firm, whose Boston-based business was the design, construction, and sale of execution machinery to state penal systems.

In 1988 Leuchter conducted a widely reviled investigation of Nazi gas chambers. Analysis quickly revealed the flaws in his "report" (as well as revealing he had no engineering training). Leuchter Associates collapsed in the early 1990s as former customers, wary of bad publicity and abashed by his lack of credentials, abandoned him.

27. Julius and Ethel Rosenberg were convicted of espionage for the Soviet Union following a month-long trial in 1951. They were executed in June 1953 after legal appeals spanning two years proved unsuccessful. The case has been reexamined often by legal scholars, most exhaustively in the late 1990s following the public release of nearly three thousand "Venona" documents in 1995–96 and access to archives opened in 1997 after the collapse of the Soviet Union. Writing in his study *The Trial in American Life* (Chicago: University of Chicago Press, 2007), Robert A. Ferguson has highlighted some of the parallels between the trials of the two women, Mary and Ethel, beginning with his view that neither woman was guilty.

28. There were others who were not caught up in Stanton's dragnet. Thomas Harbin, a former local postmaster like Surratt, was another conspirator in Booth's plot to kidnap Lincoln. Harbin, a Confederate agent who also knew safe routes across the Potomac from Maryland, was introduced to the actor by Doctor Mudd and recruited into the plot in December 1864. Harbin last saw Booth briefly on April 23, when Booth and Herold finally arrived on Virginia's northern neck during their escape. He never was brought to trial.

CHAPTER 2. "FLIGHT IS THE CRIMINAL'S INARTICULATE CONFESSION"

The epigraph is from Assistant District Attorney Nathaniel Wilson's address to the Surratt trial jury on Monday, June 18, 1867: "When the last blow had been struck, when [Surratt] had done his utmost to bring anarchy and desolation upon his native land, he turned his back upon the abomination he had wrought, he turned his back upon his home and kindred, and commenced his shuddering flight. We shall trace that flight, because *in law flight is the criminal's inarticulate confession* and because it happened in this case as it always happens, and always must happen, that in some moment of fear or of elation or of fancied security, he, too, to others confessed his guilty deeds."

1. William M. Stewart and George Rothwell Brown, eds., *Reminiscences of Senator William M. Stewart of Nevada* (New York: Neale Publishing, 1908), 177–79.

2. Surratt was described in the wanted poster issued on April 20 as "about 5 feet, 9 inches. Hair rather thin and dark; eyes rather light; no beard. Would weigh 145 or 150 pounds. Complexion rather pale and clear, with color in his cheeks. Wore light clothes of fine quality. Shoulders square; cheekbones rather prominent; chin narrow; ears projecting at the top; forehead rather low and square, but broad. Parts hair on right side; neck rather long. His lips are firmly set. A slim man."

3. Robin W. Winks, *The Civil War Years: Canada and the United States*, 4th ed. (Montreal: McGill-Queen's University Press, 1998), 368.

4. Lincoln's first call for volunteers to augment the North's sixteen-thousand-man regular army and put down the rebellion was for seventy-five thousand men. These few enlisted to serve for only three months. He almost certainly would have asked for more to stay longer, but this first mobilization was limited by statute. Not until mid-year did Congress pass a law permitting three-year enlistments.

5. The rebellion of slaves on Haiti eventually concluded in Haitian independence in 1804. The United States benefitted handsomely if indirectly from their uprising. The revolt, terrific losses of French soldiers to yellow fever on the island during the suppression attempt, and his preoccupation with the war in Europe led Napoleon to propose the sale of the French Louisiana Territory to the Americans in 1803. The deal was done on April 30 and it enlarged the new country by more than eight hundred thousand square miles, a vast expanse comprising all or parts of fifteen future American states.

6. Joshua Coffin's book was *An Account of Some of the Principal Slave Insurrections, and Others, Which Have Occurred, or Been Attempted, in the United States and Elsewhere, During the Last Two Centuries* (New York: American Anti-Slavery Society, 1860), online at http://gutenberg.org/etext/18601 (accessed March 19, 2008). Coffin (1792–1864), a Massachusetts educator, historian, and genealogist, was also an ardent abolitionist. He served as the first president of the American Anti-Slavery Society.

7. Debby Applegate, *The Most Famous Man in America: The Biography of Henry Ward Beecher* (New York: Three Leaves Press, 2006), 310.

8. "Parole," adopted from European military tradition, required the paroled prisoner to return home under his word of honor, and to remain there rather than at his regiment as a noncombatant under certain restrictions (e.g., to stay a fixed distance from military forts and camps of the other side) until officially notified of his exchange. Only after being formally exchanged was he permitted to return to the fight. Parole managed the asymmetric number of POWs a battle produced, and freed captors from the expensive obligation of accommodating and feeding their prisoners.

9. Interrupted prisoner exchange programs and large camps were new to warfare in North America, but not elsewhere. During the Napoleonic wars, for example, Great Britain operated such camps for captured French sailors, of which it held some eighty thousand at the peak in 1814. The several biggest British camps for seamen contained roughly seven thousand prisoners each, large even by the standards of the American Civil War sixty years later.

10. Allan Line schedule and fare details are from an advertisement in the *Quebec Morning Chronicle and Commercial and Shipping Gazette*, Friday, September 3, 1865, 3. Available online at http://bibnum2.banq.qc.ca/bna/qc/.

11. Subsidies for carrying the mail were an important part of the Allan Line's business plan, typically contributing two thousand dollars per crossing, a sum equivalent

to the gross revenues from thirty first-class passengers. In exchange, however, her majesty's government expected timely departures and arrivals with substantial penalties imposed for delays. This pressure forced the creation of special procedures at both ends of the voyage for expedited mail handling.

CHAPTER 3. "SUCH A WRETCH OUGHT NOT TO ESCAPE"

1. Quebec to Moville was 2,460 nautical miles and Moville to Liverpool added another 190 nautical miles to the crossing. Counting the Montreal-Quebec leg in the *Montreal*, Surratt's eastbound cruise covered 2,810 nautical miles. Distances from James Croil, *Steam Navigation, and Its Relation to the Commerce of Canada and the United States* (Toronto: William Briggs, 1898), 177.

2. As reported in Lee's diary for those dates.

3. The first crossing of the Atlantic with steam power assisting sails was from Savannah to Liverpool in May 1819, by the paddle-wheel steamer *Savannah*. Although Canadians like to credit Quebec-built *Royal William*'s Atlantic transatlantic voyage from Pictou, Nova Scotia, in August 1833 as the first ocean crossing entirely under steam power, most other sources cite two in April five years later, by the paddle-wheel steamers *Sirius* and *Great Western*, as the inauguration of the new era in transportation.

4. According to *Gore's Liverpool Directory*, the population of the city and its immediate suburbs in 1861 totaled 462,749, not counting an estimated 13,000 itinerant seamen at the port. There were just over 75,000 houses in the same place, of which nearly 5 percent were uninhabited.

5. The schedule of the reinforcement of Canada with British regulars in 1861 and their postwar redeployment to the United Kingdom in 1865 is from Winks, *Civil War Years*, 52.

6. Liverpool's historic ties might have been to the American South, but the city came around. Six months after that fund-raising bazaar, the same splendid space on Lime Street was the scene of a eulogy delivered by Liverpool's lord mayor, Edward Lawrence, during a mass "indignation meeting" after news of Lincoln's assassination finally reached England. His Worship, the mayor, spoke from a dais set in front of the great Willis Organ, a forest of nearly eight thousand blued and gilded organ pipes, some as large as trees, to an audience standing on a floor made of thirty thousand Minton ceramic tiles. Their nautical design, as lush as an oriental carpet, matched the splendor of the arched and painted ceiling above. Gaslight illuminated the room. (The hall's brilliant stained glass windows, the southern one depicting St. George in armor slaying a dragon, would not be installed until nearly twenty years later.) It's unlikely that Lincoln's death was noted in any grander room.

Lawrence ended his speech with "Fellow-townsmen, in the name of this great meeting, in the name of the people of Liverpool, in the names of my nation and my race—with a loathing and horror for which language fails me—I denounce this foul crime against our common humanity, and I pray God that he will so dispose the hearts of the American nation to righteous judgment that the worst consequences may be averted from the land which President Lincoln loved so wisely and so well." The mayor's denunciation was quickly converted into a parliamentary motion, which passed those assembled by acclamation. *Liverpool Mercury*, April 27, 1865, 7.

7. The *Alabama* was purchased by James Bulloch (who also had procured the CSS *Florida* in Liverpool for the Confederacy). She was commissioned in August 1862 under the command of Captain Raphael Semmes, CSN, and immediately put to sea on her first and only war patrol. During the next twenty-two months *Alabama* preyed on Union merchant shipping in the Atlantic, the Gulf of Mexico, and the West and East Indies, capturing or sinking some sixty vessels, including the USS *Hatteras*, the only commissioned ship taken by a raider during the war.

In mid-June 1864 the CSS *Alabama* was caught in port at Cherbourg, France, by the USS *Kearsarge*. Their duel, fought on June 19, was close enough to shore to be observed by fascinated Frenchmen sailing about the port and in its local waters. (One observer of the gunfight might have been the brilliant impressionist painter, Edouard Manet, whose generally accurate 1864 painting of their battle, "The Kearsarge at Boulogne," is owned by New York's Metropolitan Museum of Art.)

The *Alabama* was fatally holed after an hour's close combat and sank in two hundred feet of water. Some survivors were captured by the *Kearsarge*, but Captain Semmes and forty-one others were rescued by a British yacht and escaped to England. *Alabama*'s wreck was found in 1984 seven miles off Cherbourg and positively identified soon thereafter. Her bell was recovered in June 2002. The CSS *Shenandoah*'s end came later. Built in 1863 she was sold in 1866 to the Sultan of Zanzibar, who had her renamed *El Majidi*. She was lost at sea in the 1870s.

8. Dolin quotes whaling historian John Backstoce as saying in his *Whales, Ice and Men* (1986) that Shenandoah's captain knew from other sources that the war was over well before he met up with the *Barracouta* August 2. Eric J. Dolin, *Leviathan: The History of Whaling in America* (New York: W. W. Norton, 2007), 331.

9. In 1865 cities in the United States and the capitals of Europe were connected to one another by telegraph, but there was no telegraphic connection between the two continents. The first attempt at an intercontinental telegraph connection had been made in 1857. The first complete connection quickly failed in 1858. The steamship *Great Eastern* laid the first durable transatlantic undersea cable in 1866, between western Ireland and eastern Newfoundland. Initially the rates set by the cable operator, the New York, Newfoundland and London Telegraph Company, were very high: one hundred dollars for a twenty-word message between the United States and Great Britain (counting five letters as a "word" and including the address, date, and signature in the count). Encoded messages were charged double the plain language rate. All paid in advance.

10. Holy Cross was seriously damaged the night of December 21, 1940, during a Luftwaffe air raid. An attack the following May, one of sixty-eight against the port city during World War II, completed the church's destruction. The church was rebuilt in 1954 but demolished again fifty years later during a spasm of urban renewal. The records of Holy Cross Church were transferred to Liverpool's Central Library on William Brown Street in March 1975. The library also holds two relevant documents, a book, *Holy Cross Church Centenary, 1849–1859* (published in 1949), and a summary of the centenary volume history contained in the *Cathedral Record* 24, no. 7 (July 1954): 155–58, 167.

11. *London Times*, December 28, 1866, 6.

12. This route from Great Britain to Rome was not especially well worn by aspirants to join the Pontifical Zouaves. In mid-1868 there were only 161 Zouaves from Britain, a small percentage of the total force. Predictably, most came from Ireland.

CHAPTER 4. "THE ESCAPE OF WATSON SAVORS OF A PRODIGY"

1. During the late 1860s the scope of the pope's temporal rule shrank from the Papal States to little more than the walled precinct surrounding St. Peter's Basilica, but the contraction was not formalized until 1929. That's when the state of Vatican City was established by the Lateran Pacts, three agreements between the Kingdom of Italy and the Holy See that also settled the Catholic Church's financial claims dating back sixty years and formally established Catholicism as Italy's state-supported religion. Benito Mussolini, then prime minister, signed for the kingdom.

2. In early 1362 the property on Via di Monserrato became an English pilgrims' hospice dedicated to the martyr St. Thomas Becket, who as archbishop of Canterbury was slain by royal order of King Henry II in December 1170. Approaching the end of the sixteenth century the two-hundred-year-old refuge and hospice had declined into a residence for a small handful of chaplains "who spent their time card playing, drinking, betting, entertaining dubious company and quarrelling among themselves." Michael Williams, a historian of the college, explained this aberrant behavior by observing tolerantly, "A strange climate, unusual food, an alien tongue, and remoteness from the constraints of family and home often lead the Englishman to lose his head and behave in an untypical manner."

Although none of these enabling conditions changed as the centuries rolled over, what had descended in midlife into something like a fraternity house was revitalized under new leadership as the English College, a school for English seminarians who would graduate to become missionaries to their home country, while still preserving its place as a hostel and sanctuary for pilgrims from England to the holy city.

Ten Venerable graduates were canonized between 1581 and 1679; during the same years twenty-seven others were beatified and titled "blessed" and another four were named "venerable" in formal recognition of their heroic virtue and terrible deaths. Every December 1 students meet in front of the "Martyrs' picture" in the College Church to sing a Te Deum in their memory.

3. Canon Frederick Robert Neve (1806–1886) converted to Roman Catholicism in October 1845 at age thirty-nine.

4. Quoted in Leo Francis Stock, "An American Consul Joins the Papal Zouaves," *Catholic World* 132 (November 1930): 147. On Zouave pay, see Cowan to Cerruti in Howard R. Murraro, "Canadian and American Zouaves in the Papal Army, 1868–1870," Canadian Catholic Historical Association *Report* 12 (1944–45): 96.

5. The quote and the analysis are both from Randall M. Miller, "Catholic Religion, Irish Ethnicity, and the Civil War," in *Religion and the American Civil War*, ed. Randall M. Miller, Harry S. Stout, and Charles Reagan Wilson (New York: Oxford University Press, 1998), 263.

6. Murraro, "Canadian and American Zouaves in the Papal Army," 91.

7. However it really happened, Surratt's embarrassing escape did not cast a shadow on Allet's military career. A few months later, on January 1, 1867, the regiment of Zouaves was constituted as two battalions of six companies each, with Allet in overall command as a full colonel.

8. Cited in Alfred Isaacson, *The Travels, Arrest, and Trial of John H. Surratt* (Middletown, N.Y.: Vestigium Press, 2003), 22fn.

9. Samuel F. B. Morse, *Letters and Journals* (Boston: Houghton Mifflin, 1914), 2:416.

10. Edward Beecher began with an informal census of the Roman Catholic Church in the United States ("seven archbishops, thirty-two bishops, 1,574 priests . . . numerous and dangerous organized societies sworn to defend and extend the authority of the Pope of Rome ") and went from there to describe the church as a "system designed to exterminate Protestantism by argument and conviction." Edward Beecher, *The Papal Conspiracy Exposed, and Protestantism Defended, in the Light of Reason, History and Scripture* (Boston: Stearns, 1855). One Catholic reviewer called Beecher's book "the quintessence of Evangelical acidity double distilled." The genre was (and still is) popular. See also the anonymous *Pope or President? . . . Facts for Americans* (New York: R. L. Delisser, 1859).

CHAPTER 5. "I BELIEVE YOUR NAME IS SURRATT"

1. The SS *Tripoli's* routing for autumn 1866 is from Lloyd's List. The ship's official number was 45997, and other information about the ship can be found referencing that number.

2. Michel B. Oren, *Power, Faith and Fantasy: America in the Middle East 1776 to the Present* (New York: W. W. Norton, 2007), 152.

3. From James A. Morgan III, "Searching for Redemption in the Deserts of Egypt," *Civil War Times*, February 2007, 39–45.

4. Mark Twain, *The Innocents Abroad; or the New Pilgrims Progress* (New York: New American Library, 1966), 257.

5. In a single, run-on sentence in the October 4, 1868, issue of the *Cleveland Leader* George Thompson described looking at Surratt this way: "I searched his long, hooked nose, long oblique dark brows, keen blue eyes with eyelids hidden under the brows, outflapping pointer's ears, head, flat on top, huge and swelling behind the ears, mobile, sensitive, pointed, haughty chin, a type of face expressed in the portraits of the stern and gloomy Stuart Calverts and their pioneers in Catholic Maryland, pear shaped with cruciform, florid goatee and moustache, the Saxon crossed by the Spaniard." Somehow in Thompson's eyes Surratt had acquired a distinctly Catholic physiognomy despite the fact that his parents were converts to the faith. The quotation is from the September 1988 *Surratt Courier*, published by the Surratt Society of Clinton (formerly Surrattsville), Maryland.

Papal records contained a less colorful description of Zouave No. 1857, Giovanni Watson:

Altezza: 1 Piedi e 80 pollici
viso: ovale
fronte: leopetra?
occhi: castagne
bocca: media
mento: tondo
capelli:
sopraciglia: bionda

From Ministro delle Armi, Reg. 1636, Battaglione dei Zuavi, vol. 2. Zouave records listed Surratt's date of birth as April 13, 1844. My thanks to Janna Israel for this information.

6. In July 1880, when Surratt was thirty-six and memories of the 1860s had dimmed, the *Washington Post* described him as "slightly above medium height but rather of slender build. His face is long and somewhat 'pinched' but not unpleasantly so. A large Roman nose and a ponderous underjaw, denoting personal courage, are the striking points of his features, which are ornamented by a red moustache and goatee. He has piercing gray eyes set under heavy eyebrows, and his years of combat with the world has made them unusually restless, and his movements quick and emphatic." In fifteen years Surratt had migrated from sly cowardice to possessing "unusual personal courage," all as revealed by his appearance.

7. Geoffrey Wall, *Flaubert: A Life* (New York: Farrar, Straus & Giroux, 2002), 155.

8. In 1977, Durrell returned to Alexandria, escorting a film team intent on making a documentary. He found the international entrepôt he had known barely visible beneath the Egyptian metropolis it had become. Durrell concluded that fabulous, cosmopolitan Alexandria had been destroyed by "Nasser's puritanical socialist

revolution," but he had changed, too. Now sixty-five, married four times, and internationally famous, Durrell wasn't who he had been decades before either, and his disappointing return proved anew that one cannot step in the same water twice.

9. From Hale to Seward, No. 72, December 27, 1866. This and other quotations from Hale's correspondence with the secretary of state between December 1866 and June 1867 (despatch Nos. 70, 72, 79, and 90) are from Department of State, *The Foreign Relations of the United States.*

10. From Edwards Pierrepont's closing statement to the jury, August 3, 1867, in *Trial of John H. Surratt in the Criminal Court for the District of Columbia,* vol. 2 (Washington, D.C.: GPO, 1867), 1257.

11. Unpardonably, she and her three sister ships were built from unseasoned white oak. These green hull timbers deteriorated quickly, and barely six years after commissioning the *Swatara* was judged unserviceable. In December 1871 the ship began a comprehensive, keel-up rebuilding at the New York Navy Yard. The work was disguised as a "repair" in reports to Congress by President Grant's long-service and devious secretary of the navy, George Robeson. The ship that emerged from the yard in September 1873 retained the same name but was entirely new otherwise: bigger and heavier, with new engines, more guns, and requiring a much larger crew.

12. Jeffers provided the House's Committee on the Judiciary with a copy of his orders to the crew when he testified before Boutwell on February 20, 1867, the day after Surratt was delivered to Marshal Gooding in Washington. House, H. Rept. 33, 39th Cong., 2nd sess., 15–16, March 2, 1867.

13. From Secretary of the Navy Gideon Welles's diary entry for January 25, 1867. Gideon Welles, *Diary of Gideon Welles Secretary of the Navy under Lincoln and Johnson with an introduction by John T. Mercer, Jr., and with Illustrations* (Boston: Houghton Mifflin, 1911).

14. *Chicago Tribune,* February 20, 1867, 1.

15. Sharpe's report of July 1867 to the secretary of state was provided by President Johnson to Congress that December. House, Ex. Doc. 68, 40th Cong., 2nd sess., December 19, 1867.

CHAPTER 6. "SEDUCED BY THE INSTIGATION OF THE DEVIL"

1. "The Killing of Thomas Keating, An Address from Irishmen of Washington City to the Citizens of the United States," from the private collection of Louis Becker, Villanova University School of Law. Herbert, a native Alabaman and one-term congressman, lived in California from 1850 to 1859. He then relocated to West Texas. During the Civil War he served as an officer with the 7th Texas Cavalry. He died in Louisiana in July 1864 from wounds received at the Battle of Mansfield several months earlier. Herbert's biographical sketch on the web site of the U.S. Congress (http://bioguide.congress. gov) manages to make no mention of Keating's murder or the trial that followed.

2. "Trial of John Surratt," *New York Herald*, June 31, 1867.

3. John D. Lawson, *American State Trials: A Collection of the Important and Interesting Criminal Trials Which Have Taken Place in the United States from the Beginning of Our Government to the Present Day, with Notes and Annotations*, vol. 9 (St. Louis: F. H. Thomas Law Book, 1918), 4.

4. Theodore Calvin Pease and James G. Randall, *The Diary of Orville Hickman Browning*, vol. 1 (Springfield: Illinois State Historical Library, 1925), 487, entry for July 27, 1861.

5. Brig. Gen. Thomas Harris was the author of *Assassination of Lincoln: A History of the Great Conspiracy and Trial of the Conspirators by a Military Commission and a Review of the Trial of John H. Surratt*, published earlier. It was Harris's belief that "every citizen, and every sojourner in our country, who is loyal to the Roman Catholic Church is an enemy to our government, of necessity, for he yields his highest allegiance to the Pope of Rome, a foreign potentate, who has time and again anathematized every fundamental principle of our government" (from his 1897 pamphlet *Rome's Responsibility for the Assassination of Lincoln*).

6. A. G. Riddle's report to Secretary Seward, n.d., Entry 9D, Records of the Attorney General's Office, Letters Received, 1809–1870, Records of the Department of Justice, RG 60, NA.

7. The archived record of trial documents contains an annotated list of the ninety-six talesmen in the pool from which the twelve jurors were selected. Thirty-nine were excused from jury duty because they had earlier formed or expressed an opinion as to Surratt's guilt. Twenty-three others were challenged by counsel and dismissed for that reason. Only three claimed "conscientious scruples" against the death penalty as a reason not to serve.

CHAPTER 7. "A NEW TRIAL WILL DOUBTLESS FOLLOW"

1. Witnesses were listed in the government trial record in four categories: "Government," "Defendants," "Rebutting testimony," and "Sub-rebutting testimony." There were 85, 97, 94, and 23, respectively, for a total of 299. This count includes some witnesses who testified in more than one category. Louis Weichmann, for example, appeared first as a government witness and then later (very briefly) as a subrebutting witness.

2. Swedenborgians, followers of Swedish theologian Emanuel Swedenborg (1688–1772), were present in the United States beginning in the late eighteenth century, concentrated largely in the East (especially Pennsylvania) and Midwest. The reference is to the mystical aspects of Swedenborg's beliefs, which included a spiritual afterlife.

3. The case file is in Entry 77, Case File No. 4,851, "United States v. William Cleaver," Box 16, Criminal Case Files, 1863–1938, Records of the District Courts of the United States, District of Columbia, RG 21, NA.

4. Winks, *Civil War Years*, 61.

5. Osborn H. Oldroyd and T. M. Harris, *The Assassination of Abraham Lincoln: Flight, Pursuit, Capture and Punishment of the Conspirators* (Rahway, N.J.: Hershon, 1901), 238.

6. Alfred Isaacson wrote about Fisher's appraisal of the trial in the May 1987 issue of the *Surratt Courier*, and this is his conclusion. Fisher's essay on the trial was discovered by Father Isaacson among the judge's papers in the Manuscript Division of the Library of Congress, control number MM75020636.

CHAPTER 8. "PRESIDENT JOHNSON WAS A DRUNKARD"

1. Jefferson Davis managed to fall into three of Johnson's fourteen exempted classes, those peopled by "pretended civil officers," by men who left seats in the Congress to aid in the rebellion, and by those Southerners who owned more than twenty thousand dollars of taxable real estate. The text of President Johnson's proclamation can be found at the Civil War Interactive web site, http://www.civilwarinteractive.com/DocsAmnmestyProcJohnson.htm.

2. Maybe as much as $775,000 all told, in everything from copper pennies to gold $20 double eagles, including a crate of silver jewelry contributed to the cause by patriotic women. The total included several tons of bagged coins and hundreds of millions in bales of near worthless Confederate scrip. Between April 2 and May 4 the Treasury was slowly drained to pay troops. A month out of Richmond in Washington, Georgia, the cache was down to about $145,000. Of that, $56,000 was further distributed as payroll. Writing in the *Surratt Courier* of September 2007 (vol. 32, no. 9), Marshall Waters says that most of what was left ($86,000) was pocketed by a Lieutenant Commander Semple, CSN, who took it with him to Florida as a nest egg.

3. Pease, *Diary of Orville Hickman Browning* 2:100, entry of Tuesday, October 16, 1866.

4. R. F. Nichols, "United States vs. Jefferson Davis, 1865–1869," *American Historical Review* 31, no. 2 (January 1926): 276.

5. A sixty-four-page graphic version of Chiniquy's 368-page book, *The Big Betrayal*, is published by Chick Publications, an anti-Catholic publishing house.

6. From Johnson's veto message to the House of Representatives of the First Reconstruction Act, March 2, 1867. Earlier he had observed, "The negroes have not asked for the privilege of voting; the vast majority of them have no idea what it means." Johnson's veto was overridden by both houses.

7. Stephen's "corner-stone speech" on March 21, 1861, in Savannah as reported by the *Savannah Republican* was later quoted by Henry Cleveland in his *Alexander H. Stephens in Public and Private: With Letters and Speeches, Before, During, and Since the War* (Philadelphia: National Publishing, 1866). Available on line at the University of Michigan's Making of America Books web site, http://quod.lib.umich.edu/m/moa/.

8. Hans L. Trefousse, *The Impeachment of a President: Andrew Johnson, the Blacks, and Reconstruction* (New York: Fordham University Press, 1999), 5.

CHAPTER 9. "A VERDICT OF ACQUITTAL"

1. Yellow fever had been present in the Americas since the mid-seventeenth century. After the first recorded outbreak in the New World in 1647–48, later epidemics washed across great parts of the two continents on an apparently random schedule. During the seventeenth, eighteenth, and nineteenth centuries yellow fever erupted as far north as Nova Scotia and as far south as Brazil. In the first half of the nineteenth century, yellow fever epidemics visited New Orleans two out of every three years.

A callous *New York Times* correspondent writing in Richmond, Virginia, on the last day of October 1867 foresaw that the "twin plagues" of yellow fever and the freedmen's franchise would eventually force a salutary population redistribution in the newly reunited country, thus solving "the negro question" that the Civil War apparently had left unresolved. Under pressure from yellow fever's "fearful ravages" in the South during 1867, he thought, those of Saxon and German blood would relocate to the healthy and industrious North. Meanwhile, Latins, Ethiopians, and "embrowned Indians," all believed immune to the disease, would cluster "within the charmed circle of perennial Summer, which is swept by cyclones, hurricanes, and that avenging cruiser Bronze John (or Yellow Jack)."

2. At some time during the subsequent legal process, Albert Riddle was replaced on the government's team of prosecutors by an "N. Wilson," about whom I have found nothing other than mention of his name in the appeals court decision dated November 6, 1868.

3. Pierrepont to Seward, May 18, 1868, Entry 9D, Records of the Attorney General's Office, Letters Received, 1809–1870, Records of the Department of Justice, RG 60, NA.

4. The writing is crabbed and irregular, with words crossed out and lines crushed at the bottom of a page. It is almost certainly in Carrington's hand and not that of a professional clerk, who would have produced a more legible and elegant script.

5. Surratt was out of prison on bail in summer and autumn 1868, something his attorneys had accomplished relatively easily once Judge Wylie took the bench. They seemingly had no problem in finding bondsmen, either. But there's a hint, at least, that Merrick and Bradley lacked confidence in their now footloose client. A small note in the *Chicago Tribune* of October 4 announced, "The counsel of Surratt deny the statement that they have assured the District Attorney that their client would appear and answer any indictment found against him. He having been discharged, they have no control over his movements, and are in no way responsible therefore."

6. Executive clemency is defined in a spare half-sentence in Article 2, Section 2 of the Constitution: "[The president] shall have the Power to grant Reprieves and Pardons for Offenses against the United States, except in Cases of Impeachment." The power, with deep roots in English history and law, was uncontroversial when the Constitution was drafted in 1787.

Whatever quiet reservations any delegates to the constitutional convention might have left Philadelphia with were seemingly put away the next year by Alexander Hamilton, who argued anonymously in Federalist Paper 74, "Humanity and good policy conspire to dictate, that the benign prerogative of pardoning should be as little as possible fettered or embarrassed . . . without an easy access to exceptions in favor of unfortunate guilt, justice would wear a countenance too sanguinary and cruel." Hamilton must have been convincing. The pardon power wasn't an issue in the state ratification conventions.

CHAPTER 10. "FREE AS AN INNOCENT CHILD"

1. At the time, Barbee (1874–1958) was writing features for the *Washington Post*. During 1928–33 Barbee interrupted his career in journalism to work with the Roosevelt administration. After 1942 he researched and wrote books and articles about the Civil War. Barbee did not come to his John Surratt story entirely open-minded. In the same article he said he believed that "the military commission that tried [Mary Surratt] *unanimously voted to acquit her*, but Judge Joseph E. Holt, the Judge Advocate-General of the Army, got them to change their verdict, *'in order that he might get President Johnson to pardon her.'* Holt never brought that matter to the President's attention. I . . . have unearthed records which make the hanging of poor Mrs. Surratt the most awful crime in American history." Barbee's papers are at Georgetown University.

2. Roy Z. Chamblee, *Lincoln's Assassins: A Complete Account of Their Capture, Trial, and Punishment* (Jefferson, N.C.: McFarland, 1990), 537.

3. Alfred Isaacson, *The Travels, Arrest and Trial of John H. Surratt* (Middletown, N.Y.: Vestigium Press, 2003), 33.

4. The letter quoted is from "Fact and Information," *Surratt Society News*, August 1977.

5. After first appearing at nearby Fort Meade, Maryland, the flu struck Baltimore hard. The disease came to the city in September 1918. At the peak the following month (October was the worst month countrywide), perhaps two thousand in the city exhibited new symptoms and one-tenth as many died each day. By then, public assemblies had been banned, schools closed, and Baltimore's hospitals, overwhelmed by staff losses and ward crowding, had long since closed their doors. Statistics are incomplete, but the estimate is that two thousand died from flu in the city, several hundred times the annual toll from a typical flu season during that period.

BIBLIOGRAPHY

Contemporary reporting, including that of the *Liverpool Mercury*, the *Liverpool Telegraph and Shipping Gazette*, the *Washington Evening Star*, the *New York Times*, the *New York Herald*, the *Quebec Morning Chronicle* and *Commercial and Shipping Gazette*, the *Chicago Tribune*, and the *London Times*, has been used throughout. So too has *Harper's Weekly*.

The National Archives holds selected documents from "the United States vs. John Harrison Surratt," but not a trial transcript, in Record Group 21 under Criminal Cases Nos. 4,731 (ninety-one pages), 5,920 (forty-five pages), and 6,594 (fourteen pages). Most are in manuscript form.

A verbatim trial transcript, *Trial of John H. Surratt in the Criminal Court for the District of Columbia, Hon. George H. Fisher, Presiding*, was printed in one thousand two-volume copies in Washington, D.C., by the Government Printing Office in 1867 (just six years after the GPO was established). This is the official record of trial as taken by Francis Smith, the reporter of the House of Representatives, but it is not error free. Gen. Edwin Lee's testimony, for example, does not appear in this record, although his name is in the index of defense witnesses.

Another published verbatim record of the trial, one that is both more complete and easier to use (thanks to a superior index), is in R. Sutton, D. F. Murphy, and James J. Murphy, "Trial of John H. Surratt, in the Supreme Court of the District of Columbia, Sitting for the Trial of Crimes and Misdemeanors, on an Indictment for Murder of President Lincoln," *Reporter: A Periodical Devoted to Religion, Law, Legislation, and Public Events* 47 (June 17, 1867) to 102 (Sept. 21, 1867). Sutton and the Murphys described themselves as chief and principal members, respectively, of the Senate's Official Corps of Reporters, doing business out of offices above the Adams Express Company at 514 Pennsylvania Avenue, Washington City.

A transcript of the extended statements by the presiding judge and counsel on both sides, but not the testimony of witnesses, is in John D. Lawson, ed.,

American State Trials: A Collection of the Important and Interesting Criminal Trials Which Have Taken Place in the United States from the Beginning of Our Government to the Present Day, with Notes and Annotations, vol. 9 (St. Louis: F. H. Thomas Law Book, 1918), 1–336. Lawson's preface to this volume contains his revealing observation that "when political passion is strong in a community the only way to convict for a political crime is to have a jury of the right political faith."

Letters among the attorney general, the secretary of state, the district attorney, and others about Surratt's trials can be found in Entry 9D, Records of the Attorney General's Office, Letters Received, 1809–1870, Records of the Department of Justice, RG 60, NA.

Many contemporary newspapers covered the Surratt trial extensively. The *New York Herald* published daily stories on its first page, as did the *Washington Intelligencer, Philadelphia Daily Inquirer, Washington Evening Star*, and *Chicago Tribune*. Coverage of the Surratt trial competed with domestic political news and the two big international stories of the day: the execution of Emperor Maximilian of Mexico (slain by a revolutionary firing squad in June 1867) and the birth of the Dominion of Canada (signed into being in London as the Constitution Act in 1867).

Congressional and National Archives Records

Deck logs of the screw sloop of war USS *Swatara*. July 1, 1866–December 31, 1866, and January 1, 1867–June 30, 1867. Vols. 4 and 5 of 60. Logs of U.S. Naval Ships, 1801–1915. Records of the Bureau of Naval Personnel. RG 24, NA.

Habeas Corpus Case No. 46. "Concerning an attempt to free Mary E. Surratt by habeas corpus proceedings after her conviction by military commission." Nineteen pages. A record of the Supreme Court for the District of Columbia (now the U.S. District Court for the District of Columbia). Letters Received by the Office of the Adjutant General, 1861–1870. M619. RG 21, NA.

House Executive Document No. 9. 39th Cong., 2nd sess. Dec. 10, 1866. *Message from the President of the United States Transmitting a Report of the Secretary of State Relating to the Discovery and Arrest of John H. Surratt*.

House. Executive Document No. 25. 39th Cong., 2nd sess. Jan. 7, 1867. *Message from the President of the United States Transmitting Further Copies of Papers in Answer to Resolution of the House of 3d Ultimo, Relative to the Arrest of John H. Surratt*.

House Executive Document No. 68. 40th Cong., 2nd sess. Dec. 19, 1867. *Message from the President of the United States Transmitting a Report of George H. Sharpe Relative to the Assassination of President Lincoln.*

House Report No. 33. 39th Cong., 2nd sess. Mar. 2, 1867. *John H. Surratt.*

Published Sources

Adams, Henry. *The Education of Henry Adams: An Autobiography.* Boston: Houghton Mifflin, 1918. A complete digital text is available from the University of Virginia's American Studies program at http://xroads.virginia.edu/~HYPER/hadams/ehaheader.html/.

Applegate, Debby. *The Most Famous Man in America: The Biography of Henry Ward Beecher.* New York: Three Leaves Press, 2006.

Appleton, Thomas E. *Ravenscrag: The Allan Royal Mail Line.* Toronto: McClelland & Stewart, 1974.

Bellesiles, Michael A., ed. *Lethal Imaginations: Violence and Brutality in American History.* New York: New York Univ. Press, 1999.

Benedict, Michael Les. *The Impeachment and Trial of Andrew Johnson.* New York: W. W. Norton, 1973.

Black, Robert C. *The Railroads of the Confederacy.* Chapel Hill: Univ. of North Carolina Press, 1952.

Booth, Bradford A. "Trollope and the 'Pall Mall Gazette.'" Pts. 1 and 2. *Nineteenth-century Fiction* 4, nos. 1 and 2 (June and Sept. 1949): 51–69, 137–58.

Boyd's Directory of Washington and Georgetown. Washington, D.C.: Boyd and Waite, 1867.

Boyd's Directory of Washington and Georgetown. Washington, D.C.: Boyd and Waite, 1868.

Brown, Alexander Crosby. *The Old Bay Line, 1840–1940.* Richmond: Dietz Press, 1940.

Canfield, Eugene B. *Civil War Naval Ordnance.* Washington, D.C.: GPO, 1969.

Cashin. Joan E. *First Lady of the Confederacy: Varina Davis's Civil War.* Cambridge: Harvard Univ. Press, 2006.

The Catholic Encyclopedia. 1913. Available online at New Advent. http://www.newadvent.org/cathen/index.html/.

Chamblee, Roy Z. *Lincoln's Assassins: A Complete Account of Their Capture, Trial, and Punishment.* Jefferson, N.C.: McFarland, 1990.

Clephane, James E. *Official Report of the Trial of Mary Harris . . . for the Murder of Adoniram J. Burroughs . . . July 3, 1865.* Washington, D.C.: W. H & O. H. Morrison, 1865.

Cliff, Nigel. *The Shakespeare Riots: Revenge, Drama, and Death in Nineteenth-Century America.* New York: Random House, 2007.

Cole, Simon. *Suspect Identities: A History of Fingerprinting and Criminal Identification.* Boston: Harvard Univ. Press, 2002.

A Complete List of the Students Entered at Saint Charles' College, Ellicott City, Maryland, from the Opening, October 31st, 1848, until the Golden Jubilee, June 15th, 1898. Staten Island, N.Y.: Press of the Mission of the Immaculate Virgin, 1898.

Cox, Frederick J. "The American Naval Mission in Egypt." *Journal of Modern History* 26, no. 2 (June 1954): 173–78.

Crombe, V. *Régiment des zouaves pontificaux: Liste des zouaves ayant fait partie du régiment du 1er janvier 1861 au 20 septembre 1870.* Lille, France: N.p., 1910–20.

Crosby, Molly Caldwell. *The American Plague: The Untold Story of Yellow Fever, the Epidemic that Shaped Our History.* New York: Berkley Books, 2006.

Cumming, Carmen. *Devil's Game: The Civil War Intrigues of Charles A. Dunham.* Urbana: Univ. of Illinois Press, 2004.

Davis, Jefferson. *The Rise and Fall of the Confederate Government.* 2 vols. New York: D. Appleton, 1881.

Davis, William. *An Honorable Defeat: The Last Days of the Confederate Government.* New York: Harcourt, 2001.

———. *Look Away: A History of the Confederate States of America.* New York: Free Press, 2002.

Dolin, Eric Jay. *Leviathan: The History of Whaling in America.* New York: W. W. Norton, 2007.

Dorris, J. T. "Pardoning the Leaders of the Confederacy." *Mississippi Valley Historical Review* 15, no. 1 (June 1928): 3–21.

Doster, William E. *Lincoln and Episodes of the Civil War.* New York: G. P. Putnam's Sons, 1915.

Durrell, Lawrence. *The Alexandria Quartet (Justine, Balthazar, Mountolive, Clea).* New York: Penguin Books, 1991.

Epperson, James. "The POW Cartel." Civil War Interactive. http://www.civilwarinteractive.com/POWCartel.htm/.

Farr, Grahame. *West Country Passenger Steamers.* Lancashire, UK: T. Stephenson & Sons, 1967.

Faust, Drew Gilpin. *This Republic of Suffering: Death and the American Civil War.* New York: Alfred A. Knopf, 2008.

Ferguson, Robert A. *The Trial in American Life.* Chicago: Univ. of Chicago Press, 2007.

Fisher, Louis. *Military Tribunals and Presidential Power*. Lawrence: Univ. Press of Kansas, 2005.

Foner, Eric. *Reconstruction: America's Unfinished Revolution, 1863–1877*. New York: Harper and Row, 1988.

Forster, E. M. *Alexandria: A History and a Guide*. Gloucester, Mass.: Peter Smith, 1968.

———. *Pharos and Pharillon*. New York: Alfred A. Knopf, 1962.

Frank, Seymour J. "The Conspiracy to Implicate the Confederate Leaders in Lincoln's Assassination." *Mississippi Valley Historical Review* 40, no. 4 (Mar. 1954): 629–56.

Garrett, Laurie. *The Coming Plague, Newly Emerging Disease in a World Out of Balance*. New York: Penguin Books, 1994.

Gray, John A. "The Fate of the Lincoln Conspirators: The Account of the Hanging, Given by Lieutenant-Colonel Christian Rath, the Executioner." *McClure's Magazine* 37, no. 6 (Oct. 1911): 626–36.

Gray, Michael P. *The Business of Captivity: Elmira and Its Civil War Prison*. Kent, Ohio: Kent State Univ. Press, 2001.

The Great Conspiracy: A book of absorbing interest!, startling developments, eminent persons implicated, full secret of the assassination plot, John H. Surratt and his mother; with biographical sketches of J. B. Booth and John Wilkes, and the life and extraordinary adventures of John H. Surratt, the conspirator. Philadelphia: Barclay, 1866.

Greenhill, Basil, and Ann Giffard. *Travelling by Sea in the Nineteenth Century: Interior Design in Victorian Passenger Ships*. New York: Hastings House, 1974.

Groebner, Valentin. *Who Are You: Identification, Deception and Surveillance in Early Modern Europe*. New York: Zone Books, 2007.

Guttridge, Leonard, and Ray Neff. *Dark Union*. Hoboken, N.J.: John Wiley & Sons, 2003.

Hatfield, Mark O. *Vice Presidents of the United States, 1789–1993*. Washington, D.C.: GPO, 1997.

Holmes, Clay W. A. M. *The Elmira Prison Camp: A History of the Military Prison at Elmira, N.Y. July 6, 1864 to July 10, 1865*. New York: G. P. Putnam's Sons, 1912. Reprint, Salem, Mass.: Higginson, 1997.

Horigan, Michael. *Elmira, Death Camp of the North*. Mechanicsburg, Pa.: Stackpole Books, 2002.

Howe, Daniel Walker. *What Hath God Wrought: The Transformation of America, 1815–1848*. New York: Oxford Univ. Press, 2007.

Isaacson, Alfred. *The Travels, Arrest, and Trial of John H. Surratt*. Middletown, N.Y.: Vestigium Press, 2003.

Jackson, E. Hilton. "John H. Surratt and the Great Conspiracy." *Virginia Law Register* 10, no. 1 (June 1904): 95–106.

Johnson, Ludwell H. "Beverley Tucker's Canadian Mission." *Journal of Southern History* 29, no.1 (Feb. 1963): 88–99.

Johnston, Angus James II. *Virginia Railroads in the Civil War*. Chapel Hill: Univ. of North Carolina Press, 1961.

Karabell, Zachary. *Parting the Desert: The Creation of the Suez Canal*. New York: Alfred A. Knopf, 2003.

Kauffman, Michael W. *American Brutus: John Wilkes Booth and the Lincoln Conspiracies*. New York: Random House, 2004.

Kennedy, John F. "Edmund G. Ross." In *Profiles in Courage*, by John F. Kennedy, chap. 6. New York: Harper & Brothers, 1956.

Kennedy, Joseph C. G. *Population of the United States in 1860; Compiled from the Original Returns of the Eighth Census*. Washington, D.C.: GPO, 1864.

Kertzer, David I. *Prisoner of the Vatican: The Pope's Secret Plot to Capture Rome from the New Italian State*. Boston: Houghton Mifflin, 2004.

Leech, Margaret. *Reveille in Washington, 1860–1865*. New York: Time, 1962.

Lemann, Nicholas. *Redemption: The Last Battle of the Civil War*. New York: Farrar, Straus & Giroux, 2006.

Leonard, Elizabeth. *Lincoln's Avengers: Justice, Revenge, and Reunion after the Civil War*. New York: W. W. Norton, 2005.

Levin, Alexandra Lee. "Who Hid John H. Surratt, the Lincoln Conspiracy Case Figure?" *Maryland Historical Magazine* 60, no. 2 (1965): 175–84.

Life and Extraordinary Adventures of John H. Surratt, the Conspirator: A Correct Account and Highly Interesting Narrative of His Doings and Adventures from Childhood to the Present Time. Philadelphia: Barclay, 1867.

Loring, W. W. *Confederate Soldier in Egypt*. New York: Dodd, Mead, 1884.

Man, Albon P. "The Church and the New York Draft Riots of 1863." *Records of the American Catholic Historical Society of Philadelphia* 62, no. 1 (Mar. 1951): 33–50.

Marraro, Howard R. "Canadian and American Zouaves in the Papal Army, 1868–1870." Canadian Catholic Historical Association *Report* 12 (1944–45): 83–102.

———. "The Closing of the American Diplomatic Mission to the Vatican and Efforts to Revive It, 1868–1870." *Catholic Historical Review* 33 (Apr. 1947–Jan. 1948): 423–47.

McCulloch, Hugh. *Men and Measures of Half a Century: Sketches and Comments.* New York: Charles Scribner's Sons, 1888.

Miller, Randall M. "Catholic Religion, Irish Ethnicity, and the Civil War." In *Religion and the American Civil War,* ed. Randall M. Miller, Harry S. Stout, and Charles Reagan Wilson. New York: Oxford Univ. Press, 1998, 261–91.

Moreau, Louis Edmond. *Nos Croises ou Histoire Anecdotique de l'Expedition des Voluntaires Canadiens a Rome pour la Defense de l'Eglise.* Montreal: Fabre & Gravel, 1871.

Murphey, Hermon King. "The Northern Railroads and the Civil War." *Mississippi Valley Historical Review* 5, no. 3 (Dec. 1918): 324–38.

Nichols, R. F. "United States vs. Jefferson Davis, 1865–1869." *American Historical Review* 31, no. 2 (Jan. 1926): 266–84.

Nickles, David Paull. *Under the Wire: How the Telegraph Changed Diplomacy.* Cambridge: Harvard Univ. Press, 2003.

Nott, Charles, and Archibald Hopkins. *Cases Decided in the Court of Claims at the December Term, 1873, with the Rules of Practice and the Acts of Congress Relating to the Court.* Washington, D.C.: W. H. & O. H. Morrison, 1874.

Oldroyd, Osborn H., and T. M. Harris. *The Assassination of Abraham Lincoln: Flight, Pursuit, Capture and Punishment of the Conspirators.* Rahway, N.J.: Hershon, 1901.

Oren, Michael B. *Power, Faith, and Fantasy: America in the Middle East 1776 to the Present.* New York: W. W. Norton, 2007.

Owensbey, Betty J. *Alias Paine: Lewis Thornton Powell, the Mystery Man of the Lincoln Conspiracy.* Jefferson, N.C.: McFarland, 1993.

Parrott, Kay. *Pictorial Liverpool: The Art of WG and William Herdman.* Liverpool: Bluecoat Press, 2005.

Pease, Theodore Calvin, and James G. Randall, eds. *The Diary of Orville Hickman Browning.* 2 vols. Springfield: Illinois State Historical Library, 1925.

Peterson, Todd David. "Congressional Power over Pardon and Amnesty: Legislative Authority in the Shadow of Presidential Prerogative." *Wake Forest Law Review* 38 (2003): 1225–2003.

Powell, J. H. *Bring Out Your Dead: The Great Plague of Yellow Fever in Philadelphia in 1793.* Philadelphia: Univ. of Pennsylvania Press, 1949.

Powell, Joseph, Z. P. *Two Years in the Pontifical Zouaves: A Narrative of Travel, Residence, and Experience in the Roman States.* London: R. Washbourne, 1871. Digitized by Google Books. http://books.google.com/.

Rehnquist, William H. *Grand Inquests: The Historic Impeachments of Justice Samuel Chase and President Andrew Johnson.* New York: Harper Perennial, 1999.

Reid, Thomas. *America's Fortress: A History of Fort Jefferson, Dry Tortugas, Florida.* Gainesville: Univ. Press of Florida, 2006.

Reimer, Michael J. "Colonial Bridgehead: Social and Spatial Change in Alexandria, 1850–1882." *International Journal of Middle East Studies* 20, no. 4 (Nov. 1988): 531–53.

Richardson, James D., ed. *A Compilation of the Messages and Papers of the Confederacy Including the Diplomatic Correspondence, 1861–1865.* 2 vols. Nashville: United States Publishing, 1905.

Ross, Edmund G. *History of the Impeachment of Andrew Johnson, President of the United States, by the House of Representatives, and His Trial by the Senate, for High Crimes and Misdemeanors in Office, 1868.* Santa Fe, N.M.: Edmund G. Ross, 1896. On line at Yale Law School's Avalon Project. http://www.yale. Edu/lawweb/avalon/treatise/andrew_johnson/johnson.htm/.

Rothman, Sheila M. *Living in the Shadow of Death: Tuberculosis and the Social Experience of Illness in American History.* New York: HarperCollins, 1994.

Schofield, Nicholas, ed. *A Roman Miscellany: The English in Rome, 1550–2000.* Herefordshire, UK: Gracewing, 2002.

Serpell, David R. "American Consular Activities in Egypt." *Journal of Modern History* 10, no. 3 (Sept. 1938): 344–63.

Seymour, Mark Wilson, ed. *The Pursuit and Arrest of John H. Surratt: Despatches from the Official Record of the Assassination of Abraham Lincoln.* Austin, Tex.: Civil War Library, 2000.

Sifakis, Stewart. *Compendium of the Confederate Armies: Texas.* New York: Facts on File, 1995.

Steers, Edward, Jr. *Blood on the Moon: The Assassination of Abraham Lincoln.* Lexington: Univ. Press of Kentucky, 2001.

———, ed. *The Trial: The Assassination of President Lincoln and the Trial of the Conspirators.* Lexington: Univ. Press of Kentucky, 2003.

Stern, Philip Van Doren, ed. *The Life and Writings of Abraham Lincoln.* New York: Modern Library, 1999.

Stock, Leo Francis. "An American Consul Joins the Papal Zouaves." *Catholic World* 132 (Nov. 1930): 146–50.

———, ed. *United States Ministers to the Papal States: Instructions and Despatches, 1848–1868.* Washington, D.C.: Catholic Univ. Press, 1933.

Swanson, James L. *Manhunt: The Twelve-Day Chase for Lincoln's Killer.* New York: William Morrow, 2006.

Talbot, Margaret. "Duped: Can Brain Scans Uncover Lies?" *New Yorker,* July 2, 2007, 52–61.

Thayer, Lucius Ellsworth. "The Capitulations of the Ottoman Empire and the Question of Their Abrogation as It Affects the United States." *American Journal of International Law* 17, no. 2 (Apr. 1923): 207–33.

Thompson, Holland, ed. *Prisons and Hospitals*. Vol. 7 of *The Photographic History of the Civil War*. New York: Review of Reviews, 1911.

Tidwell, William A., James O. Hall, and David Winfred Gaddy. *Come Retribution: The Confederate Secret Service and the Assassination of Lincoln*. Jackson: Univ. Press of Mississippi, 1988.

Trefousse, Hans L. *The Impeachment of a President: Andrew Johnson, the Blacks, and Reconstruction*. New York: Fordham Univ. Press, 1999.

Trindal, Elizabeth Steger. *Mary Surratt: An American Tragedy*. Gretna, La.: Pelican Publishing, 1996.

Trollope, Anthony. *North America*. 2 vols. New York: St. Martin's Press, 1986.

———. *The West Indies and the Spanish Main*. New York: Carroll & Graf, 1999.

Tucker, Neely. "Swept Away by History: Virginia's Museum of the Confederacy Is Struggling Not to Become a Relic of the Past." *Washington Post*, Apr. 4, 2007, C1.

Wade, William. "The Man Who Stopped the Rams." *American Heritage Magazine* 14, no. 3 (Apr. 1963). http://www.americanheritage.com/articles/magazine/ah/1963/3/1963_3_18.shtml/.

Warner, Ezra J. *Generals in Blue: Lives of the Union Commanders*. Baton Rouge: Louisiana State Univ. Press, 1964.

Weichmann, Louis J. *A True History of the Assassination of Abraham Lincoln and of the Conspiracy of 1865*. Edited by Floyd E. Risvold. New York: Alfred A. Knopf, 1975.

Welles, Gideon. *Diary of Gideon Welles Secretary of the Navy under Lincoln and Johnson with an Introduction by John T. Mercer, Jr., and with Illustrations*. Boston: Houghton Mifflin, 1911.

Welsh, Jack D. *Medical Histories of Confederate Generals*. Kent, Ohio: Kent State Univ. Press, 1995.

Williams, Michael E. *The Venerable English College Rome: A History, 1579–1979*. Dublin: Cahill, 1979.

Williams, Stephen K. *Cases Assigned and Decided in the Supreme Court of the United States, December Terms 1870, 1871*. Book 20. Rochester, N.Y.: Lawyers Co-operative Publishing, 1912.

Winks, Robin W. *The Civil War Years: Canada and the United States*. 4th ed. Montreal: McGill-Queen's Univ. Press, 1998.

INDEX

ABOUT THE AUTHOR

Andrew Jampoler lives in the Lost Corner of Loudoun County, Virginia, with his wife, Susan, a professional geographer, and their two golden retrievers. They have married children in Pennsylvania and Iowa. He is an alumnus of Columbia College and the School of International and Public Affairs, both of Columbia University in New York City, and of the U.S. State Department Foreign Service Institute's School of Language Study. During more than twenty years on active duty with the U.S. Navy Jampoler commanded a land-based maritime patrol aircraft squadron and a naval air station. Later he was a senior sales and marketing executive in the international aerospace industry. Jampoler has been writing full-time for nearly ten years.

His first book, *Adak: The Rescue of Alfa Foxtrot 586*, is the true story of a U.S. Navy maritime patrol aircraft ditching in the North Pacific Ocean in October 1978. A review in May 2003 in the *Wall Street Journal* described the book as "an adventure story to rival the best you've ever read." *Adak* later won Jampoler recognition as the Press's "author of the year." The crew's story based on this book has been the subject of television specials in Russia and Japan.

His second book, *Sailors in the Holy Land: The 1848 American Expedition to the Dead Sea and the Search for Sodom and Gomorrah*, recounts the Navy's small boat expedition down the River Jordan and across the Dead Sea in the mid-nineteenth century. Nathaniel Philbrick, author of the award-winning *Sea of Glory*, described the book in 2005 as telling "the fascinating story of one of the most improbable operations ever mounted by the U.S. Navy. . . . A meticulously researched account."

Jampoler also writes for periodicals. One of his articles in the U.S. Naval Institute's *Naval History* magazine, about Lt. Emory Taunt and his expedition up the Congo River in 1885, was recognized by the publisher as its best piece of writing in 2006.

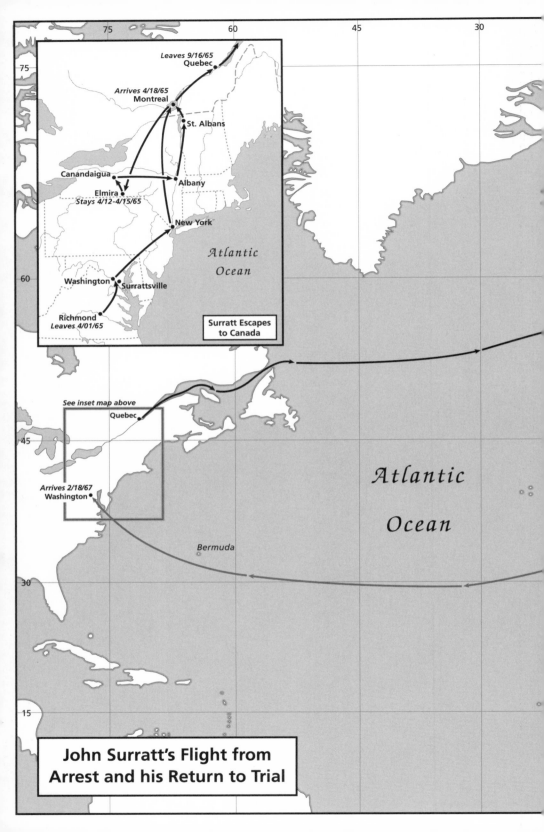

75 · 60 · 45 · 30

Leaves 9/16/65
Quebec

Arrives 4/18/65
Montreal

St. Albans

Canandaigua · Albany

Elmira
Stays 4/12-4/15/65

New York

*Atlantic
Ocean*

Washington · Surrattsville

Richmond
Leaves 4/01/65

**Surratt Escapes
to Canada**

See inset map above
Quebec

45

Arrives 2/18/67
Washington

30

Bermuda

*Atlantic

Ocean*

15

**John Surratt's Flight from
Arrest and his Return to Trial**